Perspectives on Women in Management and the Global Labor Market

Elisabete S. Vieira
GOVCOPP, University of Aveiro, Portugal

Mara Madaleno
GOVCOPP, University of Aveiro, Portugal

João Teodósio
Polytechnic Institute of Santarém, Portugal

A volume in the Advances in Logistics, Operations, and Management Science (ALOMS) Book Series

IGI Global
PUBLISHER of TIMELY KNOWLEDGE

Published in the United States of America by
IGI Global
Business Science Reference (an imprint of IGI Global)
701 E. Chocolate Avenue
Hershey PA, USA 17033
Tel: 717-533-8845
Fax: 717-533-8661
E-mail: cust@igi-global.com
Web site: http://www.igi-global.com

Library of Congress Cataloging-in-Publication Data

Names: Vieira, Elisabete S., editor. | Madaleno, Mara, 1981- editor. | Teodósio, João, 1979- editor.
Title: Perspectives on women in management and the global labor market / Elisabete Vieira, Mara Madaleno, and João Teodósio, editor.
Description: Hershey, PA : Business Science Reference, [2023] | Includes bibliographical references and index. | Summary: "This book investigates the gender effect on the management decision-making process and the respective consequences, showing similarities and striking differences in the practices of different countries and economies by offering a compilation of ideas in new trends associated with the presence of women in management and the global labor market"-- Provided by publisher.
Identifiers: LCCN 2022031273 (print) | LCCN 2022031274 (ebook) | ISBN 9781668459812 (hardcover) | ISBN 9781668459829 (paperback) | ISBN 9781668459836 (ebook)
Subjects: LCSH: Women executives--Case studies. | Labor supply--Case studies.
Classification: LCC HD6054.3 .P46 2023 (print) | LCC HD6054.3 (ebook) | DDC 658.4/09082--dc23/eng/20220803
LC record available at https://lccn.loc.gov/2022031273
LC ebook record available at https://lccn.loc.gov/2022031274

This book is published in the IGI Global book series Advances in Logistics, Operations, and Management Science (ALOMS) (ISSN: 2327-350X; eISSN: 2327-3518)

British Cataloguing in Publication Data
A Cataloguing in Publication record for this book is available from the British Library.
All work contributed to this book is new, previously-unpublished material.
The views expressed in this book are those of the authors, but not necessarily of the publisher.
For electronic access to this publication, please contact: eresources@igi-global.com.

Advances in Logistics, Operations, and Management Science (ALOMS) Book Series

ISSN:2327-350X
EISSN:2327-3518

Editor-in-Chief: John Wang, Montclair State University, USA

MISSION

Operations research and management science continue to influence business processes, administration, and management information systems, particularly in covering the application methods for decision-making processes. New case studies and applications on management science, operations management, social sciences, and other behavioral sciences have been incorporated into business and organizations real-world objectives.

The **Advances in Logistics, Operations, and Management Science** (ALOMS) Book Series provides a collection of reference publications on the current trends, applications, theories, and practices in the management science field. Providing relevant and current research, this series and its individual publications would be useful for academics, researchers, scholars, and practitioners interested in improving decision making models and business functions.

COVERAGE

- Production Management
- Services management
- Computing and information technologies
- Risk Management
- Marketing engineering
- Political Science
- Finance
- Operations Management
- Networks
- Information Management

IGI Global is currently accepting manuscripts for publication within this series. To submit a proposal for a volume in this series, please contact our Acquisition Editors at Acquisitions@igi-global.com or visit: http://www.igi-global.com/publish/.

The Advances in Logistics, Operations, and Management Science (ALOMS) Book Series (ISSN 2327-350X) is published by IGI Global, 701 E. Chocolate Avenue, Hershey, PA 17033-1240, USA, www.igi-global.com. This series is composed of titles available for purchase individually; each title is edited to be contextually exclusive from any other title within the series. For pricing and ordering information please visit http://www.igi-global.com/book-series/advances-logistics-operations-management-science/37170. Postmaster: Send all address changes to above address.

Titles in this Series

For a list of additional titles in this series, please visit:
http://www.igi-global.com/book-series/advances-logistics-operations-management-science/37170

Futuristic Technology Perspectives on Entrepreneurship and Sustainable Innovation
Sanjay Misra (Ostfold University, Norway) Amit Jain (Amity University, India) Manju Kaushik (Amity University, India) and Chitreshh Banerjee (Amity University, India)
Business Science Reference • © 2023 • 300pp • H/C (ISBN: 9781668458716) • US $250.00

Cases on Managing Dairy Productive Chains
Eduardo Guilherme Satolo (São Paulo State University, Brazil) and Priscilla Ayllen Bustos Mac-Lean (São Paulo State University, Brazil)
Engineering Science Reference • © 2023 • 320pp • H/C (ISBN: 9781668454725) • US $235.00

Perspectives and Strategies of Family Business Resiliency in Unprecedented Times
Hotniar Siringoringo (Gunadarma University, Indonesia) and Ravindra Hewa Kuruppuge (University of Peradeniya, Sri Lanka)
Business Science Reference • © 2023 • 300pp • H/C (ISBN: 9781668473948) • US $240.00

Moving From R&D Development to Production and Sales in Start-Up Companies
Amiram Porath (APC, Israel)
Business Science Reference • © 2023 • 181pp • H/C (ISBN: 9781799856856) • US $195.00

Advanced Research and Real-World Applications of Industry 5.0
Mahmoud Numan Bakkar (Abu Dhabi Vocational Education and Training Institute (ADVETI), Institute of Applied Technology (IAT), UAE) and Elspeth McKay (Cogniware.com.au, Australia)
Business Science Reference • © 2023 • 315pp • H/C (ISBN: 9781799888055) • US $250.00

For an entire list of titles in this series, please visit:
http://www.igi-global.com/book-series/advances-logistics-operations-management-science/37170

IGI Global
PUBLISHER of TIMELY KNOWLEDGE

701 East Chocolate Avenue, Hershey, PA 17033, USA
Tel: 717-533-8845 x100 • Fax: 717-533-8661
E-Mail: cust@igi-global.com • www.igi-global.com

Editorial Advisory Board

List of Reviewers

Huseyin Karsili, *Bahcesehir Cyprus University, Cyprus*
Fernanda Matias, *University of Algarve, Portugal*
Catarina Alexandra Neves Proença, *Polytechnic Institute of Coimbra, Portugal*
Udaya Raj Paudel, *Quest International College, Nepal*
Liliana Pimentel, *University of Coimbra, Portugal*
Subrata Kumar Ray, *University of Calcutta, India*
Sutapa Ray, *University of Calcutta, India*
Aleff dos Santos Santana, *Federal University of Pará, Brazil*
Lidiane Nazaré da Silva Dias, *Federal University of Pará, Brazil*
Juliene do Socorro e Silva Pereira, *Federal University of Pará, Brazil*
Jessika Jhenniffer da Silva Carvalho, *Federal University of Pará, Brazil*
Mustafa Toycan, *Bahçeşehir Cyprus University, Cyprus*
Achour Zyed, *University of Carthage, Tunisia*

Table of Contents

Detailed Table of Contents

In this chapter, the impact of board gender diversity on overall firm risk was investigated. Drawing on social identity theory, upper echelons theory, and agency theory, a hypothesis of a negative link between gender diversity on the board of directors and firm risk has been put forward. Using a panel data regression on a sample of large Tunisian companies listed on the Tunis Stock Exchange (BVMT) over the period 2016-2020, the author was able to provide empirical evidences supporting the existence of a significant negative impact of the percentage of women on boards of directors on stock return volatility as global firm risk proxy.

This chapter aims to assess the role of gender diversity on banking performance in Kathmandu Valley. The study adopted descriptive approach. Respondents were sampled from employees of a commercial banks in Kathmandu Valley. Simple random sampling techniques was used to select 300 employees. The questionnaire was used for data collection. Descriptive statistics, correlation, regression, pre-estimation, post-estimation techniques within binary logistic model were used for data analysis. The study found that gender diversity has positive significant influence on enhancing banking performance. Gender diverse teams could help organization enhance creativity in its practice and increase its performance level. This study concluded that gender diversity has been one of the important issues in the world, and enhancing it could result higher productivity and higher performance of an organization. Hence, the chapter recommends that there should be inclusive climate in the workplace and policies supporting work-life balance should be forwarded.

Preface

ABOUT THE SUBJECT

The topics on the perspectives on women in management and the global labor market have gained pertinent international relevance. As more women achieve management positions across the world, it is essential to understand women's roles in management in different countries and economies as well as their relationships to the global market and the gender effect on management. Women's leadership and the challenges that they face look very different globally. It is important to research the role of women in management to strengthen equality and efficiency.

Perspectives on Women in Management and the Global Labor Market provides a clear idea of the effect of gender on the management decision-making process and the respective consequences, showing similarities and striking differences in the practices of different countries and economies. This book serves as a compilation of ideas on the new trends associated with the presence of women in management and the global labor market. Covering topics such as firm debt maturity, change management, and wage inequality, this premier reference source is an excellent resource for business managers and leaders, human resource managers, entrepreneurs, government officials, sociologists, students and educators of higher education, librarians, researchers, and academicians.

There is empirical evidence stating that the management decision-making process is different according to gender. There are several reasons to explain these differences, such as the style of management, the predisposition for risk aversion, and behavioral reasons. The differences in the decision-making process led to different consequences in firms' management, profitability, and firms' value. The institutional environment providing women quotas in management can influence the presence of women on the board of management and, consequently, on management decisions.

Female directors can develop trust leadership, which requires managers to share information and are more likely to be risk-averse in what concerns management decisions, such as capital structure and investment decisions.

As women have increased their presence in the business world, their participation in management teams has been reinforced. However, their participation in management mostly takes place in small and medium-sized companies, and the number of women who assume the role of CEOs in larger organizations is still low.

It is extremely important to highlight the role of gender diversity in the case of business as well as their presence in business and management. However, it is necessary to understand that there are several obstacles that women still must face in reaching CEO and board positions in companies. They remain often excluded from the high-level economic process of decision-making, despite their activism over the last years to break this barrier. However, we highlight the fact that the presence of women in the labor market is increasingly relevant for economic growth and development. It is relevant to understand the need to focus on gender diversity in organizations. It is necessary to implement measures and policies able to decrease gender inequality and reduce the wage gap for the same roles and tasks being executed. Recruitment and retention of talents should also be a concern and an agenda need.

The global labor market faces several challenges, namely, to achieving Sustainable Development Goals, such as the evidence that unemployment remains above pre-pandemic levels, the increase of workers associated with informal employment, the significance of young people that are not in education, employment, or training (NEET), and the gender parity in managerial positions. Although the share of women in management has been rising all over the world, progress is still slower than desired.

Consequently, it is fruitful to investigate and disseminate the results of theoretical and empirical studies that explore the role of women in management, and its impacts on the global market, to obtain insightful knowledge on how to effectively promote women's access to decision-making positions such as managerial functions, namely as CEOs, and their contribution to the economic development.

This book folds several coherent chapters which allow, on a scientific basis, to discuss, at an international level, the new directions in the presence of women in management, and their role in the labor market.

Expectations

The editors intend this book to be useful for regulatory authorities and researchers in the field of women in management and the global labor market.

Through dissemination of the research findings on the rigor of finance, this publication could also be valuable to develop and inspire further studies by researchers and students in postgraduate courses, whose research interests are related to gender diversity and the global market.

The book intends to provide a clear comparison of major trends regarding the presence of women in management and the global labor market, showing similarities and striking differences in the practices of different countries and economies. The idea of this book is to be a compilation of ideas in new trends that are currently shaping economic development. According to the economies, there are different mechanisms to ensure the presence of women on board, and the consequences are useful to provide new highlights into a new direction in gender topics.

This book aims to be a reference source that discusses the gender effects in management decisions, and their consequences, in different dimensions. It can have an impact on the academy since the subjects are of increasing importance. We would like to collect studies that allow researchers to understand the new directions of investigation in the proposed subjects. Besides, it allows comparing the different practices all over the world, given the international focus.

Relating these subjects and going to new avenues of research is an asset of this book. As such, it has a variety of crucial issues of gender effects in management, contributing to a better expansion of both theoretical and empirical works applied on this subject.

ORGANIZATION OF THE BOOK

This book is organized into 13 chapters. The first chapter is focused on the literature review of gender in management. Thus:

- Chapter 1, "Management and Gender in the Global Labor Market: A Bibliometric Analysis," offers a literature review on gender in management and the global labor market, based on the bibliometric analysis methodology.

The next six chapters provide studies analyzing the issue of management gender, focusing on specific economic realities, such as different countries or regions. In this way:

- Chapter 2, "The Work-Family Conflict in the Accounting Profession: A Study on the Female Gender in Portugal," focuses on a bank-based system country, Portugal, investigating the conflicts in the accounting profession in the context of the family businesses.
- Chapter 3, "Does Board Gender Diversity Influence Firm Debt Maturity? Evidence From Portuguese Hotel Industry SMEs," focuses on a specific sector of the Portuguese market, analyzing whether gender diversity affects debt maturity, since there is evidence that women and men take different decisions about the capital structure of companies.

- Chapter 4, "Change Management as a Tool to Implement Gender Equality: The Spanish Banking Sector Case," explores the relationship between gender equality and the management of change experienced, considering the financial sector of another bank-based system country, Spain, focusing on the banking sector.
- Chapter 5, "Board Diversity Evolution in the Iberian Stock Markets: Is the Evidence Supporting Governance Regulators?" analyzes the evolution of gender diversity and the state of the firm's accomplishment of quotas through time in two neighboring countries, Portugal and Spain, which compose the Iberian market.
- Chapter 6, "Female Presence on Boards of Directors and Firm Risk: Case of Listed Tunisian Firm," deals with gender diversity on the firms' performance, examining the impact of the diversity of boards of directors on the risk of the company, considering the Tunisian context, given the socio-cultural differences of Tunisian women compared to Western women, and the status enjoyed by women in this country compared to other Arab-Muslim countries.
- Chapter 7, "Assessment of Gender Diversity on Banking Performance in Nepal: Evidence From Binary Logit Estimation," assesses the role of gender diversity on banking performance in Kathmandu valley, based on a descriptive approach. The chapter considers a questionnaire for data collection, and descriptive statistics, correlation, regression, pre-estimation, and post-estimation techniques within a binary logistic model for data analysis.

The next chapter focuses on wage inequality:

- Chapter 8, "Between Pay and Performance: A Perspective on Wage Inequality in the Accounting Profession," analyses the wage differences based on gender, as well as the professionals' academic degrees, age, time of profession, and job situation, based on a survey applied to Portuguese Certified Accountants. Although the accounting profession has been dominated by men until 2010, since then, it has been noticed an increase in women's enrolment in the Professional Order, surpassing men.

The last five chapters cover diverse issues, such as the creative crafts entrepreneurship, the COVID-19 effects on management decision and gender discrimination, the Foucaultian assumptions of governmentality, the emancipatory power of accounting effects on the ruptures of hegemonies in the context of entrepreneurial women, and racial diversity. Thus:

- Chapter 9, "Women's Entrepreneurship in Creative Crafts: The Case of 'Benim Küçük Atölyem'," analyzes the specific case of creative crafts entrepreneurship to focus on why an entrepreneur decides to become a creative crafts entrepreneur and how she is performing it, based on qualitative research, combining observatory research and interviews to explore the phenomenon of creative crafts entrepreneurship.
- Chapter 10, "From Struggle to Strength: Gender Parity in Top-level Leadership," explores the difficulties women experience in attaining and being seen as effective in top leadership positions. Besides, it will also highlight the COVID-19 effects on management decisions and gender discrimination, considering the gender-differential impact of COVID-19 in relation to the response strategies, challenges, and policies at the management level and in the global labor market.
- Chapter 11, "Tearing the Veil of Hegemonies: The Emancipatory Power of Accounting for Entrepreneurial Women in the Amazon," examines how the emancipatory power of accounting enables ruptures of hegemonies in the context of entrepreneurial women in the Amazon, collecting data through interviews.
- Chapter 12, "Dealing With Mavericks in the Workplace," emphasizes the role of black women's skills in Corporate America, medium to small businesses, non-profits, academia, politics, and healthcare, to obtain leadership status, trying to answer how Black women can navigate to be successful in their chosen professions.
- Chapter 13, "Breaking the Glass Ceiling: Oral History of the Professional Trajectories of Women in Public Accounting," analyzes the professional trajectories of women working in public accounting in light of the glass ceiling phenomenon, in the Northern region of Brazil.

Elisabete S. Vieira
GOVCOPP, University of Aveiro, Portugal

Mara Madaleno
GOVCOPP, University of Aveiro, Portugal

João Teodósio
Polytechnic Institute of Santarém, Portugal

Acknowledgment

The editors would like to thank all the people involved in this project for all the help provided, especially to the authors and reviewers. We sincerely appreciate the contributions provided by all of you. It was an excellent and relevant input to the publication process. Without your support, this project would not be possible to achieve.

The editors would like to thank each of the authors of the chapters who contributed deeply dispending their time and expertise to this book, making it so special.

It is never too much to thank and recognize the valuable work of the members of the IGI Editorial Advisory Board in improving the quality, consistency, and presentation of the content of the chapters, which has ensured the highest accuracy in the double-blind review process. We would like to thank the Editorial Advisory Board for its precious collaboration, as well as some of the authors who have taken on a double task, serving as well as referees for their pairs.

To all, our most sincere thank you.

Chapter 1
Management and Gender in the Global Labor Market:
A Bibliometric Analysis

Elisabete S. Vieira
GOVCOPP, University of Aveiro, Portugal

Mara S. Madaleno
University of Aveiro, Portugal

João Teodósio
Polytechnic Institute of Santarém, Portugal

ABSTRACT

Achieving gender equality and women's empowerment is integral to each of the 17 sustainable development goals (SDGs). Notwithstanding that, goal five is fully applied to gender equality. In this chapter, the authors attempt to collate and understand the disjointed research on female management around the world, reviewing the literature at the macro, meso, and microanalysis levels. Simultaneously, the authors address the obstacles, challenges, motivations, and characteristics of women in management and the global labor market. The analysis is based on a gender-aware and a bibliometric analysis, appropriate methods when aggregating studies of different methodological approaches, and different empirical version analyses which have emerged from 2010 up to the present, thus covering broad and fragmented topics in different settings. Therefore, the present chapter analyzes the areas that have received sufficient research attention and those which are still under-developed, contributing with suggestions to decrease the gap in this area of research.

DOI: 10.4018/978-1-6684-5981-2.ch001

INTRODUCTION

Persistent differences considering "typical" women's and men's jobs, underrepresentation in higher management, a high women's part-time rate, persistent non-implementation of gender quotas, and considerable gender pay gap for the same activity or education level, remain nowadays (Clark et al., 2021; Halliday et al., 2021). Despite the already conducted efforts worldwide, it remains to be solved individually at the country level the substantial remaining differences in employment patterns (Ahrens & Scheele, 2022).

This chapter intends to analyse the women's status in management around the world and to study the influence of women in management in the global labor market. For that, we propose a bibliometric analysis considering the most recent empirical works which emerged in the field. The Scopus bibliographic source will be used, and the articles included go from 2010 to 2021. Some insights from the recent literature which emerged in the first half of 2022 will also be analyzed. The goal is to register the most recent literature on the topic and to provide a summary of findings with important policy implications. Therefore, a review of knowledge areas and research gaps are to be provided. Based on the findings, we provide an analysis of the status quo, a summary of the existing gaps, and suggestions for future research directions.

This chapter's bibliometric analysis will be divided, into methodological terms, regarding the main key terms to be searched within the bibliometric databases. First, we explore the current literature on women in management and the global labor market. Second, the empirical and theoretical literature which emerged on gender diversity on boards and management teams. Third, considering the recent literature on women in management and diversity within the board, including issues such as the gender pay gap and management roles. Fourth, by linking individual country analysis to regional analysis of women in management and the global labor market. Fifth, by searching the emergent literature on women in management, the global labor market, and individual characteristics.

By showing the complementarity of these factors, and how the literature has explored them, we intend to contribute to the institutional, organizational, public, and private policy regulation, and corporate governance pieces of literature. Similar to previous recent studies (Clark et al., 2021; Datta et al., 2021; Fleischer, 2022; Kirsch, 2021; Loyning, 2021; Sidhu et al., 2020; Singh et al., 2021; Wang et al., 2021), we note the need for policymakers to go beyond mere codification of rules via quotas and simultaneously work towards raising national and organizational social consciousness levels on issues of gender equality.

This chapter ends by indicating further avenues for future research identifying the existing gaps. First, there is a clear lack of theoretical foundations. Second, there exists an over-emphasis on macro-level indicators, like culture and religion, probably due to data availability whereas a lot less is known at the organizational level variables. Third, there is still evidence of a lack of studies that analyze women in management within ethnic groups or studies that acknowledge the complex social, cultural, and religious diversity. Fourth, different country and region contexts dictate women in management and the global labor market, imposing that diversity contexts should be taken into account. Fifth, there is particular inattention given to regional experiences like the refugee crisis, being the recent invasion of Russia to Ukraine an important avenue for future research, as well as other emerging trends such as the Covid-19 pandemic and similar. Sixth, the evolution of board diversity literature which emerged reached different conclusions leading to important analysis to be further developed in this regard, particularly in what respects the credit risk, bankruptcy risk, and risk of information disclosure. Seventh, board diversity will also dictate corporate social responsibility or even sustainability disclosures, implementation, and additional costs. Different perspectives are pointed up to this moment, deserving additional and careful analysis in the emerging literature. Finally, gender diversity considering foreign directors, internationalization, foreign direct investment, and independent directors are areas of research that require deeper analysis.

The rest of the chapter is organized as follows. The next section presents the materials and methods used in the study. Afterward, the results are presented, followed by a discussion. A final section concludes the article and offers some future research agendas regarding gender diversity and leadership.

MATERIALS AND METHODS

The bibliometric analysis consists of the application of statistical methods to analyze the evolution of a scientific research topic, founding the profile of publications and perceiving trends in future research, based on the evidence progress and the perceived gaps (De Bakker et al., 2005).

We select the Scopus database (https://www.scopus.com/search/) to implement the bibliometric method to understand the core of management and gender in the global labor market for several reasons. First, Aksnes and Sivertsen (2019) and Nawaz et al. (2020) argue that the Scopus database is suitable for carrying out bibliometric analysis. Second, it is one of the favorite databases for academic researchers (Marlowe & Clarke, 2022). Third, it offers a nonstop admission to research output all over the world (Elsevier, 2021). Finally, Scopus covers a wide range of scientific articles in the area of business and management (Aksnes & Sivertsen, 2019), which is the focus of this study. Additionally, while jointly using the Web of Science (WoS) database, for the final filters used, it was possible to be noticed that almost articles presented in Scopus were also included in the WoS.

The next step is to select the filters to implement the bibliometric analysis, which was carried out on June 8th, 2022. We define several filters to conduct the analysis: i) limit the period between 2010 and 2021; ii) limit the study fields to "Business, Management and Accounting" and "Economics, Econometrics, and Finance"; iii) consider only articles and iv) set the language to "English".

Table 1 shows the combinations of keywords mentioned in the introduction and the number of articles found with the filters mentioned above.

Table 1. Number of articles, considering different keyword combinations

N.º	Keywords	N.º articles without filters	N.º articles with filters
1	Women and "labor market" and management	472	80
2	"Gender diversity" and board and "management team"	45	24
3	"Gender pay gap" and management	89	31
4	"Women in management" and "country analysis"	1	1
5	"Women in management" and "labor market"	15	3
6	"Women in management" and "individual characteristics"	1	1
7	"Women in management" and "ethnic groups"	1	1
8	Cultural and social and religious and women and management	133	7
9	Women and "labor market" or management and "gender diversity"	437	213
10	"Refugee crisis" or "invasion of Russia" or covid and women	13,754	318
11	"Board diversity" or "gender diversity" and "credit risk"	8	7
12	Women and "Corporate Social Responsibility" or CSR	577	203
13	Women or "gender diversity" and internationalization or "foreign direct investment"	377	81

Source: Own elaboration.

Considering the different keyword combinations, we can see distinct kinds of results. First, there are cases with an insufficient number of papers for analysis (numbers 4; 5; 6; 7; 8; 11). The searches number 1; 3; 9; 10 and 13 have a great difference between the results without filters, and with filters, representing the last result of about 16%, 34.8%, 48.7%, 55.1%, and 21,5%, respectively. The difference is mainly justified by the study fields, in which a significant number of studies are associated with the domain of, for example, Medicine, Psychology, Social Sciences and Biology. From the last two keywords combinations (numbers 2 and 12), we opt to analyze the search number 12 - Women and "Corporate Social Responsibility"

(CSR), mainly because it is related to the labor market, and it is one of the fundamental issues currently associated with sustainability.

Choosing the subject to implement the bibliometric analysis, we go along the following filters to conduct the analysis:

1) Starting with the following criteria: (TITLE-ABS-KEY (gender OR female OR women OR "gender diversity") AND TITLE-ABS-KEY (management AND leadership)), we obtain 577 results;
2) Considering the period from 2010 to 2021, the results decline to 466;
3) Limiting the study fields to "Business, Management and Accounting" and "Economics, Econometrics, and Finance" (because finance is assotiated with management), the results decline to 282;
4) Choosing only "articles", we obtain 211 results;
5) Finally, set the language to "English", and we finish with 203 articles.

Considering the filters 1 to 5: (title-abs-key (women) and title-abs-key ("corporate social responsibility" or csr)) and (limit-to (pubyear, 2021) or limit-to (pubyear, 2020) or limit-to (pubyear, 2019) or limit-to (pubyear, 2018) or limit-to (pubyear, 2017) or limit-to (pubyear, 2016) or limit-to (pubyear, 2015) or limit-to (pubyear, 2014) or limit-to (pubyear, 2013) or limit-to (pubyear, 2012) or limit-to (pubyear, 2011) or limit-to (pubyear, 2010)) and (limit-to (doctype, "ar")) and (limit-to (subjarea, "busi") or limit-to (subjarea, "econ")) and (limit-to (language, "english")), the final collection used in this review comprises 203 articles, from 2010 to 2021.

Figure 1 shows the methodological approach to conducting the bibliometric analysis.

Figure 1. Methodological approach to determine the sample selection process
Source: Own elaboration.

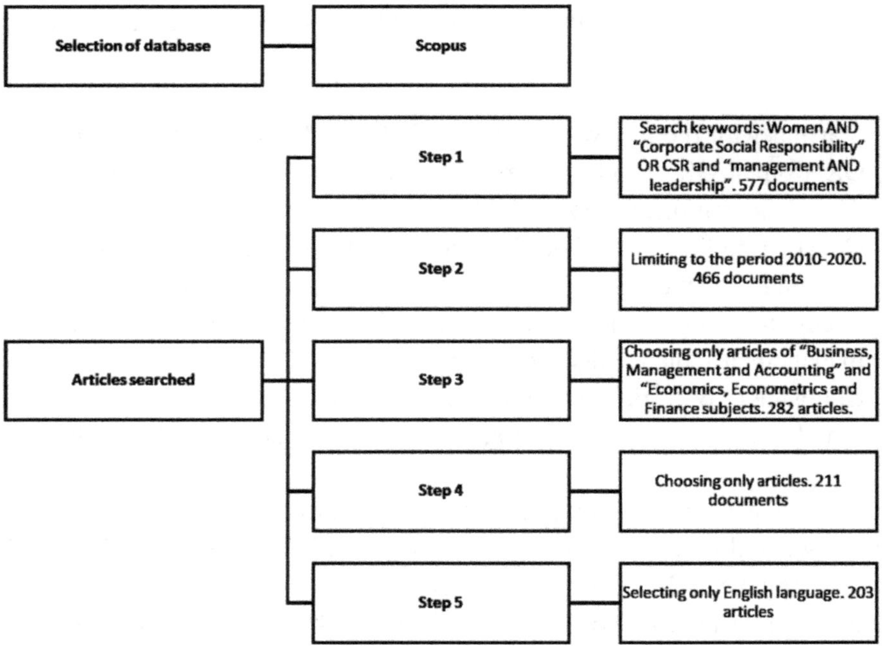

The final dataset consists of the analysis of 203 articles, considering also 5 articles published in 2022, and already with citations. In the following, we resort to graphical and table analysis of the research outputs, using also WordClouds.

RESULTS OF BIBLIOMETRIC ANALYSIS

Based on the sample selection process, we start the bibliometric analysis by focusing on the 203 papers published in the period 2010-2021. Figure 2 shows the number of articles published each year.

Figure 2. The number of articles published by year: 2010-2021
Source: Own elaboration.

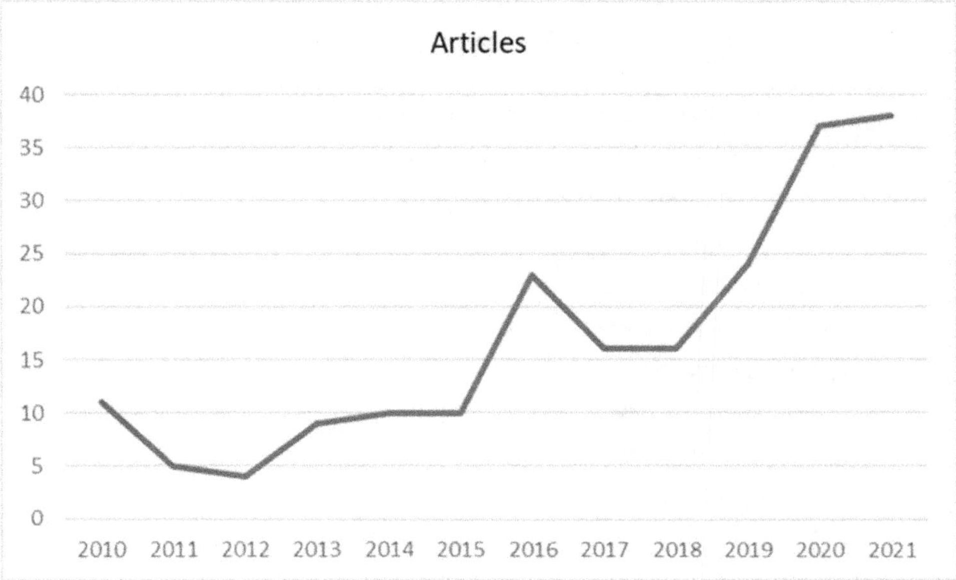

Considering the period from 2010 to 2021, the articles range between 4, in 2012 and 38, in 2021. Overall, the number of articles about women and CSR has increased continuously. The accelerated ascendant evolution of publications during the last four years (2018-2021) suggests that these topics have attracted many researchers, which leads to a significant increase in published articles. The articles published in the last four years represent about 56,7% of the articles, and considering the last six years, they represent 75.9% of the total publications. For curiosity, the first paper published on these subjects registered in Scopus is dated 1973 (49 years ago).

Figure 3 displays the documents by country or territory during the period 2010-2021.

Figure 3. Documents by country or territory: 2010-2021
Source: Own elaboration.

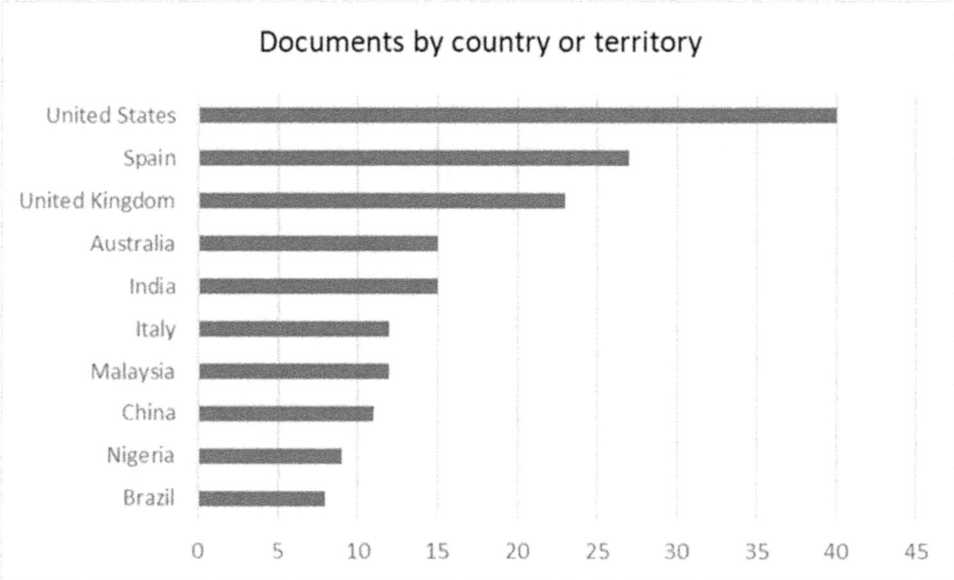

Regarding the articles published by country or territory, it is clear that the research is concentrated in the United States, with 40 publications, followed by Spain and the United Kingdom, with 27 and 23 publications, respectively. Australia and India present 15 publications, followed by Italy and Malaysia, both with 12 articles published. The other countries on the top ten documents by country are China (11), Nigeria (9), and Brazil (8).

Considering the respective continents, the studies are concentrated in Western Europe (Spain, the United Kingdom, and Italy), which represents 36% of the publications, followed by North America (the United States), with 23%, and Asia (India, Malaysia, and China), with 22% of the published papers. Oceania (Australia), Africa (Nigeria), and South America (Brazil) represent, respectively, 9% and 5% of the last two countries.

There is still a scarcity of research on these topics on several continents and regions, such as South America, East Europe, some Western Europe, and African countries.

Figure 4 presents the top 10 documents published by affiliation under the sample selection method.

Figure 4. Documents by affiliation: 2010-2021
Source: Own elaboration.

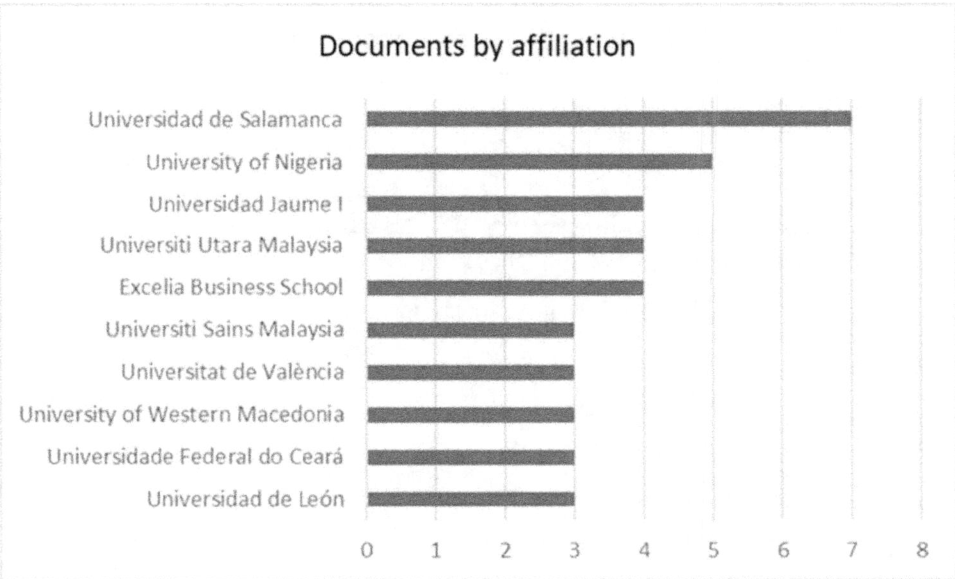

Concerning the affiliation of the authors, the Spanish Universities (Salamanca, Valência, Léon, and University Jaume I) stand out from the others, with 17 publications, followed by two organizations from Malaysia (7). The last four Universities (University of Nigeria; Excelia Business School, France; University of Macedonia and Ceará University, Brazil) with 5, 4, 3, and 3 articles published, respectively.

Figure 5 shows the documents published by source title, considering the five sources with more publications.

Figure 5. Documents per year by source title: 2010-2021
Source: Own elaboration.

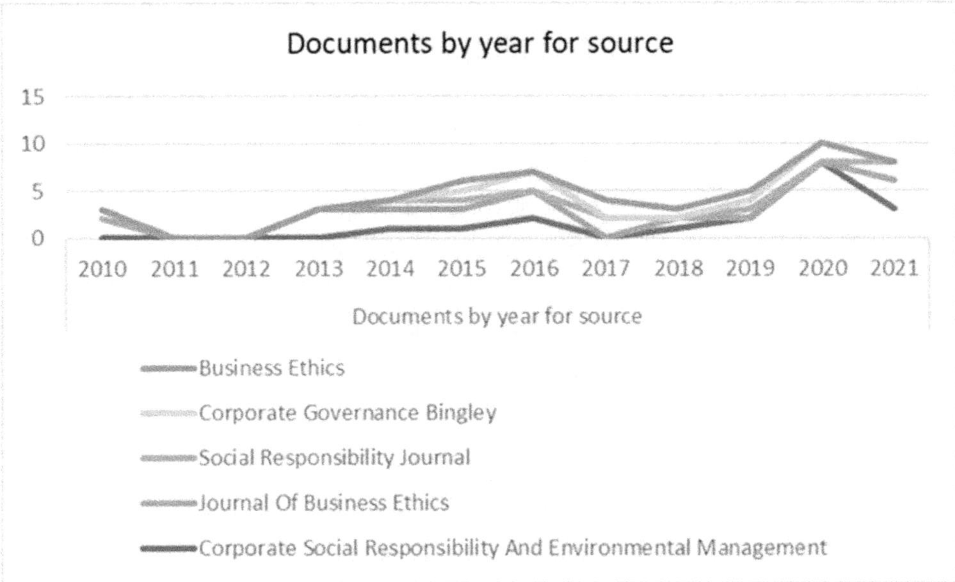

The five-top journals with more publications in the domain of women and CSR during the 2010-2021 period, are the Corporate Social Responsibility and Environmental Management (18 documents), the Journal of Business Ethics (16), the Social Responsibility Journal (8), the Corporate Governance Bingley (6) and the Business Ethics (5). The years with more publications are 2020 and 2021, representing, these two tears, almost 34% of the total publications, suggesting this is a hot topic, with more relevance in the last years, which is also evident in Figure 2.

Figure 6 highlights the authors with more published papers during the period 2010-2021.

Figure 6. Documents per year by author: 2010-2021
Source: Own elaboration.

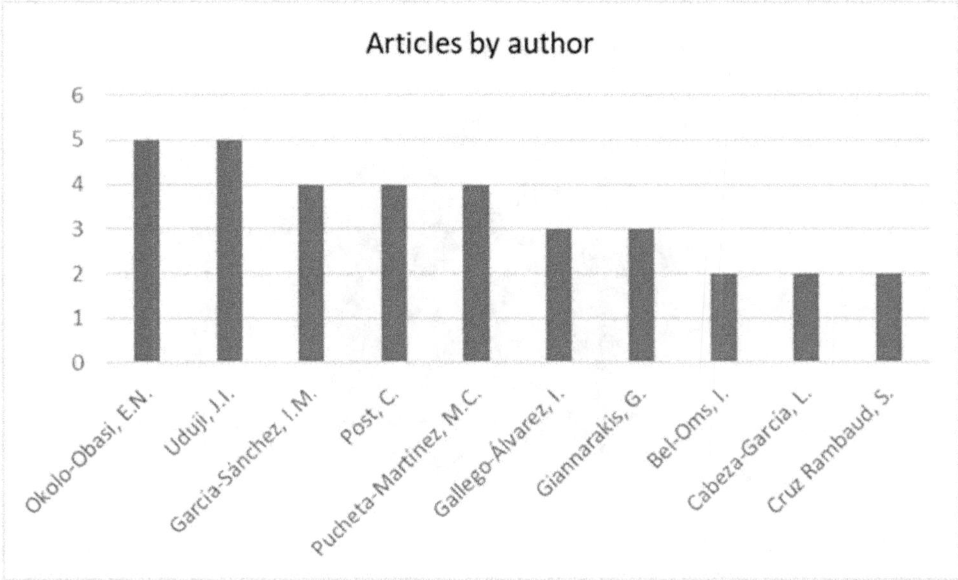

The authors with more publications in the period under study are Okolo-Obasi, E.N. and Uduji, J.I., with five articles each one; García-Sánchez, I.M., Post, C. and Pucheta-Martínez, with four pulications each. M.C., Gallego-Álvarez, I., and Giannarakis, G. are responsible for three articles. Three of the 10 authors have two articles published (Bel-Oms, I.; Cabeza-García, L.; Cruz Rambaud, S.).

Finally, Figure 7 shows the articles by subject area during the period 2010-2021.

Figure 7. Articles by subject area: 2010-2021
Source: Own elaboration.

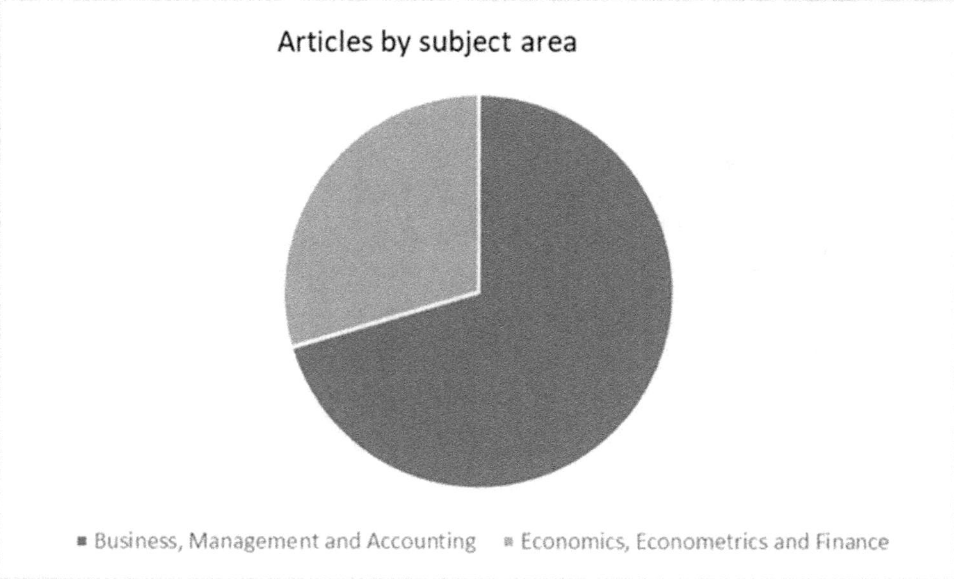

As we can see, the majority of the articles are published in the journals of Business, Management, and Accounting, followed by the ones of Economics, Econometrics, and Finance, representing 70.5% and 29.5%, respectively.

After a brief characterization of the articles about women and CSR between 2010 and 2021, we narrow our analysis, ranking the publications by the number of citations. Consequently, we identify the h-index (Hirsch, 2005), which combines the number of publications and the number of citations (excluding the self-citations), in the option "view citation overview" of the Scopus database. The results are presented in Figure 8.

Figure 8. h-index: 2010-2021
Source: Own elaboration.

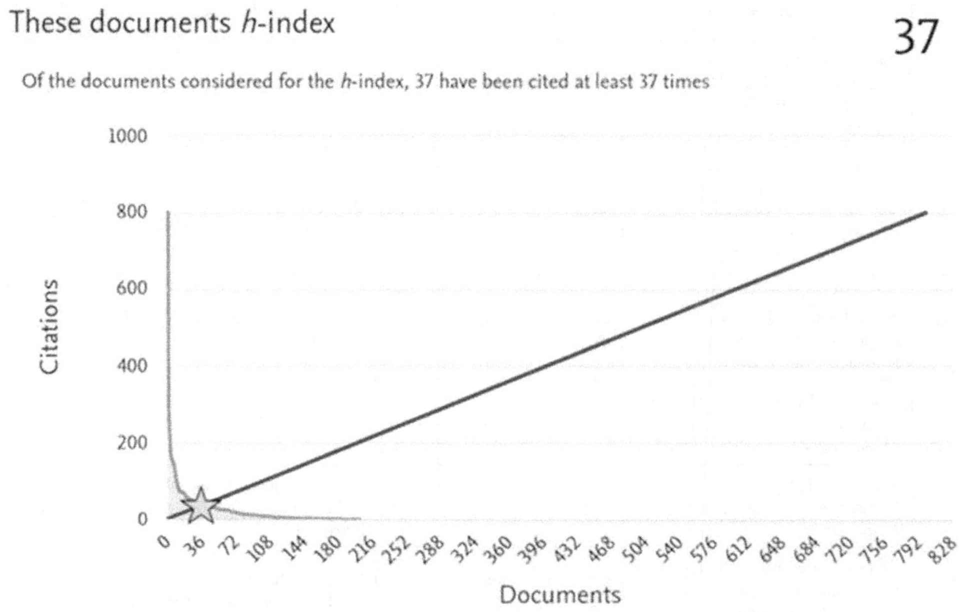

The h-index is 37, which means that of the 203 articles obtained from Scopus, 37 have at least 37 citations. As 37 is a high number of articles, we will focus our analysis on the top 20 cited articles, between 2010 and 2021. However, we must be aware that this choice can conditioning the discussion.

DISCUSSION

Table 2 presents the top 20 articles ranked by citations.

Table 2. Top 20 cited articles during the period 2010-2021

	Document title	Authors	Year	Source	Cited by
1	The Impact of Board Diversity and Gender Composition on Corporate Social Responsibility and Firm Reputation	Bear, S., Rahman, N., Post, C.	2010	Journal of Business Ethics, 97(2), 207-221	800
2	The effect of corporate governance elements on corporate social responsibility (CSR); reporting: Empirical evidence from private commercial banks of Bangladesh	Khan, H.-U.-Z.	2010	International Journal of Law and Management, 52(2), 82-109	266
3	Board Composition and Corporate Social Responsibility: An Empirical Investigation in the Post Sarbanes-Oxley Era	Zhang, J.Q., Zhu, H., Ding, H.-B.	2013	Journal of Business Ethics, 114(3), 381-392	228
4	Women on Boards of Directors and Corporate Social Performance: A Meta-Analysis	Byron, K., Post, C.	2016	Corporate Governance: An International Review, 24(4), 428-442	174
5	The Relationship between Women Directors and Corporate Social Responsibility	Setó-Pamies, D.	2015	Corporate Social Responsibility and Environmental Management, 22(6), 334-345	161
6	Diversity of Board of Directors and Environmental Social Governance: Evidence from Italian Listed Companies	Cucari, N., Esposito De Falco, S., Orlando, B.	2018	Corporate Social Responsibility and Environmental Management, 25(3), 250-266	155
7	Women on boards: Do they affect sustainability reporting?	Fernandez-Feijoo, B., Romero, S., Ruiz-Blanco, S.	2014	Corporate Social Responsibility and Environmental Management, 21(6), 351-364	148
8	Board reputation attributes and corporate social performance: An empirical investigation of the US Best Corporate Citizens	Mallin, C.A., Michelon, G.	2011	Accounting and Business Research, 41(2), 119-144	137
9	From Board Composition to Corporate Environmental Performance Through Sustainability-Themed Alliances	Post, C., Rahman, N., McQuillen, C.	2015	Journal of Business Ethics, 130(2), 423-435	121
10	Is Board Gender Diversity Linked to Financial Performance? The Mediating Mechanism of CSR	Galbreath, J.	2018	Business and Society, 57(5), 863-889	101
11	Corporate governance and financial characteristic effects on the extent of corporate social responsibility disclosure	Giannarakis, G.	2014	Social Responsibility Journal, 10(4), 569-590	93
12	Financial, governance and environmental determinants of corporate social responsible disclosure	Giannarakis, G., Konteos, G., Sariannidis, N.	2014	Management Decision, 52(10), 1928-1951	84
13	Board gender diversity and ESG disclosure: evidence from the USA	Manita, R., Bruna, M.G., Dang, R., Houanti, L.	2018	Journal of Applied Accounting Research, 19(2), 206-224	74

Continued on following page

Table 2. Continued

	Document title	Authors	Year	Source	Cited by
14	Board composition and corporate social responsibility in an emerging market	Sundarasen, S.D., Je-Yen, T., Rajangam, N.	2016	Corporate Governance (Bingley), 16(1), 35-53	74
15	Corporate governance and corporate social responsibility disclosure: evidence from Pakistan	Lone, E.J., Ali, A., Khan, I.	2016	Corporate Governance (Bingley), 16(5), 785-797	74
16	The Legitimacy of CSR Actions of Publicly Traded Companies Versus Family-Owned Companies	Panwar, R., Paul, K., Nybakk, E., Hansen, E., Thompson, D.	2014	Journal of Business Ethics, 125(3), 481-496	71
17	Going green: women entrepreneurs and the environment	Braun, P.	2010	International Journal of Gender and Entrepreneurship, 2(3), 245-259	71
18	The effect of corporate governance elements on corporate social responsibility (Csr) disclosure: An empirical evidence from listed companies at kse Pakistan	Majeed, S., Aziz, T., Saleem, S.	2015	International Journal of Financial Studies, 3(4), 530-556	68
19	Does having women managers lead to increased gender equality practices in corporate social responsibility?	De Celis, I.L.-R., Velasco-Balmaseda, E., De Bobadilla, F.S., Alonso-Almeida, M.D.M., Intxaurburu-Clemente, G.	2015	Business Ethics, 24(1), 91-110	66
20	Corporate philanthropy and productivity: Evidence from an online real effort experiment	Tonin, M., Vlassopoulos, M.	2015	Management Science, 61(8), 1795-1811	60

The 20 articles have been cited 3,026 times. The first one (Bear et al., 2010) stands out quite a bit from all the others, with 800 citations, which represents 26.4% of the total citations. There are 10 papers with more than 100 citations. The citations of the other publications in the top 20 range from 60 to 93.

Concerning the years of publication, it varies between 2010 and 2018, being the major number of papers from 2015 (25%) and 2014 (20%), showing that, although the increase of publications in the last years of the sample (2018-2021 - Figure 2), they are not so cited than the ones from 2014 and 2015.

Concerning the publication's sources, three journals appear on the list more than once: Corporate Governance (2), Corporate Social Responsibility and Environmental Management (3), and the Journal of Business Ethics (4). Indeed, several studies focus on the relationship between Corporate Governance (CG) characteristics and CSR (Khan, 2010; Mallin & Michelon, 2011; Zhang et al., 2013; Majeed et al., 2015; Sundarasen et al., 2016).

Khan (2010) analyzes the relationship between CG elements and CSR, considering a sample of Bangladeshi commercial banks. Overall, the results show that the banks cover their CSR activities in different segments, such as education and health. Concerning the impact of CG on CSR, the authors find evidence that non-executive directors and nationality diversity have a positive impact on CSR reporting. However, they find no relationship between women's representation on board and CSR reporting. Based on data from the Top 100 Best Corporate Citizens, for the period between 2005 and 2007, Mallin and Michelon (2011) find evidence that the percentage of independent, community influential, and female directors impact positively on CSR, but the CEO duality and community influential directors with multiple directorships impact negatively on CSR. Zhang et al. (2013) focus on the presence of outside directors and women directors on the board, and their impact on CSR in the Post-SOX period, considering a sample of listed firms in the US, finding evidence that women directors and outside directors impact positively on the CSR performance. Majeed et al. (2015) focus their study on the impacts of CG characteristics on CSR disclosure, based on a sample of Pakistani listed firms, between 2007 and 2011, concluding that board size, institutions ownership, and ownership concentration affects positively the CSR reporting. However, the women and foreign directors' representation on the board impacts negatively on the CSR reporting. Analyzing the context of Malaysian listed firms, the evidence of Sundarasen et al. (2016) shows that role duality, non-executive directors, and independent non-executive directors exert a negative impact on CSR. In contrast, women on board have a positive effect on CSR.

Summarising the results concerning the relationship between women and CSR, some studies find a positive effect of the presence of women on board and CSR (Mallin & Michelon, 2011; Zhang et al., 2013; Sundarasen et al., 2016). However, Majeed et al. (2015) find a contrary effect, existing also evidence of no association amid these variables (Khan, 2010), which indicates that the results are not consensual.

Some research focuses more specifically on the relationship between women on board and CSR (Bear et al., 2010; De Celis et al., 2015; Setó-Pamies, 2015; Byron & Post, 2016).

Bear et al. (2010) investigate the potential effect of the number of women on boards on CSR ratings for a sample of firms carefully chosen from the Fortune most admired 2009 list, concluding that the number of women on board has a positive relationship with CSR ratings. Using a sample of Spanish companies, De Celis et al. (2015) conclude that the presence of women on board has a positive effect on CSR activities. Setó-Pamies (2015) studied whether women on the board of directors can reinforce the improvement of CSR in firms, contributing to sustainable development. Considering a sample of companies from 22 countries, the results show that gender diversity has a positive impact on CSR. Based on a meta-analysis of 87 independent samples from 20 different countries, Byron and Post's (2016) results show that female representation on board has a positive association with CSR performance.

These four studies find a positive effect on the existence of women on board and CSR. Comparing with previous studies' evidence, we can wonder if the absence of the other CG determinants is influencing the empirical results.

Five of the top 20 studies focus their analysis on the relationship between CG factors and CSR disclosure (Fernandez-Feijoo et al., 2014; Giannarakis, 2014; Giannarakis et al., 2014; Lone et al., 2016; Cucari et al., 2018). Fernandez-Feijoo et al. (2014) examine the association between sustainability reporting and the existence of at least three women on the board of directors. Overall, the authors find evidence that countries with higher gender equality are more likely to have firms with at least three women on the board of directors. More specifically, the results show evidence of a positive association between the board of directors with at least three women and the extent of CSR reporting.

Giannarakis (2014) explores the impact of CG elements on the extent of CSR disclosure, in the US context, concluding that the board commitment influences positively the levels of CSR disclosure. Giannarakis et al. (2014) examine the role of CG elements on CSR disclosure for the US market, considering the period from 2009 to 2012. Overall, the results show that CEO duality and female representation on board are not determinants of the extent of CSR disclosure. The authors conclude that a possible reason for the evidence of a non-significant association between women on board and CSR disclosure is the circumstance that, in developed counties, both women and men have equal access to education, training, and work. Lone et al. (2016) study the impact of CG characteristics on CSR disclosure, in the Pakistani context in the 2010-2014 period, concluding that independent directors, female directors, and board size impacts positively on the degree of CSR disclosure. In contrast, Cucari et al. (2018) find evidence of a negative association between the representation of females on board and the extent of CSR disclosure.

Consequently, the evidence of the potential impact of CG elements and the CSR disclosure has mixed results.

The studies of Post et al. (2015) and Galbreat (2018) have in common the fact that they analyze the relationship between CG elements and companies' performance. Post et al. (2015) find evidence that both the presence of women and independent directors on board impacts positively on US companies' environmental performance. In the same vein, Galbreat (2018) analyses a sample of Australia's listed firms, finding evidence that the representation of women on board is positively related to CSR and that CSR impacts financial performance.

The remaining studies of the top-20 cited articles explore distinct subjects. Braun (2010) investigates whether female entrepreneurs are more involved in green issues than their male counterparts, in the Australian context. The empirical evidence shows that females are more involved in environmental attitudes than males, which suggests that women entrepreneurs are more involved in green issues than men entrepreneurs. Panwar et al. (2014) focus on the legitimacy of CSR actions, considering a sample of family firms, as compared to non-family firms that belong to the US forest products firms, finding that family firms present a higher legitimacy for CSR actions, compared to their counterparts.

Concerning social issues, Tonin and Vlassopoulos (2015) analyze the effectiveness of social incentives that take the form of a donation to a charity. The results show a positive relationship between social incentives and the productivity of organizations, regardless of whether they assume a fixed or performance-related value. When individuals can choose the combination of incentives, half sacrifice some of their private compensation to increase social compensation, with women being more likely to do so than men.

In the US context, and covering the period from 2010 to 2015, Manita et al. (2018) find no significant association between board gender diversity and the environmental, social, and governance (ESG) disclosure. However, when the women directors on the board are below three, this relationship is not statistically significant. This evidence somewhat follows the results of Fernandez-Feijoo et al. (2014), for CSR disclosure.

Figure 9 presents a word cloud based on the 203 article titles, the subject of the current analysis. Female disclosure, women, CSR, corporate, responsibility, social, board, performance, and diversity are among the most used words within the titles. As to the most used keywords within articles, we have the corporate reputation, corporate social responsibility, board diversity, boards of directors, gender composition, financial reporting, corporate governance, disclosure, board composition, women, sustainability, sustainable development, women directors, board of directors, gender diversity, female talent, corporate social performance, women on board, environment, CSR, and environmental management. After exploring this literature some future research avenues are noticed. Future lines of research include studying the women's labor market according to the type of enterprises (public or private), to try to demonstrate if in the public sector there is less inequality on boards and management than in the private sector in the women's collective. Still, there remains a lack of information on the part of private companies to provide anonymous information about their workers (salary, productivity, working hours, etc.), leaving fewer possibilities to explore incentives and management allowed behaviors to carry out deeper investigations.

Moreover, there is still a lack of studies exploring legislation regarding women on board quotas in a cross-country comparison. Including developed and developing countries, or distinguishing between emerging economies would provide useful insights into the literature on management and gender in the global labor market. As for now, hot topics are highlighted, such as CSR and ESG, which are related to sustainability issues. Therefore, not only SDG 5 deserves deeper analysis as to the psychological and sociodemographic characteristics of the board of directors composition, but sustainability has raised increased attention in gender-management-related thematics. Also, it becomes highlighted the need to increase the study period of analysis, since when we deal with companies, financial data is used and these are limited to availability. Moreover, different ways of measuring variables emerge in the literature, and comparing in empirical terms all the results obtained up to the present would raise valuable policy directions and still deserve deeper analysis.

Figure 9. Word-cloud of the 203 article titles: 2010-2021
Source: Own elaboration.

After the analysis of the top 20 cited articles between 2010 and 2021, we will examine the published articles from 2022, which have already been cited. Table 3

summarizes the four articles from 2022 that have already been cited in the literature and belong to the data collection collected from Scopus.

The empirical evidence of the most trending articles of 2022 (already with citations) shows evidence that researchers and academics are concerned with the study of gender diversity, CSR, and, more recently, ESG concerns. The ESG topic is also explored within the 203 articles which have been the subject of our analysis. This is the case of Manita et al. (2018) discussing board gender diversity and ESG disclosure in the context of USA firms, and Velte (2016) in the context of two European countries, Germany and Austria. The latter finds that female members on the management board do have a positive impact on ESG performance, but that CSR expertise does not have a significant impact on ESG performance. However, Velte (2016) states that the implementation of a CSR committee has a positive and significant link with ESG performance. Also, Cucari et al. (2018) investigate the association between ESG disclosure and diversity of the board of directors (BoD) in Italian listed companies.

Results point out that a firm's CSR disclosure is associated with independent director and committee CSR. In addition, women on BoDs are negatively correlated, whereas the age of the board is not significant. Friede et al. (2015) study combines the findings of about 2200 individual studies on the relationship between ESG and corporate financial performance. Results point out that roughly 90% of studies find a nonnegative relation and that the large majority of studies report positive findings. The authors even argue that the positive ESG impact on corporate financial performance appears stable over time. Based on these studies we may state that shareholders and policymakers will have a deeper knowledge of the significant roles that board diversity is playing as a determinant of ESG disclosure if the literature is further explored. Additionally, results applied for one country may not be expanded to others, leaving room for the country and cross-country analysis.

Table 3. Cited articles on women and CSR in 2022

Authors	Findings	Citations
Nicolò et al. (2022)	- This study examines the effect of gender diversity on ESG disclosure in the context of European listed companies; - The results show a positive relationship between the female presence on the board of directors and the ESG disclosure.	4
Srivastav and Tang (2022)	- This study develops a structural equation model to analyze the Matthew effect in talent management; - The authors conclude that talent management strategy (TMS) increases job satisfaction more than life satisfaction in the distal context; - In the omnibus context, TMS indirectly improves borderline spanners' sales commission via life satisfaction, but not job satisfaction; - The model succeeds for the whole sample, for males, but not for females.	3
Saeed et al. (2022)	- The study explores whether top management team (TMT) gender diversity influences the implementation of environmental standards in the context of emerging countries; - The results show that the presence of women in TMT influences positively the likelihood of ISO 14001 certification and renewal; - There is evidence that women in management improve the environmental strategy.	2
Khidmat et al. (2022)	- This study explores the influence of gender diversity on CSR activities, in the Chinese context; - The results show that women's representation on the board of directors influences positively the firm performance, corporate governance, family ownership, institutional ownership, and managerial ownership - There is evidence that Chinese companies with gender diversity on board are socially responsible.	1

Source: Own elaboration.

CONCLUSION

This chapter intended to report on women's status in management around the world and to consider the influence of women in management in the global labor market. For the effect, a bibliometric analysis was presented considering the most recent empirical and theoretical research works which emerged in the field. The Scopus bibliographic source was used, and the articles included go from 2010 to 2021. Some insights from the recent literature which emerged in the first half of 2022 were also analyzed. It was possible to infer from the analysis the need for deeper exploration of the topic and important future research avenues are highlighted during the discussion of the results. The most evident is the need to explore different country contexts considering the laws which emerged concerning quotas on the board of directors.

Limitations to the female's role within companies are a reality and there is room for policy intervention to reduce gender inequality.

The explored literature through bibliometric analysis also allows understanding that sustainability issues are at the forefront of recent studies. It became evident that CSR and ESG are now deserving deeper understanding and exploration from research. Interesting would be to understand if psychological and intellectual capital would lead to entrepreneurship in management and contribute to gender differences decreases. For that, salary gaps need to be exploited and the differences should be taken into account by policymakers to fulfill the imposed legislation requirements of quotas on the board of directors. Attention should be given to equalizing countries' requirements in gender quotas and only then SDG goal 5 would become a reality. As for now, large differences remain and the recent literature turns them evident. The present chapter also highlights the positive contributions that CSR and ESG companies' practices impose on companies' financial performance. Finally, a gendered workforce seems to present similar capabilities (skills, ability to detect opportunities, and networks) to engage in corporate entrepreneurship, reinforcing good management practices and promoting financial performance, thus increasing profits and contributing to weighted development and growth. Therefore, it is argued that any gender differences could be explained by the influence of country-level conditions (gender equality levels, culture, and social norms), which should be decreased and/or eliminated to fulfill gender quotas requirements and promote equal human capital opportunities, both in regular jobs or at the management teams or board of directors levels. The future research can also be developed in order to develop aspects that have not yet received due attention in the studies carried out so far. There is evidence of a lack of studies that analyze women in management within ethnic groups or studies that acknowledge the complex social, cultural, and religious diversity. In addition, different country and region contexts dictate women in management and the global labor market, imposing that diversity contexts should be taken into account. Another research avenue can be based on the regional experiences like the refugee crisis and the invasion of Russia to Ukraine. The evolution of board diversity literature which emerged reached different conclusions, in need of further research. Among other perspectives, gender diversity considering foreign directors, internationalization, foreign direct investment, and independent directors are areas of research that require deeper analysis.

REFERENCES

Ahrens, P., & Scheele, A. (2022). Game-Changers for Gender Equality in Germany's Labour Market? Corporate Board Quotas, Pay Transparency and Temporary Part-Time Work. *German Politics*, *31*(1), 157–176. doi:10.1080/09644008.2021.1984428

Aksnes, D. W., & Sivertsen, G. A. (2019). Criteria-based assessment of the coverage of Scopus and Web of Science. *Journal of Data and Information Science*, *4*(1), 1–21. doi:10.2478/jdis-2019-0001

Bear, S., Rahman, N., & Post, C. (2010). The Impact of Board Diversity and Gender Composition on Corporate Social Responsibility and Firm Reputation. *Journal of Business Ethics*, *97*(2), 207–221. doi:10.100710551-010-0505-2

Braun, P. (2010). Going green: Women entrepreneurs and the environment. *International Journal of Gender and Entrepreneurship*, *2*(3), 245–259. doi:10.1108/17566261011079233

Byron, K., & Post, C. (2016). Women on Boards of Directors and Corporate Social Performance: A Meta-Analysis. *Corporate Governance*, *24*(4), 428–442. doi:10.1111/corg.12165

Clark, C. E., Arora, P., & Gabaldon, P. (2021). Female Representation on Corporate Boards in Europe: The Interplay of Organizational Social Consciousness and Institutions. *Journal of Business Ethics*. doi:10.100710551-021-04898-x

Cucari, N., Esposito De Falco, S., & Orlando, B. (2018). Diversity of Board of Directors and Environmental Social Governance: Evidence from Italian Listed Companies. *Corporate Social Responsibility and Environmental Management*, *25*(3), 250–266. doi:10.1002/csr.1452

Datta, S., Doan, T., & Toscano, F. (2021). Top executive gender, board gender diversity, and financing decisions: Evidence from debt structure choice. *Journal of Banking & Finance*, *125*, 106070. doi:10.1016/j.jbankfin.2021.106070

De Bakker, F. G., Groenewegen, P., & Den Hond, F. (2005). A bibliometric analysis of 30 years of research and theory on corporate social responsibility and corporate social performance. *Business & Society*, *44*(3), 283–317. doi:10.1177/0007650305278086

De Celis, I. L.-R., Velasco-Balmaseda, E., De Bobadilla, F. S., Alonso-Almeida, M. D., & Intxaurburu-Clemente, G. (2015). Does having women managers lead to increased gender equality practices in corporate social responsibility? *Business Ethics (Oxford, England)*, *24*(1), 91–110. doi:10.1111/beer.12081

Elsevier. (2021). *Scopus: Who uses Scopus*. Elsevier. https://www.elsevier.com/solutions/scopus/who-uses

Fernandez-Feijoo, B., Romero, S., & Ruiz-Blanco, S. (2014). Women on boards: Do they affect sustainability reporting? *Corporate Social Responsibility and Environmental Management*, *21*(6), 351–364. doi:10.1002/csr.1329

Fleischer, D. (2022). Does gender diversity in supervisory boards affect gender diversity in management boards in Germany? An empirical analysis. *German Journal of Human Resource Management*, *36*(1), 53–76. doi:10.1177/2397002221997148

Friede, G., Busch, T., & Bassen, A. (2015). ESG and financial performance: Aggregated evidence from more than 2000 empirical studies. *Journal of Sustainable Finance & Investment*, *5*(4), 210–233. doi:10.1080/20430795.2015.1118917

Galbreath, J. (2018). Is Board Gender Diversity Linked to Financial Performance? *The Mediating Mechanism of CSR Business and Society*, *57*(5), 863–889.

Giannarakis, G. (2014). Corporate governance and financial characteristic effects on the extent of corporate social responsibility disclosure. *Social Responsibility Journal*, *10*(4), 569–590. doi:10.1108/SRJ-02-2013-0008

Giannarakis, G., Konteos, G., & Sariannidis, N. (2014). Financial, governance and environmental determinants of corporate social responsible disclosure. *Management Decision*, *52*(10), 1928–1951. doi:10.1108/MD-05-2014-0296

Halliday, C. S., Paustian-Underdahl, S. C., & Fainshmidt, S. (2021). Women on Boards of Directors: A Meta-Analytic Examination of the Roles of Organizational Leadership and National Context for Gender Equality. *Journal of Business and Psychology*, *36*(2), 173–191. doi:10.100710869-019-09679-y

Khan, H.-U.-Z. (2010). The effect of corporate governance elements on corporate social responsibility (CSR); reporting: Empirical evidence from private commercial banks of Bangladesh. *International Journal of Law and Management*, *52*(2), 82–109. doi:10.1108/17542431011029406

Khidmat, W. B., Habib, M. D., Awan, S., & Raza, K. (2022). Female directors on corporate boards and their impact on corporate social responsibility (CSR): Evidence from China. *Management Research Review*, *45*(4), 563–595. doi:10.1108/MRR-09-2020-0560

Kirsch, A. (2022). Revolution From Above? Female Directors' Equality-Related Actions in Organizations. *Business & Society*, *61*(3), 572–605. doi:10.1177/00076503211001843

Lone, E. J., Ali, A., & Khan, I. (2016). Corporate governance and corporate social responsibility disclosure: Evidence from Pakistan. *Corporate Governance (Bingley), 16*(5), 785–797. doi:10.1108/CG-05-2016-0100

Løyning, T. (2021). Regulating for gender equality in business: The law on gender quotas and the network of interlocking directorates in Norway, 2008–2016. *Review of Social Economy*, 1–27. doi:10.1080/00346764.2021.1901139

Majeed, S., Aziz, T., & Saleem, S. (2015). The effect of corporate governance elements on corporate social responsibility (Csr) disclosure: An empirical evidence from listed companies at kse Pakistan. *International Journal of Financial Studies, 3*(4), 530–556. doi:10.3390/ijfs3040530

Mallin, C. A., & Michelon, G. (2011). Board reputation attributes and corporate social performance: An empirical investigation of the US Best Corporate Citizens. *Accounting and Business Research, 41*(2), 119–144. doi:10.1080/00014788.2011.550740

Manita, R., Bruna, M. G., Dang, R., & Houanti, L. (2018). Board gender diversity and ESG disclosure: Evidence from the USA. *Journal of Applied Accounting Research, 19*(2), 206–224. doi:10.1108/JAAR-01-2017-0024

Marlowe, J., & Clarke, A. (2022). Carbon accounting: A systematic literature review and directions for future research. *Green Finance, 4*(1), 71–87. doi:10.3934/GF.2022004

Nawaz, K., Saeed, H. A., & Sajeel, T. A. (2020). Covid-19 and the state of research from the perspective of psychology. *International Journal of Business and Psychology, 2*(1), 35–44.

Nicolò, G., Zampone, G., Sannino, G., & De Iorio, S. (2022). Sustainable corporate governance and non-financial disclosure in Europe: Does the gender diversity matter? *Journal of Applied Accounting Research, 23*(1), 227–249. doi:10.1108/JAAR-04-2021-0100

Panwar, R., Paul, K., Nybakk, E., Hansen, E., & Thompson, D. (2014). The Legitimacy of CSR Actions of Publicly Traded Companies Versus Family-Owned Companies. *Journal of Business Ethics, 125*(3), 481–496. doi:10.100710551-013-1933-6

Post, C., Rahman, N., & McQuillen, C. (2015). From Board Composition to Corporate Environmental Performance Through Sustainability-Themed Alliances. *Journal of Business Ethics, 130*(2), 423–435. doi:10.100710551-014-2231-7

Saeed, A., Riaz, H., Liedong, T. A., & Rajwani, T. (2022). The impact of TMT gender diversity on corporate environmental strategy in emerging economies. *Journal of Business Research, 141*, 536–551. doi:10.1016/j.jbusres.2021.11.057

Setó-Pamies, D. (2015). The Relationship between Women Directors and Corporate Social Responsibility. *Corporate Social Responsibility and Environmental Management, 22*(6), 334–345. doi:10.1002/csr.1349

Sidhu, J. S., Feng, Y., Volberda, H. W., & Van Den Bosch, F. A. J. (2021). In the Shadow of Social Stereotypes: Gender diversity on corporate boards, board chair's gender and strategic change. *Organization Studies, 42*(11), 1677–1698. doi:10.1177/0170840620944560

Singh, A. K., Kota, H. B., Sardana, V., & Singhania, S. (2021). Does Gender Diversity on Board Promote Corporate Social Responsibility? An Empirical Analysis of Sustainable Development Goals, *Australasian Accounting. Business and Finance Journal, 15*(5), 22–40.

Srivastava, R. V., & Tang, T. (2022). The Matthew effect in talent management strategy: Reducing exhaustion, increasing satisfaction, and inspiring commission among boundary spanning employees. *Journal of Business and Industrial Marketing, 37*(3), 477–496. doi:10.1108/JBIM-06-2020-0296

Sundarasen, S. D., Je-Yen, T., & Rajangam, N. (2016). Board composition and corporate social responsibility in an emerging market. *Corporate Governance (Bingley), 16*(1), 35–53. doi:10.1108/CG-05-2015-0059

Tonin, M., & Vlassopoulos, M. (2015). Corporate philanthropy and productivity: Evidence from an online real effort experiment. *Management Science, 61*(8), 1795–1811. doi:10.1287/mnsc.2014.1985

Velte, P. (2016). Women on management board and ESG performance. *Journal of Global Responsibility, 7*(1), 98–109. doi:10.1108/JGR-01-2016-0001

Wang, Y., Wilson, C., & Li, Y. (2021). Gender attitudes and the effect of board gender diversity on corporate environmental responsibility. *Emerging Markets Review, 47*, 100744. doi:10.1016/j.ememar.2020.100744

Zhang, J. Q., Zhu, H., & Ding, H.-B. (2013). Board Composition and Corporate Social Responsibility: An Empirical Investigation in the Post Sarbanes-Oxley Era. *Journal of Business Ethics, 114*(3), 381–392. doi:10.100710551-012-1352-0

KEY TERMS AND DEFINITIONS

Board of Directors: The board of directors of a public company is elected by shareholders. The board makes key decisions on issues such as mergers and dividends, hires senior managers, and sets their pay. Responsible for helping a corporation set broad goals, supporting senior management in pursuit of those goals, and ensuring the company has adequate, well-managed resources at its disposal.

Corporate Diversity and Inclusion: Corporate diversity is when organizations intentionally employ a workforce of employees of varying characteristics (sexual orientation, gender, race, ethnicity, religion, age, physical abilities, political ideologies, or socioeconomic status). Inclusion is defined as "the achievement of a work environment in which all individuals are treated fairly and respectfully, have equal access to opportunities and resources, and can contribute fully to the organization's success."

Corporate Governance: Corporate Governance refers to how companies are governed and for what purpose. Identifies who has power and accountability, and who makes decisions. A toolkit that enables management and the board to deal more effectively with the challenges of running a company. Corporate governance ensures that businesses have appropriate decision-making processes and controls in place so that the interests of all stakeholders (shareholders, employees, suppliers, customers, and the community) are balanced.

Corporate Social Responsibility: Corporate social responsibility (CSR) is a self-regulating business model that helps a company be socially accountable to itself, its stakeholders, and the public. Corporate social responsibility is also called corporate citizenship, through which companies can be conscious of the kind of impact they are having on all aspects of society, including economic, social, and environmental.

Environmental, Social, and Governance (ESG): ESG is based on a framework that helps stakeholders understanding how an organization is managing risks and new opportunities related to ESG. The Environmental pillar is related with the environmental impacts and risk management practices on the organizations, such as gas emissions, stewardship over natural resources, and the climate risks. The Social concerns are associated with human rights, consumer protection, animal welfare, and adherence to health and safety standards. Finally, the Governance component refers to the way a firm is managed and controlled, in order to make organizations more transparent to investors.

Gender: Gender refers to the characteristics of women, men, girls, and boys that are socially constructed. This includes norms, behaviors, and roles associated with being a woman, man, girl, or boy, as well as relationships with each other. As a social construct, gender varies from society to society and can change over time.

Global Market: Represents activities of trading and providing various types of services in all countries of the world. In the context of management and gender, represents all types of activities pursued all over the world.

Management: Management is a process of planning, decision making, organizing, leading, motivating, and controlling the human resources, financial, physical, and information resources of an organization to reach its goals efficiently and effectively.

Chapter 2
The Work-Family Conflict in the Accounting Profession:
A Study on the Female Gender in Portugal

Ana Rita Alves
Universidade de Aveiro, Portugal

Carla Carvalho
Universidade de Aveiro, Portugal

ABSTRACT

This chapter presents a study that analyzes the Portuguese certified accountant's perception on the difficulties that certified accountant (CA) women face in their professional life, more specifically regarding the work-family conflict. To achieve this goal, an empirical study was conducted by applying a questionnaire survey to Portuguese CAs. This study is structured in six sections. After this introduction, in section two is presented the literature review on the subject of this study. Section three is dedicated to the presentation of the methodology used to conduct the empirical study. Sections four and five present the analysis and interpretation of the data collected, as well as the discussion of the results obtained, respectively. In section six is presented the main conclusions and contributions of the study.

DOI: 10.4018/978-1-6684-5981-2.ch002

1. INTRODUCTION

The way each individual, man or woman, perceives and presents him/herself before the society, constitutes de basis that's supports the construction of his/her interpersonal and intergroup relations, thus the relevance in studying certain phenomena through an approach that introduces gender issues (Nunes, 2007).

Throughout history, efforts have been made to combat male domination and to promote the emancipation of woman, seeking to create a space truly common to men and women, where gender differences are blurred.

In the years following the revolution of April 1974, Portugal underwent major transformations, namely in terms of democratization, access to education and work, witnessing the emergence of new opportunities to invest in women's education and professional careers. It was with the end of the dictatorship that women "*moved from domesticity to active life, testing their skills and revealing their talents*" (Rebelo, 2011: 1), claiming their identity and autonomy. As a result, Portuguese women have been achieving professional positions that were traditionally reserved for men.

If on one hand, for long-time women were denied rights such as education, work or even the right to vote (Sousa, 1998), on the other hand, we are currently moving towards a reality in which women are able to exercise their rights (UNESCO, 2022a: viii). However, despite these achievements there are still systematic differences, particularly in terms of salary, career progression opportunities and the work-family conflict (Guebara & Ravache, 2021; UNRIC, 2021a; Vicente, 2000).

In fact, despite the growing participation of women in the labor market, society still has the traditional perception that domestic work and taking care of the family are primarily female tasks. In line with this reality, several studies have highlighted that women's career focus is primarily determined by their parental status and by aspects related to the family role (*e.g.* Ibrahim & Al Marri, 2015; Whiting, 2008). As such, the factors that appear to most influence career are family and personal aspirations, with family responsabilities varying with the presence of children and, personal aspirations depending on spousal support (Vidwans & Cohen, 2019).

Despite all the obstacles they face in professional terms, it is undeniable that, currently, women play a key role, not only in society, but also in the companies where they work (Arioglu, 2020; Leszczyńska, 2018; Prates, 2021), namely in the profession of Certified Accountant (CA), contributing substantially to the development of those companies and appreciation of the profession itself.

Gender is a global and complex issue in accounting research (Vidwans & Cohen, 2019). So much so that, notwithstanding the fact that a century has passed since women were admitted to the accounting profession in some of the developed countries of the world, researchers continue to study the nature of gender in this profession (Del Baldo et al., 2018).

According to data provided by the Ordem dos Contabilistas Certificados (OCC), the organization that regulates the accounting profession in Portugal, at national level, the CA profession is mostly performed by women (54%) (OCC, 2021).

Given the importance that women have been gaining in the profession of CA in Portugal, and the fact that the relationship between the female gender and this profession in this country has been little studied, the importance of this study is justified. This research became even more relevant through the global pandemic context, during which many female accountants have seen their professional sphere coexist with their personal life, namely in the reconciliation of their profession through home office, with their role as mother and home caregiver (Reimann & Diewald, 2022).

Thus, the overall goal of this study is to analyze the Portuguese CA's perception of the difficulties that CA women face in their professional life, more specifically regarding the work-family conflict.

To achieve this goal, an empirical study was conducted by applying a questionnaire survey to Portuguese CA's. The final sample consists of 469 respondents.

This study is structured in six sections. After this introduction, in section 2 is presented the literature review on the subject of this study. Section 3 is dedicated to the presentation of the methodology used to conduct the empirical study. Sections 4 and 5 present the analysis and interpretation of the data collected, as well as the discussion of the results obtained, respectively. In section 6 is presented the main conclusions and contributions of the study.

2. LITERATURE REVIEW

2.1. Women's Rights in Society and the Work-Family Conflict

The *United Nations Regional Information Centre for Western Europe* - UNRIC (2021b), from the United Nations, states that "*women represent half of the world's population and therefore also half of its potential. Gender equality, besides being a fundamental human right, is essential to achieve peaceful societies with full human potential and a sustainable development. Moreover, it has been proven that women's empowerment stimulates productivity and economic growth*".

Although many efforts are being done to reduce inequalities between men and women (*e. g.* UNRIC, 2021c), it is important to mention some aspects where these differences still emerge, namely in access to education and work.

In some developing countries, the minimum conditions for access to education are not guaranteed, and this obstacle is even bigger when referring to the female gender, which is why we continue to witness cases of inequality that are demarcated by gender (Guebara & Ravache, 2021; UNRIC, 2021a; Vicente, 2000). However, fact sheet on girls' education published by UNESCO showed that girls' enrolment rates in primary and secondary school have almost doubled in low-income countries over the past 25 years (UNESCO, 2022b).

Regarding the access to higher education, in the past, in most countries the access to the academy was restricted to the male gender (Mischau, 2001). In fact, if we go back a few decades, we can see that women were a minority in universities, in Europe. However, since the mid-1990s, more women than men have completed higher education (UNESCO, 2020).

Between 1933 and 1974, Portugal was ruled by a dictatorship regime, marked by illiteracy, oppression and a mentality that considered that "*the prestige of the home requires the future mother to have an education according to women's natural mission*" (Sousa, 1998: 141). Thus, it can easily be seen that the end of this political era influenced positively and significantly the presence of women in access to education.

In fact, it was with the end of the dictatorship that, more expressively, Portuguese women "*emerged from domesticity into active life, put their capacities to the test and revealed talents*" (Rebelo, 2011: 1), affirming their identity and autonomy. The achievements of April 1974 revolution freed Portugal from "*isolation from the world and gave voice to a whole silenced people*" (Rebelo, 2011: 3), ensuring access to health, education and culture, without discrimination of gender, ethnicity and religion. The April revolution also allowed women other important achievements, such as (Rebelo, 2011):

- The exercise of the right to vote without any restrictions;
- Equal opportunities at work;
- Access to positions in the local administrative career, diplomatic and magistracy;
- The abolition of the right of the husband to open his wife's mail;
- Equal rights and duties with regard to civil and political capacity and raising of children;
- The recognition of the value of maternity, through maternity leave without loss of pay or other advantages.

These achievements did not only occur in Portugal, but also in other countries such as Italy, Germany, France and many others outside of Europe, which for years were ruled by undemocratic regimes (Fundação Francisco Manuel dos Santos, 2018).

It is undeniable that, with the achievement of these rights, the status of women in Portuguese society has improved (Lisboa et al., 2006), as a result of several initiatives, among which the authors highlight the publication of the Portuguese Law no. 62/2017, of 1st of August, which forced public and listed companies to hire more women for supervisory positions and for their boards of directors. However, the enshrinement in the law is not enough to dissipate all discriminatory practices that still continue to exist today, reflecting the legacy of our past, with evident salary discrimination (European Commission, 2020) and career progression (Marques, 2018; Tiron-Tudor & Faragalla, 2018).

Despite the increasing participation of women in the labor market, society still has the traditional perception that domestic work and caring for the family are primarily female tasks (Pinto, 2019; Vilela, 2015). In line with this reality, several studies have highlighted that women's career focus is primarily determined by their parental status and by aspects related to the family role (*e.g.* Ibrahim & Al Marri, 2015; Thomas & Ganster, 1995; Whiting, 2008).

In this respect, Whiting (2008) has documented some changes in society regarding work-family conflict, whether at the level of employing organizations, the family sphere or at the individual level. With the increasing participation of women in society, traditional roles have gradually been deconstructed and diversity is more prevalent. These changes are important for both genders, as they allow for the integration of the personal spheres (Whiting, 2008).

The work-family conflict is identified as a potentiator of several negative consequences, which extend to increased health risks for working parents (ranging from depression, heart problems, among others), decreased performance of parental roles and productivity, as well as absenteeism and personal and professional dissatisfaction (Thomas & Ganster, 1995).

2.2. The Research on the Work-family Conflict in the Accounting Profession

In most countries, the accounting profession has always been predominantly male (Ried et al., 1987; Wootton & Kemmerer, 2000). However, since the 1970s, globally the gender structure of the profession has changed dramatically, with women currently representing a relevant percentage of accounting professionals worldwide (Del Baldo et al., 2018; Flynn et al., 2015; Khlif & Achek, 2017).

In Portugal, the CA profession is mostly performed by women (OCC, 2021), as it can be seen in the Figure 1.

Figure 1. CA's distribution by gender in Portugal
Source: OCC (2021)

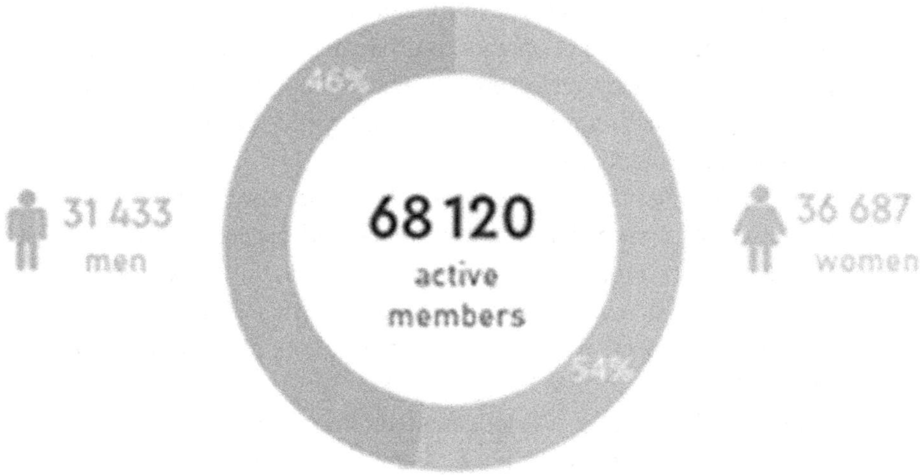

As consequence of the feminization of the profession, women began to be as numerous, or even more numerous, than the number of men in the profession (Del Baldo et al., 2018). However, women's progression up the hierarchical ladder was, and still is, difficult, starting from the gender stratification within the organizations, but also due to the glass ceiling phenomenon, which explains the invisible barrier existing in organizations, beyond which only a few women could overcome (Lucas & Dias, 2020; Siboni et al., 2016; Tiron-Tudor & Faragalla, 2018). Another discriminatory factor, which cuts across most professions, including the accounting profession, is the gender salary differences. In this regard, studies show that within the European Union women earn, on average, 14,1% less per hour than men (European Commission, 2020).

A large part of the studies related to gender are focused on the role of women, as they have been throughout history, the target of more discrimination, compared to men in similar conditions (Haynes, 2017). This focus on women is replicated on the literature of accounting and gender, which tends to highlight the difficulties of women in the accounting profession, due to the fact that there is a greater propensity for their exclusion and oppression, compared to the opposite gender (Haynes, 2008).

The accounting profession has been investigated from various perspective, particularly with regard to gender (Haynes, 2017; Lucas & Dias, 2020; Pinto, 2019; Walker, 2008). Empirical evidences from these studies has suggested that women continue to experience gender discrimination, mostly in aspects such as career progression (Atena & Tiron-Tudor, 2020; Cimirotić et al., 2017; Lucas & Dias, 2020; Tiron-Tudor & Faragalla, 2018; Wood & Lindorff, 2001), salary differences (Atena & Tiron-Tudor, 2020; Cimirotić et al., 2017; Lucas & Dias, 2020; Tiron-Tudor & Faragalla, 2018; Wood & Lindorff, 2001) and the work-family conflict (Cimirotić et al., 2017; Kokot-Blamey, 2021; Pinto, 2019; Whiting, 2008).

With regard to work-family conflict and its consequences for career success, Whiting (2008) conducted interviews with sixty-nine New Zealand accountants to find out their strategies to reconcile their family and professional responsibilities and achieve professional success. As with many other professions, the accounting profession in New Zealand has also welcomed a growing number of women. In this country, although mothers in accounting are mainly devoted to their families and work part-time, organizations are adapting to the female presence in the profession. However, the data shows that these organizations have been practicing a subtle form of discrimination. The interviewees reported that, in order to achieve higher positions within the profession, long hours of dedication to work, total availability and few career breaks are required. As a way of bridging the conflict, changes have occurred, namely in terms of the growing participation of women and the consequent gradual deconstruction of the traditional role. So much so that diversity is now becoming more prevalent, particularly among female accountants, and companies have been adopting flexible working policies as a way of making higher hierarchical positions attainable.

Life-work balance and working hours, in particular, represent difficulties for women in accounting, considering the possibility of becoming mothers an obstacle to their career progression (Cimirotić et al., 2017). Although most Austrian women have flexible working hours, they admit that there is still a disparity between work and their personal life, due to the difficulty they feel in disconnecting from the former in their leisure time or even on holidays. They acknowledge, however, that this is not an obstacle to attaining top or leading career positions (Cimirotić et al., 2017). Sule (2019), also studied the life-work balance of Nigerian men and women and their stress management in order to determine the gender differences on that balance. The data collected indicates that stress management has a positive impact on the work-life balance, whereas the academic level, marital status and work experience have a significant variation on that balance. In specific, the results show that the daily routine impedes work for women more than men, mostly because at a certain age women have a greater family commitment than men (Sule, 2019).

In another culture, Ibrahim and Al Marri (2015) conducted interviews with married female accountants in the United Arab Emirates in order to study the effects of gender and their degree of satisfaction with organizational policies aimed at supporting work-family conflict. The results highlight that married accountant women experience work-family conflict more than men, as it is a relatively new concept in the country for women to work. Ibrahim and Al Marri (2015) consider that organizational practices aimed at reducing gender conflict are important tools for reducing such evidence.

Very recently, Kokot-Blamey (2021) conducted a study on the maternity experiences of sixty women partner accountants in Germany and the UK, as women partners in these countries remain a minority. It was found that women in Germany are able to reconcile motherhood with their careers, as it is expected that women in Germany will work part-time during motherhood. However, they admit that part-time is irreconcilable with becoming a partner, and motherhood is often seen as a "burden" on other colleagues at work. In the UK, respondents were reluctant to take maternity leave and return to work for fear of having to claim their rights such as breastfeeding leave.

Having in mind the pandemic context that the world experienced, Reimann et al. (2022) conducted a study in order to evaluate the impact of COVID on the daily routine of German accountants. The results showed that the experiences existent prior to the pandemic played a very important role in the current perception of the conflict. Whereas the work-family conflict was more susceptible of increasing during the pandemic, the past experiences helped to mitigate the already existent conflict in the new conditions. In general, the work-family conflict increased during the pandemic, but this only happened in the direction of work to home, and not the opposite, for example through the need of having to compensate the lack of daycare and taking care of their children while working from home.

Vidwans and Cohen (2019) studied the women's accounting revolution and concluded that the barriers - individual, family and organizational - to their achievements within the profession have changed little, forcing women to find ways to overcome or compensate for them, particularly in terms of integrating their family and professional lives. From this study, it becomes clear that individuals are influenced by social forces and external factors. In this aspect, the impact of the family on career takes on a substantial role, differing according to gender, responsibilities, family support and individual aspirations.

Finally, in the Portuguese context, Pinto (2019) studied the perception of work-family conflict between men and women in a Portuguese company. The perception of the conflict is essentially in the sense that work interferes with the family, but that the family does not interfere with work, considering that there are gender differences. However, contrary to the previous study, this research shows that men are the ones who perceive the work-family conflict the most, despite the fact that women generally have a greater variety of tasks. Regarding to the companies' response to combating work-family conflict, takes the form of policies to make work and its hours more flexible, as well as support for children and parental leave.

3. METHODOLOGY

The overall goal of this study is to analyze the CAs' perception of the difficulties that CA women face in their professional life, more specifically regarding the work-family conflict.

In addition to this general goal, two specific goals and two research questions were defined, as presented in Figure 2.

Figure 2. Goals and research questions of the study

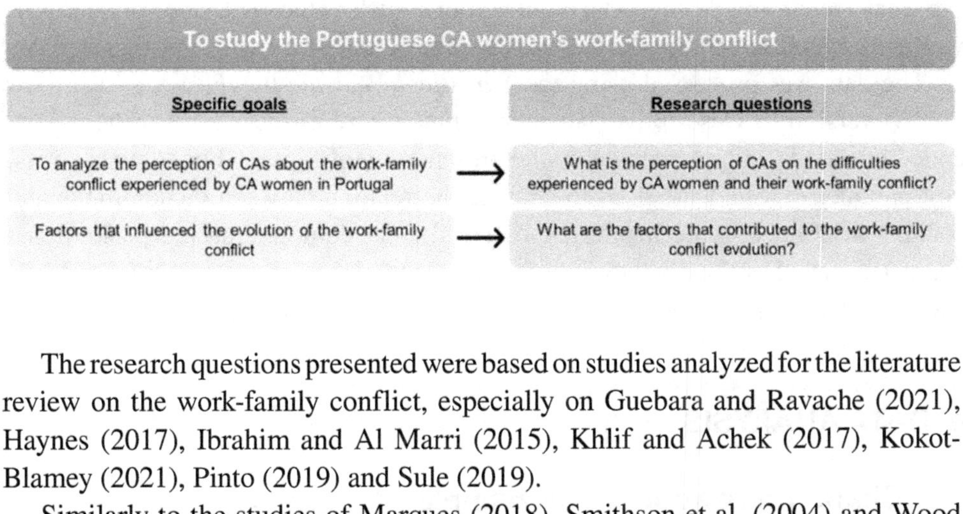

The research questions presented were based on studies analyzed for the literature review on the work-family conflict, especially on Guebara and Ravache (2021), Haynes (2017), Ibrahim and Al Marri (2015), Khlif and Achek (2017), Kokot-Blamey (2021), Pinto (2019) and Sule (2019).

Similarly to the studies of Marques (2018), Smithson et al. (2004) and Wood and Lindorff (2001), this empirical study is, as regards to the data collection, of a qualitative nature, since data were generated from the perceptions of Portuguese CAs, gathered through a questionnaire.

The construction of the questionnaire, which is original, was based on the previously conducted literature review of the studies of Ibrahim and Al Marri (2015) and Pinto (2019). As this study focused on the collection of perceptions, most questions in the questionnaire are presented according to a *Likert* scale with 5 levels of response: "Strongly disagree", "Disagree", "Neither agree nor disagree", "Agree" and "Strongly agree". Respondents were informed of the guarantee of anonymity and confidentiality of their answers.

The questionnaire consists of two parts, the first one being dedicated to the respondents' sociodemographic and professional characterization and the second one containing two sections that seek to answer the specific goals of the study.

The questionnaire was previously validated in order to identify possible inconsistencies or ambiguities in the elaborated questions, the existence of superficial questions and adjust its dimension. Since this was a questionnaire developed from scratch, this step was particularly important to obtain higher quality data.

Thus, the questionnaire was tested by six CAs of different genders, age groups and with different professional activities. After analyzing the feedback received from this pre-test, the necessary adjustments were made to the questions. The questionnaire was created on the electronic platform *FormsUA* and was active between October 18th 2020 and November 2nd 2020. The link to the questionnaire was sent by email to several Portuguese educational institutions that teach accounting courses, and also to several Portuguese accounting firms. Additionally, it was disclosed in websites of different accounting professional organizations, such as the OCC and APOTEC, as well as in several accounting forums and Facebook groups formed by Portuguese CAs.

The data was processed using the *Statistical Package for the Social Sciences (SPSS)*, version 26. Descriptive statistical techniques were used to analyze the closed-ended questions, complemented by the presentation of figures. For some answers, non-parametric tests were used to analyze the relation between dichotomous and ordinal variables, considering the respondents' socio-demographic and professional characteristics. For the dichotomous variables the *chi-square* test of independence was performed and for the ordinal variables the *Kruskal-Wallis* test.

4. DATA ANALYSIS

4.1. Charachterization of the Sample

The population of this study is all active Portuguese CAs. At the time of this study, there were 68 278 active members registered in the OCC in Portugal (OCC, 2020). After the questionnaire distribution process, 649 complete responses were obtained. However, to ensure that only CA data would be processed, the first question of the questionnaire asked respondents to tick whether or not they were CA. For those respondents who answered "No" the questionnaire ended at that question. Of those 649 answers, 180 were not CA, therefore the final sample is composed of 469 respondents (higher than the 382 which corresponds to the ideal sample size, for a confidence level of 95% and a margin of error of 5%).

Figure 3. Sample by gender

As it can be seen in Figure 3, the respondents are mostly female, representing around 92% of the sample. Although CA women are in a larger number in Portugal, the percentage of women who answered the questionnaire is much higher than the proportion of Portuguese CA women. This high female participation in the questionnaire responses may be explained by the theme of the study, which has certainly aroused greater interest in female CAs.

Figure 4. Sample by age

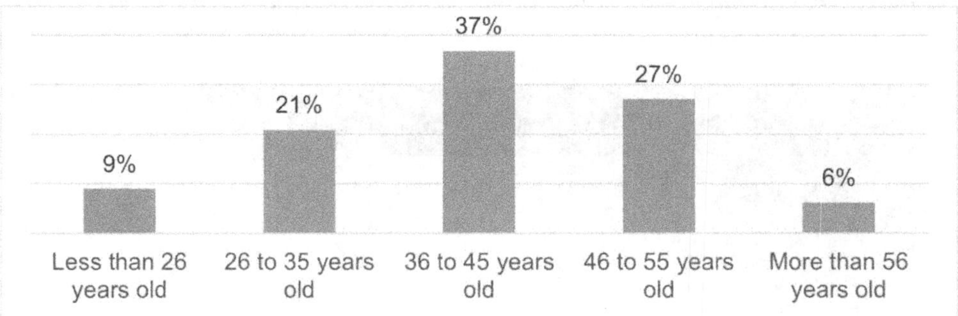

Regarding the age distribution of the sample (Figure 4), 85% of the respondents are aged between 26 and 55 years, which includes the three main age groups: 26 to

35 years (21%), 36 to 45 years (37%) and 46 to 55 years (27%). Thus, the sample is mostly composed of CAs from the age groups with more active working lives.

Regarding the respondents' marital status (Figure 5), most of them are married (61%), with the second largest group represented by singles (27%).

Figure 5. Sample by marital status

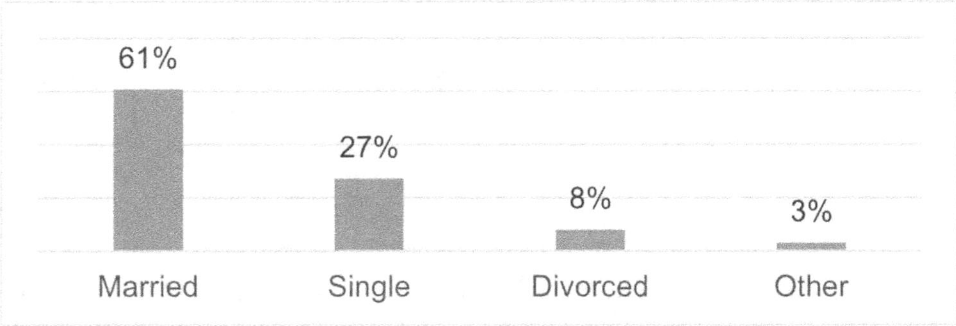

About the geographical distribution of the sample (Figure 6), the five districts with the highest response rate are Lisbon (21,5%), Aveiro (18,3%), Porto (15,6%), Braga (8,3%) and Leiria (6%), which make up approximately 70% of the total sample. There is consequently an approximation to the distribution by national territory of

Figure 6. Geographical distribution of the sample by district of residency

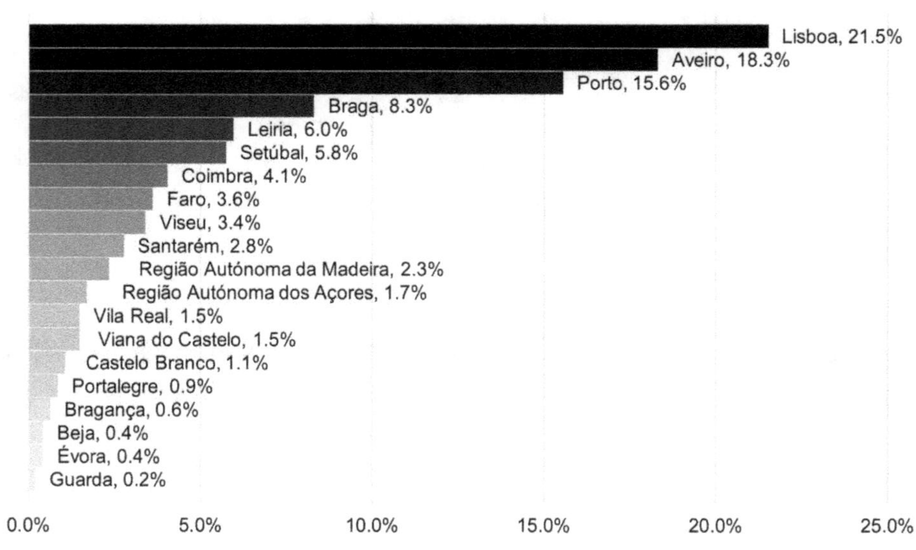

the number of CAs carrying out activity in each of those districts. In fact, according to data made available by the OCC, these five districts total 45 536 active members, which corresponds to approximately 67% of the active members (OCC, 2020).

It is also relevant to note that responses were obtained from all 18 districts in mainland Portugal, as well as from the Autonomous Region of Madeira and the Autonomous Region of the Azores. In other words, in terms of geographical distribution, the sample tends to be representative of the population.

In terms of academic qualifications (Figure 7), around 80% of the respondents have a Bachelor's degree, followed by Masters (15%), If 1% of the respondents with a Doctorate are added to these, it can be concluded that 96% of the respondents have a higher education degree.

Figure 7. Academic qualification of the sample

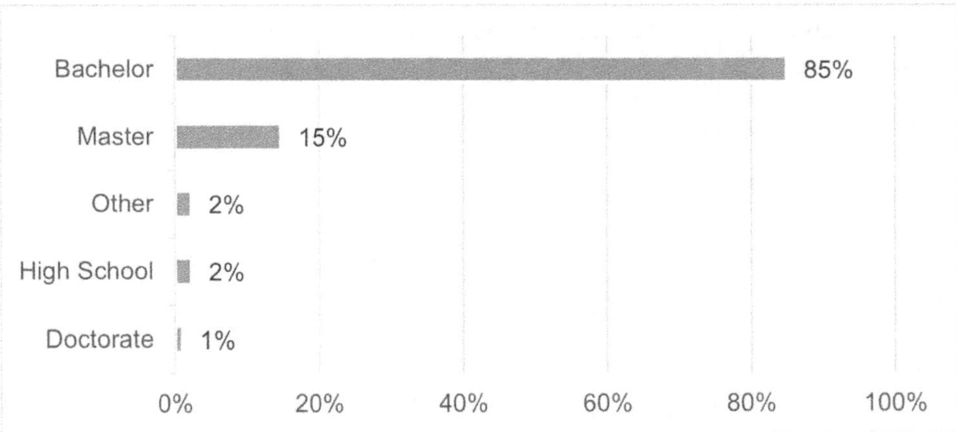

About the type of professional activity (Figure 8), the majority (65%) perform their professional activity as employees and 33% as self-employed. This evidence is very relevant for the study, since employees are the ones most affected by the work-family conflict since they are more dependent on third parties to manage these two aspects.

At last, concerning the number of years that the respondents have been performing his/her current professional activity (Figure 9), it was found that the interval with the most answers (148) is between 10 and 20 years of experience, followed by the interval of 21 to 30 years (108). These data are consistent with the age of the respondents, since most respondents are between 36 and 55 years old. But they also

Figure 8. Type of professional activity of the sample

seem to reveal that, on average, the seniority of the respondents in their current position tends to be high: in fact, 281 respondents (60% of the sample) have held the

Figure 9. Seniority of the sample in its current activity

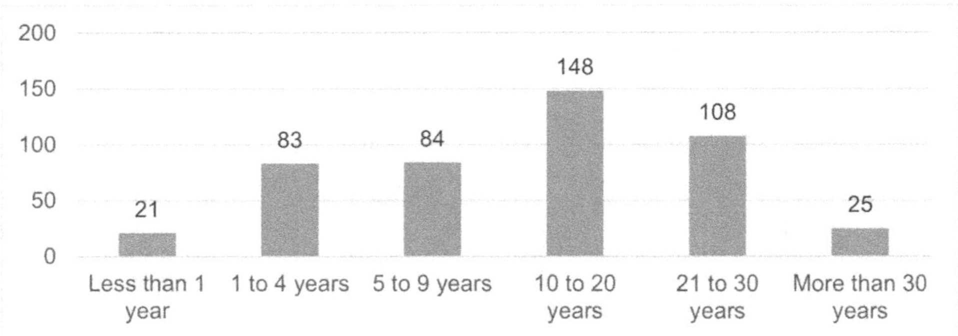

same position for more than 10 years, while 133 respondents (28% of the sample) have held it for more than 21 years.

4.2. The Certified Accountant Women and the Performance of Their Activity

This section presents the respondents' perceptions of the conditions of CA women in the performance of their duties. For that, the respondents were asked to assess, on a scale reflecting their degree of agreement (1 - strongly disagree and 5 - strongly agree), a set of situations in which CA women may present more or less advantage or difficulty in the exercise of their profession, due to their female condition (Table 1).

Table 1a. CA women's condition on the performance of their job

Expression Degree of agreement		Lower level of stress		Less pressure at work		More employer tolerance		Higher level of demand		Easier communication		More tired		Less time available	
Strongly Disagree	1	227	48%	247	53%	193	41%	57	12%	33	7%	40	9%	38	8%
Disagree	2	166	35%	161	34%	174	37%	99	21%	63	13%	77	16%	93	20%
Neither agree nor disagree	3	55	12%	49	10%	77	16%	123	26%	164	35%	107	23%	69	15%
Agree	4	18	4%	10	2%	20	4%	133	28%	166	35%	155	33%	174	37%
Strongly Agree	5	3	1%	2	0%	5	1%	57	12%	43	9%	90	19%	95	20%
Total		469	100%	469	100%	469	100%	469	100%	469	100%	469	100%	469	100%
Mode		1		1		1		4		4		4		4	
Median		2		1		2		3		3		4		4	
Mean		1,73		1,63		1,87		3,07		3,16		3,38		3,42	
Standard deviation		0,86		0,79		0,91		1,21		1,03		1,21		1,24	

Table 1b. (continuation) - CA women's condition on the performance of their job

Expression Degree of agreement		Less workload		More flexibility in working hours		Postpone maternity		Postpone marriage		Fewer responsibility		More opportunities	
Strongly Disagree	1	226	48%	134	29%	55	12%	62	13%	255	54%	144	31%
Disagree	2	182	39%	181	39%	76	16%	112	24%	163	35%	183	39%
Neither agree nor disagree	3	51	11%	102	22%	104	22%	137	29%	39	8%	108	23%
Agree	4	8	2%	45	10%	159	34%	111	24%	9	2%	27	6%
Strongly Agree	5	2	0%	7	1%	75	16%	47	10%	3	1%	7	1%
Total		469	100%	469	100%	469	100%	469	100%	469	100%	469	100%
Mode		1		2		4		3		1		2	
Median		2		2		3		3		1		2	
Mean		1,67		2,17		3,26		2,93		1,6		2,08	
Standard deviation		0,77		1		1,24		1,18		0,77		0,95	

As can be seen about the expression "Lower level of stress", most respondents disagree (84%) that women have lower levels of stress, a trend that is confirmed by the mode, which is located at level 1. Likewise, the great majority also disagrees that CA women have "less pressure at work", with the mode being at level 1 "strongly disagree" and no great dispersion of values (standard deviation 0,79).

The vast majority of respondents either strongly disagree (41%) or disagree (37%) that CA women benefit from "more employer tolerance". However, in this expression, the neutral opinion assumes some expression, representing 16% of the respondents.

With regard to the expression "Higher level of demand", there is a great dispersion of values (standard deviation of 1,21), with the mean being in agreement level 3. In other words, the opinions are divergent, with 33% of the respondents disagreeing or strongly disagreeing on women being more demanding, against 41% who agree or strongly agree with this expression.

As for CA women being considered as to having "easier communication", on average, only 46% of the respondents agree that this is a characteristic of CA women. Slightly more consensus (52% and 57% agreement) exists on CA women being "more tired" and having "less time available" respectively.

When asked whether CA women enjoy "less workload", 87% of the CA respondents disagreed with such statement (mean degree of agreement of 1,67).

As regards women having "more flexibility in their working hours", the results indicate that the mode of agreement was at level 2, corresponding to 39% of the answers obtained. In this particular case, there is a symmetrical distribution, given that the mode, mean and medians are equal, with a value of 2.

When asked about the need for women to "postpone maternity" and "postpone marriage", the answers obtained were diverse. Regarding the need to postpone maternity, 34% of the respondents agree that this is, in fact, a situation that CA women must consider, since maternity requires greater dedication to a dependent. As for the need to postpone marriage, opinions are not at all consensual, as 29% neither agree nor disagree with the statement, 24% disagree and another 24% agree that CA women may have to postpone marriage because they are women.

Confronted with the statement that CA women have "fewer responsibilities", due to the fact of being women, the great majority of the respondents (89%) disagree and only a minority (3%) agree with this possibility.

Finally, with regard to the fact that CA women may have "more opportunities" because they are women, the distribution of the answers is also symmetrical, with the mean, mode and median being around level 2 of agreement. In fact, 70% of the respondents disagree with the fact that CA women have more opportunities in the exercise of their functions and 23% have a neutral opinion.

4.3. The Certified Account Women and the Work-Family Conflict

The respondents were asked whether they considered if, because of being women, CA women experience the work-family conflict. Of the 469 respondents, 76% said yes, 19% said no and the remaining 5% did not know (Figure 10).

Figure 10. Do you think CA women experience the work-family conflict?

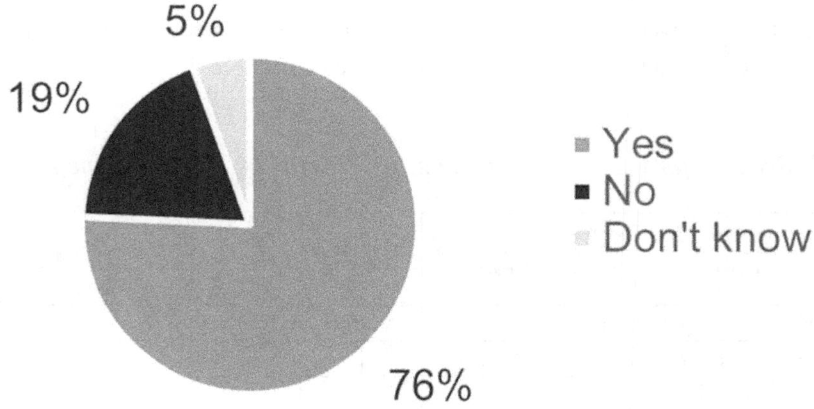

In order to assess the statistical relevance of the answers to the question: *Do you think CA women experience work-family conflict?* in relation to the socio-demographic and professional variables under analysis, the *Kruskal-Wallis* and *Chi-square* tests were applied. The results of these tests are presented in the tables in Appendix A.

We found that the values of the *chi-square* test for the CAs' experience on the work-family conflict and the variables gender, marital status, region and professional activity are equal to 285,091, 33,980, 255,364 and 160,364, respectively, with a *p-value* < 0,05, so, for all these variables, the null hypothesis, which states that the variables are independent, is rejected. Therefore, it is concluded that there is a statistically significant association between those variables.

For the remaining variables, age, academic qualification and seniority, *the Kruskal-Wallis* test was applied, concluding that there is no significant association, since the *p-value* is 0,210, 0,496 and 0,088, respectively (which means, *p-value* always higher than 0,05).

It is the older respondents who least consider that CA women experience work-family conflict, the same being observed in terms of seniority. This result is not surprising, since it is expected that the older respondents are those who have also been working longer, as the relation between age and seniority in the profession could be done in general terms. Regarding academic qualifications, those with doctorates are the ones who most expressively show that CA women experience the work-family conflict.

In order to assess the reasons that may be at the origin of the work-family conflict experienced by CA women, the 355 respondents who replied positively to the previous question were asked to assess different factors according to their degree of agreement. The answers are the ones presented in Table 2.

Table 2. Reasons for the work-family conflict experienced by CA women

Factors Degree of agreement		Support to children and other dependents		Support from spouse/family		Responsibility for the home		Culture of women's role in society		Excess of responsibility of the profession		Demand of time in the profession	
Strongly Disagree	1	2	1%	12	3%	2	1%	5	1%	1	0%	1	0%
Disagree	2	10	3%	73	21%	21	6%	24	7%	29	8%	8	2%
Neither agree nor disagree	3	16	5%	92	26%	25	7%	53	15%	53	15%	23	6%
Agree	4	228	64%	148	42%	233	66%	193	54%	152	43%	159	45%
Strongly Agree	5	99	28%	30	8%	74	21%	80	23%	120	34%	164	46%
Total		355	100%	355	100%	355	100%	355	100%	355	100%	355	100%
Mode		4		4		4		4		4		5	
Median		4		4		4		4		4		4	
Mean		4,16		3,31		4		3,9		4,02		4,34	
Standard deviation		0,68		1		0,75		0,87		0,92		0,72	

As can be seen, the justifying factor which received greater agreement from the respondents was the time demand in the exercise of the profession. In effect, 46% of the respondents strongly agreed and 45% agreed that this factor is very relevant and the most determinant, among the six presented, for the existence of work-family conflict, with a high mean value for the degree of agreement (4,34) and the mode at level 5 (Strongly agree). Note that only 2% of the respondents do not agree that this is the case.

Related to this, another factor that may be justifiable for the convergence of the personal and professional spheres, and consequent conflict, is the excessive responsibility associated with the performance of the accounting profession. The vast majority of respondents considered this factor to potentiate work-family conflict, with 43% of respondents agreeing and 34% strongly agreeing.

With regard to factors related to the family, both the support to underage children or other dependents and the responsibility for the home were considered by the respondents as two factors that significantly contribute to these conflicts, with a mean degree of agreement of around 4 points. In fact, 92% and 93%, respectively, agree or strongly agree that the time or resources spent supporting children or other dependents, as well as the responsibility for the home, have a considerable weight in the conflict between the personal and professional sphere. In contrast, at the level of spousal support, only 50% of the respondents considered that the lack of spousal support aggravates the work-family conflict, while 24% disagreed and 26% expressed a neutral opinion. In fact, of all the factors presented in this question, this was the one with the lowest mean (3,31).

Finally, with regard to the factor related to the established level of culture of the role of women in society (which reflects the idea that women are responsible for everything related to the housework, educate children or the idea that they should be devoted to the family), 54% of the respondents agree and 23% strongly agree that this factor contributes to the work-family conflict of CA women.

Figure 11. Has the CA women's work-family conflict diminished over time?

In order to understand if the work-family conflict experienced by CA women has diminished over time, this question was asked to the respondents (Figure 11). It was found that 23% of the CA respondents said yes, whilst the majority (59%)

Figure 12a. Factors that contributed to the decrease in work-family conflict for CA women

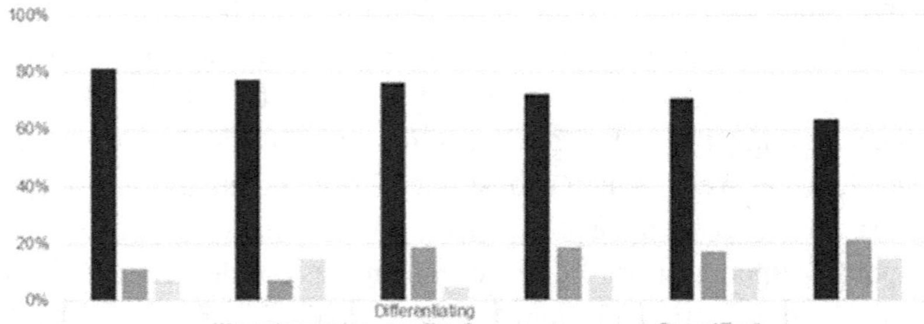

	Personal skills	Women increased training	Differentiating capacities of women in the profession	Social skills	Spousal/Family support	OCC
■ Strongly Agree / Agree	81%	78%	76%	73%	71%	64%
■ Neither agree nor disagree	11%	8%	19%	19%	18%	21%
■ Strongly Disagree / Disagree	8%	15%	5%	9%	11%	15%
Mode	4	4	4	4	4	4
Median	4	4	4	4	4	4
Mean	3,91	3,78	3,83	3,79	3,73	3,59
Standard deviation	0,85	1	0,79	0,85	0,87	0,98

Figure 12b. (continuation) - Factors that contributed to the decrease in work-family conflict for CA women

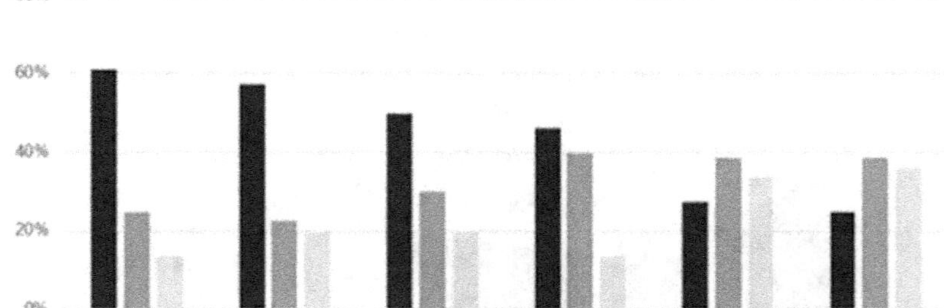

	Support to dependents	OCC Bastonary	Schedule flexibility	Companies' internal policies	Decreasing number of men in the profession	Governmental measures
■ Strongly Agree / Agree	61%	58%	50%	46%	28%	25%
■ Neither agree nor disagree	25%	23%	30%	40%	39%	39%
■ Strongly Disagree / Disagree	14%	20%	20%	14%	34%	36%
Mode	4	4	4	3	3	3
Median	4	4	4	3	3	3
Mean	3,58	3,49	3,35	3,36	2,81	2,83
Standard deviation	0,93	1,15	0,98	0,87	1,01	1

consider that the work-family conflict has not diminished, which leaves open the possibility of this conflict having increased or maintained. Finally, the remaining 18% did not know how to answer this question.

In order to identify the reasons that may have contributed to the reduction of work-family conflict, the respondents who answered affirmatively to the previous question (23%) were asked to evaluate different factors according to their degree of agreement (Figure 12).

About the personal and social skills, 81% and 73%, respectively, agreed that these factors were determinants for the reduction of the conflict-family-work experienced by the CA woman. Regarding the last factor mentioned, "personal skills", it was found that, among the six factors under analysis in this section, this was the one with the highest mean agreement (3,91).

Also, 76% of the respondents agree that the differentiating capacity of women in the exercise of the CA profession was determinant for the decrease of the work-family conflict. In addition, it should be noted that the percentages of disagreement (levels of agreement 1 and 2) amount to a very small share of the opinions (6%).

In terms of the increase in the training of women, 78% of the CA respondents agree that this factor was relevant for the reduction of the work-family conflict. With a mean, mode and median around agreement level 4, the answers obtained are close to a symmetrical distribution.

When questioned about support, the majority, around 71%, agreed that the support from the spouse or family was determinant in reducing the conflict experienced by the CA women, with support for dependents following the same trend, with 61% agreeing with its influence in reducing the conflict. It should be noted that the position "neither agree nor disagree" presents a relevant share of the answers to the factor "support to dependents", while 25% of the respondents demonstrate a position of neutrality.

About the contribution that the OCC and its Bastonary (who is a woman) have in reducing the work-family conflict experienced by women in the CA profession, both factors had the dominant position of agreement grade 4 ("agree"). Thus, 64% and 58%, respectively, of the professionals agree or strongly agree that the OCC and its Bastonary have a relevant impact on reducing the conflict.

Regarding "schedule flexibility", 50% of the respondents agree that this factor had an impact on the decrease of the conflict, although 30% neither agree nor disagree and 20% strongly disagree.

At the level of the companies' internal policies, degree of agreement 3 ("neither agree nor disagree") takes the dominant position, representing 40% of the responses obtained. However, the favorable opinions overlap for approximately 46% of the respondents.

On the possibility that the decrease in the percentage of men in the profession is a justifying factor, 39% of the CA respondents neither agree nor disagree. However, it is perceived that there is a dispersion of values, with standard deviation equal to 1,01, which is due to the fact that opinions are slightly heterogeneous. More specifically, this dispersion is reflected in the 14% and 20% of CAs who strongly disagree and disagree, respectively, that this factor has had any influence in reducing the conflict, and also, in the 28% of respondents who agree or strongly agree that the decrease in the number of men in the profession has positively impacted the conflict experienced. For this point in analysis, the factor "decreasing number of men in the profession" was the one with the lowest average agreement (2,81).

Finally, the opinions are similar with regard to governmental measures, a factor for which 39% of the respondents demonstrated a neutral position. However, the standard deviation of 1 reveals a slight dispersion of the data. This is reflected in the 25% and 36% who agree and disagree, respectively, that the measures adopted by the Government may have had an effect in reducing the work-family conflict.

5. DISCUSSION OF RESULTS

Before discussing the responses to the two research questions, it is interesting to analyze the response percentages of each gender. As presented in the characterization of the sample, about 92% of the respondents are women. This information is relevant for the analysis of the results, as it may be an indicator that women are more concerned with work-family conflict than men, as they are traditionally more affected by these difficulties.

It should also be noted that the majority of respondents have more than ten years of professional experience. In other words, this analyses it is based on the opinion of individuals who have been working in the profession for some time, thus obtaining a better perception of the evolution of the work-family conflict.

What is the perception of CAs on the difficulties experienced by CA women and their work-family conflict?

The study showed that most respondents considered that CA women experience a work-family conflict, so it was sought to identify the factors justifying this phenomenon, those are namely the support to children or other dependents, the demand for time at work, and the responsibility for the home.

According to the literature analyzed, society still has the perception that domestic work and caring for the family are tasks of the female domain (Pinto, 2019; Vilela, 2015), which is in line with the results that show the culture established in society, concerning the role of women and the responsibility for the home, as factors justifying the work-family conflict of CA women. Nevertheless, Whiting (2008) mentions that the so-called traditional role of women has been gradually deconstructed as a result of women's increasing participation in society.

Two other factors, highlighted in the results of the study and which generate work-family conflict, are supporting children and other dependents and the time demands of the profession. In fact, the accounting profession demands a lot of dedication and time from the professional, and it is common for accountants to give up their free time to deal with professional issues, whether accounting and tax returns, or applications for economic support programs, or even studying to keep up to date with new laws or procedures. However, raising a child also requires time and dedication, and this is where the conflict comes in. This is in line with some research that state that the life-work-balance as well as seeking a better position at work are affected by the possibility of women becoming mothers (Cimirotić et al., 2017, Kokot-Blamey, 2021).

In contrast to these factors, the excessive responsibility of the profession, the support of the spouse/family and the time demands of the profession did not contribute substantially to triggering the conflict.

What are the factors that contributed to the work-family conflict evolution?

Most of the respondents do not consider that work-family conflict has decreased over time. That might be because over the past years we lived in a period of global pandemic where accountants were forced to reconcile family and work in the same space. This intensified the conflict, with women often showing some difficulty in disconnecting on their off time of their professional role, but also the need to compensate the external childcare support (children's daycare) that during the pandemic was not working as it normally would be (Cimirotić et al., 2017; Reimann et al., 2022). On the other hand, the authors tried to understand which factors contributed to the reduction of the conflict, from the perspective of those who considered that there had been a positive evolution. According to the respondents, the factors that contributed most to reducing work-family conflict were the differentiating capacity of women, the increase in women's education, personal skills, social skills, and the support of the spouse/family.

The perception of work-family conflict is essentially that the professional sphere interferes with the personal sphere, but that the personal sphere does not interfere with the professional sphere (Pinto, 2019). With regard to this aspect, the respondents considered that the support of the spouse or family was essential to mitigate the conflict. If the origin of the conflict is related to a question of time, in which the profession is demanding, the partner's support is essential, not only in the children's education, but also in household chores. According to Vidwans and Cohen (2019), the impact of family on career is substantial and differs according to personal aspirations. The results are therefore in line with the author's argument that family responsibilities vary according to the presence of children, and personal aspirations vary according to spousal support.

As far as skills are concerned, these are once again reinforced as determining factors for the evolution of any of the issues under analysis. The strength of women, their character and all the characteristics that come from what it means to be a woman, are an added value to the profession and another tool in the fight against gender discrimination.

As for the increase in women's education, this was considered to be a factor that contributes to the reduction of the work-family conflict. This may be due to the fact that higher academic qualifications tend to enable women to have a more comfortable position in the performance of their professional activity, both in terms of remuneration and in terms of working hours. This may be reflected in a greater willingness to hire help with domestic tasks, for example, or a greater availability of time that allows the personal and professional spheres not to clash. The fact that the level of education has an impact on the conflict was confirmed by Sule (2019). The findings confirm that age, education level, marital status and professional experience have a significant variation on the balance between work and family.

For the remaining factors, namely support for dependents, OCC and its Bastonary, flexible working hours and internal policies of the organization, the respondents considered that these had some influence on reducing conflict. In regard to the two entities representing the CAs, the opinions are in harmony as already mentioned. It is expected that the role of these two factors have impacted the professional sphere, however this does not make it less important and does not prevent them from also acting in the personal sphere. An example of this could be the promotion of informal moments aimed at bringing professionals and their families together, the annual Christmas party of the OCC being an example of action in the personal sphere.

Finally, factors related to the decrease in the percentage of men in the profession and governmental measures have little or no influence on the positive evolution of the work-family conflict.

6. CONCLUSION

This study allows us to conclude that the respondents do not consider that, because they are women, CA women enjoy conditions that, from a first perspective, could be more favorable to them than, for example, men, such as: having a lower level of stress or pressure at work; having greater tolerance from the employer; lower workload; greater flexibility in working hours; fewer responsibilities; and more opportunities. On the contrary, the respondents consider that, as they are women, CAs have less time available, are more tired and may feel pressured to postpone maternity or even marriage (although there is less consensus on the latter). Finally, as more favorable aspects, the respondents recognize that, because they are women, CAs have greater ease of communication and are more demanding in the performance of their professional activity.

On the other hand, the vast majority (76%) of the study participants consider that, because they are women, CAs experience the work-family conflict, with the main justifying factor for this conflict being the time demands in the exercise of the profession. Related to this, another factor that may be justifiable for the convergence of the personal and professional spheres, and consequent conflict, is the excessive responsibility associated with the performance of the accounting profession. Another important factor that contributes to this conflict is related to the established culture of the role of women in society, which reflects the idea that women are responsible for everything related to domestic chores, raising children or the idea that they should be devoted to the family. Finally, with regard to family-related factors, both the support for underage children or other dependents, and the responsibility for the home, were also considered as contributing significantly to those conflicts. The support (or lack of it) of the spouse also seemed to contribute to that conflict, although there was less consensus on this factor.

This study also allows us to conclude that there is a perception of a pessimistic evolution related to the decrease of the work-family conflict experienced by CA women. However, some respondents (23%) consider that this conflict has been decreasing over time. Such decrease seems to come from the personal characteristics and attitudes of CA women themselves, specifically their personal and social skills, the differentiating capacity of women and the increase in their training. Next are the factors related to family support, specifically the support from the spouse and family and the support for dependents. With regard to the intervention of organizations, the OCC and its Bastonary, as well as the internal policies of the companies and flexible working hours, contributed to reducing this conflict. The contributions arising from government measures were not considered by the respondents as a factor that contributes to reducing the inadequacy of women's pay.

As a consequence of women's emancipation, their role in the family sphere needed to be adjusted as they took on an active role in the labor market. Consequently, personal life often clashes with professional life, as a result of situations of greater stress, pressure, tiredness or even lack of time. Women have had and always will have a very important role in the family sphere, so it is necessary to adopt practices that aim to ensure a healthy balance between their personal life and their professional life, so that they are able to play their role not only as professionals, but also within the family. Now more than ever, the work-family conflict is of particular importance. In fact, during the pandemic context, many CAs saw their professional sphere cohabiting with their personal life, namely in the reconciliation of their profession through homme office, with their role as mother and care giver.

This study provides important contributions to theory and practice. Firstly, it contributes to the literature on the evolution of women in the accounting profession, by highlighting the difficulties and challenges that Portuguese CA women face in the performance of their activity, more specifically the work-family conflict. This study also contributes to the practice, namely to state authorities, women's rights defense organizations, as well as to the regulatory body of the profession in Portugal, the OCC, so that, in a future, that is expected to be short, measures may be identified in order to mitigate the difficulties that CA women experience, and to take advantage of the challenges that are foreseen for the accounting profession.

The main limitation of this study is that the questionnaire was mostly answered by Portuguese CA women, lacking answers from men. As consequence of this limitation, the study is not able to present a comparison between the perception of both genders. For future investigations, a deeper study could be conducted with the comparison of both gender perceptions' as well as a study on the factors that could justify such perceptions on both genders, using more robust statistical methods.

REFERENCES

Arioglu, E. (2020). Female board members: The effect of director affiliation. *Gender in Management*, *35*(2), 225–254. doi:10.1108/GM-05-2019-0080

Atena, F., & Tiron-Tudor, A. (2020). Gender as a dimension of inequality in accounting organizations and developmental HR strategies. *Administrative Sciences*, *10*(1), 1–24. doi:10.3390/admsci10010001

Cimirotić, R., Duller, V., Feldbauer-Durstmüller, B., Gärtner, B., & Hiebl, M. R. W. (2017). Enabling factors that contribute to women reaching leadership positions in business organizations: The case of management accountants. *Management Research Review*, *40*(2), 165–194. doi:10.1108/MRR-10-2014-0233

de Sousa, J. F. (1998). O Estado Novo e a Contabilidade: contributo para o estudo do Ensino Técnico e da profissão de Contabilista na década de 30. *Estudos do ISCA*, *3/4*, 112–170.

Del Baldo, M., Tiron-Tudor, A., & Faragalla, W. (2018). Women's role in the accounting profession: A comparative study between Italy and Romania. *Administrative Sciences*, *9*(1), 1–23. doi:10.3390/admsci9010002

European Commission. (2020). *Equal Pay? Time to close the gap!* EC. https://ec.europa.eu/info/sites/default/files/aid_developmen t_cooperation_fundamental_rights/2020_factsheet_on_the_gende r_pay_gap.pdf

Flynn, A., Earlie, E. K., & Cross, C. (2015). Gender equality in the accounting profession: One size fits all. *Gender in Management*, *30*(6), 479–499. doi:10.1108/GM-06-2015-0048

Guebara, R. K. M. & Ravache, R. L. (2021). Desigualdade de género os desafios encontrados pelas mulheres na sociedade. *Connection line-revista eletrónica do Univag, 24*, 154-159. doi:10.18312/connectionline.v0i24.1642

Haynes, K. (2008). Power and politics in gender research: A research note from the discipline of accounting. *Gender in Management*, *23*(7), 528–532. doi:10.1108/17542410810908875

Haynes, K. (2017). Accounting as gendering and gendered: A review of 25 years of critical accounting research on gender. *Critical Perspectives on Accounting*, *43*, 110–124. doi:10.1016/j.cpa.2016.06.004

Ibrahim, M. E., & Al Marri, A. (2015). Role of gender and organizational support in work-family conflict for accountants in UAE. *International Journal of Commerce and Management, 25*(2), 157–172. doi:10.1108/IJCoMA-03-2013-0026

Khlif, H., & Achek, I. (2017). Gender in accounting research: A review. *Managerial Auditing Journal, 32*(6), 627–655. doi:10.1108/MAJ-02-2016-1319

Kokot-Blamey, P. (2021). Mothering in accounting: Feminism, motherhood, and making partnership in accountancy in Germany and the UK. *Accounting, Organizations and Society, 91*, 1–16. doi:10.1016/j.aos.2021.101255

Leszczyńska, M. (2018). Mandatory quotas for women on boards of directors in the european union: Harmful to or good for company performance? *European Business Organization Law Review, 19*(1), 35–61. doi:10.100740804-017-0095-x

Lisboa, M., Frias, G., Roque, A., & Cerejo, D. (2006). Participação das mulheres nas elites políticas e económicas no Portugal democrático (25 de abril de 1974 a 2004). *Revista da Faculdade de Ciências Sociais e Humanas, 18*, 163–187.

Lucas, A., & Dias, D. (2020). Glass Ceiling in accounting profession: Myth or reality? *INTED2020 Proceedings, 1*, 5499–5504. 10.21125/inted.2020.1483

Manuel dos Santos, F. F. (2018). *Igualdade de género ao longo da vida: Portugal no contexto Europeu.* FFMS. https://www.ffms.pt/FileDownload/97de6517-2059-46b4-967a-f3b8a15ef139/igualdade-de-genero-ao-longo-da-vida

Marques, I. A. (2018). *A mulher nas carreiras de topo* [Dissertação de mestrado, Universidade Autónoma de Lisboa]. http://hdl.handle.net/11144/3868

Mischau, A. (2001). Women in higher education in Europe - A Statistical overview. *The International Journal of Sociology and Social Policy, 21*(1/2), 20–31. doi:10.1108/01443330110789529

Nunes, M. T. A. (2007). *Género e cidadania nas imagens de História: estudos de manuais escolares e software educativo.* Comissão para a Cidadania e Igualdade se Género.

Ordem dos Contabilistas, C. (2020). *Relatório e Contas 2020.* OCC. https://www.occ.pt/pt/a-ordem/relatorio-e-contas-plano-de-at ividades-e-orcamento/

Ordem dos Contabilistas, C. (2021). *Relatório e Contas 2021*. OCC. https://www.occ.pt/news/Documentos/RC2021.pdf

Pinto, A. M. (2019). *As Diferenças de Género na Percepção do Conflito Trabalho-Família* [Dissertação de mestrado, Instituto Politécnico de Castelo Branco]. http://hdl.handle.net/10400.11/1226

Prates, S. (2021, 29 de junho). O papel das mulheres na resiliência das empresas. *Lider Magazine*. https://lidermagazine.sapo.pt/o-papel-das-mulheres-na-resiliencia-das-empresas/

Rebelo, D. (2011). *As conquistas democráticas da mulher portuguesa*. http://www.25abril.org/a25abril/get_document.php?id=240

Reimann, M., Peters, E., & Diewald, M. (2022). COVID-19 and Work–Family Conflicts in Germany: Risks and Chances Across Gender and Parenthood. *Front. Sociol.*, *6*, 780740. doi:10.3389/fsoc.2021.780740 PMID:35071402

Ried, G. E., Acken, B. T., & Jancura, E. G. (1987). An historical perspective on women in accounting. *Journal of Accountancy*, *163*(5), 338–355.

Rodrigues, S. (2016). *Salários e desigualdade de género em Portugal* [Dissertação de mestrado, Universidade dos Açores]. http://hdl.handle.net/10400.3/4093

Siboni, B., Sangiorgi, D., Farneti, F., & De Villiers, C. (2016). Gender (in) accounting: Insights, gaps and an agenda for future research. *Meditari Accountancy Research*, *24*(2), 158–168. doi:10.1108/MEDAR-04-2016-0054

Smithson, J., Lewis, S., Cooper, C., & Dyer, J. (2004). Flexible working and the gender pay gap in the accountancy profession. *Work, Employment and Society*, *18*(1), 115–135. doi:10.1177/0950017004040765

Sule, D. F. (2019). Work-family balance and stress management among accountants in Obafemi Awolowo University Ile-Ife, Nigeria. *Gender Actualization of the SDGD: The African experience*, 60.

Thomas, L. T., & Ganster, D. C. (1995). Impact of Family-supportive work variables on work-family conflict and strain: A Control perspective. *The Journal of Applied Psychology*, *80*(1), 6–15. doi:10.1037/0021-9010.80.1.6

Tiron-Tudor, A., & Faragalla, W. (2018). Women career paths in accounting organizations: Big4 scenario. *Administrative Sciences*, *8*(4), 62. doi:10.3390/admsci8040062

UNESCO. (2020). *Gender evolution in education*. UNESCO. https://tellmaps.com/uis/gender/#!/tellmap/79054752

UNESCO (2022a). *Global education monitoring report 2022: gender report, deepening the debate on those still left behind*. Global Education Monitoring Report Team.

UNESCO. (2022b). *UNESCO in action for gender equality, 2020-2021*. UNESCO.

UNRIC. (2021a). *A (des)igualdade de género e o (des)equilíbrio de poder*. UNESCO. https://unric.org/pt/a-desigualdade-de-genero-e-o-desequilibrio-de-poder/

UNRIC. (2021b). *Igualdade de género*. UNRIC. https://unric.org/pt/mensagem-do-secretario-geral-da-onua-conferencia-internacional-contra-o-terrorismoriade-5-8-de-fevereiro-de-2005proferida-pelo-sr-javier-ruperez-director-executivodireccao-do-comite-cont-3

UNRIC. (2021c). *Objetivo 5: Igualdade de género*. UNRIC. https://unric.org/pt/objetivo-5-igualdade-de-genero-2/

Vicente, A. (2000). *Direitos das mulheres/direitos humanos*. Cadernos Condição Feminina, 59. Comissão para a Igualdade e para os Direitos das Mulheres.

Vidwans, M., & Cohen, D. A. (2019). Women in accounting: Revolution, where art thou? *Accounting History*, *1963*. doi:10.1177/1032373219873686

Vilela, C. V. (2015). *O acesso das mulheres ao estudo da Contabilidade: comparação entre o caso britânico e o caso português* [Dissertação de mestrado, Instituto Superior de Contabilidade e Administração do Porto]. http://hdl.handle.net/10400.22/7871

Walker, S. P. (2008). Accounting histories of women: Beyond recovery? *Accounting, Auditing & Accountability Journal*, *21*(4), 580–610. doi:10.1108/09513570810872932

Whiting, R. H. (2008). New Zealand chartered accountants' work/family strategies and consequences for career success. *Pacific Accounting Review*, *20*(2), 111–137. doi:10.1108/01140580810892472

Wood, G. J., & Lindorff, M. (2001). Sex differences in explanations for career progress. *Women in Management Review*, *16*(4), 152–162. doi:10.1108/09649420110392136

Wootton, C. W., & Kemmerer, B. E. (2000). The changing genderization of the accounting workforce in the US, 1930–90. *Accounting Business & Financial History*, *10*(2), 169–190. doi:10.1080/095852000411023

APPENDIX: RESULTS OF THE *KRUSKAL-WALLIS* AND CHI-*SQUARE TESTS*

Table 3. The Work-family Conflict of CA Women

Gender	***Chi-square*** [a]	***P-value***
	285,091	<0,001
Marital Status	***Chi-square*** [a]	***P-value***
	33,980	<0,001
Region	***Chi-square*** [a]	***P-value***
	255,364	<0,001
Professional activity	***Chi-square*** [a]	***P-value***
	160,364	<0,001

[a]0 cells (0,0%) have expected frequencies lower than 5. The minimum expected cell frequency is 221,5.

Table 4.

Variable		**Mean of the orders**	*Kruskal-Wallis* **Test**	
			Kruskal-Wallis **H**	*P-value*
Age	Less than 26 years old	218,11	5,864	0,210
	26 to 35 years old	228,69		
	36 to 45 years old	222,25		
	46 to 55 years old	226,06		
	More than 56 years old	183,96		
Academic qualification	High school	245,86	3,380	0,496
	Bachelor	234,36		
	Licentiate	218,49		
	Master	223,65		
	Doctorate	266,00		
Seniority	Less than 1 year	199,55	9,570	0,088
	1 to 4 years	219,37		
	5 to 9 years	227,24		
	10 to 20 years	220,44		
	21 to 30 years	235,89		
	More than 30 years	179,33		

Chapter 3
Does Board Gender Diversity Influence Firm Debt Maturity?
Evidence From Portuguese Hotel Industry SMEs

Fernanda Inácio Matias
ESGHT, University of Algarve, Portugal

Sandra Cristina Rebelo
CITUR, University of Algarve, Portugal

Celísia Isabel Baptista
University of Algarve, Portugal

Georgette dos Santos Andraz
University of Algarve, Portugal

ABSTRACT

This chapter examines the effect of board gender diversity on corporate debt maturity It analyses a gender-based behavioral dimension for corporate debt maturity choice. The study finds that firms with a larger female representation on the board of directors and managers tend to have a larger proportion of short-maturity debt. The evidence also shows that when a woman holds the position of chair of the board and simultaneously is a shareholder, the chance for issuing a short-term debt is higher. These findings meet the argument that boards with female directors and leaders are more likely to issue short-term debt. This method of financing decision can be considered as a corporate governance device with potential impact on reducing managerial opportunism.

DOI: 10.4018/978-1-6684-5981-2.ch003

INTRODUCTION

Over time there has been a differentiation between genders, overvaluing the male sex over the female and creating a different social role depending on gender. Nevertheless, in the last century there has been significant legislative contributions to gender equality in the labor field, with the European union's policies providing conditions for promoting the right to gender equality. In addition, in recent decades there has been an improvement in the educational level of women and an increase in their participation in the labor market, occupying leadership positions, which have traditionally been controlled by men. These factors have contributed to the interest of research on different issues regarding gender on corporate board of directors.

The topic of female representation in the corporate board of directors has gained relevance since the beginning of this century, giving rise to research and implementation of regulations that provide minimum quotas for the under-represented gender. Kirsch (2018) refers in his literature review, focused on large, listed companies, that in the period of 2015, only 21% of directors were female in the European Union, 20% in the United States and 3% in Japan. According to Informa D&B (2022), female represented 28.3% of directors in the Portuguese companies in 2021.

Several behavioral finance studies have focused their attention on how the characteristics of corporate managers influence business decisions. Following this theoretical approach, a growing body of research provides evidence of differences in women's behavior compared to men's: they are more prudent (Huang & Kisgen, 2013), more conservative in their predictions (Lonkani, 2019), their participation makes boards more influential in management (Fondas & Sassalos, 2000) and have greater risk aversion and ethical sense (Ho, Li, Tam, & Zang, 2015). Also, in line with these findings, recent literature on the board gender diversity suggests that differences in women behavior, compared to men can influence financial decisions (e.g., Huang & Kisgen, 2013; Hérnandez-Nicolás, Martin-Ugedo, & Mínguez-Vera, 2015). However, there is scarce and controversial evidence of the role of female directors in this field (Garcia & Herrero, 2021).

Several empirical studies show that boards with a higher percentage of women directors are associated with lower debts levels (e.g., Alves, Couto & Francisco, 2015; Hernández-Nicolás et al., 2015), following the arguments of agency theory, that greater board diversity leads to a reduction in information asymmetries. This circumstance improves firm's proportion of external equity in the capital structure, leading to lower leverage. Based on the theories of gender differences which suggest that female directors are less overconfidence and have greater risk aversion then male directors, López-Delgado and Diéguez-Soto (2020), Fenoy-Castaño, Martínez-Romero and Martínez-Alonso (2021) also found a negative relation between gender diversity and leverage. La Rocca, Neha and La Rocca (2020) argue that female managers, being less overconfident and more conservative, in line with their personal traits (higher risk aversion and more ethical constraints), prefer to preserve financial flexibility to avoid missing any growth opportunities, and choose to have less debt in the capital structure.

In fact, the role of women in performing functions at a high level of management is still a controversial issue and the results are not consistent. Although some studies have concluded that gender diversity has a positive effect on business performance (e.g., Carter, Simkins, & Simpson, 2003; Srinidhi, Gul, & Tsui, 2011; Reguera-Alvarado, Fuentes, & Laffarga, 2017),) others have found a negative effect (e.g., Adams & Ferreira, 2009; Minguez-Vera & Martin, 2011; Shehata, Salhin, & El-Helaly (2017), or a non-significant effect (e.g., Menicucci, Paolucci, & Paoloni, 2019).

This study aims to extend the literature on this issue, providing evidence on the effect of the female presence on the board of directors on the company debt maturity. To the best of the author's knowledge, only a few studies maturity (e.g., La Rocca et.al., 2020; Datta, Doan, & Toscano, 2021). have analysed female's role in shaping the nature of the decisions in terms of debt. The main objective of this chapter is to investigate the effect of female presence on the corporate board on the debt maturity of the firms, specifically, whether companies with greater female representation in senior positions tend to have a greater proportion of short-term debt. According to Li and Zhang (2019), the objective of this financing option is to introduce a control instrument that reduces the company's agency costs. The use of short-term debt increases the company's liquidity risk and, consequently, the need to monitor managers' decisions to avoid risky behavior, such as the over-investment. Another reason for this financing option is put forward by the debt maturity theories, according to which the debt maturity structure is associated with the company's discretion, that is, it is the result of rational and coherent decision-making taken by its managers to develop the organization (Barclay & Smith, 1995). The empirical analysis relies on a sample of Portuguese public limited small and medium enterprises (SMEs) from the hotel industry, for the period 2015-2019, collected from the Orbis database. In this study, a panel data regression methodology was used for the empirical study.

The reason for this sample selection lies on the SMEs relevance for the development process of the Portuguese economy. The Portuguese business structure is characterized by small firms' units, not listed on the stock exchange. In most SMEs there is a coincidence between ownership and management. In 2018, SMEs accounted for 99.9% of the total number of companies, 78.5% of total employment and 64.1% of added value (INE, 2020), highlighting the micro-enterprises which represent 96.1% of the total number of companies. Regarding the gender diversity, SMEs are the type of company with the highest percentage of women in management positions, 31%, 25% and 21% in micro, small and medium-sized enterprises, respectively, against 19% in large companies (Informa D&B, 2022). Contrary to the large companies, the

SMEs have singular characteristics which impact their loan strategies (e.g., Ang, 1991; López-Gracia & Aybar-Arias, 2000).

The hotel industry is a structuring segment of tourism, which in Portugal assumes special economic relevance. In 2018, tourism accounted for 14.6% of GDP Portuguese, according to data provided by INE (2020). During the last years of the last decade, there was substantial dynamics in the Portuguese hotel industry, for example, in the period from 2014 to 2018, there was an increase of 20% in hotel establishments, 36.5% of guests, 69% of total income and 56% of average income per room (Filipe, 2020). The labor market in the hotel industry incorporates a high female presence, but few women occupy top positions in business management (Segovia-Pérez, Figueroa-Domecq, Fuentes-Moraleda, & Muñoz-Mazón, 2019). However, the Portuguese hotel industry is one of the three industries with more female members in the boardroom (Informa D&B, 2022), Additionally it has specific characteristics, such as, those related to the product, business management models and intensity of capital and labor (Wood, 2015).

This study is grounded on the agency theory and contributes to extend the literature on female presence on the corporate boards in several ways. First, it contributes to the understanding of the effect of gender diversity decisions on hotel firms' debt maturity. To the best of the author's knowledge, no other study has been conducted regarding this issue applied in the Portuguese hotel industry. Second, reinforces the argument that female directors and managers are more likely to use short-term debt as a governance device, reducing the likelihood of overinvestment and managerial opportunism, supporting the hypothesis of the agency theory that gender diversity is associated with a more efficient monitoring of the firm decisions. Third, it adds evidence that the presence of female on corporate boards has significant effects on firms' total debt, supporting the theory of agency concerning the lower asymmetry of information associated with gender diversity. Finally, at a practical level, our results support the efforts of policymakers in continuing to contribute to gender equality on firm's boardroom.

This chapter is structured as follows. A literature review and research hypotheses is first presented, followed by a description of the data and variables measurement. Then, we present the regression models and the results, and finally the conclusions.

LITERATURE REVIEW AND HYPOTHESES

Role of Female Directors and Managers

Gender diversity on corporate boardroom is an instrument with great potential in contributing to mitigate the agency problem within the firm, because of the separation between management and ownership of capital. This fact is quite evident in the hotel industry where the separation between property ownership and management generates conflicts of interest between agents and owners (Guilding 2003). The agency theory, particularly adopted in the research of corporate governance, argues that women play an important role in governance: their participation makes boards more influential in management (Fondas & Sassalos, 2000) and enriches them in terms of information, perspectives, debate and decision-making (Burke, 1997); are more concerned with the prior preparation of meetings (Huse & Solberg, 2006)) and contribute to the efficiency of the staff due to the decrease in conflict (Nielsen & Huse, 2010).

Although the empirical research shows differences in women's behaviour compared to that of men, which seems to be favourable to the company performance, the issue of female directorships is still relatively inconclusive. At the empirical level, the results on the role of women in performing functions at a high level of management are not consistent. Carter et al. (2003) examined the relationship between the diversity of the board of directors and the value of the company, focused on the 1000 largest U.S. companies available in Fortune 1000. Using control variables such as, size, industry and some corporate governance measures, the authors show evidence of a significant positive relationships between the percentage of women or minorities on the board and the value of the company. Srinidhi et al. (2011) studied the association between female participation on the board of directors and the quality of results. The results show evidence of improvement in the quality of results and a better level of supervision of the board. Based on a sample of 125 non-financial companies listed on the Madrid Stock Exchange from 2005 to 2009, Reguera-Alvarado et al. (2017) showed that the increase in the number of women on boards was more than 98% and that this has a positive relation with the economic results. Based on French companies listed in CAC 40, the results of Ahmadi, Nakaa and Bouri (2018) show a positive association between board gender diversity and ROE and ROA, suggesting that financial performance increases with gender diversity. In the same line of results, the study of Ting, Wang, Lu and Chen (2021), using a sample of companies in the financial sector, conclude that female directors in a specific management position can influence a firm's corporate governance.

Using a sample of U.S. listed companies Adams and Ferreira (2009) suggest that the female directors 'participation has a positive impact on firms' results, but on average they perform worse the greater is the gender diversity of the board, suggesting that the mandatory representation quotas of the female gender for directors can reduce the value of the company. Based on data from Spanish SMEs, for the period of 1998-2003, Minguez-Vera and Martin (2011) demonstrate that the presence of women on the company's board of directors impacts negatively on their performance, suggesting that this result may be motivated by the greater risk aversion of women in the formulation of strategy. Also, the study by Shehata et al. (2017) show a significant negative association between gender diversity and company performance using a sample of SMEs located in the U.K. Considering these results the authors state that the decisions on board gender diversity should be made with great caution. On the other hand, some studies (e.g., Menicucci, et al., 2019) show no significant effect, stating that studies using multivariate analyses with relative performance indicators (e.g., ROA and ROE), unlike bivariate analyses with absolute indicators, there are no significant differences between companies controlled by men and women. Also, study of Marinova, Plantenga and Remery (2016), based on data from Dutch and Danish listed companies from 2007, show that board diversity does not influence performance.

The results of empirical studies conducted with samples from different countries concerning the effect of board diversity on the company's performance are mixed (Post & Byron, 2015). Carmo, Alves e Quaresma (2022) present two main reasons for the mixed results: the differences between the period of the study, countries and/or companies which represent institutional contexts with different agency problems and the use of different measures of financial performance and gender diversity.

Female Directors and Managers and Debt Maturity

Managers are faced with a multiplicity of decisions, such as the financing of the company which sources, in a simplified way, fall into equity or capital of others. The composition of these fund sources configures the company's capital structure. The study of the capital structure has aroused special interest in the scientific community and attracted a substantial part of the financial literature in the last six decades, particularly since the publication of Modigliani and Miller (1958).

One of the main issues that have sustained the investigation is related to the factors that determine the level of indebtedness of the company. Nevertheless, the results based on the paradigm of traditional finance have been inconclusive, so the theory of behavioral finance has been developed. This approach questions the pillars of financial theory, namely rationality in decision-making (Barberis & Thaler, 2003). The theory of behavioral finance, as well as other considerations such as of corporate governance, may be an appropriate complement to traditional theories to deepen knowledge about capital structure decisions, debt level, and debt maturity.

The optimal structure of debt maturity is influenced by the investment and financing policies of companies, but also by agency costs resulting from conflicts between managers, shareholders, and creditors. As short-term debt implies constant renegotiations, and imposes more disciple for managers and market control, reducing debt agency costs. However, if there is a separation between ownership and management, managers are not expected to opt for optimal debt maturity for the company and impose constant monitoring on themselves (Datta, et al., 2021). Thus, managers are expected to prefer long-term debt, eventually deviating from optimal debt maturity for the company and its shareholders.

Debt maturity is investigated as an important corporate governance monitoring device. The lower the maturity of the debt, the greater the liquidity risk of the company, associated with the fulfillment of its commitments to pay capital and financial and refinancing charges. Therefore, short-term debt plays a disciplinary role in controlling investments and in avoiding overinvestment (Jensen, 1986). On the other hand, the opening of the company's capital to new investors contributes to the optimal level of investment that maximizes its wealth is lower, generating an underinvestment problem (Jensen & Meckling, 1976). This means that partially financed companies with debt have an incentive to reject investment projects with positive net value. Myers (1977) suggested that this problem can be mitigated by reducing debt maturity which serves as a mechanism to alleviate the agency costs of control and obligation.

The literature that relates ethics to gender argues that women are more concerned with ethical issues, such as information dissemination, integrity, and conflicts of interest, and have higher moral standards than men (Ho et al., 2015). Based on these characteristics, in the context of debt maturity, it is expected that female executives have less preference for debt with a long maturity than men because they do not care so much about the market valuation, and this way, they do not move away from the optimal structure of debt maturity. García and Herrero (2021), Datta et al. (2021), La Rocca et al. (2020), Li and Zhang (2019), Huang and Kisgen (2013), and others have observed that boards with a higher percentage of women directors are more likely to use short-term debt. Datta et al. (2021), using a sample of data from a panel of U.S. companies, suggest that women choose capital structure with a higher proportion of short-term debt than men, meeting the interest of shareholders. Li and Zhang (2019), with a sample of companies in the S&P 1500 index, 1997-2016, obtained similar results, suggesting that women directors are likely to use short-term debt as a control mechanism. In addition, Huang and Kisgen (2013) and La Rocca et al. (2020) support greater use of short-term debt because it offers greater financial flexibility in business management.

An opposite argument is presented by Briozzo, Cardone-Riportella and García-Olalla (2019), based on a study with Spanish SMEs. These authors argue that gender diversification on boards generates improvements in the level of monitoring, performance, independence, and consequently more long-term debt. Also, Hernández-Nicolás et al. (2015) report a positive relationship between gender diversity and debt maturity and Li and Zhang (2019) observe that the companies that use more short-term debt have the poorest governance.

The various economic agents interacting within the company do not share the same information suggesting the existence of asymmetric information, a situation whereby in a transaction one of the parties has more and/or better information than the other party. In the context of the agency theory, gender diversity on the firms boardroom contributes to reducing information asymmetry and, therefore, agency costs and facilitates access to different sources of funding. The fact that women were more concerned than men about the dissemination of information (Ho et al., 2015) will help to ensure that the greater participation of female directors in the board is associated with less asymmetric information, ease of access to external sources of funding, including increases in equity and, consequently, lower level of debt. As demonstrated in the previous studies, female is more conservative, more prudent and more risk-averse, demotivating characteristics of indebtedness. In this line of research, regarding the relationship between female presence in boards and total indebtedness, several studies have observed that boards with a higher percentage of women directors are associated with lower levels of corporate indebtedness: Garcia and Herrero (2021), Adusei and Obeng (2019), Alves, et al. (2015), Hernández-Nicolás et al. (2015) and others.

Also, Huang and Kisgen (2013) report that companies with female executives are less likely to issue debt than companies with executive men. According to these authors, this situation shows greater confidence and lower risk aversion of men, compared to women, in making most of the decisions in companies, suggesting a negative relationship between female presence on boardroom and leverage. However, the empirical findings regarding total indebtedness are mixed, with authors reporting a positive relationship, such as Nisiyama and Nakamura (2018) and a non-significant relationship like Detthamrong, Chancharat and Vithessonthi (2017).

Based on the arguments that female representation on firm boards and management is associated with greater monitoring, greater risk aversion and greater information dissemination than male directors, the following hypothesis are tested:

Hypothesis one: The intensity of female gender in the board of directors and managers has a positive effect on short-term debt.

Hypothesis two: The presence of female gender as chair of the board has a positive effect on short-term debt.

Hypothesis three: The intensity of female gender in the board of directors and managers has a negative effect on total debt.

METHODOLOGY

Data Sources and Variables

This research is based on quantitative and qualitative secondary data, for the period from 2015 to 2019, collected from the Orbis database, by Bureau van Dijk. Although data from 2020 and 2021 were already available, it was decided not to include them because they corresponded to a period strongly influenced by the pandemic crisis caused by the SARS-CoV-2 virus.

The study focuses on small and medium-sized Portuguese hotel companies. Companies classified under the code NACE Rev 2 - 551 - Hotels and similar accommodations that comply with the SME conditions set out in Commission Recommendation 2003/361/EC of 6 May 2003, namely: i) number of employees less than 250 and, (ii) turnover less than or equal to EUR 50 million or total annual balance sheet less than or equal to EUR 43 million.

A non-probabilistic sample was extracted from the database, composed of hotel SMEs active in the research period, which had quality information for the operationalization of the variables to be studied, and which were not in a situation of technical bankruptcy. The final sample contains 1,903 observations, concerning 386 hotel SMEs.

The effect of gender on the debt maturity of SMEs in the Portuguese hotel industry was tested using three independent variables related to gender, defined considering the literature review and available data. This study used control variables related to characteristics of companies that could influence indebtedness, according to capital structure financial theories (trade-off theory and pecking-order theory) and empirical research (e.g., Palacín-Sánchez, Ramírez-Herrera, & Pietro, 2013; Serrasqueiro & Caetano, 2015; Sogorb-Mira, 2005). The capital structure was analyzed in terms of short-term debt and total debt. Table 1 presents the research variables and the respective measures. Similar to Tang and Jang (2007), interactive variables were tested in order to better understand the effect of each variable on the capital structure of Portuguese hotel SMEs. Transformed variables were also tested to verify the monotony of the effect of the base variable on the debt maturity.

Table 1. Variables

Variables	Measures
Dependent variables	
Total leverage ($TLEV_{i,t}$)	Total liabilities/ Total assets
Short debt ($SDEBT_{i,t}$)	Current liabilities/ Total liabilities
Independent variables	
Female directors and managers (FDM_{it})	Number of female directors and managers
Female chair of the board (FCB_{it})	Dummy: 1 for female chair of the board; 0 other wise
Female chair of the board and shareholder ($FCBS_{it}$)	Dummy: 1 for female chair and shareholder; 0 other wise
Control variables	
Size ($SIZE_{i,t}$)	Log total assets
Profitability ($ROA_{i,t}$)	Net income / Total assets
Free cash-flow ($FCF_{i,t}$)	Net income and depreciations and amortizations/ Turnover
Tangibility ($TANG_{i,t}$)	Fixed assets / Total assets
Liquidity ($LIQ_{i,t}$)	Current assets / Current liabilities
Age ($AGE_{i,t}$)	Data age – Establishment year

Given the availability of data, independent variables (gender variables) are based on information from the last year available in the Orbis database. According to Informa D&B (2022), gender diversity has remained constant in the accommodation and food service sector.

Model Specification

We use panel data models to analyze the effect of gender in the SMEs hotel industry debt maturity. These models present various advantages over sectional data models, namely, enabling more precise statistics and more efficient statistical tests, by allowing control of the unobservable fixed effects that can bias the estimates of the coefficients. Panel data models work with a greater amount of information and a greater number of degrees of freedom. We estimate the following models:

$$TLEV_{it} = \beta_0 + \beta_1 FDM_{it} + \beta_2 FCB_{it} + \beta_3 FCBS_{it} + \beta_4 SIZE_{it} + \beta_5 ROA_{it} + \beta_6 ROA^2_{it} + \beta_7 TANG_{it} + \beta_8 AGE_{it} + \mu_{i,t},$$

$$SDEBT_{it} = \beta_0 + \beta_1 FDM_{it} + \beta_2 FCB_{it} + \beta_3 FCBS_{it} + \beta_4 SIZE_{it} + \beta_5 ROA_{it} + \beta_6 FCFxROA_{it} + \beta_7 TANG_{it} + \beta_8 LIQ_{it} + \mu_{i,t},$$

Where: i represents each of the firms, t represents the time, $\mu_{i,t}$, represents the error or idiosyncratic disturbance, varying over i and t. All variables are defined and explained in Table 1 in the previous subsection.

It was applied different diagnostics tests: the White test and Breusch-Pagan test to check for the homoscedasticity of the residual, the variance inflation factor (VIF) to check for multicollinearity, the Breusch-Pagan Lagrange Multiplier test to check firms' individual effects, and the Wooldridge test to check first-order autocorrelation, confirm that the random effects GLS (Generalized Least Squares) regression model with AR(1) disturbances is the most suitable.

The use of dummy variables invalidates the use of the fixed effects model since these variables are omitted. Estimations are made with the software Stata SE 13.1.

EMPIRICAL RESULTS

Descriptive Statistics and Correlation Matrix

Graph 1 shows that 82% of Portuguese SMEs in the hotel industry, under analysis, have female members in their boardroom and executive management.

Figure 1. % SME of hotel industry with female director or manager

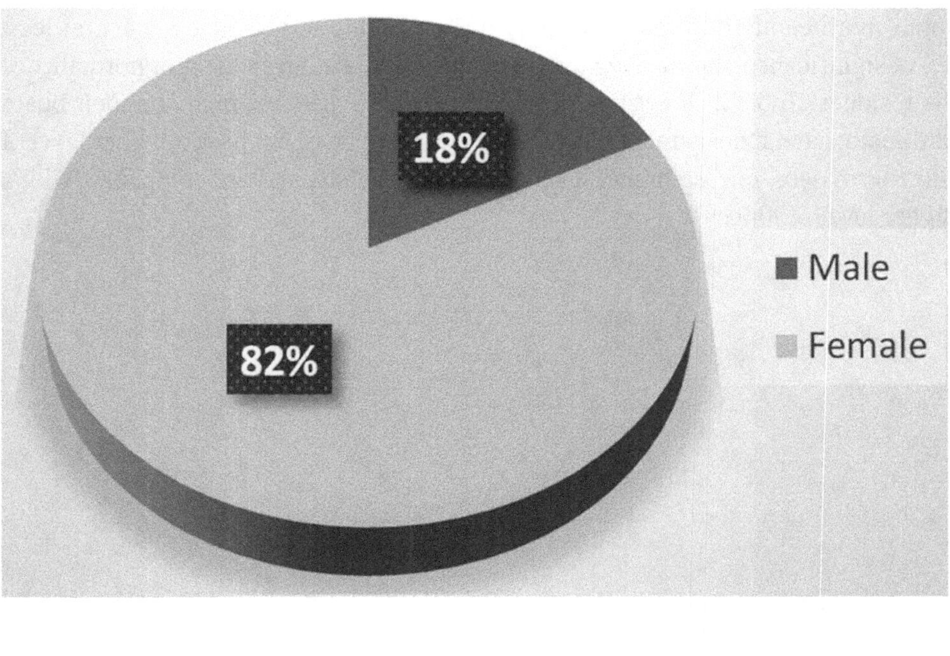

Regarding the leadership of SMEs in the hotel industry, Graph 2 shows that only 13% have a woman as chair of the board and 10% of them are also shareholders of the companies.

Figure 2. % SME of hotel sector with female chair of the board

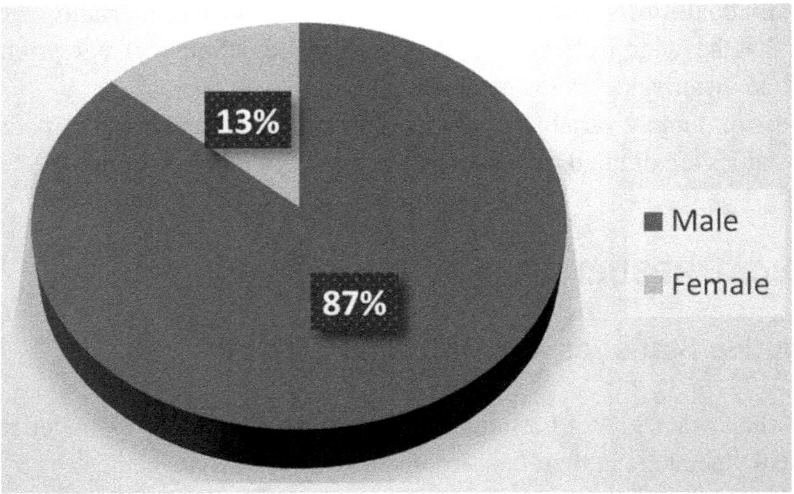

Tables 2, 3, and 4 show descriptive statistics. The hotel SMEs in the study have some significantly different characteristics according to gender diversity, at least 5% of significance, considering the Mann-Whitney test, given the non-normality of the residues. Table 2 shows that hotel SMEs with female members on their board of directors and management are generally less indebted, but have a higher level of short-term debt, release higher levels of free cash flow, and are companies with a higher level of longevity.

Table 2. Descriptive statistics – presence of female directors and managers

Variáveis	Yes		No		Mann-Whitney test – P-value
	Mean	Std. Dev.	Mean	Std. Dev.	
$TLEV_{i,t}$	0.5275	0.2424	0.5710	0.2666	0.0022***
$SDEBT_{i,t}$	0.4507	0.3206	0.4223	0.3568	0.0168**
$SIZE_{i,t}$	4.0049	0.5253	4.0068	0.5923	0.6101
$ROA_{i,t}$	0.0326	0.0911	0.0375	0.1097	0.5422
$FCF_{i,t}$	0.0640	0.0773	0.0602	0.0969	0.0151**
$TANG_{i,t}$	0.7488	0.2606	0.7275	0.3073	0.2236
$LIQ_{i,t}$	5.7704	44.7258	9.3726	86.9438	0.7933
$AGE_{i,t}$	26.6415	18.7920	17.8971	15.3784	0.0001***

1. All variables are explained in Table 1.
2. * Statistical significance at 10%; ** Statistical significance at 5%; *** Statistical significance at 1%.

Table 3 reports significant differences between hotel SMEs run by men and women. Hotel SMEs whose chair of the board is female have a higher level of short-term debt and have smaller size, tangibility and liquidity.

Table 3. Descriptive statistics – chair of the board is female

Variáveis	Yes		No		Mann-Whitney test – P-value
	Mean	Std. Dev.	Mean	Std. Dev.	
$TLEV_{i,t}$	0.5329	0.2531	0.5355	0.2465	0.9329
$SDEBT_{i,t}$	0.4999	0.3059	0.4373	0.3298	0.0003***
$SIZE_{i,t}$	3.8878	0.5155	4.0233	0.5388	0.0002***
$ROA_{i,t}$	0.0311	0.0734	0.0339	0.0976	0.8534
$FCF_{i,t}$	0.0673	0.0731	0.0627	0.0823	0.0871*
$TANG_{i,t}$	0.6736	0.2702	0.7561	0.2678	0.0001***
$LIQ_{i,t}$	5.9168	32.3765	6.4848	57.3035	0.0023***
$AGE_{i,t}$	25.4423	16.9127	25.0479	18.7795	0.3166

1. All variables are explained in Table 1.
2. * Statistical significance at 10%; ** Statistical significance at 5%; *** Statistical significance at 1%.

Table 4 shows that when hotel SMEs are run by female shareholders, they are globally less indebted, but with higher levels of short-term debt. They also have a lower level of investment in fixed assets and lower liquidity.

Table 4. Descriptive statistics – chair of board is a female and shareholder

Variáveis	Yes		No		Mann-Whitney test – P-value
	Mean	Std. Dev.	Mean	Std. Dev.	
$TLEV_{i,t}$	0.3353	0.2684	0.5376	0.2462	0.0005***
$SDEBT_{i,t}$	0.7719	0.2425	0.4417	0.3263	0.0001***
$SIZE_{i,t}$	3.8993	0.4386	4.0065	0.5386	0.2676
$ROA_{i,t}$	0.0526	0.1280	0.0333	0.0942	0.2313
$FCF_{i,t}$	0.0814	0.1028	0.0631	0.0808	0.2006
$TANG_{i,t}$	0.6651	0.2344	0.7460	0.2698	0.0054***
$LIQ_{i,t}$	2.1134	1.6093	6.4613	54.9572	0.0245**
$AGE_{i,t}$	31.0000	17.9583	25.0236	18.5349	0.0576*

1. All variables are explained in Table 1.
2. * Statistical significance at 10%; ** Statistical significance at 5%; *** Statistical significance at 1%.

Table 5 reports the correlation matrix of all variables in the study. The correlation between total leverage and independent variables reports statistically significant correlations with more than 66% of the explanatory variables under analysis, with at least 5% significance. Correlations are quite low, with the highest being related to the correlation between the dependent variable (TLEV) and the variables age ($r=-0.2107$; $p<0.01$), free cash flow ($r=-0.1833$; $p<0.01$) and profitability (ROA) ($r=-0.1651$; $p<0.01$). The analysis of short-term debt reveals that it is linearly associated with more than 77% of the explanatory variables, considering a significance level of 1%. However, the level of association is low, showing a maximum of 42.06% for the variable tangibility (TANG).

Among the explanatory variables, the correlation level is also low, except for the correlation between the variables profitability (ROA) and free cash flow (FCF), whose coefficient is 88.91%, with a significance level of 1%. To avoid multilinearity problems, the free cash flow variable was not considered isolated in the models.

Table 5. Correlation matrix

	TLEV	SDEBT	FDM	FCB	FCBS	SIZE	ROA	FCF	TANG	LIQ	AGE
TLEV	1										
SDEBT	-0.3159***	1									
FDM	-0.0846***	-0.0159	1								
FCB	-0.0035	0.0651***	0.1301***	1							
FCBS	-0.0892***	0.1102***	-0.0337	0.2903***	1						
SIZE	0.0731***	-0.4042***	0.1811***	-0.0858***	-0.0218	1					
ROA	-0.1651***	0.2123***	0.0057	-0.0098	0.0223	-0.1088***	1				
FCF	-0.1833***	0.2582***	0.0109	0.0192	0.0246	-0.1772***	0.8891***	1			
TANG	0.0034	-0.4206***	0.0558**	-0.1042***	-0.0328	0.3004***	-0.2759***	-0.2357***	1		
LIQ	0.0089	-0.0834***	-0.0528**	-0.0035	-0.0087	-0.0413*	-0.0207	-0.0566**	-0.1358***	1	
AGE	-0.2107***	0.0359	0.1833***	0.0073	0.0365	0.1905***	-0.02	-0.0371	0.0796***	-0.0687***	1

1. All variables are explained in Table 1.
2. * Statistical significance at 10%; ** Statistical significance at 5%; *** Statistical significance at 1%.

Results

Tables 6 and 7 present the results of the panel data models. To ensure the robustness of the results, in addition to the estimation of random effects GLS (Generalized Least Squares), regression model with AR (1) disturbances, the results of fixed effects and random effects models are also presented in the robust version.

Table 6 shows the panel regressions findings for three models that analyze the effect of diversity gender on total leverage. The significant level of the Wald chi2 test indicates the rejection of the null hypothesis, that is, the explanatory variables, together, do not explain the total leverage. So, the selected explanatory variables in this study can be considered explanatory of the debt maturity of SMEs in the Portuguese hotel industry. The coefficient of determination (within R^2) is 18.58%.

Table 6. Panel data regression – total leverage

	Random effects AR(1)		Fixed effects vce		Random effects vce	
	β	z	β	t	β	z
FDM	-0.01244**	-2.03	Omitted		-0,01111*	-1,73
FCB	0.04188	1.27	Omitted		0,04161	1,19
FCBS	-0.17591*	-1.78	Omitted		-0,16233	-1,56
SIZE	0.14557***	11.37	0.22296***	5,25	0,12162***	3,93
ROA	-0.46915***	-13.01	-0.44978***	-5,60	-0,50997***	-6,81
ROA2	-0.22210***	-7.52	-0.24242***	-5,37	-0,26963***	-6,33
TANG	-0.01465	-0.69	0.04256	0,83	0,02531	0,56
AGE	-0.0045***	-7.88	-0.02400***	-8,19	-0,00488***	-7,28
_cons	0.11787***	2.28	0.23026	1,46	0,19279	1,58
Wald chi2 / F	373.97 (0.0000)		29.51 (0.0000)		145.64 (0.0000)	
R^2	0.1858		0.2380		0.1897	

1. All variables are explained in Table 1.
2. * Statistical significance at 10%; ** Statistical significance at 5%; *** Statistical significance at 1%.
3. Wald chi2 test for random effects models and F test for fixed effects model; significance levels in parentheses.

The results in Table 6 display that the coefficients of all independent variables are found to be statistically significant at least 5%, except female chair and shareholder at 10%. The ones referring to the chair of the board and tangibility are not statistically significant. The results show that the intensity of the female gender in the boardroom and management has a negative effect on the level of total leverage of Portuguese SMEs in the hotel industry, as presented in hypothesis three. The profitability (ROA) and the firm's age (AGE) also negatively impact the total leverage. The size of the firm seems to be the only independent variable with a positive effect on the dependent variable.

Table 7. Panel data regression – short debt

	Random effects AR(1)		Fixed effects vce		Random effects vce	
	β	z	β	t	β	z
FDM	0.01432**	2.21	Omitted		0,01504**	2,28
FCB	-0.03659	-1.04	Omitted		-0,03454	-1,06
FCBS	0.31753***	3.01	Omitted		0,31069***	4,86
SIZE	-0.25255***	-14.36	-0.33312***	-9,11	-0,25856***	-11,64
ROA	0.18417***	3.29	0.21884***	3,32	0,21599***	3,79
FCFxROA	0.36025***	2.61	0.43883***	2,64	0,47384***	3,32
TANG	-0.29489***	-9.32	-0.22039***	-2,95	-0,29880***	-5,56
LIQ	-0.00039***	-4.25	-0.00028**	-2,18	-0,00042**	-2,54
_cons	1.64233	23.45	1.93622***	15,14	1,66503***	21,27
Wald chi2 / F	463.61 (0.0000)		33.26 (0.0000)		451.32 (0.0000)	
R^2	0.1711		0.1772		0.1708	

1. All variables are explained in Table 1.
2. * Statistical significance at 10%; ** Statistical significance at 5%; *** Statistical significance at 1%.
3. Wald chi2 test for random effects models and F test for fixed effects model; significance levels in parentheses.

Table 7 shows the results of panel data models that analyze the effect of diversity gender on short-term debt. The significant level of the Wald chi2 test, confirms the selected explanatory variables in this study can be considered as explanatory of the short-term debt of SMEs in the Portuguese hotel industry. The coefficient determination R^2 of this model is lower than the total leverage model (17.11%) but higher than other similar studies (e.g., Datta et al., 2021).

The coefficients of all independent variables are found to be statistically significant, at least 5%, except the one referring to the chair of the diversity of the board of directors. The results presented in Table 7 report that the intensity of the female gender in the board of directors and managers has a positive effect on the level of short-term debt of Portuguese SMEs, supporting our hypothesis one. Hypothesis two is only confirmed when the chair of the board of directors is female and simultaneously is a shareholder of the company, according to the positive coefficient of the variable FCBS. Regarding the control variables, it is observed that profitability exerts a positive effect on the short-term debt, which becomes more pressing in the presence of free cash flow. The size of the company, as well as its tangible assets and the level of liquidity, have a negative effect on the short-term debt.

DISCUSSION AND CONCLUSION

The empirical research suggests that the role of women on corporate boards remains a controversial issue. Nevertheless, the literature on the gender diversity board suggests that differences in women behaviour compared to men can influence business decisions. The empirical research regarding this issue shows the relevance of gender diversity on the performance of the company, which encourages the development of public policies to provide conditions for the promotion of the right to equality between genders.

As mentioned earlier, most empirical research still ignores the effect of board gender diversity on financial decision, particularly on debt maturity. This study aims to investigate the effect of female presence in corporate boards on debt maturity, specifically whether companies with greater female representation at the top level of the corporate hierarchy tend to have a greater proportion of short-term debt. We expect that increase of women participation on boards reduces the level of total debt and increases the level of short-term debt.

The empirical study is based on a sample of public limited small and medium enterprises (SMEs) from Portuguese hotel industry, for the period of 2015-2019. Consistent with the expectations and previous empirical studies, the results show that firms with larger female representation on the board of directors and managers tend to have more short-term debt. This finding supports hypothesis one which states that the intensity of the female gender in the boardroom has a positive effect on short-term indebtedness. Overall, it suggests a more adverse management profile to investment, which is an option that is generally financed by long-term indebtedness. Empirical evidence on the relationship between short-term debt and female prevalence on the boardroom supports a positive relationship (e.g., García & Herrero, 2021; Datta et al., 2021; La Rocca et al., 2020; Li & Zhang, 2019). This outcome is suitable related to the general economic and financial literature on gender differences which claims that a more gender diversified firm (higher percentage of women) is more risk-averse, which influences their debt maturity. Jensen (1986) emphasizes the monitoring role of short-term debt in monitoring overinvestment behavior. Under these circumstances, the characteristic of more excellent monitoring of women directors is desired to lead to lower debt maturities. These results may have been boosted, as was the case with Li and Zhang (2019), by the fact that companies with women in charge have greater governance needs, as we pointed out earlier, are smaller and have lower liquidity. This fact drives women to see short-term debt as a governance mechanism.

Further analysis shows that when a woman holds the position of chair of the board and is simultaneously a shareholder, the chance of issuing a short-term debt is higher. That is, given the position of ownership and control it is expected for managers to voluntarily choose the optimal debt maturity structure and self-impose monitoring. This result partially supports hypothesis two, which predicts that the presence of female women at the highest level of the managerial hierarchy has a positive effect on short-term debt.

Taken together, the findings meet the argument that boards with female directors and leaders are more likely to issue short-term debt. This strategy is considered a corporate governance device, which potentially reduces managerial opportunism, supporting the agency's theory hypothesis that gender diversity improves the level of monitoring of the company. Our results confirm that the intensity of the female gender in the boardroom and management has a negative effect on the level of total leverage of Portuguese SMEs in the hotel industry, as presented in hypothesis three. This result reinforces the empirical evidence reported by García and Herrero (2021), Adusei and Obeng (2019), Alves et al. (2015), Hernández-Nicolás et al. (2015) and supports the theory of agency regarding the reduction of asymmetric information associated with women's participation on corporate boardroom.

The control variables effects on the dependent variable show that larger companies have a more indebted capital structure, on the other hand they show evidence of a lower short-term debt. In fact, larger companies tend to diversify their businesses further, diluting the level of risk of their creditors, and making them less exposed to the possibility of bankruptcy, which will positively affect their capacity and conditions of indebtedness (Ang, 1991). In small businesses, the typical informational opacity between internal and external agents of the company becomes particularly severe (López-Gracia & Aybar-Arias, 2000), which often drives them to finance themselves with short-term debt. Profitability is negatively related to total indebtedness, but positively to short-term indebtedness, although with less impact. These results partially support the pecking-order theory, according to which the most profitability companies tend to use less debt (Myers, 1984) and show that in the event of insufficient results, SMEs will opt for debt that less reduces managers' flexibility, i.e., short-term debt (Sogorb-Mira, 2005).

The results also provide evidence that tangible assets have a negative effect on short-term debt, suggesting that SMEs with lower fixed assets need to contract more short-term debt. However, Palacín-Sánchez, Ramíres-Herrera and Pietro (2013) argued that financial institutions may not consider tangibility very important when financing a SMEs. Finally, the findings report that older companies are likely to accumulate higher levels of own funds and lower capital needs, supporting the prediction that the longevity of small companies influences their financing decisions and that companies that have been operating in the market for more years probably acquire greater self-financing capacity (Serrasqueiro & Caetano, 2015).

This chapter corroborates with the theory of agency and contributes to the empirical literature on female presence on corporate boards in several ways. First, it sheds light on the conflicting evidence on the relationship between female board leadership and firm debt maturity. In addition, to the best of the author´s knowledge, this is the first attempt to investigate empirically the impact of female board leadership on firm debt maturity on SMEs from the Portuguese hotel industry. Second, it reinforces the argument that female directors and managers are more likely to use short-term debt as a governance device, reducing the likelihood of overinvestment and managerial opportunism, supporting the hypothesis of the agency's theory that gender diversity is associated with a more efficient monitoring of the firm decisions. Third, it adds evidence that the presence of female in corporate boards has significant effects on firms' total debt, supporting the agency theory regarding the lower asymmetry of information associated with gender diversity. Finally, at a practical level, the empirical findings of this chapter support the efforts of policymakers and regulators in continuing to contribute to gender equality at firm's boardroom.

LIMITATIONS AND FUTURE RESEARCH DIRECTIONS

This study also features limitations that can be fruitful avenues for future research. Firstly, the sample used in this study is based on secondary data rather than on primary data collected in the field. Hence, the sample has some limitations, namely the data of the gender variables remained unchanged and refers to the last year of data available, mostly to 2021, and does not include specific variables of the hotel industry. Also, the analysis was based on accounting and not on market data and last, the conclusions drawn in this study may not be applicable to other industries. Therefore, future studies can expand this research by including other industries to examine how the impact of gender diversity on debt maturity differs by industries.

REFERENCES

Adams, R., & Ferreira, D. (2009). Women in the boardroom and their impact on governance and performance. *Journal of Financial Economics*, *94*(2), 291–309. doi:10.1016/j.jfineco.2008.10.007

Adusei, M., & Obeng, E. Y. T. (2019). Board gender diversity and the capital structure of microfinance institutions: A global analysis. *The Quarterly Review of Economics and Finance*, *71*, 258–269. doi:10.1016/j.qref.2018.09.006

Ahmadi, A., Nakaa, N., & Bouri, A. (2018). Chief executive officer attributes, board structures, gender diversity and firm performance among French CAC 40 listed firms. *Research in International Business and Finance*, *44*, 218–226. doi:10.1016/j.ribaf.2017.07.083

Alves, P., Couto, E. B., & Francisco, P. M. (2015). Board of directors' composition and capital structure. *Research in International Business and Finance*, *35*, 1–32. doi:10.1016/j.ribaf.2015.03.005

Ang, J. (1991). Small business uniqueness & the theory of financial management. *Journal of Small Business Finance*, *1*(1), 1–13. doi:10.57229/2373-1761.1108

Barberis, N., & Thaler, R. (2003). A survey of behavioral finance. In G. M. Constantinides, M. Harris, & R. M. Stulz (Eds.), *Handbook of the Economics of Finance* (Vol. 1, pp. 1053–1128). Elsevier Science B.V.

Barclay, M. J., & Smith, C. W. Jr. (1995). The maturity structure of corporate debt. *The Journal of Finance*, *50*(2), 609–631. doi:10.1111/j.1540-6261.1995.tb04797.x

Briozzo, A., Cardone-Riportella, C., & García-Olalla, M. (2019). Corporate governance attributes and listed SMEs' debt maturity. *The International Journal of Business in Society*, *19*(4), 735–750. doi:10.1108/CG-11-2017-0272

Burke, R. J. (1997). Women on corporate boards of directors: A needed resource. *Journal of Business Ethics*, *16*(9), 909–915. doi:10.1023/A:1017987220508

Carmo, C., Alves, S., & Quaresma, B. (2022). Women on boards in Portuguese listed companies: Does gender diversity influence financial performance? *Sustainability*, *14*(10), 6186. doi:10.3390u14106186

Carter, D. A., Simkins, B. J., & Simpson, W. G. (2003). Corporate governance, board diversity and firm value. *Financial Review*, *38*(1), 33–53. doi:10.1111/1540-6288.00034

Datta, S., Doan, T., & Toscano, F. (2021). Top executive gender, board gender diversity, and financing decisions: Evidence from debt structure choice. *Journal of Banking & Finance*, *125*, 1–17. doi:10.1016/j.jbankfin.2021.106070

Detthamrong, U., Chancharat, N., & Vithessonthi, C. (2017). Corporate Governance, Capital Structure and Firm Performance Evidence from Thailand. *Research in International Business and Finance*, *42*, 689–709. doi:10.1016/j.ribaf.2017.07.011

Fenoy-Castaño, C., Martínez-Romero, M. J., & Martínez-Alonso, R. (2021). Does the female presence in corporate governance influence the level of indebtedness in agri-food family firms? [Switzerland]. *Agriculture, 11*(11), 1135. doi:10.3390/agriculture11111135

Filipe, G. (2020). *Determinantes da Estrutura de Capital: Efeito de Variáveis Micro e Macroeconómicas no Setor Hoteleiro em Portugal - Uma Análise de Dados em Painel,* [Master's thesis, University of Algarve].

Fondas, N., & Sassalos, S. (2000). A different voice in the boardroom: How the presence of women directors affects board influence over management. *Global Focus, 12*, 13–22.

García, C. J., & Herrero, B. (2021). Female directors, capital structure, and financial distress. *Journal of Business Research, 136*, 592–601. doi:10.1016/j.jbusres.2021.07.061

Guilding, C. (2003). Hotel owner/operator structures: Implications for capital budgeting process. *Management Accounting Research, 14*(3), 179–199. doi:10.1016/S1044-5005(03)00049-0

Hernández-Nicolás, C., Martín-Ugedo, J., & Minguez-Vera, A. (2015). The influence of gender on financial decisions: evidence from small start-up firms in Spain. *E & M Economie and Management, 18*(4), 93-107.

Ho, S., Li, A., Tam, K., & Zhang, F. (2015). CEO gender, ethical leadership, and accounting conservatism. *Journal of Business Ethics, 127*(2), 351–370. doi:10.100710551-013-2044-0

Huang, J., & Kisgen, D. J. (2013). Gender and corporate finance: Are male executives overconfident relative to female executives? *Journal of Financial Economics, 108*(3), 822–839. doi:10.1016/j.jfineco.2012.12.005

Huse, M., & Solberg, A. (2006). How Scandinavian women make and can make contributions on corporate boards. *Women in Management Review, 21*(2), 113–130. doi:10.1108/09649420610650693

Informa D&B. (2022). Diversidade de género nas empresas em Portugal. Informa D&B. https://biblioteca.informadb.pt/read/document.aspx?id=2639# Instituto

de Estatística, N. (INE). (2020). Empresas em Portugal 2018. Lisboa: Instituto Nacional de Estatística

Jensen, M. C. (1986). Agency Costs of Free Cash Flow, Corporate Finance, and Takeovers. *The American Economic Review*, *76*(2), 323–329.

Jensen, M. C., & Meckling, W. H. (1976). Theory of the firm: Managerial behavior, agency costs and ownership structure. *Journal of Financial Economics*, *3*(4), 305–360. doi:10.1016/0304-405X(76)90026-X

Kirsch, A. (2018). The gender composition of corporate boards: A review and research agenda. *The Leadership Quarterly*, *29*(2), 346–364. doi:10.1016/j.leaqua.2017.06.001

La Rocca, M., Neha, N., & La Rocca, T. (2020). Female management, overconfidence and debt maturity: European evidence. *The Journal of Management and Governance*, *24*(3), 713–747. doi:10.100710997-019-09479-9

Li, Y., & Zhang, X. (2019). Impact of board gender composition on corporate debt maturity structures. *European Financial Management*, *25*(5), 1–35. doi:10.1111/eufm.12214

Lonkani, R. (2019). Gender differences and managerial earnings forecast bias: Are female executives less overconfident than male executives? *Emerging Markets Review*, *38*, 18–34. doi:10.1016/j.ememar.2018.11.012

López-Delgado, P., & Diéguez-Soto, J. (2020). Indebtedness in family-managed firms: The moderating role of female directors on the board. *Review of Managerial Science*, *14*(4), 727–762. doi:10.100711846-018-0307-y

López-Gracia, J., & Aybar-Arias, C. (2000). An empirical approach to the financial behaviour of small and medium sized companies. *Small Business Economics*, *14*(1), 55–63. doi:10.1023/A:1008139518709

Marinova, J., Plantenga, J., & Remery, C. (2016). Gender diversity and firm performance: Evidence from Dutch and Danish boardrooms. *International Journal of Human Resource Management*, *27*(15), 1777–1790. doi:10.1080/09585192.2015.1079229

Menicucci, E., Paolucci, G., & Paoloni, N. (2019). Does gender matter for hotel performance? Evidence from the Italian hospitality industry. *International Journal of Tourism Research*, *21*(5), 625–638. doi:10.1002/jtr.2286

Minguez-Vera, A., & Martin, A. (2011). Gender and management on Spanish SMEs: An empirical analysis. *International Journal of Tourism Research*, *22*(14), 2852–2873.

Modigliani, F., & Miller, M. H. (1958). The cost of capital, corporation finance and the theory of investment. *The American Economic Review*, *48*(3), 261–297.

Myers, S. C. (1977). Determinants of corporate borrowing. *Journal of Financial Economics*, *5*(2), 147–175. doi:10.1016/0304-405X(77)90015-0

Myers, S. C. (1984). The Capital Structure Puzzle. *The Journal of Finance*, *39*(3), 575–592. doi:10.2307/2327916

Nielsen, S., & Huse, M. (2010). The contribution of women on boards of directors: Going beyond the surface. *Corporate Governance*, *18*(2), 136–148. doi:10.1111/j.1467-8683.2010.00784.x

Nisiyama, E. K., & Nakamura, W. T. (2018). Diversidade do Conselho de Administração e a Estrutura de Capital. *Revista de Administração de Empresas*, *58*(6), 551–563. doi:10.15900034-759020180604

Palacín-Sánchez, M., Ramírez-Herrera, L., & Pietro, F. (2013). Capital structure of SMEs in Spanish Regions. *Small Business Economics*, *41*(2), 503–519. doi:10.100711187-012-9439-7

Post, C., & Byron, K. (2015). Women on boards and firm financial performance: A meta-analysis. *Academy of Management Journal*, *58*(5), 1546–1571. doi:10.5465/amj.2013.0319

Reguera-Alvarado, N., de Fuentes, P., & Laffarga, J. (2017). Does board gender diversity influence financial performance? Evidence from Spain. *Journal of Business Ethics*, *141*(2), 337–350. doi:10.100710551-015-2735-9

Segovia-Pérez, M., Figueroa-Domecq, C., Fuentes-Moraleda, L., & Muñoz-Mazón, A. (2019). Incorporating a gender approach in the hospitality industry: Female executives' perceptions. *International Journal of Hospitality Management*, *76*(Part A), 184–193.

Serrasqueiro, Z., & Caetano, A. (2015). Trade-off theory *versus* pecking order theory: Capital structure decisions in a Peripheral Region of Portugal. *Journal of Business Economics and Management*, *16*(2), 445–466. doi:10.3846/16111699.2012.744344

Shehata, N., Salhin, A., & El-Helaly, M. (2017). Board diversity and firm performance: Evidence from the UK SMEs. *Applied Economics*, *49*(48), 4817–4832. doi:10.1080/00036846.2017.1293796

Sogorb-Mira, F. (2005). How SME uniqueness affects capital structure: Evidence from a 1994–1998 Spanish data panel. *Small Business Economics*, *25*(5), 447–457. doi:10.100711187-004-6486-8

Srinidhi, B., Gul, F. A., & Tsui, J. (2011). Female directors and earnings quality. *Contemporary Accounting Research*, *28*(5), 1610–1644. doi:10.1111/j.1911-3846.2011.01071.x

Tang, C. H., & Jang, S. (2007). Revisit to the determinants of capital structure: A comparison between lodging firms and software firms. *International Journal of Hospitality Management*, *26*(1), 175–187. doi:10.1016/j.ijhm.2005.08.002

Ting, I. W. K., Wang, W., Lu, W., & Chen, Y. (2021). Do female directors will have impact on corporate performance? *Review of Managerial Science*, *15*(3), 611–631. doi:10.100711846-019-00351-6

Wood, R. C. (2015). *Hospitality management: A brief introduction.* SAGE Publications. doi:10.4135/9781473920521

Chapter 4
Change Management as a Tool to Implement Gender Equality:
The Spanish Banking Sector Case

Susana Diaz-Iglesias
Universidad Rey Juan Carlos, Spain

Carmen Orden-Cruz
Universidad Rey Juan Carlos, Spain

Alicia Blanco-Gonzalez
Universidad Rey Juan Carlos, Spain

ABSTRACT

Although numerous studies on gender equality, and change management (CM) exist, the connection between the constructs remains largely unexplored. This paper aims to narrow the research gap that links elements of gender equality and the management of change experienced by companies in the Spanish financial sector when implementing their gender equality policies. Using a longitudinal analysis as a methodological approach, the content of the sustainability reports disclosed on the websites of the Spanish banks was analyzed. The results show preliminary indications that CM could play an important role in the development of gender policies in organizations. This study contributes to understanding how companies, in the financial sector, have developed their gender equality policies over the last decade, providing clues for the improvement of future gender policies.

DOI: 10.4018/978-1-6684-5981-2.ch004

INTRODUCTION

Companies are continually searching for competitive advantages to adapt to changing situations. One of their main priorities is to adjust their business operations and strategies to align with the 17 Sustainability Development Goals (SDGs) established by the United Nations in its 2015 summit "Transforming Our World: The 2030 Agenda for Sustainable Development" (Tsalis et al., 2020), and to integrate sustainability to guarantee their long-term success (Redman, 2018).

One of the SDGs that has generated the most interest is goal 5, which is dedicated to promoting gender equality (United Nations, 2019b). To address this challenge, firms develop and implement CSR strategies, and how they adopt and embed CSR practices is a crucial competitive strategic factor that motivates new ways to achieve better CSR performance (Rao & Tilt, 2016).

Companies are the best drivers to facilitate the transition to a sustainable society because they concentrate more power than even weaker countries (Brown, 1981). This explains the increasing importance of the study of their sustainability (Chang et al., 2017). On one hand, small and medium enterprises and non-governmental organizations are the actors that boost social engagement. On the other hand, multinational enterprises use institutional voids as drivers to develop new inclusive business models and invest in education, training, and health services to improve their employees' capabilities on this subject (Arnold, 2018).

More ambitious frameworks and specific policies should be developed to face the current sustainability challenge (Queisser, 2016). Companies need to manage change optimally to gain a competitive advantage to drive them to organizational success (Todnem By, 2008). And, where reducing women's workplace discrimination is a key challenge and the potential source of that competitive advantage (Gartzia, 2021).

Although there are numerous studies on gender equality, and CM with the CSR implications, the connection between the concepts remains largely unexplored. Therefore, there is a need for more empirical studies (Nadeem et al., 2017; van den Brink & Benschop 2018) and more meaningful research to help policymakers to make decisions about gender equality (Ferreira, 2015). This study aims to narrow the research gap between the elements of CSR in companies and CM to implement gender equality policies through the experience of companies in the Spanish financial sector when implementing their CSR policies.

This study explores how CM may be used as a resource when implementing corporate sustainability strategies involving gender equality policies. In this way, this study aims to evaluate the impact that CM has on the achievement of gender equality in financial companies, as well as to measure the real impact of their actions toward gender equality. Six case studies were examined using a longitudinal analysis methodology by analysing the sustainability reports for the six leading banking companies in Spain. The analysis tries to understand how those banks have developed gender equality policies in the last ten years. The banking sector was selected because it has a more homogeneous reference population, and it is one of the main engines that drive the achievement of a more diverse and inclusive economy (Birindelli et al., 2018; Delgado-Piña et al., 2020).

The ten most important categories related to gender equality in the working and professional environment were identified from different sources such as the Demetriades (2007); Dijkstra & Hanmer (2000); World Economic Forum (2020) created for CM. Finally, the data was obtained and analyzed using the CADQAS software Atlas.ti tool.

Therefore, the research objectives are as follows:

Research objective 1: To assess the evolution of gender equality in the sample analyzed.

Research objective 2: To assess the relationship between CM and gender equality programs

Research objective 3: To evaluate the relationship over time between CM and the implementation of gender equality programs.

BACKGROUND

CSR & Gender Equality

Today, gender equality has become an issue for all businesses and one of the main internal motivators for CSR. Women's empowerment and gender equality are some of the main concerns for global sustainable development. The United Nations highlighted these items as a priority in "The 2030 Agenda for Sustainable Development" (2015). In modern economies, those organizations that integrate ODSs into their operations experience greater business success (Dyllick & Hockerts, 2002). Research shows that investing in women and girls can lead to increases in productivity, organizational effectiveness, return on investment, and higher consumer satisfaction (United Nations Global Compact, 2022).

Just to present some data about the gender at work, according to the UN (2019a), women represent 39% of the workforce, but only 27% occupy managerial positions. Further, according to The Global Gender Gap Report (2020), the gap in the labour market is wider at higher seniority levels. Worldwide, 36% of senior private sector managers and public sector officials are women. In comparison, the presence of women on corporate boards or as top business leaders is even more limited: only 18.2% of firms globally are led by women. Similarly, the Global Gender Gap Report 2020, published by the World Economic Forum (2020), presents the framework for gender-based disparities and tracks their progress over time on economic participation and opportunity, educational attainment, health and survival, and political empowerment dimensions. This year, the worldwide average (population-weighted) distance completed to parity is 68.6%. This means that the gender gap is narrower, but no country has yet achieved full gender parity to date. Likewise, this year's report, which marks the 14th edition, is the first time that shows gender gaps in emerging jobs. Eight professions have been identified (people and culture, content production, marketing, sales, product development, data, AI, engineering, and cloud computing) with increasing employment prospects across 20 leading economies. This report analyses the information gathered on LinkedIn during the last five years to indicate hiring trends. Only two groups, people and culture, and content production have shown more significant employment for women than men.

According to the social categorization theory, the classification of individuals in an organizational context shows preferences to work with similar social demographic groups, for example, members of the same gender, because they are perceived as open to ideas that are similar to their own (Harjoto et al., 2018).

Most of the academic literature studies on gender equality are centred on women's inclusion on boards or on executive teams (Dezsö & Ross, 2012; Furlotti et al., 2019; Liao et al., 2015). In the sector analyzed in this study, most of the literature are focused on gender diversity mainly within the composition of boards of directors in international banks (Birindelli et al., 2018; De Cabo et al., 2012; Gallego-Álvarez & Pucheta-Martínez, 2020) or Spanish banks (Delgado-Piña et al., 2020; Zurdo et al., 2013). The increasing interest of women on boards occurred after the European Commission issued a proposal for a Directive in November 2012. They established the goal to push companies listed on the stock exchange to reach 40% of the gender least represented in non-executive positions on boards of directors for 2020 (Zurdo et al., 2013). Moreover, the Code of Corporate governance for Spanish listed companies (2015 version) included a recommendation for achieving 30% board seats occupied by women by 2020. This type of change as planned, is implemented from a top-down direction. They are driven by the management team, and goals are detailed in advance of their implementation (By, 2005).

Van der Walt and Ingley (2003) state that while there is no universal acceptance of arguments supporting boardroom diversity, they mention two reasons: ethical and economic. The first emphasizes that it is unfair to exclude people for performance-related characteristics. The second is based on performance according to the boardroom composition with the underlying assumption that board composition affects the development of their functions and partial economic benefits of firm performance (De Cabo et al., 2012). Nonetheless, some authors, that defend the potential benefits of promoting women in business, focus on the social benefits in general and not just on firm profitability (Ferreira, 2015). Economic impact is one of the main topics analyzed regarding board diversity; that is, whether board gender diversity improves corporate financial performance. Some empirical studies found a positive association between the two variables, but almost none found causation (Cunningham, 2020). Carter et al., (2010) (cited in De Cabo et al., 2012) warned that, according to contingency theory, the net effect of gender diversity can be either positive or negative from a financial performance perspective. In many studies, they are positively linked because they contribute to effective governance of firms and, at the same time, have a positive influence on CSR (Galbreath, 2018; Setó-Pamies, 2015). Also, the higher the number of female members on boards likely led to more actions to promote gender diversity which consequently increased the number of women on the boards (Figueroa-Domecq et al., 2020). Specifically, in the banking sector, some studies prove that only gender-balanced boards positively impact a bank's sustainability performance (Birindelli et al., 2018). So, it is better to be prudent when stating blunt assertions to avoid being self-defeating (Cunningham, 2020).

But boards should reflect a more comprehensive social environment because diversity per se is not enough to result in more effective corporate boards, as Van der Walt and Ingley (2003) argued. They should be formed by merit criteria as selected by directors, and their expertise in selecting qualified individuals reflects the diversity of their team. In fact, their challenge is to gain the balance of expertise and perspectives needed for effective functioning and decision-making. Likewise, a similar challenge exists for minority representation in the boardroom for their voices to be heard.

One of the integral welfare functions of boards of directors is seeking sustainability according to the law. There is evidence of a positive relationship between more diverse boards and adopting more sustainable business practices. Companies interested in pursuing sustainability objectives should prioritize the appointment of women on their boards (Kassinis et al., 2016). There is also a positive association with women in the position of chairperson if one sees the prevalence of females in the job scheme (Furlotti et al., 2019). Although diversity may occur voluntarily or through quotas, the different effects still need to be understood (Hillman, 2015).

Policy-makers and researchers argue that a cultural change is needed alongside legal changes to establish organization-wide diversity, not only at the Board of Directors level, but also as a lever to implement initiatives, policies, and measures that incorporate more gender diversity on demographic and structural aspects (Kassinis et al., 2016).

Gender Equality & the Tool of Change Management

Among the different elements that make up CSR in organizations, gender is gaining more importance and a positive influence, not just in a financial impact but also on a firm's socially responsible behaviour (Setó-Pamies, 2015). Thus, efficient CM when implementing CSR strategies, such as gender equality, can improve chances of success leading to competitive organizational advantages. CM is one of the most strategic aspects of achieving organizational success within the challenging and complex changing environment in which organizations find themselves today (Al-Haddad & Kotnour, 2015; Guimaraes & Armstrong, 1998; Todnem By, 2008).

For some authors, the driver of change is that which generates the desire or need for change in an organization, including leadership, regulations, or laws (Whelan-Berry & Somerville, 2010).

Much has been written about leadership when studying change management in organizations and the difference in styles between female and male leaders. Starting with Rosener (1990), for example, that assessed that women normally use a transformational leadership, being this one better for economical turbulent situations against the command-and-control style preferred by men. Late, same author Rosener (1997), affirm that women in senior positions in organizations make increases productivity, innovation, and profits through their aptitude for ambiguity and willingness to empower others. Therefore, being a woman in organizational change processes and talking about management styles attributed to women perpetuates women in a secondary position (Tyler, 2005).

Related to Change theory, Lewin (1947, 1951) was the first author with his "unfreezing-refreezing" model being the origin point for future approaches. And today still there are parts of the change practice that need further works in order to advance the knowledge of gender and change in practice (Linstead et al., 2005).

The early versions of CM literature provided lines of study about management and technology implementation, but lately, it has been focused on roles of organizational development, strategy, decision making, and Model, this last one related to CSR (Diaz-Iglesias et al., 2019). Scholars across many disciplines seek to explain organizational changes and their reasons. Ideally, the different perspectives will integrate without nullifying one another. To better foster change towards sustainability within companies, the research carried out by Lozano et al., (2016) shows that an understanding of the holistic nature of change is needed (Lozano, 2012) to promote adequate strategies and remove obstacles. The main obstacle for gender change is resistance (van den Brink & Benschop, 2018).

Similarly, the origin of planning organizational change for sustainability begins with reporting, and reciprocally those changes optimize future sustainable reporting. Thus, the department responsible for producing sustainability reporting is the motor that facilitates change in companies (Lozano et al., 2016). A sustainability report can help organizations measure, understand, and communicate their economic, social, environmental, and governance performance, and then set goals and manage change more effectively (GRI webpage).

The links between sustainability reporting and organizational CM for gender equality also need to be understood. A company's first sustainability report is published as a result of a company's internal motivations with subsequent reports being issued with a mix of internal and external motivating factors. Thus, a company's decision to create and publish a sustainability report is the starting point that promotes an organizational change, making those changes part of the organization until the publication of a follow-up report (Lozano et al., 2016). Even creating a committee responsible for developing and implementing CSR is a mechanism that proves a commitment to sustainable economic development and brings value to the organization (Hussain et al., 2018).

According to Al-Haddad and Kotnour (2015), there are eleven systematic change methods and six different CM methods. Selecting the adequate change method is a requisite for organizational CM success and must align with the organizational change type. Having strategic objectives and well-defined change objectives to measure change is also requisite. However, there is currently no framework that scientifically unifies knowledge and its influence on organizations' preparation strategies for successful change (Burnes & Jackson, 2011; Rafferty et al., 2013). Nor is there research that explains all the approaches to change in a unified way (Nyström et al., 2013). Nevertheless, it has become more recognized in recent years that one or even two methods cannot cover the myriad of different change situations (Burnes & Jackson, 2011).

The lack of knowledge of how to effect organizational change toward gender equality should be a core competency to be developed to understand the mechanisms by which organizational culture and climate can change (Coe et al., 2019). Also, companies implement same programs that other previous, due to the lack of collaborative frameworks, in this sense, they obtain slow results on the reducing the women's discrimination in organizations (UN 2021).

The situation in the work environment of gender inequality, especially in the private sector, suggests that actions beyond the simplistic view of gender should be promoted, (Eagly et al., 1995). In this sense, i.e., Grosser and Moon (2008) address the complementary roles of social action and self-regulation of private companies in becoming inherently more engaged and concerned with social issues. The role of women in change management not only impacts organizational change from a marginalized position, but also in the change process itself (Tyler 2005.)

In this document, the authors try to cover the gap in the literature and understand, in an empirical way, how organizations in the financial sector in Spain have been managing change during the last ten years through the analysis of their CSR strategies when implementing gender equality policies.

METHODOLOGY AND DATA COLLECTION

This paper examines the areas of sustainability, CM, and gender equality. To accomplish this, it explored how the largest Spanish banking organizations on the stock exchange: Santander, BBVA, Bankia, Bankinter, Sabadell, and Caixabank, managed change when reporting on gender equality in their sustainability reports (Torres et al., 2013).

The current outlook regarding sustainability reports and gender equality in organizations is broad. In some cases, the sector is an important factor differentiating the development and the commitment to the sustainability goals. In the case of banking, the sector is formed by large companies, which generally develop and communicate their sustainability reports (Bonilla-Priego et al., 2014) and examine gender equality in the composition of their staff.

As Morley and Crossouard (2016) point out, gender equality "cannot be reduced to a number." "Neither is it just about increasing quantitative representation." Therefore, this study performed comparative content analyses of the annual reports and online public documents (corporate governance, sustainability reports, etc.) retrieved from the corporate websites of the banks. This source of information allows for data collection and is understandable for the stakeholders (Bonilla-Priego et al., 2014; Ilinitch et al., 1998).

As shown in Table 1, all documents refer to the period from 2010 (except in the case of Bankia, which refers to 2012 and Caixabank to 2013) to 2019. Also, it is important to note that they have different formats, titles, lengths, and structures.

Table 1. Sample and sampling criteria

Bank and year	Name of the document	Number of pages
BANKIA 2012	Report BFA-Bankia	94
BANKIA 2019	Annual Report	78
BANKINTER 2010	Corporate Responsibility Report	121
BANKINTER 2019	Consolidated non-financial information statement	114
SANTANDER 2010	Sustainability Report	70
SANTANDER 2019	Annual Report	802
BBVA 2010	Corporate Responsibility Report	105
BBVA 2019	Annual Report	525
SABADELL 2010	Corporate Social Responsibility Report	121
SABADELL 2019	Non-financial Information Report	39
CAIXABANK 2013	Integrated Corporate Report	223
CAIXABANK 2019	Socioeconomic Impact of the CaixaBank Group	68

Source: (Own elaboration)

Following other authors (Baumann-Pauly et al., 2016; Bono et al., 2008; Rao & Tilt, 2016), a longitudinal study was conducted to understand the impact of CM on gender equality strategies implemented in the period selected from 2010 to 2019. Likewise, a case study approach was used as part of our methodology. The authors conducted a qualitative and interpretative semantic content analysis based on text coding, in which themes are classified through objective variables (Friese, 2011; Olabuénaga, 2012). The categories of the codes for the content analysis were defined and selected taking into consideration the items included in the following sources: "SDG 5" indicators (UN Global Compact, 2022); "Gender-related Development Index," "Development Index and Gender Empowerment Measure" and the "Gender Gap Index" (GGI) elaborated by the World Economic Forum (2020). The indicators analyzed were selected from previous research such as Demetriades (2007); Dijkstra and Hanmer (2000); Furlotti et al., (2019); Galbreath (2018), and Miotto and Vilajoana-Alejandre (2019). Thus, the most important categories related to gender equality in the working and professional environment considered were: access to education, salary gap, women's health and working conditions, equal opportunities for professional development, sexual harassment protocol, work-life balance, female employment rate, social actions for women's communities, and women on boards of directors. The last one, given the importance of previous research (Birindelli et al., 2018; Liao et al., 2015), the authors decided to examine it specifically instead of women in management positions.

Thus, to analyze the content of the reports and to systematize data in the same manner employed in previous research, the authors used Computer Assisted Qualitative Data Analysis CADQAS software Atlas.ti (Miotto & Vilajoana-Alejandre, 2019; Raigada, 2002; Valles, 2002; Van der Voet et al., 2015). In Atlas.ti, this means creating "codes of the primary document's Table," coding the documents by bank and year, 2010 and 2019.

The first step was encoding the content of the sustainability reports in a deductive way. It was necessary to reduce the large number of words by coding them and linking them with the defined categories to be later the subject of the semantic analysis (Friese, 2011; Olabuénaga, 2012). According to Demetriades (2007), indicators are the point of reference or basis used to measure and evaluate changes. They usually are numbers, facts, opinions, etc., that mark the changes or progress to gain objectives. There is a lack of standardization of the descriptors that designate the indicators. Depending on the relevance that each entity gives to gender equality policies and on their style of communication, in the search, authors used keywords explicit a priori in the categories.

The second step was inductively encoding the content. Authors were immersed in the semantic texts, searching for synonymous keywords to avoid missing relevant text parts. Such is the case of root words designated differently in Spanish, for example,

"Mujer, femen, directiv, maternidad, or igualdad, diversid etc." Also, there are text quotes that mention different topics. In those cases, they can be assigned to more than one code. Also, in many cases, the indicators "Female Access to employment" and "Equal Opportunities of Development" mean or are included in the same quotations, so they are added to both codes. The connections of the codes of the central concepts were made within the same bank in 2019 and in 2010, in order to account the relationships between them (Corbin & Strauss, 1990).

To finalize, a second author of this study revised the coding. This peer revision avoided the possibility of subjectivity when using this methodology (Olabuénaga, 2012). The result variable used was the number of times that each entity, directly or indirectly, mentioned a concept or topic related to gender equality or CM in the report. The assumption is that as in previous studies such Miotto, & Vilajoana-Alejandre (2019) the more often a topic is mentioned, the more importance the report authors attribute to it.

RESULTS AND DISCUSSION

This document is aimed at analyzing how CM may be used as a resource when implementing corporate sustainability strategies in gender equality policies. It has tried to enrich the understanding of gender equality-related topics in the narrative of the Spanish financial industry. Our research was conducted through the methodology of longitudinal analysis, following the recommendations laid out by Rao and Tilt (2016) and Nadeem et al., (2017) to develop a better understanding of the relationship between CSR and gender equality. This study also contributes to building methodological strength of the CM literature and the existing gender equality. The longitudinal analysis encompasses the evolution of a decade of the six leading and most representative Spanish banks in the stock exchange as case studies. The authors conducted a content analysis of the main documents and reports of the entities of the sample retrieved from their web pages. In particular, the research was focused on the information related to gender equality matters through several previously defined indicators for the analysis. The times that banks mention the different indicators of gender equality within their official documents help to determine their priorities in attaining the UN Sustainability Development Goals.

Research objective 1: To assess the evolution of gender equality in the sample analyzed. As in previous studies (Grosser & Moon, 2008), the study results show a significant increase in interest in gender equality, during the last ten years. The Spanish banking sector has increased the number of times that entities mention the different indicators in their official publications. In some cases, it even showed that the structure of some banks assimilated and consolidated their policies of gender equality into normal operations.

The absolute values for each indicator between 2010 and 2019 are shown in Table 2. Regarding this information, all codes together experienced a significant increase in importance during the last decade, going from 114 mentions to 190. The codes that decreased were "access to education," "sexual harassment protocols," "women's health and working conditions," and "work-life balance"; finally, "equal opportunities for professional development" did not change.

Table 2. Differences on codes' frequency in absolute terms

Codes	Absolute 2010	Absolute 2019	Differences
Access to education	1	0	-1
Equal opportunities for professional development	25	25	0
Female employment access	11	33	22
Salary gap information	9	28	19
Sexual harassment protocols	11	9	-2
Social Action for Women's Communities	9	28	19
Women's health and working condition	6	4	-2
Women image	10	20	10
Women on Boards of Directors	9	22	13
Work-life balance	23	21	-2
Totals	114	190	76

Source: (Own elaboration)

The evolution of gender equality was evaluated by analyzing the change in interest among different topics during the periods. In 2010, importance was given to "Equal opportunities for the professional development of women" implemented mainly by Bankinter with almost half of the absolute mentions. It was followed by "Work-life balance" an indicator whose importance was similar between all entities (except Bankia, which mentioned this topic once). Ten years later, "Female employment access" was mentioned most frequently in the BBVA report and this topic showed the highest increase in attention from 2010 to 2019. It was followed by "salary gap information" and the initiatives undertaken to promote "social actions for women's communities" implemented mainly by Santander and BBVA. These last two were also the second topics that gained more relevance in 2019.

Figure 1 shows the absolute values for the six entities separately. Considering the overall results, in 2010, Bankinter and Caixabank were the banks that registered the most mentions related to gender equality, while in 2019, Santander and BBVA recorded the most mentions related to gender equality. Regarding the topics, the most important in 2010 was "equal opportunities for professional development," followed by "work-life balance," with the remaining topics being much less important in a generalized way with the exception of "access to education," which was mentioned just once. In 2019 the topics that were most frequently mentioned were: "female employment access" followed by "salary gap information," and "social action for women's communities." The rest of the codes were considered closely with less importance. Meanwhile, "women's health and working conditions" and "sexual harassment protocols" gained in importance with an increase of 4 and 9 number of absolute mentions, respectively, and "access to education" was not even mentioned.

Figure 1. Evolution of codes from 2010 to 2019 by banks in absolute terms
Source: (Own elaboration)

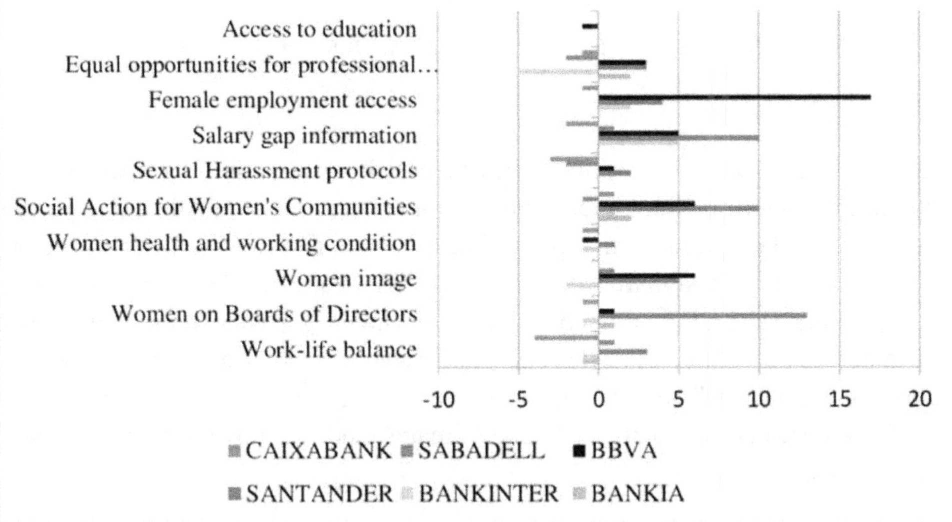

Figure 2 shows the results in 2010 by bank, with Bankinter and Bankia concentrating their attention mainly on topics related to "equal opportunities for professional development," while BBVA focused on "work-life balance" and Sabadell on "salary gap information." On the other hand, Santander had a more fragmented narrative, reporting mainly information about "equal opportunities for professional development," "social action for women's communities," and "work-life balance."

Caixabank mentioned the topics of "women image" and "work-life balance" the most often.

Figure 2. Code frequency results 2010
Source: (Own elaboration)

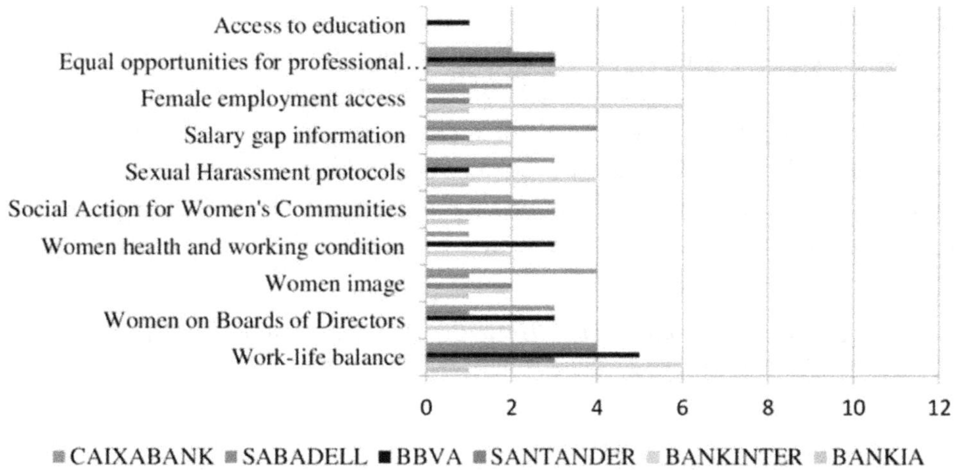

A decade later (see Figure 3), all entities increased their attention to gender equality with different interests. Bankinter focused its information on "female employment access" and "salary gap information," while Bankia maintained a focus on "equal opportunities for professional development." BBVA focused on "female employment access," while Sabadell continued to focus on "salary gap information" and also gave more mentions to "work-life balance." Santander concentrated on "women on boards of directors" and "social action for women's communities," and finally, Caixabank continued to focus on "women image" and "social action for women's communities."

Figure 3. Code frequency results 2019
Source: (Own elaboration)

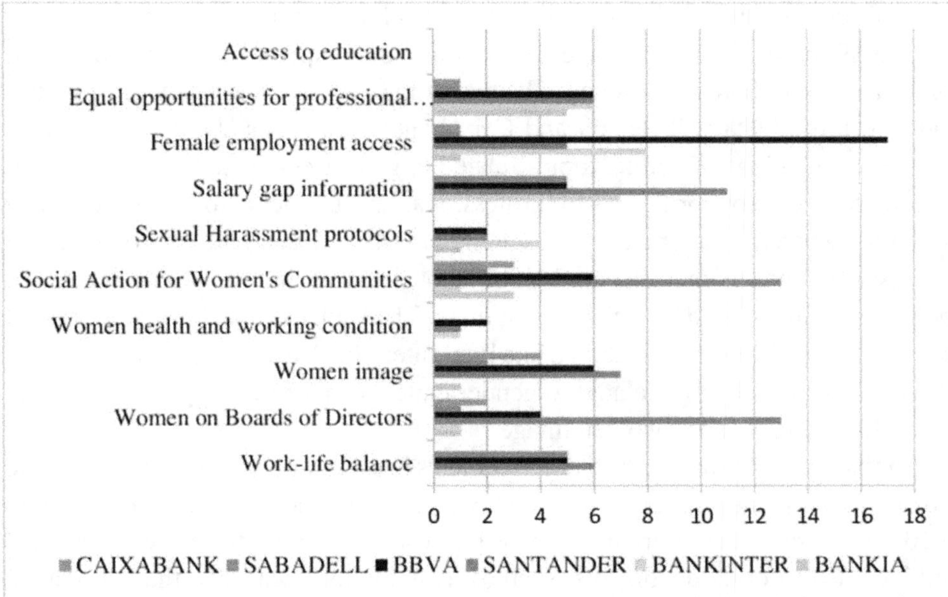

The information by banks shows how each of them treats gender equality in their sustainability reports. Starting with Santander, during the ten years analyzed, it is the only bank that presented an increase in all indicators except "access to education," which was maintained at 0. Also, it is the bank with the highest number of gender equality mentions in its 2019 report (64 of 190). The highest level of attention for this entity went to the terms "women on boards of directors" and "social action for women's communities," followed by "salary gap information." The rest of the codes registered increases but with fewer mentions. BBVA was the second bank with the highest number of gender equality mentions in 2019 (53 of 190). The evolution of its focus went from "work-life balance" (maintaining the number of mentions of this topic in the 2019 report) to "female employment access" in the last decade. Mentions of "access to education and women's health" and "working condition" decreased by 1.

The third entity in giving relevance to gender equality in 2019 was Bankinter (33 of 190), which experienced a decrease in the number of mentions of topics related to gender equality in general with 5 indicators that showed negative values. The highest differences were found with "equal opportunities for professional development" followed by "women image," "women health and working condition," "women on boards of directors" and finally "work-life balance." The main increase in the numbers of times that an indicator was mentioned was 5, in this case "salary gap information," followed by "female employment access" and "social action for women's communities." Sabadell, the fourth bank that mentioned gender equality in its 2019 report, showed a tendency toward a more equalized distribution of the importance of each topic in general. Its main topics were "salary gap information" and "work-life balance." Bankia and Caixabank were the banks with the lowest number of mentions of coding topics related to gender equality. The first one was focused on "equal opportunities for professional development" followed by "social action for women's communities," each increasing by 2 absolute numbers. It also increased by 1 on "women on boards of directors." "Work-life balance" was the only indicator that decreased by 1 absolute number. The bank did not show variations on the rest of the indicators. Caixabank, like Bankinter, showed a decrease in the number of mentions of indicators related to gender equality in 7 of the topics, principally "work-life balance" and "women image."

Another aspect to highlight is that "women's health and working conditions" and "sexual harassment protocols" obtained two fewer mentions in 2019 compared to 2010. This decline in importance may be because these topics have been developed and included in other documents, such as: conciliation measures, the harassment protocol, the gender equality plan, or the occupational risk prevention plan. These specific regulations stimulate the internalization of such topics in the very structure of the organizations, indicating normalization since they are not expressly addressed in sustainability reports.

Regarding "Women Image" authors found a gain in relevance after a decade to the same extent as the topic of "women in management boards." Mainly it is in relation to women in leadership positions in the reports. Authors interpretation is that banks are considering women for leadership positions. Although they know that it will be a slow change process. The priority is to achieve an equality percentage (40%) in the management board, as requested by the European Commission. "Access to education" was mentioned only once in the 2010 reports and not at all in 2019. It is possible that this topic is not contemplated because Spain is a developed country where the entire population has access to education.

Table 3 displays our results concerning the composition of the boards of directors. The evolution shows that in all the six banks. the number of women increased during the last decade. In 2019. Santander stood out with women representing 40% of the board members. followed by Caixabank with 37.50%. Bankinter with 33.30%. BBVA with 26.67%. and Sabadell with 20%. Bankia is the bank with the lowest representation of the feminine gender on its board of directors, with 16.66%. Santander recorded the highest increase in the number of women with 30% followed by Bankinter with 24.30%. BBVA with 17.01%. Bankia and Caixabank with 15.66% and 15.28% respectively and Sabadell with the lowest increase of 6.67%.

Table 3. Percentage of women on boards of directors

	2010	2019	Evolution
BANKIA	1%	16.66%	15.66%
BANKINTER	9%	33.30%	24.30%
SANTANDER	10%	40%	30.00%
BBVA	9.66%	26.67%	17.01%
CAIXABANK	22.22%	37.50%	15.28%
SABADELL	13.33%	20%	6.67%

Source: (Own elaboration)

The presence of women on the board of directors was another priority issue in the reports of the entities. According to recent research, less than half of the Spanish banks (of a sample of 63% of the Spanish Banking System) have a woman on the board. Only 15% have three or more women, so, it is important to consider the masculine characteristics of the Spanish management culture. which make female representation on boards very low (Delgado-Piña et al., 2020). Similarly. in the six entities analyzed, the concept of women on the board of directors gained relevance in their 2019 reports (going from 9 to 22 times mentioned). The European Commission issued a directive on November 11, 2012. which established the objective of achieving 40% participation of the least represented gender in the non-executive positions on the boards of companies listed in the stock market. All entities analyzed have implemented changes in their strategies according to this objective. Despite the challenges, the evolution in this aspect has been quick. However, most corporate directors are open and would accept reasonable proposals to advance gender diversity on their boards (Cunningham, 2020).

Among the entities, Santander demonstrated the greatest attention to this matter in recent years because this indicator is most often mentioned in their official sustainability document. Santander has shown a practical increase in women on its board, going from the 10% to 40% of female representation in 2019. Sabadell did not present variations in mentions over the last decade but increased its female representation by 15.28% to 37.50% of women on its board. On the other hand, Bankinter and Caixabank reported a decrease in mentions of the theme of "Women on Boards of Directors." This reduction may mean that these institutions have been consolidating their organizations because paradoxically. They showed an increase in the number of women in their boards of directors from 9% to 33.3% and from 13.33% to 20% respectively in the last decade. Similarly, for BBVA, the indicator does not reflect the practical manner in which the bank is working on the issue. One explanation could be that the number of women on its board of directors has increased by more than 17% from 2010, achieving almost 27% of the female representation in 2019. Finally, Bankia is the bank that worked the slowest to achieve "gender equality" on its board of directors. The bank increased female representation to 16.7% of board members. Likewise, Bankia showed a slight increase in the number of times this indicator is mentioned in its official documents.

Finally, the analysis of the relationship between gender equality and CM is included in Table 4.

Table 4. Interaction frequency between CM - gender equality

Indicator related	Absolute 2010	Absolute 2019
Salary gap information	1	2
Empowerment of women	0	1
Work-life balance	2	2
Female employment access	0	2
Equal opportunities for professional development	0	1

Source: (Own elaboration)

There are 44 interactions between CM and sustainability. But only 11 are explicit about gender equality. In 2010 CM was related to "salary gap information" and "work-life balance"; and in 2019, the links increased to more topics such as "empowerment of women," "female employment access," and "equal opportunities for professional development." Examining the results, the authors found that gender equality and CM are present in the analyzed reports. However, it has a different definition depending on the weight of the indicators and the years studied.

The authors highlight CM's role as the lever for achieving the SDGs. During the content analysis, the authors detected that CM appears in the text as an approach to strategy, challenge, or initiatives that organizations establish to achieve said objectives in their reports. But CM only appears 11 times among the 44 mentions concerning gender equality. Likewise, according to Research **objective 2** (to assess the relationship between CM and gender equality programs), in this study, a tenuous relationship between both elements was found. This relationship appears in 2010 reports with less frequency and almost no link between Organizational CM and gender equality measures. The Sabadell and Caixabank reports are the only ones to include CM as it relates to "salary gap information" and "work-life balance." Nevertheless. CM is present in the reports of all entities in 2019. The aspects in which the organizational change is being implemented to improve gender equality are "incorporation of women into employment," "work-life balance," "empower women," "reduce the salary gap," and "equal professional development." Still resistance to change

The analysis **of Research objective 3** evaluates the relationship in time between CM and the implementation of gender diversity programs. There is an increase in the number of times that both elements are linked in the documents. In 2010, only two gender equality indicators in two banks were linked. Whereas in 2019, five indicators were present in all entities.

CONCLUSION

Summarizing, this study shows that there has been a significant increase in the interest in gender equality during the last ten years in the Spanish banking sector. The most relevant topics in 2010 are: "equal opportunities for the professional development of women" and "work-life balance." While in 2019, the most frequently mentioned topics are: "access to female employment," "salary gap information," and "social actions for women's communities." The decrease in mentions of "women's health and working condition" and "sexual harassment protocols" in the last decade is something to analyze further in future empirical research. This trend could be a sign of the internalization of those topics in the company structure as they are addressed in different policies or official documents such as conciliation measures. the harassment protocol itself, the gender equality plan, or the occupational risk prevention plan. In some cases, it may even show that the structure of some banks might have assimilated and consolidated their policies of gender equality as something normalized. "Access to education" is another indicator that did not prove to be relevant. The authors hypothesize that this may be because the entire population has access to education in Spain.

Finally, in general, all entities analyzed are increasing the female representation on their boards of directors. In line with the goal to achieve the 40% established by the European Commission. Still, this new scenario will probably stimulate a drag effect on the rest of the organization. One of the reasons why CM in implementing gender equality is not included more often in the 2010 reports is because the SDGs were not set until 2015. This highlights the need to do something to effectively drive change in organizations to meet this goal, CM can be that tool. As the shift towards a more sustainable company is already underway. Likewise, sharing best practices is essential because entities do not specify how changes were developed. Examples can include: if they define an action plan to reduce the salary gap between males and females within their staff or implement a procedure to achieve the increased presence of women on the boards of directors, or develop a policy to guarantee non-discrimination about professional development.

Limitations and Future Propositions

One of the limitations of this study is the sample size for the content analysis was limited to six of the most important banks included in the Spanish stock exchange. Despite this limitation, a smaller data set allowed for fewer choices and enabled the analysis of exactly the same documents (Friese, 2011). Authors future research agenda includes increasing the number of banks examined with consideration given to including the smallest ones. It would be interesting to obtain information regarding the way the firms are managing the change of implementing gender equality into their structures. It could be through interviews of CSR directors, focus groups of professionals within the sector or, even, analysing other official documents such as equality plans and harassment protocol procedures in which companies include information related to gender equality.

Likewise, after the COVID-19 situation, it would be interesting to analyze how companies manage the change to the new situation and how it affects their gender equality strategies. There is still a lack of empirical research to analyze different sectors, their evolution, and the impact that good CM brings to the development and implementation of gender equality policies.

Conflict of Interest

The authors of this publication declare there is no conflict of interest.

Funding Agency

This research received no specific grant from any funding agency in the public commercial, or not-for-profit sectors.

REFERENCES

Al-Haddad, S., & Kotnour, T. (2015). Integrating the organizational change literature: A model for successful change. *Journal of Organizational Change Management, 28*(2), 234–262. doi:10.1108/JOCM-11-2013-0215

Arnold, M. G. (2018). Sustainability value creation in frugal contexts to foster Sustainable Development Goals. *Business Strategy & Development, 1*(4), 265–275. doi:10.1002/bsd2.36

Baumann-Pauly, D., Scherer, A. G., & Palazzo, G. (2016). Managing institutional complexity: A longitudinal study of legitimacy strategies at a sportswear brand company. *Journal of Business Ethics, 137*(1), 31–51. doi:10.100710551-014-2532-x

Birindelli, G., Dell'Atti, S., Iannuzzi, A. P., & Savioli, M. (2018). Composition and activity of the board of directors: Impact on ESG performance in the banking system. *Sustainability, 10*(12), 4699. doi:10.3390u10124699

Bonilla-Priego, M. J., Font, X., & Pacheco-Olivares, M. R. (2014). Corporate sustainability reporting index and baseline data for the cruise industry. *Tourism Management, 44*, 149–160. doi:10.1016/j.tourman.2014.03.004

Bono, R., Arnau, J., & Vallejo, G. (2008). Analysis techniques applied to longitudinal data in psychology and health sciences in the period 1985-2005. *Papeles del Psicólogo, 29*, 136–146.

Brown, L. R. (1981). Building a sustainable society. WW Norton & Company.

Burnes, B., & Jackson, P. (2011). Success and failure in organizational change: An exploration of the role of values. *Journal of Change Management, 11*(2), 133–162. doi:10.1080/14697017.2010.524655

By, R. T. (2005). Organisational change management: A critical review. *Journal of Change Management, 5*(4), 369–380. doi:10.1080/14697010500359250

Chang, R. D., Zuo, J., Zhao, Z. Y., Zillante, G., Gan, X. L., & Soebarto, V. (2017). Evolving theories of sustainability and firms: History, future directions, and implications for renewable energy research. *Renewable & Sustainable Energy Reviews, 72*, 48–56. doi:10.1016/j.rser.2017.01.029

Coe, I. R., Wiley, R., & Bekker, L. G. (2019). Organisational best practices towards gender equality in science and medicine. *Lancet, 393*(10171), 587–593. doi:10.1016/S0140-6736(18)33188-X PMID:30739694

Corbin, J., & Strauss, A. (1990). Grounded theory research: Procedures, canons and evaluative criteria. *Qualitative Sociology, 13*(1), 3–21. doi:10.1007/BF00988593

Cunningham, L. A. (2020). Board gender diversity: debate and practice. *Legal Studies Research Paper Series.* George Washington University Law School.

De Cabo, R. M., Gimeno, R., & Nieto, M. J. (2012). Gender diversity on European bank's board of directors. *Journal of Business Ethics, 109*(2), 145–162. doi:10.100710551-011-1112-6

Delgado-Piña. M. I., Rodríguez-Ruiz. Ó., Rodríguez-Duarte. A., & Sastre-Castillo. M. Á. (2020). Gender Diversity in Spanish Banks: Trickle-Down and Productivity Effects. *Sustainability. 12*(5). 2113.

Demetriades, J. (2007). Gender Indicators: What. Why and How? OECD. https://www.oecd.org/dac/gender-development/43041409.pdf

Dezsö, C. L., & Ross, D. G. (2012). Does female representation in top management improve firm performance? A panel data investigation. *Strategic Management Journal, 33*(9), 1072–1089. doi:10.1002mj.1955

Diaz-Iglesias. S.. Blanco-Gonzalez. A.. & Orden-Cruz. C. (2019). Science mapping analysis of change management. *Revista ESPACIOS. 40*(32).

Dijkstra, A. G., & Hanmer, L. C. (2000). Measuring socio-economic gender inequality: Toward an alternative to the UNDP gender-related development index. *Feminist Economics, 6*(2), 41–75. doi:10.1080/13545700050076106

Dyllick, T., & Hockerts, K. (2002). Beyond the business case for corporate sustainability. *Business Strategy and the Environment, 11*(2), 130–141. doi:10.1002/bse.323

Eagly, A. H., Karau, S. J., & Makhijani, M. G. (1995). Gender and the effectiveness of leaders: A meta-analysis. *Psychological Bulletin, 117*(1), 125–145. doi:10.1037/0033-2909.117.1.125 PMID:7870858

Ferreira, D. (2015). Board diversity: Should we trust research to inform policy? *Corporate Governance, 23*(2), 108–111. doi:10.1111/corg.12092

Figueroa-Domecq, C., Palomo, J., Flecha-Barrio, M. D., & Segovia-Pérez, M. (2020). Technology double gender gap in tourism business leadership. *Information Technology & Tourism, 22*(1), 1–32. doi:10.100740558-020-00168-0

Friese, S. (2011). Using ATLAS. ti for analyzing the financial crisis data. *In Forum Qualitative Sozialforschung/Forum: Qualitative. Social Research, 12*(1), 1–24.

Furlotti, K., Mazza, T., Tibiletti, V., & Triani, S. (2019). Women in top positions on boards of directors: Gender policies disclosed in Italian sustainability reporting. *Corporate Social Responsibility and Environmental Management, 26*(1), 57–70. doi:10.1002/csr.1657

Galbreath, J. (2018). Is Board Gender Diversity Linked to Financial Performance? The Mediating Mechanism of CSR. *Business & Society, 57*(5), 863–889. doi:10.1177/0007650316647967

Gallego-Álvarez, I., & Pucheta-Martínez, M. C. (2020). Environmental strategy in the global banking industry within the varieties of capitalism approach: The moderating role of gender diversity and board members with specific skills. *Business Strategy and the Environment*, *29*(2), 347–360. doi:10.1002/bse.2368

Gartzia, L. (2021). Gender Equality in Business Action: A Multi-Agent Change Management Approach. *Sustainability*, *13*(11), 6209. doi:10.3390u13116209

GRI. (2023). *Home*. Global Reporting Initiative. https://www.globalreporting.org/information/sustainability-reporting/Pages/default.aspx

Grosser, K., & Moon, J. (2008). Developments in company reporting on workplace gender equality?: A corporate social responsibility perspective. *Accounting Forum*, *32*(3), 179–198. doi:10.1016/j.accfor.2008.01.004

Guimaraes, T., & Armstrong, C. (1998). Empirically testing the impact of change management effectiveness on company performance. *European Journal of Innovation Management*, *1*(2), 74–84. doi:10.1108/14601069810217257

Harjoto, M. A., Laksmana, I., & Yang, Y. W. (2018). Board diversity and corporate risk taking.

Hillman, A. J. (2015). Board diversity: Beginning to unpeel the onion. *Corporate Governance*, *23*(2), 104–107. doi:10.1111/corg.12090

Hussain, N., Rigoni, U., & Orij, R. P. (2018). Corporate governance and sustainability performance: Analysis of triple bottom line performance. *Journal of Business Ethics*, *149*(2), 411–432. doi:10.100710551-016-3099-5

Ilinitch, A. Y., Soderstrom, N. S., & Thomas, T. E. (1998). Measuring corporate environmental performance. *Journal of Accounting and Public Policy*, *17*(4–5), 383–408. doi:10.1016/S0278-4254(98)10012-1

Kassinis, G., Panayiotou, A., Dimou, A., & Katsifaraki, G. (2016). Gender and Environmental Sustainability: A Longitudinal Analysis. *Corporate Social Responsibility and Environmental Management*, *23*(6), 399–412. doi:10.1002/csr.1386

Lewin, K. (1947). Frontiers in group dynamics: II. Channels of group life; social planning and action research. *Human Relations*, *1*(2), 143–153. doi:10.1177/001872674700100201

Lewin, K. (1951). *Field theory in social science: selected theoretical papers* (D. Cartwright, Ed.).

Liao, L., Luo, L., & Tang, Q. (2015). Gender diversity. board independence. environmental committee and greenhouse gas disclosure. *The British Accounting Review*, *47*(4), 409–424. doi:10.1016/j.bar.2014.01.002

Linstead, S., Brewis, J., & Linstead, A. (2005). Gender in change: Gendering change. *Journal of Organizational Change Management*, *18*(6), 542–560. doi:10.1108/09534810510628495

Lozano, R. (2012). Towards better embedding sustainability into companies' systems: An analysis of voluntary corporate initiatives. *Journal of Cleaner Production*, *25*, 14–26. doi:10.1016/j.jclepro.2011.11.060

Lozano, R., Nummert, B., & Ceulemans, K. (2016). Elucidating the relationship between sustainability reporting and organisational change management for sustainability. *Journal of Cleaner Production*, *125*, 168–188. doi:10.1016/j.jclepro.2016.03.021

Miotto, G., & Vilajoana-Alejandre, S. (2019). Gender equality: a tool for legitimacy in the fast fashion industry. *Harvard Deusto Business Research*. *8*(2), 134–147.

Morley, L., & Crossouard, B. (2016). Women's Leadership in the Asian Century: Does Expansion Mean Inclusion? *Studies in Higher Education*, *41*(5), 801–814. doi:10.1080/03075079.2016.1147749

Nadeem, M., Zaman, R., & Saleem, I. (2017). Boardroom gender diversity and corporate sustainability practices: Evidence from Australian Securities Exchange listed firms. *Journal of Cleaner Production*, *149*, 874–885. doi:10.1016/j.jclepro.2017.02.141

Nyström, M., Höög, E., Garvare, R., Weinehall, L., & Ivarsson, A. (2013). Change and learning strategies in large scale change programs: Describing the variation of strategies used in a health promotion program. *Journal of Organizational Change Management*, *26*(6), 1020–1044. doi:10.1108/JOCM-08-2012-0132

Olabuénaga. J. I. R. (2012). Metodología de la investigación cualitativa. *Universidad de Deusto. 15*.

Queisser, M. (2016). Gender equality and the Sustainable Development Goals. In Love. P. (Ed.). *Debate the Issues: New Approaches to Economic Challenges*. OECD Publishing. Paris.

Rafferty, A. E., Jimmieson, N. L., & Armenakis, A. A. (2013). Change readiness: A multilevel review. *Journal of Management*, *39*(1), 110–135. doi:10.1177/0149206312457417

Raigada, J. L. P. (2002). Epistemología. metodología y técnicas del análisis de contenido. *Sociolinguistic Studies*, *3*(1), 1–42. doi:10.1558ols.v3i1.1

Rao, K., & Tilt, C. (2016). Board composition and corporate social responsibility: The role of diversity, gender, strategy and decision making. *Journal of Business Ethics*, *138*(2), 327–347. doi:10.100710551-015-2613-5

Redman, A. (2018). Harnessing the Sustainable Development Goals for businesses: A progressive framework for action. *Business Strategy & Development, 1*(4), 230–243.

Rosener, J. B. (1990). Way females lead. *Harvard Business Review*, *68*, 119–125. PMID:10107957

Rosener, J. B. (1997). *America's competitive secret: Women managers*. Oxford University Press on Demand.

Setó-Pamies, D. (2015). The Relationship between Women Directors and Corporate Social Responsibility. *Corporate Social Responsibility and Environmental Management*, *22*(6), 334–345. doi:10.1002/csr.1349

Todnem, By. R. (2008). Organisational change management: A critical review. *Journal of Change Management, 5*(4), 369–380.

Torres. M. J. M. Izquierdo. M. Á. F. & Olmedo. E. E. (2013). Responsabilidad social corporativa e internacionalización bancaria: el caso de la banca española en Argentina. Brasil y Chile. *Harvard Deusto Business Research, II*(2), 143–164.

Tsalis, T. A., Malamateniou, K. E., Koulouriotis, D., & Nikolaou, I. E. (2020). New challenges for corporate sustainability reporting: United Nations' 2030 Agenda for sustainable development and the sustainable development goals. *Corporate Social Responsibility and Environmental Management*, *27*(4), 1617–1629. doi:10.1002/csr.1910

Tyler, M. (2005). Women in change management: Simone De Beauvoir and the co-optation of women's Otherness. *Journal of Organizational Change Management*, *18*(6), 561–577. doi:10.1108/09534810510628503

United Nations. (2015). *World Summit on Sustainable Development "Transforming our World: The 2030 Agenda for Sustainable Development."* UN. https://www.un.org/sustainabledevelopment/summit/

United Nations. (2019a). *Report of the Secretary-General on SDG Progress.* UN. https://sustainabledevelopment.un.org/content/documents/24978Report_of_the_SG_on_SDG_Progress_2019.pdf

United Nations. (2019b). *Sustainable Development Goal 5: Achieve gender equality and empower all women and girls.* UN. https://sustainabledevelopment.un.org/sdg5

United Nations Global Compact. (2022). *UN Sustainable Development Goals.* UN. https://www.unglobalcompact.org/sdgs/17-global-goals

Valles. M. S. (2002). Ventajas y desafíos del uso de programas informáticos (eg ATLAS. Ti y MAXqda) en el análisis cuantitativo: una reflexión metodológica desde la grounded theory y el contexto de la investigación social española. *Fundación Centro de Estudios Andaluces.* 1–26.

Van den Brink, M., & Benschop, Y. (2018). Gender interventions in the Dutch police force: Resistance as a tool for change? *Journal of Change Management, 18*(3), 181–197. doi:10.1080/14697017.2017.1378695

Van der Voet, J., Kuipers, B., & Groeneveld, S. (2015). Held back and pushed forward: Leading change in a complex public sector environment. *Journal of Organizational Change Management, 28*(2), 290–300. doi:10.1108/JOCM-09-2013-0182

Van der Walt, N., & Ingley, C. (2003). Board dynamics and the influence of professional background. gender and ethnic diversity of directors. *Corporate Governance, 11*(3), 218–234. doi:10.1111/1467-8683.00320

Whelan-Berry, K. S., & Somerville, K. A. (2010). Linking change drivers and the organizational change process: A review and synthesis. *Journal of Change Management, 10*(2), 175–193. doi:10.1080/14697011003795651

World Economic Forum. (2020). *Insight Report: The Global Gender Gap Report 2020.* World Economic Forum: Cologny/Geneva. Switzerland. https://www.weforum.org/reports/gender-gap-2020-report-100-years-pay-equality

Zurdo, R. J. P., Centeno, M. C. G., Fernández, M. G., & Barberis, G. M. F. (2013). Responsabilidad social corporativa y género en los consejos de administración de las cooperativas de crédito españolas. *Prisma Social: Revista de Investigación Social, 10*, 332–360.

APPENDIX 1

The results are compiled in a code frequency report, shown in Tables 5 and 6 for 2010 and 2019, respectively.

Table 5(a). Data collection: codes frequency report 2010

	BANKIA 2012			BANKINTER			SANTANDER		
	Absolute	**Comparison with the other brands**	**Comparison with the others Gender Equality Codes**	**Absolute**	**Comparison with the other brands**	**Comparison with the others Gender Equality Codes**	**Absolute**	**Comparison with the other brands**	**Comparison with the others Gender Equality Codes**
Access to education	0	0.00%	0.00%	0	0.00%	0.00%	0	0.00%	0.00%
Equal opportunities for professional development	3	12.00%	37.50%	11	44.00%	31.43%	3	12.00%	23.08%
Female employment access	1	9.09%	12.50%	6	54.55%	17.14%	1	9.09%	7.69%
Salary gap information	0	0.00%	0.00%	2	22.22%	5.71%	1	11.11%	7.69%
Sexual Harassment protocols	1	9.09%	12.50%	4	36.36%	11.43%	0	0.00%	0.00%
Social Action for Women's Communities	1	11.11%	12.50%	0	0.00%	0.00%	3	33.33%	23.08%
Women's health and working condition	0	0.00%	0.00%	2	33.33%	5.71%	0	0.00%	0.00%
Women image	1	10.00%	12.50%	2	20.00%	5.71%	2	20.00%	15.38%
Women on Boards of Directors	0	0.00%	0.00%	2	22.22%	5.71%	0	0.00%	0.00%
Work-life balance	1	4.35%	12.50%	6	26.09%	17.14%	3	13.04%	23.08%
Totals	8		100.00%	35		100.00%	13		100.00%

(Source: Own elaboration)

Table 5(b). Data collection: codes frequency report 2010

BBVA			SABADELL			CAIXABANK 2013			Totals
Absolute	Comparison with the other brands	Comparison with the others Gender Equality Codes	Absolute	Comparison with the other brands	Comparison with the others Gender Equality Codes	Absolute	Comparison with the other brands	Comparison with the others Gender Equality Codes	Absolute 2010
1	100.00%	6.25%	0	0.00%	0.00%	0	0.00%	0.00%	1
3	12.00%	18.75%	3	12.00%	15.79%	2	8.00%	8.70%	25
0	0.00%	0.00%	1	9.09%	5.26%	2	18.18%	8.70%	11
0	0.00%	0.00%	4	44.44%	21.05%	2	22.22%	8.70%	9
1	9.09%	6.25%	2	18.18%	10.53%	3	27.27%	13.04%	11
0	0.00%	0.00%	3	33.33%	15.79%	2	22.22%	8.70%	9
3	50.00%	18.75%	0	0.00%	0.00%	1	16.67%	4.35%	6
0	0.00%	0.00%	1	10.00%	5.26%	4	40.00%	17.39%	10
3	33.33%	18.75%	1	11.11%	5.26%	3	33.33%	13.04%	9
5	21.74%	31.25%	4	17.39%	21.05%	4	17.39%	17.39%	23
16		100.00%	19		100.00%	23			114

(Source: Own elaboration)

Table 6(a). Data collection: codes frequency report 2019

	BANKIA			BANKINTER			SANTANDER		
	Absolute	**Comparison with the other brands**	**Comparison with the others Gender Equality Codes**	**Absolute**	**Comparison with the other brands**	**Comparison with the others Gender Equality Codes**	**Absolute**	**Comparison with the other brands**	**Comparison with the others Gender Equality Codes**
Access to education	0	0.00%	0.00%	0	0.00%	0.00%	0	0.00%	0.00%
Equal opportunities for professional development	5	20.00%	41.67%	6	24.00%	18.18%	6	24.00%	9.38%
Female employment access	1	3.03%	8.33%	8	24.24%	24.24%	5	15.15%	7.81%
Salary gap information	0	0.00%	0.00%	7	25.00%	21.21%	11	39.29%	17.19%
Sexual Harassment protocols	1	11.11%	8.33%	4	44.44%	12.12%	2	22.22%	3.13%
Social Action for Women's Communities	3	10.71%	25.00%	1	3.57%	3.03%	13	46.43%	20.31%
Women's health and working condition	0	0.00%	0.00%	1	25.00%	3.03%	1	25.00%	1.56%
Women image	1	5.00%	8.33%	0	0.00%	0.00%	7	35.00%	10.94%
Women on Boards of Directors	1	4.55%	8.33%	1	4.55%	3.03%	13	59.09%	20.31%
Work-life balance	0	0.00%	0.00%	5	23.81%	15.15%	6	28.57%	9.38%
Totals	12		100%	33		100%	64		100%

(Source: Own elaboration)

Table 6(b). Data collection: codes frequency report 2019

BBVA			SABADELL			CAIXABANK			Totals
Absolute	Comparison with the other brands	Comparison with the others Gender Equality Codes	Absolute	Comparison with the other brands	Comparison with the others Gender Equality Codes	Absolute	Comparison with the other brands	Comparison with the others Gender Equality Codes	Absolute 2010
0	0.00%	0.00%	0	0.00%	0.00%	0	0.00%	0.00%	0
6	24.00%	11.32%	1	4.00%	5.88%	1	4.00%	9.09%	25
17	51.52%	32.08%	1	3.03%	5.88%	1	3.03%	9.09%	33
5	17.86%	9.43%	5	17.86%	29.41%	0	0.00%	0.00%	28
2	22.22%	3.77%	0	0.00%	0.00%	0	0.00%	0.00%	9
6	21.43%	11.32%	2	7.14%	11.76%	3	10.71%	27.27%	28
2	50.00%	3.77%	0	0.00%	0.00%	0	0.00%	0.00%	4
6	30.00%	11.32%	2	10.00%	11.76%	4	20.00%	36.36%	20
4	18.18%	7.55%	1	4.55%	5.88%	2	9.09%	18.18%	22
5	23.81%	9.43%	5	23.81%	29.41%	0	0.00%	0.00%	21
53		100%	17		100%	11		100%	190

(Source: Own elaboration)

APPENDIX 2

The authors included in Table 7 a sample of different texts that were codified in the software during the analysis. In some cases. the phrases were included in more than one Code. The first column includes the Bank and document where the information is located. In the second column contains the text. and in the Third column the Code or Codes that apply for the sentences are categorizes.

Table 7. Sample of the texts included into the codes

Documents	Content of the cite (original text in Spanish)	Codes
BBVA A 2010 Informacion-de-responsabilidad-corporativa_2010	"60.099 niños y niñas de familias desfavorecidas a través del apoyo a la educación primaria y secundaria. por medio de estas becas educativas".	Access to education
CAIXABANK A 2013 CaixaBank_Memoria13_es	"Política de igualdad y conciliación. El compromiso de CaixaBank con la igualdad y la conciliación se refleja en su adhesión a distintas iniciativas y certificaciones. y en el progresivo aumento de las mujeres en el equipo directivo".	Equal opportunities for professional development Women image Work-life balance
BANKINTER A 2010 informesostenibilidadbk2010	"El esfuerzo constante por tener una plantilla diversa y equilibrada se refleja en los porcentajes del desglose por sexo: un 49.5% de hombres y un 50.5% de mujeres".	Female employment access
SANTANDER C 2019 Informe anual-20-es	"Santander lidera el índice de Igualdad de Género de Bloomberg 2020 formado por 325 compañías de todo el mundo. Este índice incluye parámetros de igualdad salarial y paridad de género. integración y talento y liderazgo femeninos".	Salary gap information Women image
BANKIA C 2019 informe-anual-bankia-2019	"Programa con Fundación Integra para la integración laboral de exreclusos. víctimas de violencia de género y personas con discapacidad (90 beneficiarios)".	Social Action for Women's Communities
BBVA A 2010 Informacion-de-responsabilidad-corporativa_2010	"La tramitación de la evaluación de empleo a trabajadores. en general y mujeres embarazadas. en particular".	Women health and working condition
CAIXABANK A 2013 CaixaBank_Memoria13_es	"CaixaBank cuenta con un Protocolo para la Prevención. Tratamiento y Eliminación del Acoso Sexual y Laboral. Durante el año 2013. y a través de gestoras externas. se han realizado un total de dos intervenciones. las dos motivadas por acoso laboral. Tal y como establece el Protocolo. las gestoras han realizado informes de las denuncias formales…"	Sexual arrassment protocols
SABADELL 2010 MEMORIA RSC	"Prevenir y penalizar el acoso sexual y acoso por razón de sexo".	Sexual harrassment protocols
BANKINTER C 2019 estado_de_informacion_no_financiera_consolidada2019	"Prevención de riesgos laborales con perspectiva de género. específicamente en relación con aquellos riesgos psicosociales entre los que destacaría el acoso".	Sexual harassment protocols Women health and working condition
SABADELL 2019 Non-Financial Information Report	"Se ha consolidado la red de mujeres directivas SWING (Sabadell Women Inspiration Group). cuyo objetivo es el empoderamiento y la aportación del valor y los beneficios de la diversidad".	Women image

(Source: Own elaboration)

Chapter 5
Board Diversity Evolution in the Iberian Stock Markets:
Is Evidence Favoring Gender Quotas Defenders?

João Teodósio
Polytechnic Institute of Santarém, Portugal

Elisabete S. Vieira
University of Aveiro, Portugal

Mara Madaleno
University of Aveiro, Portugal

ABSTRACT

This study aims to analyze the impact of women's presence on the board of directors on the outcomes of Spanish and Portuguese-listed firms over the third millennium. Based on a documental analysis of 44 publications, it is concluded that female directors positively affect the quality and transparency of the firm's reporting and compliance with the corporate governance codes. However, concerning financial outcomes, the literature does not robustly document the positive effects of such directors' characteristics on firm performance. Similar conclusions may be drawn for dividend and tax policies. These findings are consistent across different time frames of this millennium, indicating that they are not directly driven by gender quotas implementation. These results should interest Iberian governments, regulators, shareholders, investors, and financial markets.

DOI: 10.4018/978-1-6684-5981-2.ch005

INTRODUCTION

Are scientific results of research based on gender diversity effects on Iberian-listed firms' outcomes over this millennium supporting the gender quotas defenders? This investigation aims to find a compelling answer to this research question by conducting a systematic literature review related to this regional context published in recognized journals.

Historically, the research interest in this subject devoured from the social pressure of the most developed western societies related to promoting women's equality rights in work-related issues. In the European context, some national governments have been answering to this social pressure by introducing hard (with penalties for those who do not comply with the law) or soft (long-term orientation goals without penalties) gender quota legislation, mainly for governmental and parliamentary structures, state-owned companies, and listed firms. According to European Union (2022), "hard" gender quotas applied to listed companies in Austria, Belgium, France, Germany, Greece, Italy, Portugal, and the Netherlands. Additionally, ten states have softer gender quota legislation that, in some cases, applies to listed companies (e.g., Spain) and in others not (e.g., Slovenia). A considerable number of countries still didn't make important decisions on the subject (e.g., Bulgaria and Croatia).

Concerning the Iberian context, Spain was the first country to introduce gender quota legislation in the region. In 2007, the Spanish parliament approved the establishment of gender quotas by the Constitutional Act 3/2007. This law defined a long-term goal of 40% of women's representation on the boards of public and private organizations. Despite the efforts made by governmental and regulatory authorities, this goal remains to be achieved 15 years later. Portugal only approved its gender equality law in 2017. With law 62/2017, the Portuguese parliament imposed a gender quota of 33% on the administration and supervisory boards of public companies and listed firms. Despite the law delay of around a decade compared to Spain, the target ratio in 2022 is almost achieved.[1]

Literature devoted to analyzing the long-term effects of gender quotas established by national authorities on listed companies is very scarce. In a recent systematic review, Yu and Madison (2021) identified only nine studies on this subject. Of those, eight were related to European companies (Nordic countries, France, Italy, and Spain), and only one to U.S. companies. Results demonstrate that the long-term effect of gender quota implementation in those countries was detrimental to firms' accounting and market performance in 7 of the 9 studies. Soare et al. (2022) analyzed the effects of gender quota legislation in the Belgium context based on 23 performance indicators. The authors concluded that firms performed worse after this political event on 10 of the 23 indicators and found no significant change in the remaining 13. As such, this study found no significant positive effects of this event on companies' performance.

Lastly, Tapver et al. (2020) analyzed the female directors' impact on commercial banks' CSR disclosure. Using a sample of 285 commercial banks from 35 countries belonging to different word geographies, the authors concluded that those directors significantly contribute to banks' CSR disclosure. Interestingly, results remain consistent for banks whose gender representation is under or above gender quotas, meaning that this effect is not gender quota contingent.

This chapter presents some interesting findings based on a sample of 44 publications related to Iberian stock markets. First, it becomes clear that research focuses mainly on the Spanish context and neglects the Portuguese context. This fact may be explained by Spain's considerably larger stock market and international economic influence. Second, the sample shows that the hot topic of gender diversity in this context is related to firms' financial outcomes, followed by disclosure issues. This conclusion may be helpful for future research to diversify the research topics. Third, the documental analysis demonstrates that female directors increase the quality and transparency of firms' reporting and compliance with corporate governance codes but do not robustly contribute to the increase of firms' financial performance. Fourth, and more importantly, results are relatively stable across the millennium, meaning that the long-term effects of gender quotas implementation show no significant changes in female directors' impact on firms' outcomes. Consequently, female directors' effects on listed firms are not contingent on gender quota implementation.

This investigation presents two main contributions: Firstly, this study covers a research gap related to a systematic analysis of the evolution of board gender diversity and its effects on Iberian-listed firms' outcomes considering gender quota implementation. Secondly, several research gaps in the Spanish and Portuguese contexts are provided to improve knowledge of corporate governance from this regional setting.

This chapter is organized in the following way: The first section provides background on Iberian legislation on gender quotas. The second section describes the methodological procedures. The results are presented and discussed in the next section, and the final section concludes.

BACKGROUND

Evolution of Gender Equality Legislation in the Iberian Countries

Gender quotas introduction in Spain resulted from the Constitutional Act 3/2007. This legislation focused on the Central Government and its associated or subordinate public bodies and private firms. The law established a minimum of 2/5 of both gender types on the administration boards covered by its scope. Along the legislation, it's possible to find two specific articles devoted to companies:

a) Article 75 states that *"Companies obliged to present unabridged financial statements of income will endeavor to include a sufficient number of women on their boards of directors to reach a balanced presence of women and men within eight years of the entry into effect of this Act. The provisions of the preceding paragraph will be taken into account when making appointments on the occasion of the finalization of the terms of directors designated prior to the entry into force of this Act."*
b) Article 78 states that *"For the intents and purposes of this Act, balanced membership will be understood to mean the presence of women and men in the context in question in a manner such that neither sex accounts for more than sixty nor less than forty percent of the total."*

In terms of listed firms, and to the best of our knowledge, the Unified Good Governance Code of Listed Firms, published in 2006, contemplates de first call of attention to gender equality issues, stating, in its recommendation 15, that *"When women directors are few or non-existent the board should state the reasons for this situation and the measures taken to correct it."* Later on, the Good Governance Code of Listed Companies, published in 2015, addressed gender equality matters by stating, in its principle 10, that *"The board of directors should have the optimal size to facilitate its efficient functioning, the participation of all members and agile decision-making. Director selection policy should seek a balance of knowledge, experience and gender in the board's membership"*, and through its recommendation 14, provides a target ratio for female board representation on the board of directors and a timetable to achieve it by stating that *"The director selection policy should pursue the goal of having at least 30% of total board places occupied by women directors before the year 2020."* In 2020, the Good Governance Code of Listed Companies 2015 was revised. Among its recommendations, they updated the female ratio target. They provided a new timetable for its accomplishment by stating that *"to promote desirable gender diversity on the board of directors, it is recommended that female directors represent at least 40% of the total number of members by 2022."*

Regarding the Portuguese context, gender quotas were imposed by law 62/2017. The scope of this law was restricted to public companies and listed firms and within those to administration and supervisory boards. Article 4 imposed a minimum of 1/3 of female representation for public companies on the boards mentioned above. Additionally, the same article states that in the case of the distinction between executive and non-executive directors on the administration boards, the same proportion should exist in both directors' categories. Article 5 from the same law imposes a minimum of 1/5 of female representation on administration and supervisory boards of listed firms and also states that in case of the distinction between executive and non-executive directors on the administration boards, the same proportion should exist in both directors' categories.

To accommodate this legislation, the Portuguese Institute of Corporate Governance published the Portuguese Corporate Governance Code in 2018 and revised it in 2020. The recommendations of the Corporate Code on gender equality are vague, and the word "gender" only appears twice in the following recommendations:

(a) Recommendation I.2.1. states, *"Companies should establish standards and requirements regarding the profile of new members of their governing bodies, which are suitable according to the roles to be carried out. Besides individual attributes (such as competence, independence, integrity, availability, and experience), these profiles should take into consideration general diversity requirements, with particular attention to gender diversity, which may contribute to a better performance of the governing body and to the balance of its composition."*;

(b) Recommendation V.3.4. states, *"The nomination committee should make its terms of reference available, and should foster, to the extent of its powers, transparent selection processes that include effective mechanisms of identification of potential candidates, and that those chosen for proposal are those who present a higher degree of merit, who are best suited to the demands of the functions to be carried out, and who will best promote, within the organization, a suitable diversity, including gender diversity."*

In sum, the Spanish Good Governance Code of Listed Companies recommends a minimum of 40% female representation on the board of directors, and Portuguese law forces female directors to fulfill at least 1/3 of the board seats. These targets are in line with those practiced by other European Union members. According to European Commission (2022), for the same type of companies, countries such as France and Italy impose a minimum gender quota of 40%, Belgium a minimum of 33%, and Germany, Austria, and Greece impose gender quotas under or equal to 30%.[2] Still within the European Union (EU) context, in October 2022, it was approved an EU directive that imposes listed companies of member states a quota of 40% of female representation on non-executive seats or a quota of 33% when member states choose to apply gender quotas on executive and non-executive positions. These targets must be achieved by 2026[3].

Figure 1 shows the evolution of board gender diversity in the Iberian stock markets over the last decade. If it is true that the trend is positive for both countries, it still is true that they need to achieve the ratio targets defined by law.

Figure 1. Evolution of board gender diversity over the last decade
Source: European Institute for Gender Equality (EIGE)

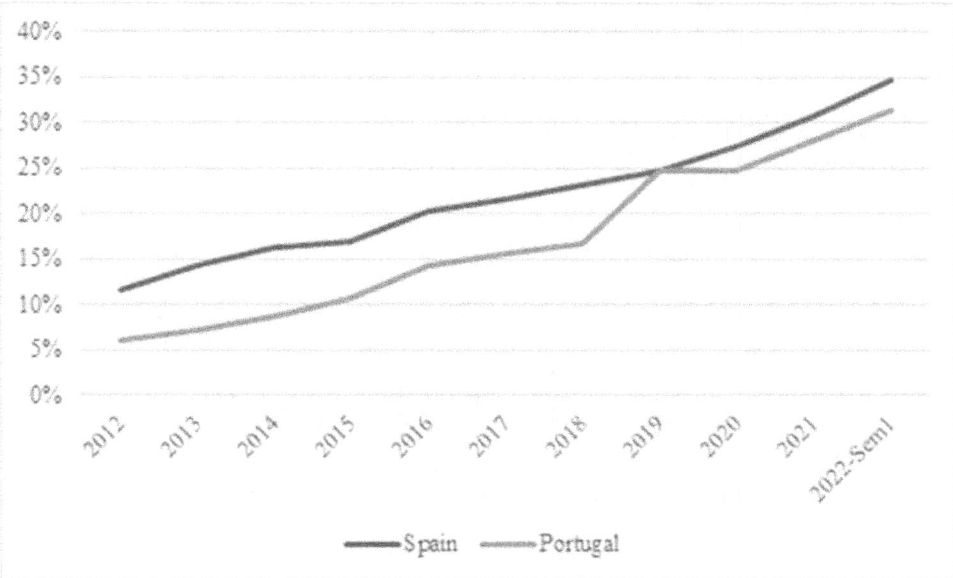

Figure 2 highlights the evolution of gender diversity in listed firms' leadership positions. In the Portuguese context, it seems that females started to occupy leadership positions in 2016. Since then, the fraction of female leaders presents some constancy except for the years 2021 and 2022, when female leaders are proportionally increasing their positions.

Figure 2. Evolution of female representation in leadership positions over the last decade
Source: European Institute for Gender Equality (EIGE)

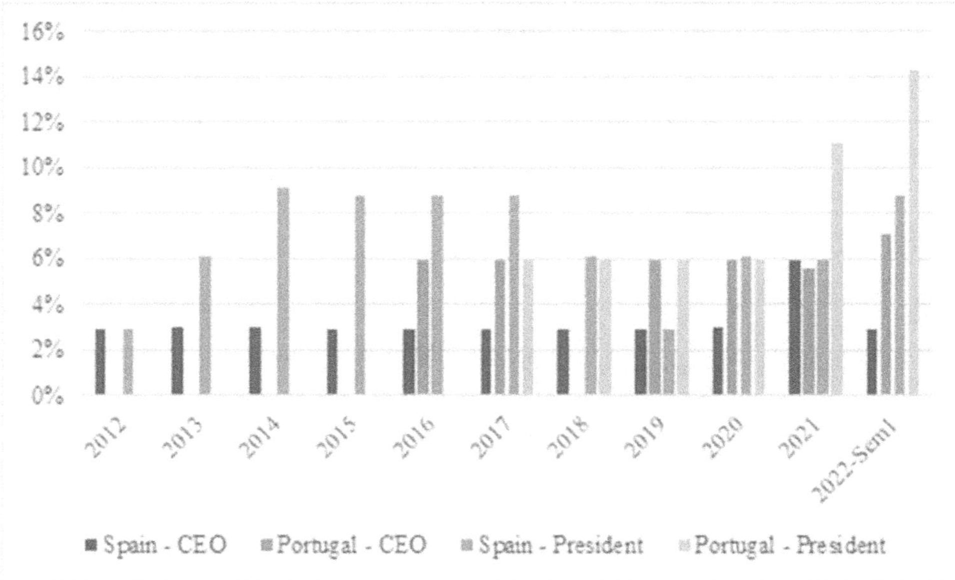

Interestingly, in the Spanish context, the proportion of female CEOs its being relatively stable over the last decade. In terms of female presidents, there was an increase between 2012 and 2014, followed by three years with similar performance. Still, between 2018 and 2021, the proportion of female presidents faced a stable decrease, only recovering in the first semester of 2022. Comparing both countries, Spain has a slightly higher fraction of female representation on the board of directors. At the same time, Portugal presents proportionally more elevated levels of females occupying the roles of President and CEO of listed firms.

METHODOLOGY

To answer the research question, *"Are scientific results of research based on gender diversity effects on Iberian-listed firms' outcomes over this millennium supporting the gender quotas defenders?"* this study follows the systematic approach as a review technique. The data collection is derived from a set of procedures. Firstly, to ensure quality research, we define that publications should have an impact factor from Web of Science and/or Scopus. Secondly, we determine the subject areas from Web of Science *(business AND business finance AND economics AND management)* and Scopus *(economics, econometrics and finance AND business, accounting, and management)* databases. We limited the document type to *"articles, review articles AND book chapters."* Thirdly, publications were searched with the following keywords: *"(Portugal OR Portuguese OR Lisbon, PSI OR Spain OR Spanish OR Madrid OR IBEX) AND (diversity OR gender OR female OR women OR woman OR male OR men OR man) AND (board OR director OR CEO OR CFO OR executive)."* The search provided 247 publications, of which 115 were derived from the Web of Science database and 132 from the Scopus database[4].

Fourthly, both databases were merged to eliminate duplications. This step results in a total of 159 publications. Fifthly, we read all the titles and abstracts to ensure that publications were related to the research question. This process determined the reduction of the sample to 124 publications. Sixthly, we conducted the download process and identified 18 publications with no free access, resulting in a total sample of 106 publications. Seventhly, we identified the publications whose sample was from listed firms or had mixed samples that presented disaggregated data for listed firms. The number of publications respecting those criteria was 63. Lastly, we selected publications that exclusively analyzed the impact of board gender diversity on firm outcomes. In this step, 19 studies were excluded due to a variety of reasons related to research type, sample characteristics, or empirical focus (e.g., non-empirical articles, empirical articles without disaggregated data per country, and empirical articles focused on gender diversity determinants). This procedure resulted in a final sample of 44 publications. Table 1 summarizes the results of the sample selection process.

Table 1. Summary of the results from the methodological procedures

Sample selection steps	Number of publications
Step 1: Initial sample from Web of Science and Scopus databases	247
Step 2: Merging databases	159
Step 3: Publications related to gender diversity	124
Step 4: Publications with free download	106
Step 5: Publications using listed firms	63
Step 6: Publications studying board gender diversity effects on firm outcomes	44

Source: Own elaboration based on Web of Science and Scopus databases

This study presents a combination of quantitative and qualitative methods. The quantitative methods were used to produce statistical information, and the qualitative approach was used to analyze the content of publications.

RESULTS AND DISCUSSION

According to Figure 3 and our sample criteria, the first published study that relates board gender diversity to firm outcomes in the Iberian Stock Markets is dated 2008. Campbell and Mínguez-Vera (2008) studied the effects of female representation on the board of directors (BOD) on the financial performance of Spanish non-financial listed firms. They reported a beneficial contribution of female directors on firm performance. Results were sensitive to gender diversity measures. Figure 3 also demonstrates that 2015 was the turning point for the considerable increase in publications in this regional context.

Figure 3. Evolution of the number of publications
Source: Own elaboration based on Web of Science and Scopus databases

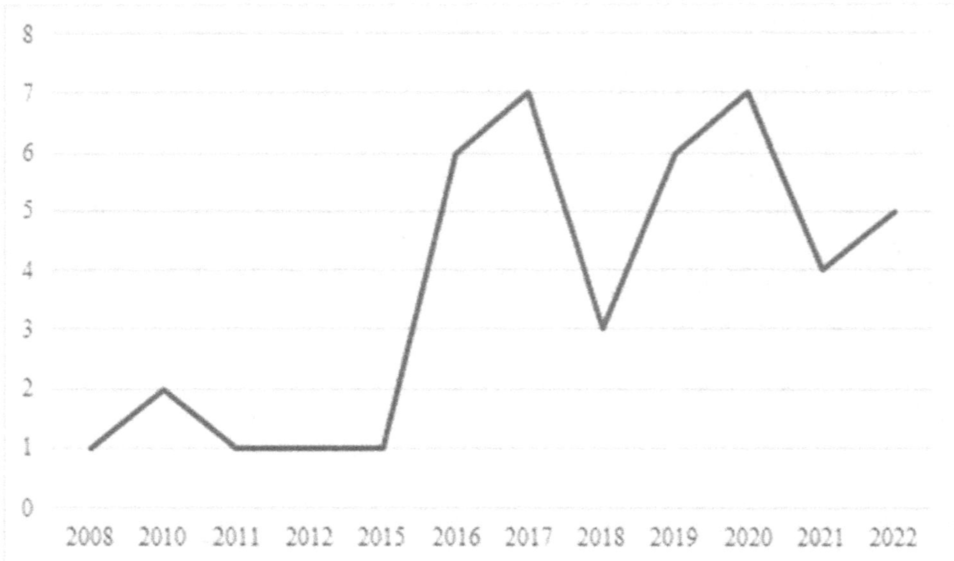

As Figure 4 shows, Spain is, by far, the most researched country in the Iberian Peninsula. Thirty single-country studies are related to Spain, and only four are associated with Portugal. Spain is also included in eight cross-national studies where data is provided by country, and only two cross-country studies focused on the Iberian market as a whole. The concentration of research on Spain compared to Portugal may result from the stock market size differences. Spain has a far higher number of listed companies (e.g., 114 in general IBEX) than Portugal (e.g., 37 in general PSI).

Figure 4. Frequency of publications by sample country
Source: Own elaboration based on Web of Science and Scopus databases

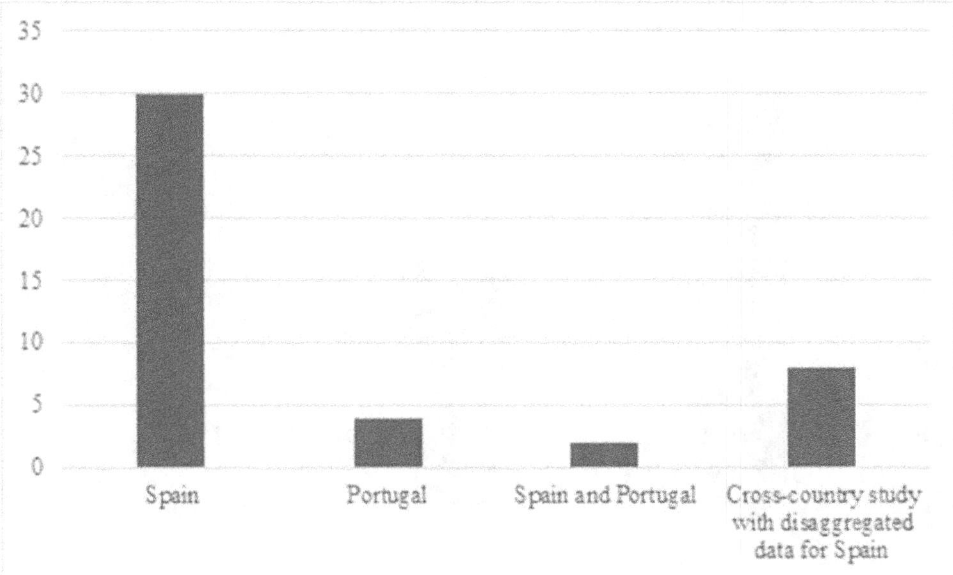

According to our systematization is possible to organize the focus of the publications into three groups, as presented in Figure 5. Research on financial issues represents 55% of the publications, 32% is devoted to information disclosure, and only 14% is associated with other fields.

Figure 5. Distribution of publications by research field
Source: Own elaboration based on Web of Science and Scopus databases

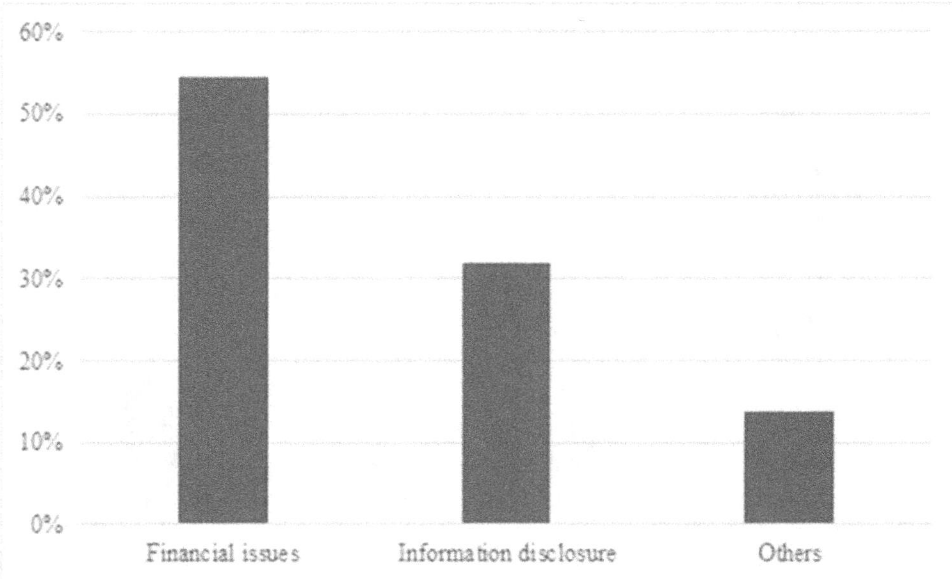

The publications on these three research fields present an erratic evolution over time. As Figure 6 demonstrates, studies devoted to the gender diversity effects on firm financial outcomes are the preferred research topic over time, with few exceptions. Publications related to the impact of gender diversity on information disclosure issues started in 2016 and achieved their top in 2017. Studies on other issues are scarce and in only three years' publications come out.

Figure 6. Evolution of publications by research field
Source: Own elaboration based on Web of Science and Scopus databases

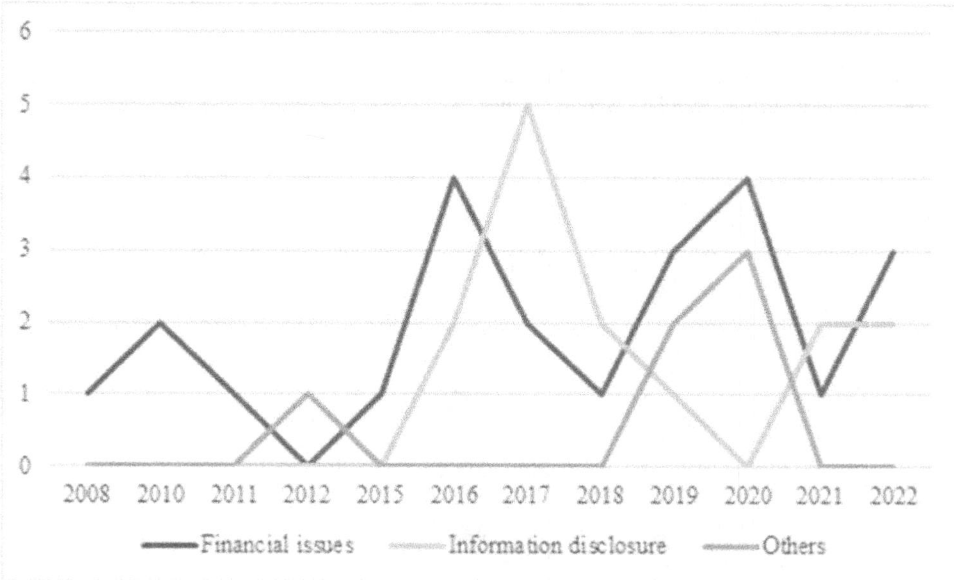

Concerning the sample periods used by Spanish-related literature, 8% of the studies consider data before gender quotas legislation, 45% present data after that event, and 47% have data from both periods. According to our analysis, those studies that use data previous to the introduction of gender quotas legislation and those that analyze data from both periods present similar conclusions to those that only consider data after introducing quotas. That is, results are relatively stable across the millennium, meaning that female directors' effects on firms' outcomes are not contingent on gender quotas implementation.

Similar conclusions cannot be drawn for the Portuguese context since no studies contain data after the introduction of gender quotas. However, considering all sampled studies, results align with those reported for the Spanish context.

In the following subsections, the results reported by research are presented according to the identified research fields: (1) board gender diversity and financial issues, (2) board gender diversity and information disclosure issues, and (3) board gender diversity and other issues.

Board Gender Diversity and Financial Issues

Literature on female board representation's effects on firms' financial outcomes presents a wide range of topics (Figure 7). Financial performance is the most researched topic, followed by firms' dividends, executive compensation, tax, capital structure, and earnings management policies.

Figure 7. Research topic on financial issues
Source: Own elaboration based on Web of Science and Scopus databases

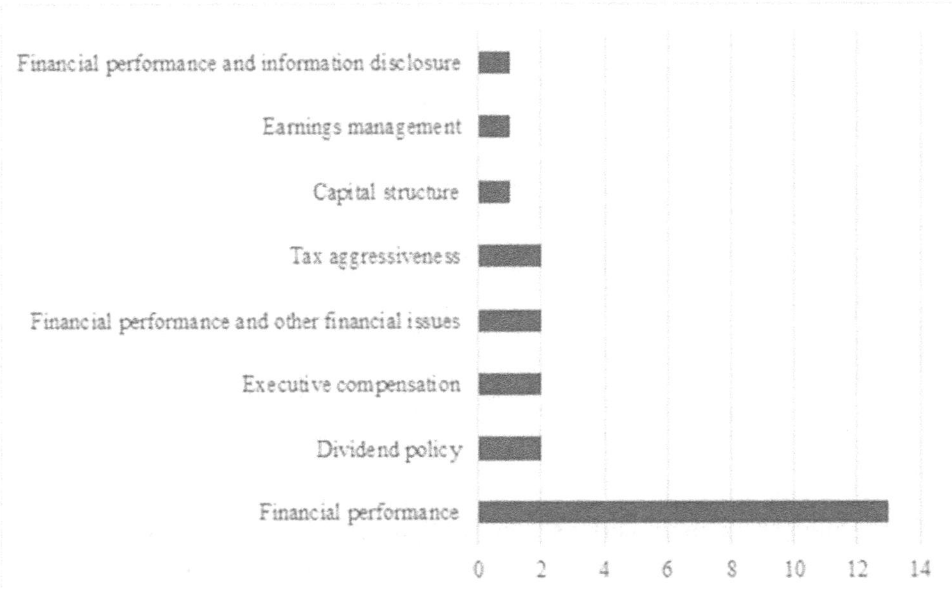

Financial Performance

Regarding firms' performance, financial performance literature presents mixed evidence. For the Spanish context, Campbell and Mínguez-Vera (2008) analyzed the effect of different board gender diversity measures on firms' Tobin's Q. Results only provide evidence for a significant and beneficial effect for the gender variable related to the female presence on the board of directors (BOD). The same authors reported in 2010 that stock markets react positively to the announcement of female appointments in the short term through the increase of cumulative abnormal returns (CAR) and confirm that board gender diversity increases firm performance over time. In the same year, Gallego-Álvarez et al. (2010) concluded for the detrimental effects of women, as a sum of all female roles analyzed, on different accounting performance measures, such as the return on assets (ROA), return on equity (ROE) and return on sales (ROS). Disaggregated gender roles (BOD, top management positions, and owners) reveal a non-significant association with firm performance.

In the same vein, Molina and Torrado (2011) concluded that exists an insignificant effect of gender diversity in firms in the financial sector.

More recently, Duppati et al. (2017) found that the impact of gender diversity on the BOD is contingent o performance measures. Female directors have a positive and significant effect on ROA. Still, an insignificant contribution to Tobin's Q. In opposition, Fernández-Gago et al. (2016) and Reguera-Alvarado et al. (2017) found robust evidence of the benefits of female directors on firm performance measured by Tobin's Q. Fernández-Temprano and Tejerina-Gaite (2020) and Martínez-García et al. (2022) found no support to the influence of female directors on performance.

The study of Spain in a cross-national sample also presents mixed evidence. While Duppati et al. (2019) demonstrated that the beneficial effects of gender diversity on firm performance are econometrically contingent, Saona et al. (2020) documented insignificant or detrimental consequences of female directors on firm performance. Martín-Ugedo et al. (2019) argued for a positive influence of women directors on firm performance. Comi et al. (2020) concluded that the introduction of gender quotas had no significant effects on firm performance.

Cross-national studies focused on the context of Iberian markets document an insignificant association between gender diversity on firm performance in both countries without differences between national samples (Lopes et al., 2016). More recently, Madaleno et al. (2021), using a similar sample, reported a consistently positive effect on female representation on the BOD, top management team, and committees only on market measures of firm performance. Vieira (2018) analyzed the Portuguese context and argued for a contingent effect of female directors on firm performance according to performance measures and crisis cycles. The author found a positive and significant association between board gender diversity on ROA in the main model. Still, robustness checks show that this effect is only significant during financial crises.

In sum, publications devoted to the Iberian stock markets do not allow us to conclude robustly about the benefits of board gender diversity on firm performance in both countries. For the Spanish context, 9 out of the 13 publications present contingent or insignificant effects on firm performance. For the Portuguese context, the only single-country study also documents a contingent impact on the link between board gender diversity and firm performance. Lastly, studies using samples from both countries also conclude for insignificant or contingent associations between board diversity and firm performance.

Dividend Policy

Literature on the effects of female representation on the BOD and firms' dividend policies is scarce. Pucheta-Martínez and Bel-Oms (2016) studied the impact of different gender variables on dividend payout. They concluded for a sample of companies without losses that the fraction of females on the BOD and the percentage of female independent directors are positively associated with dividend payout. In contrast, the fraction of executive and institutional women directors decreases dividend payout. Additionally, the authors report that female directors' ownership has an insignificant effect on firms' dividend policies. More recently, García-Meca et al. (2022) argue that the relationship between female directors and dividend policy varies according to family ties between those directors and the major shareholder. In the case of family ties, there is an inverted U-shaped relationship with dividend payout. In case of the absence of these family connections, the non-linear association turns into a U-shape type. These associations indicate that when there are family ties, an increase in female representation in the BOD decreases the dividend payout. When those ties don't exist, the effect is the opposite.

Executive Compensation

The existing literature related to the effects of board gender diversity on executive compensation is concentrated on the study of the variable component of executives' remuneration. Lucas-Pérez et al. (2015) documented that the percentage of female directors and the percentage of female outside directors are positively associated with the increase in executives' remuneration related to performance in terms of amount and percentage. Similarly, Baixauli-Soler et al. (2016) presented robust findings that this internal corporate governance mechanism measured through different gender variables promotes an increase in variable components of executives' remuneration.

Tax Aggressiveness

The study of gender diversity and tax aggressiveness is very recent in the Iberian context. García-Meca et al. (2021) showed that gender diversity in the audit committees tends to reduce aggressive tax practices measured through effective tax rate (ETR) and cash ETR promoted by CEOs with a narcissistic profile. However, Cortellese (2022) find no significant association between the fraction of female directors on the BOD and the percentage of female executives and the practices of tax aggressiveness.

Other Topics

Briozzo et al. (2019) studied the impact of board diversity on firms' definitions of financial policies, namely the capital structure. Results demonstrate that a higher proportion of females in the BOD contributes to decreased debt maturity. These results indicate that female directors tend to prefer longer debt maturity.

Saona et al. (2020) analyzed the association between female representation on the BOD and results manipulation. The authors conclude that the more female representation, the lower the probability of managing earnings through discretionary accruals.

In sum, it is possible to conclude that board gender diversity does not robustly increment firm performance, has not robustly affected firms' dividend policies, and has not robustly reduced firms' tax aggressiveness. However, it can be highlighted that female presence on the board consistently increases the variable component of executives' remuneration and decreases management earnings practices.

Board Gender Diversity and Information Disclosure Issues

The association between female board representation and information disclosure is a relevant field of research in the Iberian context. Figure 8 demonstrates that information disclosure associated with Corporate Social Responsibility is the most frequent research topic.

Figure 8. Research topics on information disclosure issues
Source: Own elaboration based on Web of Science and Scopus databases

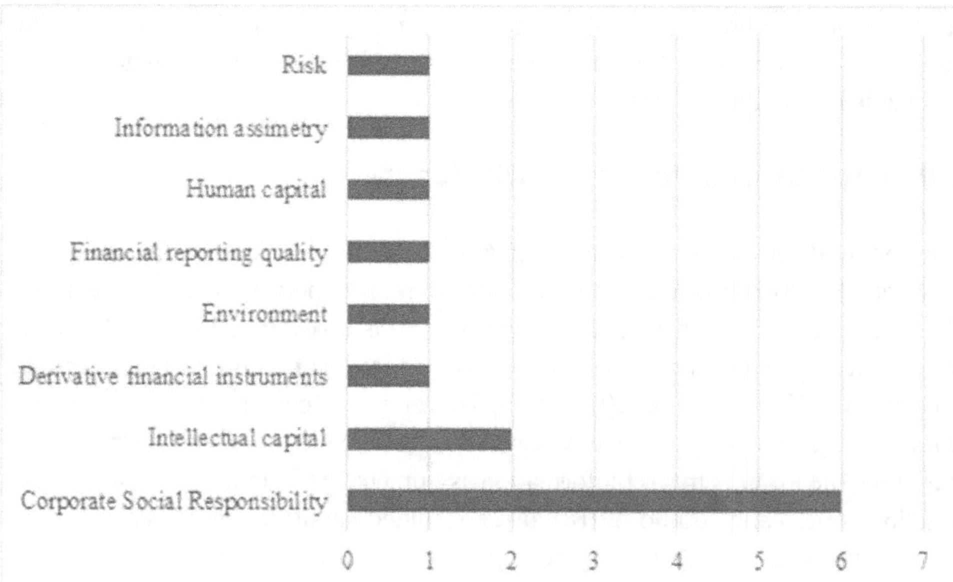

Corporate Social Responsibility indexes

Garcia-Torea et al. (2017) documented that a higher fraction of female representation on the BOD improves transparency on CSR reports. Similarly, Fuente et al. (2017) showed that the fraction of female directorships is positively related to corporate transparency about sustainability and that governance characteristics increase the probability of creating a CSR committee. Additionally, Cabeza-García et al. (2018) and Martínez et al. (2019) also confirmed the positive effect of board gender diversity on CSR disclosure by using gender measures related to the BOD as the percentage of independent and outside female directors.

Formigoni et al. (2021) presented the first study that does not confirm the beneficial effects of gender diversity on firms' CSR information disclosure. Most recent research documents a positive moderator effect of gender diversity between busy directors and CSR disclosure levels (Reguera-Alvarado & Bravo-Urquiza, 2022).

Intellectual Capital Indexes

The second most relevant research topic on information disclosure is associated with gender effects on intellectual capital disclosure. While in the Portuguese context, Rodrigues et al. (2017) documented mixed evidence on the benefits of female representation on the BOD and the Intellectual Capital Disclosure Index (ICI), Tejedo-Romero et al. (2017) found a positive contribution of that governance mechanism to ICI in the Spanish context.

Other Topics on Information Disclosure

Carmona et al. (2016) and Pucheta-Martínez et al. (2016) analyzed the consequences of board gender diversity on the level of risk disclosure and reporting quality, respectively. Findings documented that gender diversity increases risk disclosure and reduces the probability of errors, non-compliance, and omission of information in corporate reports. In 2017, Abad et al. (2017) studied the effects of gender diversity on market information asymmetry. The study concludes that the higher the representation on the BOD, the lower is market information asymmetry. Still, in the Spanish context, Tejedo-Romero and Araujo (2018) also concluded about the beneficial effects of gender diversity now in terms of the human capital disclosure index (HC).

Portuguese research also reports positive associations between board gender diversity and environmental disclosure indexes (Monteiro et al., 2021) and the level of disclosure related to derivative instruments (Serra et al., 2022). In sum, board gender diversity in the Iberian countries generally contributes to the increase in firms' reporting quality and transparency.

Board Gender Diversity and Other Issues

In this third field of research, the most prevalent topic is the study of the relationship between board gender diversity and a firm's compliance with corporate governance codes (Figure 9). Sánchez et al. (2012), and Melón-Izco et al. (2020) consistently documented that board gender diversity is a positive internal mechanism to increase firms' governance recommendations compliance. Pucheta-Martínez and Bel-Oms (2019) presented some contingencies on gender effects and the voluntary creation of committees. Results highlight the beneficial impact of independent female directors and female ownership on the voluntary creation of board subcommittees. In contrast, females representing institutional shareholders and females holding executive positions have the opposite effect.

Figure 9. Research topics on other issues
Source: Own elaboration based on Web of Science and Scopus databases

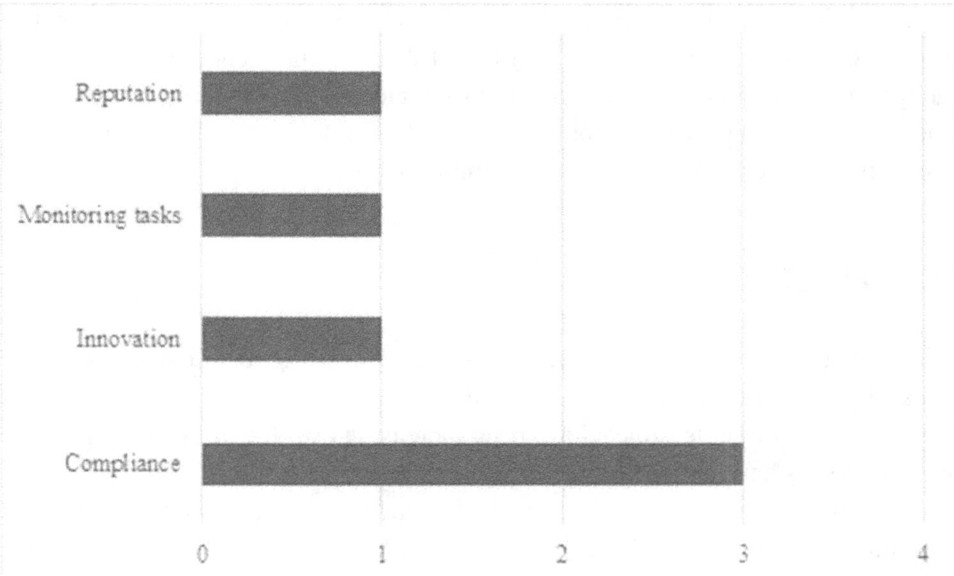

From a different perspective, Hernández-Lara and Gonzales-Bustos (2019) found a negative association between board gender diversity and a firm's innovation levels, De Masi et al. (2020) reported no significant relationship with board monitoring tasks effectiveness and Navarro-García et al. (2020) presented an incremental effect on firms' reputation. Once again, female directors produce beneficial effects, this time on firms' compliance with corporate governance codes.

Avenues for Future Research

Board gender diversity analysis is already being pursued in the Iberian market, as became clear from the analysis of research presented above. There is, however, a considerable gap in the analysis of the Portuguese context in all topics covered by this literature review, namely studies on firm performance, executive compensation, dividend and tax policies, information disclosure, and compliance with corporate governance codes. There are also research gaps for both countries regarding earnings management practices, capital structure policies, different types of firm risk-taking (e.g., financial and operational risk), and innovation performance.

Additionally, there is a gap in exploring possible mediators that might accelerate or weaken the relationship between gender quotas and company performance. The question to be answered is by which mechanisms gender quotas influence board dynamics and organizations' outcomes.

Lastly, there is a remaining need for similar studies on diversity issues besides those related to gender (age, background, race, nationality, culture, independence, etc.). For Norway, Strøm (2015) states that the government's proposal for the quota law justifies the need based on the fact that not only gender but as age and background diversity contributes to better strategic choices, higher innovation, and quicker restructuring, all driving profitability. It should also be noted that endogeneity issues should be carefully considered in future research.

CONCLUSION

This investigation intended to analyze the impact of board gender diversity on listed firms' outcomes in the Portuguese and Spanish stock markets. Descriptive data show that publications on this subject have been increasing over the last decade and that financial issues have called special attention to researchers.

Based on a sample of 44 publications, this documental analysis shows that the literature presents mixed evidence on the effects of directors' gender diversity on firm performance and other firm policies related to dividend and tax aggressiveness. However, it seems clear that female directors promote firms' reporting quality and transparency, as also firms' corporate governance codes compliance levels. These effects appear not to be directly driven by gender quotas implementation since they are reported across different time frames.

Different proposals for future research are identified in terms of firm outcomes and directors' characteristics.

A limitation that can be pointed out in this study is related to the adopted methodological procedures. By only considering literature published in Scopus or

WoS databases, the reported results, the discussion, and the conclusions may be biased.

REFERENCES

Abad, D., Lucas-Pérez, M. E., Minguez-Vera, A., & Yagüe, J. (2017). Does gender diversity on corporate boards reduce information asymmetry in equity markets? *BRQ Business Research Quarterly*, *20*(3), 192–205. doi:10.1016/j.brq.2017.04.001

Baixauli-Soler, J. S., Lucas-Perez, M. E., Martin-Ugedo, J. F., Minguez-Vera, A., & Sanchez-Marin, G. (2016). Executive directors' compensation and monitoring: The influence of gender diversity on Spanish boards. *Journal of Business Economics and Management*, *17*(6), 1133–1154. doi:10.3846/16111699.2014.969767

Briozzo, A., Cardone-Riportella, C., & García-Olalla, M. (2019). Corporate governance attributes and listed SMES' debt maturity. *Corporate Governance (Bingley)*, *19*(4), 735–750. doi:10.1108/CG-11-2017-0272

Cabeza-García, L., Fernández-Gago, R., & Nieto, M. (2018). Do Board Gender Diversity and Director Typology Impact CSR Reporting? *European Management Review*, *15*(4), 559–575. doi:10.1111/emre.12143

Campbell, K., & Mínguez-Vera, A. (2008). Gender diversity in the boardroom and firm financial performance. *Journal of Business Ethics*, *83*(3), 435–451. doi:10.100710551-007-9630-y

Carmona, P., De Fuentes, C., & Ruiz, C. (2016). Risk disclosure analysis in the corporate governance annual report using fuzzy-set qualitative comparative analysis. *RAE Revista de Administracao de Empresas*, *56*(3), 342–352. doi:10.1590/S0034-759020160307

Carter, D., D'Souza, F., Simkins, B., & Simpson, W. (2010). The gender and ethnic diversity of US boards and board committees and firm financial performance. *Corporate Governance*, *18*(5), 396–414. doi:10.1111/j.1467-8683.2010.00809.x

CNMV. (2015). *Good governance code of listed companies*. CNMV. https://www.cnmv.es/DocPortal/Publicaciones/CodigoGov/Good_Governanceen.pdf

CNMV. (2020). *Good governance code of listed companies*. CNMV. https://www.cnmv.es/DocPortal/Publicaciones/CodigoGov/CBG_2020.pdf

Comi, S., Grasseni, M., Origo, F., & Pagani, L. (2020). Where Women Make a Difference: Gender Quotas and Firms' Performance in Three European Countries. *ILR Review, 73*(3), 768–793. doi:10.1177/0019793919846450

Cortellese, F. (2022). Does the gender composition of the board of directors have any effect on tax aggressiveness in western countries? *&. Sociology, 15*(1), 2022. doi:10.14254/2071

De Masi, S., Słomka-Gołębiowska, A., & Paci, A. (2020). Women on boards and monitoring tasks: An empirical application of Kanter's theory. *Management Decision, 59*(13), 56–72. doi:10.1108/MD-10-2019-1450

Duppati, G., Sune, A., & Samanta, N. (2017). Corporate governance, research and development volatility and firm performance - Evidence from Spain and Ireland. *Cogent Economics and Finance, 5*(1), 1317117. doi:10.1080/23322039.2017.1317117

Duppati, G. R., Scrimgeour, F., & Sune, A. (2019). Relevance of corporate boards in driving performance in the period that covers financial crisis. *Corporate Governance (Bingley), 19*(2), 321–338. doi:10.1108/CG-11-2016-0204

European Commission. (2022). *2022 Report on gender equality on the EU.* Publications Office of the European Union.

Fama, E. (1980). Agency problems and the theory of the firm. *Journal of Political Economy, 88*(2), 288–307. doi:10.1086/260866

Fernández-Gago, R., Cabeza-García, L., & Nieto, M. (2016). Corporate social responsibility, board of directors, and firm performance: An analysis of their relationships. *Review of Managerial Science, 10*(1), 85–104. doi:10.100711846-014-0141-9

Fernández-Temprano, M. A., & Tejerina-Gaite, F. (2020). Types of director, board diversity and firm performance. *Corporate Governance (Bingley), 20*(2), 324–342. doi:10.1108/CG-03-2019-0096

Formigoni, H., Segura, L., & Gallego-Álvarez, I. (2021). Board of directors characteristics and disclosure practices of corporate social responsibility: A comparative study between Brazilian and Spanish companies. *Social Responsibility Journal, 17*(2), 282–298. doi:10.1108/SRJ-01-2019-0043

Fuente, J. A., García-Sánchez, I. M., & Lozano, M. B. (2017). The role of the board of directors in the adoption of GRI guidelines for the disclosure of CSR information. *Journal of Cleaner Production, 141*, 737–750. doi:10.1016/j.jclepro.2016.09.155

Gallego-Álvarez, I., García-Sánchez, I. M., & Rodríguez-Dominguez, L. (2010). The influence of gender diversity on corporate performance. *Revista de Contabilidad-Spanish Accounting Review*, *13*(1), 53–88. doi:10.1016/S1138-4891(10)70012-1

García-Meca, E., López-Iturriaga, F. J., & Santana-Martín, D. J. (2022). Board gender diversity and dividend payout: The critical mass and the family ties effect. *International Review of Financial Analysis*, *79*, 101973. Advance online publication. doi:10.1016/j.irfa.2021.101973

García-Meca, E., Ramón-Llorens, M. C., & Martínez-Ferrero, J. (2021). Are narcissistic CEOs more tax aggressive? The moderating role of internal audit committees. *Journal of Business Research*, *129*, 223–235. doi:10.1016/j.jbusres.2021.02.043

Garcia-Torea, N., Fernandez-Feijoo, B., & de la Cuesta-González, M. (2017). La influencia de la estructura de propiedad en la transparencia de la información de RSC: Evidencia del caso Español. *Revista Española de Financiación y Contabilidad*, *46*(3), 249–271. doi:10.1080/02102412.2016.1267451

Hernández-Lara, A. B., & Gonzales-Bustos, J. P. (2019). The impact of interlocking directorates on innovation: The effects of business and social ties. *Management Decision*, *57*(10), 2799–2815. doi:10.1108/MD-11-2017-1186

IPGC. (2018). *Código de Governo das Sociedades*. IPGC. https://cgov.pt/images/ficheiros/2018/codigo_de_governo_das_sociedades_ipcg_vf.pdf

IPGC. (2020). *Código de Governo das Sociedades*. IPGC. https://cam.cgov.pt/images/ficheiros/2020/revisao_codigo_pt_2018_ebook-05.11.2020.pdf

Lopes, I. T., Ferraz, D. P., & Martins, M. M. (2016). *The influence of diversity on boards on profitability: an overview across iberian non-financial listed companies* (Vol. 13). Corporate Ownership & Control.

Lucas-Pérez, M. E., Mínguez-Vera, A., Baixauli-Soler, J. S., Martín-Ugedo, J. F., & Sánchez-Marín, G. (2015). Women on the Board and Managers' Pay: Evidence from Spain. *Journal of Business Ethics*, *129*(2), 265–280. doi:10.100710551-014-2148-1

Madaleno, M., Vieira, E. S., & Teodosio, J. P. C. (2021). Corporate female leadership effects considering PSI20 and IBEX35 companies' performance. In *Research Anthology on Challenges for Women in Leadership Roles* (pp. 711–731). IGI Global., doi:10.4018/978-1-7998-8592-4.ch039

Martín-Ugedo, J. F., Mínguez-Vera, A., & Rossi, F. (2019). Female directors and firm performance in Italian and Spanish listed firms: Does masculinity matter? *Academia (Caracas)*, *32*(3), 411–436. doi:10.1108/ARLA-06-2018-0124

Martínez, M. (2019). Gender policies on board of directors and sustainable development. *Corporate Social Responsibility and Environmental Management*, *26*(6), 1539–1553. doi:10.1002/csr.1825

Martínez-García, I., Terjesen, S., & Gómez-Ansón, S. (2022). Board Gender Diversity Codes, Quotas and Threats of Supranational Legislation: Impact on Director Characteristics and Corporate Outcomes. *British Journal of Management*, *33*(2), 753–783. doi:10.1111/1467-8551.12517

Melón-Izco, Á., Ruiz-Cabestre, F. J., & Ruiz-Olalla, M. C. (2020). Diversity in the board of directors and good governance practices. *Economics and Business Letters*, *9*(2), 97–105. doi:10.17811/ebl.9.2.2020.97-105

Molina, J., M., C., & Torrado, M., N. (2011). *The efficiency of the financial sector in Spain: a gender focus.* Adm. Bogotá (Colombia).

Monteiro, A. P., Pereira, C., & Barbosa, F. M. (2021). *Environmental disclosure on mandatory and voluntary reporting of Portuguese listed firms: the role of environmental certification, lucratively and corporate governance*. Meditari Accountancy Research. doi:10.1108/MEDAR-09-2020-1001

Navarro-García, J. C., Ramón-Llorens, M. C., & García-Meca, E. (2020). *Female directors and corporate reputation.* BRQ Business Research Quarterly. doi:10.1177/2340944420972717

Pucheta-Martínez, M. C., Bel-Oms, I., & Olcina-Sempere, G.Pucheta-Martínez. (2016). Corporate governance, female directors and quality of financial information. *Business Ethics (Oxford, England)*, *25*(4), 363–385. doi:10.1111/beer.12123

Pucheta-Martínez, M. C., & Bel-Oms, I.Pucheta-Martínez. (2016). The board of directors and dividend policy: The effect of gender diversity. *Industrial and Corporate Change*, *25*(3), 523–547. doi:10.1093/icc/dtv040

Pucheta-Martínez, M. C., & Bel-Oms, I.Pucheta-Martínez. (2019). What have we learnt about board gender diversity as a business strategy? The appointment of board subcommittees. *Business Strategy and the Environment*, *28*(2), 301–315. doi:10.1002/bse.2226

Reguera-Alvarado, N., & Bravo-Urquiza, F. (2022). The influence of board social capital on corporate social responsibility reporting. *Journal of Intellectual Capital, 23*(4), 913–935. doi:10.1108/JIC-11-2020-0359

Reguera-Alvarado, N., de Fuentes, P., & Laffarga, J. (2017). Does Board Gender Diversity Influence Financial Performance? Evidence from Spain. *Journal of Business Ethics, 141*(2), 337–350. doi:10.100710551-015-2735-9

Rodrigues, L. L., Tejedo-Romero, F., & Craig, R. (2017). Corporate governance and intellectual capital reporting in a period of financial crisis: Evidence from Portugal. *International Journal of Disclosure and Governance, 14*(1), 1–29. doi:10.1057/jdg.2015.20

Sánchez, P. C., Sánchez-Ballesta, J. P., & García-Meca, E. (2012). Explanatory factors of good governance in Spanish listed firms. *Revista de Contabilidad-Spanish Accounting Review, 15*(2), 237–255. doi:10.1016/S1138-4891(12)70044-4

Saona, P., Muro, L., & Alvarado, M. (2020). How do the ownership structure and board of directors' features impact earnings management? The Spanish case. *Journal of International Financial Management & Accounting, 31*(1), 98–133. doi:10.1111/jifm.12114

Serra, S., Lemos, K. M., & Matins, M. S. (2022). The Influence of the Board of Directors and the Auditor in the Disclosure of Derivative Financial Instruments: Evidence on Portuguese Capital Market. *International Journal of Professional Business Review, 7*(1), e0240. doi:10.26668/businessreview/2022.v7i1.240

Soare, T., Detilleux, C., & Deschacht, N. (2022). The impact of the gender composition of company boards on firm performance. *International Journal of Productivity and Performance Management, 71*(5), 1611–162. doi:10.1108/IJPPM-02-2020-0073

Strøm, R. (2015). Gender discrimination before mandated quotas? Evidence from Norway: 1989–2002. *Scandinavian Journal of Management, 31*(3), 303–315. doi:10.1016/j.scaman.2015.02.006

Tapver, T., Laidroo, L., & Gurvitš-Suits, N. A. (2021). Banks' CSR reporting – Do women have a say? *Corporate Governance, 20*(4), 639–651. doi:10.1108/CG-11-2019-0338

Tejedo-Romero, F., & Araujo, J. F. F. E. (2018). Transparency, Social Responsibility and Corporate Governance: Human capital of companies. *Cuadernos de Gestión, 18*(2), 133–162. doi:10.5295/cdg.160693ft

Tejedo-Romero, F., Rodrigues, L. L., & Craig, R. (2017). Women directors and disclosure of intellectual capital information. *European Research on Management and Business Economics*, *23*(3), 123–131. doi:10.1016/j.iedeen.2017.06.003

CNMV. (2006). *Unified Good Governance Code of Listed Companies*. CNMV. https://www.cnmv.es/Portal/~/verDoc.axd?t=18470855-a84c-4b12-b67a-3c77ccef9ea3

Vieira, E. S. (2018). Board of directors characteristics and performance in family firms and under the crisis. *Corporate Governance (Bingley)*, *18*(1), 119–142. doi:10.1108/CG-01-2017-0010

Yu, J. J., & Madison, G. (2021). Gender quotas and company financial performance: A systematic review. *Economic Affairs*, *41*(3), 377–390. doi:10.1111/ecaf.12487

KEY TERMS AND DEFINITIONS

Board of Directors: The board of directors of a public company is elected by shareholders. The board makes key decisions on issues such as mergers and dividends, hires senior managers, and sets their pay. Responsible for helping a corporation set broad goals, supporting senior management in pursuit of those goals, and ensuring the company has adequate, well-managed resources at its disposal.

Corporate Diversity and Inclusion: Corporate diversity is when organizations intentionally employ a workforce of employees of varying characteristics (sexual orientation, gender, race, ethnicity, religion, age, physical abilities, political ideologies, or socioeconomic status). Inclusion is defined as "the achievement of a work environment in which all individuals are treated fairly and respectfully, have equal access to opportunities and resources, and can contribute fully to the organization's success."

Corporate Governance: Corporate Governance refers to how companies are governed and for what purpose. Identifies who has power and accountability, and who makes decisions. A toolkit that enables management and the board to deal more effectively with the challenges of running a company. Corporate governance ensures that businesses have appropriate decision-making processes and controls in place to balance the interests of all stakeholders (shareholders, employees, suppliers, customers, and the community).

Gender quotas: Refers to a positive measurement instrument aimed at accelerating the achievement of gender-balanced participation and representation by establishing a defined proportion (percentage) or a number of places or seats to be filled by, or allocated to, women and/or men, generally under certain rules or criteria.

Gender: Gender refers to the characteristics of women, men, girls, and boys that are socially constructed. This includes norms, behaviors, and roles associated with being a woman, man, girl, or boy, as well as relationships with each other. As a social construct, gender varies from society to society and can change over time.

Innovation management and performance: Innovation management is the systematic process of organizing innovative practices throughout the enterprise. When leveraged effectively, innovation management can give rise to a creative culture where breakthrough ideas are generated continuingly It can also ensure complex, large-scale innovation objectives are broken down into manageable goals that various participant groups can focus on. Thus, innovation management leads to a performance based on innovative results and management practices.

ENDNOTES

1 According to European Institute for Gender Equality (EIGE) database.

2 According to European Commission (2022) there are only seven member states imposing gender quotas for listed companies: Austria, Belgium, France, Germany, Greece, Italy and Portugal. In the same publication it is stated that *"Spain has equality legislation that recommends having at least 40% of each gender on company boards, but this recommendation is not enforceable"* (p.44).

3 https://www.consilium.europa.eu/en/policies/gender-balance-c orporate-boards/

4 Data collection was conducted on July 2022.

Chapter 6
Female Presence on Boards of Directors and Firm Risk:
Case of Listed Tunisian Firms

Zyed Achour
National Institute of Labor and Social Studies, University of Carthage, Tunisia

ABSTRACT

In this chapter, the impact of board gender diversity on overall firm risk was investigated. Drawing on social identity theory, upper echelons theory, and agency theory, a hypothesis of a negative link between gender diversity on the board of directors and firm risk has been put forward. Using a panel data regression on a sample of large Tunisian companies listed on the Tunis Stock Exchange (BVMT) over the period 2016-2020, the author was able to provide empirical evidences supporting the existence of a significant negative impact of the percentage of women on boards of directors on stock return volatility as global firm risk proxy.

INTRODUCTION

Several countries have recently adopted legislation requiring greater representation of the female gender on boards of directors (proportion of women on boards). The main objective of these policies was to tackle the gender inequality that largely dominates the composition of boards of directors. Since then, the question of the implications of gender diversity on company results has continued to arouse the interest of researchers and practitioners alike. The results have frequently remained conflicting, and the mechanisms by which gender diversity may affect firm performance in general and risk mitigation in particular remain ambiguous and poorly understood,

DOI: 10.4018/978-1-6684-5981-2.ch006

despite the abundance of research that has marked the managerial literature over the last few decades.

Furthermore, the empirical investigations were carried out mainly in Western contexts. To our knowledge, few have addressed this topic in Arab-Muslim countries. Questioning the impact of women's presence on firms' performance and firms' risk in such cultures is certainly not without interest given the specificities of the status of women that characterize Arab-Muslim societies compared to Western societies. Indeed, these societies are thought to be historically and culturally dominated by male authoritarianism and men's superiority over women. In this landscape, Tunisia would probably be an exception given that it is perceived as a leading country in guaranteeing women's rights through the adoption of avant-garde legislation (see, for example, the Code of Personal Statutes of 1956; the Tunisian Constitution of 2014). However, the proportion of female business leaders and female members of boards of directors remains low and below the averages observed in European countries. For instance, the BoardEx1 report highlights that women serving on boards of directors reached 44% in France, 29% in the United States, and 24% in Portugal in 2021.

The board of directors is undoubtedly an essential mechanism of corporate governance, but it also plays a crucial role in adopting strategies and shaping the future direction of the company. From the perspective of resource dependence theory (Pfeffer & Salancik, 2003), for example, the board of directors provides the company with advice, legitimacy, and information, facilitating preferential access to the resources essential to its proper functioning. For Hillman and Dalziel (2003), the board of directors constitutes not only human capital (providing expertise, skills, and reputation) but also relational capital through the network of relationships from which it can benefit the organization. However, it is commonly accepted that its effectiveness remains largely dependent on its size and composition. For instance, it would depend on the dualities, ages, educational levels, and origins of its members as well as their "degree of feminization."

The inclusion of women could influence the effectiveness of boards of directors for at least three reasons: The first would be in the mainstream of social feminism, suggesting that women and men do not necessarily have the same needs, experiences, skills, and values and can develop different but equally effective traits (Fischer et al., 1993). It is the process of early and continuous socialization that forges the identity of individuals and influences their behavior, particularly in decision-making and risk-taking processes. The second relates to the acquired skills that women could have for strengthening relational networks and the creation of fruitful links between the company and its environment. The third is that the inclusion of women would be a signal appreciated and valued by stakeholders outside the company (Daily & Dalton, 2003).

Even though it has been shown in numerous studies that women are psychologically more risk averse than men are (Shropshire et al., 2021; Menicucci & Paolucci, 2020; Hoang et al., 2019), it is still unclear whether having more women on boards of directors improves performance and, even less, lowers the overall risk of the company. The impact of gender diversity on financial performance in general and on the overall risk of the organization in particular has been the subject of various empirical studies (Knyazeva et al., 2021; Nadeem et al., 2019; Sila et al., 2016; Lenard et al., 2014). The findings did not make it possible to rule on a stable relationship between diversity on the board of directors and the risk of business. Indeed, while some research has reported a negative impact of the female gender on risk-taking and on the financial stability of the firm (Hutchinson et al., 2015; Lenard et al., 2014), others do not show any effect, stating that women directors do not necessarily mitigate the risk of the company, but their presence could increase the supervisory function of the board of directors (Bruna et al., 2019; Sila et al., 2016). In contrast, other research has even been able to conclude that the proportion of women on boards of directors is associated with an increased risk (Chen et al., 2019; Berger et al., 2014; Adams and Funk, 2012). Last but not least, additional studies have demonstrated that for the number of women on boards to have an effect on risk, it must reach a "critical mass" (Seebeck & Vetter, 2021).

This study aims to contribute to the literature dealing with the effect of gender diversity on firm performance by focusing on the influence of women's representation on boards on overall business risk, at least at two levels. On a theoretical level, it seeks to strengthen the hypothesis of the existence of a link between diversity in the composition of boards of directors and business risk. On an empirical level, this study, carried out in the Tunisian context, aims to enrich the debate on the consequences of diversity on the overall performance of companies. The selection of Tunisia as the example is obviously not random, given the socio-cultural differences between Tunisian and Western women as well as the higher status of women in this country compared to other Arab-Muslim countries.

The chapter's remaining sections are organized as follows: Section 2 examines the theoretical underpinnings of how gender diversity on boards affects firm risk, bolstering the research premise. Section 3 presents the methods for the empirical validation of the hypothesis. Finally, Section 4 covers the findings, conclusions, and managerial implications.

Literature Review and Hypothesis Development

The relationship between gender diversity on the board of directors and firm risk can be explored from several theoretical angles.

Social identity theory (Tajfel, 1974) provides an analytic framework to better understand the effect of diversity on group behaviors, attitudes, and interactions within the organization. It stipulates that individuals, arriving at the origin of several societies, acquire over time a characteristic that makes them easily "categorizable" in a group. It is the dominant group that will have the power to influence the less dominant groups according to its own thinking and its own system of values. This discrimination can be based on several variables, such as race, religion, nationality, level of education, or gender. As a result, a person's idea of their own identity is based on their membership in a group, and their behavior is likely to change depending on the identity of the group to which they belong. So, starting from the fact that women have distinct traits, values, and interests because of the personalities they develop during childhood, they would show more selflessness and compassion and care more about others. For instance, female managers are less likely to be lured by corruption and are more loyal to ethical standards (Ibrahim et al., 2009; Xia et al., 2018). Women are reportedly more risk-averse than men when it comes to risk preferences, particularly when making financial decisions. The decision-making processes on boards may be impacted by the participation of women, who are more risk-averse. This could be explained by the fact that men make riskier judgments than women because they are overconfident and believe in their own risk assessments and personal experiences (Loukil & Yousfi, 2016). In fact, a number of empirical findings lend credence to the idea that women are less risk-averse than men. Women tend to be more cautious when making investment decisions and favor low-risk portfolios (Croson & Gneezy, 2009; Watson & McNaughton, 2007; Hinz et al., 1996). In a similar vein, Watson & Robinson (2003) found that firms run by women saw lower profit fluctuation than firms operated by men.

Agency theory (Jensen & Meckling, 1976) emphasizes the conflicting interests between shareholders and managers; the agency hypothesis holds that managers can be driven to engage in actions that advance their own interests at the expense of shareholders due to their opportunism. The lack of effective internal control put in place by homogeneous boards of directors frequently facilitates these managerial behaviors. Male managers would therefore be more inclined to make riskier investments, indulge in discretionary spending, and incur excessive debt as a result of this poor control and overconfidence. In this regard, numerous studies have demonstrated that the participation of women on corporate boards strengthens control mechanisms, helps resolve agency conflicts, and moderates risky decision-making. For instance, Mirza et al. (2020) have demonstrated that women are able to optimize resource allocation and reduce the risks of overinvestment by acting in their supervisory roles within the board. According to Jizi & Nehme (2017), women on boards can reduce company risk by lowering the volatility of stock returns. For his part, Zhou (2019), using a sample of 2,825 Chinese enterprises, showed that female managers might cut down on cash flow risk by a quarter. The author also stresses how having female directors will improve access to bank finance and lower the likelihood of insolvency.

Upper-echelons theory (Hambrick & Mason, 1984) suggests that strategic choices are determined and influenced by the values and cognitive bases of the dominant actors in the organization. Thus, preferences and decisions are likely to be predicted by the characteristics of the managerial context. Ntim and Soobaroyen (2013) assert that the psychological characteristics of administrators have an impact on their decisions. Women on boards, who are regarded as being risk-averse, would prefer less hazardous policies. From this perspective, Jeong and Harrison (2017) argue that differences in business performance can be explained by the reduction in strategic risk-taking adopted by women. Li and Zeng (2019) were able to highlight the importance of the female gender in the financial decision-making process and the prevention of stock market crashes. Likewise, Perryman et al. (2016) found that companies with greater gender diversity in management teams display lower market risk and perform better.

According to the human capital hypothesis (Becker, 1985), board diversity can have benefits for efficiency and control. The members of the board of directors with heterogeneous skills, preferences, and backgrounds constitute a precious, unique, inimitable, and difficult-to-transfer resource. This theory thus joins the theory of dependence on resources (Pfeffer & Salancik, 2003), suggesting that administrators bring advantages to the organization (information, networks, preferential resources, and legitimacy). According to Ferreira (2010), mixed boards could have access to more resources, "connections" and would have more legitimacy and "credibility". By mobilizing this theoretical perspective, De Cabo et al., (2012) observed that European banks, while recording low risk, had a higher proportion of women on their boards of directors. Saeed et al. (2016) found that gender diversity within boards is inversely related to firm risk in both emerging and developed countries. Farag and Mallin (2017) concluded that banks' vulnerability to crises is likely to be reduced by a critical mass of female representation. In contrast, Talavera et al. (2018) did not discover any correlation between female directors and firm risk. Yang et al. (2019) reported, on the other hand, a negative impact of female representation on business performance and firm risk.

Based on the theoretical and empirical literature reviewed above, the existence of a negative impact of the presence of women on boards of directors on the overall risk of the company can be assumed. Therefore, the following hypothesis is formulated:

H: The presence of women on boards of directors has a negative impact on a firm's overall risk.

Research Methodology

Sampling and Data Collection

To test the hypothesis formulated above, a sample of Tunisian companies belonging to the Tunindex index over the period 2016–2020 was selected. The Tunindex index includes the 66 most important companies in terms of market capitalization and trading volume on the Tunis Stock Exchange (BVMT). The ability to construct a sizable panel of data through this five-year investigation improved the results and supported the econometric analyses. Financial institutions were excluded from the sample due to the differences and specificities in their governance and accounting systems. The final panel was thus made up of 34 companies, i.e., 170 company-year observations. Data on the presence of women on boards of directors and on R&D expenditure were collected manually from reference documents and annual reports available on company websites. The other data were collected from the annual reports and official bulletins of the Tunisian Stock Exchange (BVMT) and the Financial Market Council (CMF).

Description of Variables

In financial theory, two components are used to measure business risk. On the one hand, market risk generally results from factors exogenous to the company, such as fluctuations in supply and demand, interest rates, and input costs in general. On the other hand, there is a specific risk inherent in the company's operations and in its management expertise. The overall risk of an investment is commonly measured by the standard deviation of its return (Jung et al., 2019; Cox, 2008; Boudreaux, 1973). A higher standard deviation value is assumed to reflect a higher risk. Referring to similar recent research (Firmansyah et al., 2020; Heflin et al., 2022; Nathaniel et al., 2019), the standard deviation of monthly stock returns over a period of one year was used as a measure of the overall firm risk (RISK). The measure retained for the firm's overall risk is provided by Formula 1.

$$\sigma R_{it} = \sqrt{\frac{\sum_{i=1}^{n}(R_{it} - \bar{R})^2}{n-1}} \qquad (1)$$

Where,

$\sigma Ri_{t=}$ Standard deviation of company's monthly stock return,

R_{it}= Company's average monthly stock return

$\overline{R}$ = Company's average monthly stock return over 12 months
n= Number of observations

Female presence on firm boards (**FPB**) was used to measure gender diversity. This proxy, which is being used more frequently by researchers with similar interests (Chebbia et al., 2020; Yu et al., 2017; Lenard et al., 2014), enables researchers to go beyond the limitations of binary measurements of the presence of women and the issue of representativeness within boards. Additionally, some control variables that could affect the relationship under study were introduced. The first control variable was the size of the board (**BSI**), measured by the number of directors, since a large board of directors is more likely to include women. Furthermore, previous literature suggests that the size of boards is a determining factor in their effectiveness and in corporate governance. Several studies have, in fact, reported the influence of the size of the board on the protection of the company's assets, the assurance of a better allocation of resources, the limitation of managerial opportunism, the prevention of risks such as insolvency and risky investments, and the mitigation of performance volatility. For instance, Bernile et al. (2018) discovered that larger boards frequently have lower return volatility. Likewise, Mathew et al. (2016), using both market and accounting metrics of risk, reported that small boards are linked to increased risk. Second, because they can have unpredictable results, R&D expenditures and innovation activities are considered indicators of risk-taking (Sila et al., 2016). R&D efforts have also been linked to the presence of women (Rossi & Cebula, 2015). Thus, R&D intensity (**RDI**), calculated as "R&D expenditure divided by total annual sales," was introduced into the model as a control variable. Third, since indebtedness is considered a solvency indicator directly linked to the financial risk of the company, we control the model by the level of indebtedness (**LDB**). According to Bodie et al. (2014), the level of indebtedness makes it possible to assess the risk of insolvency or bankruptcy and provides information on the company's ability to honor its financial commitments. Among others, Abobakr & Elgiziry (2016), for instance, found that the percentage of women sitting on the board was negatively and significantly correlated with the debt ratio. We measure debt by the "total debt/ total assets" ratio.

Firm size (**FSI**), measured by the natural logarithm of the total assets (in millions of dinars), was also considered in the research model as a control variable. In this regard, Bruna et al. (2019), for instance, have shown that risk aversion is adversely related to firm size. Finally, economic profitability (**EPR**), defined as the ratio of total assets to profit (profit before interest, taxes, and other expenses), was the model's last controlling variable. Profitability is likely to be positively correlated with risk-taking (Boubakri et al., 2013) and gender diversity, as reported by Đặng, et al. (2020). The variables and measurement indicators are described in depth in Table 1.

Model

A regression on panel data was carried out using the following model to test the research hypothesis (Model 1).

$$RISK_{it} = \beta_0 + \beta_1\, FPB_{it} + \beta_2\, BSI_{it} + \beta_3\, EPR_{it} + \beta_4\, FSI_{it} + \beta_5\, DEB_{it} + \beta_6\, RDI_{it} + \mu_i + e_{it} \quad (2)$$

In Model 1, the index t presents the year of the observation, while the index i refers to the company. The risk variable (**RISK**) is the dependent variable. FPB is the proportion of women on the board of directors. BSI, EPR, FSI, DEB, and RDI are control variables as defined above. The βj with j ϵ {0… 6) are the parameters of the model. μ is the fixed effect over time, and e is the idiosyncratic error term.

Table 1. Description of variables

Variable	Abbreviation	Measure	Authors
Overall firm risk	RISK	Standard deviation of monthly stock return	Asteriou & Bashmakova (2013); Perryman et al. (2016); Khan & Vieito (2013)
Female presence on board	FPB	Percentage of women on the board of directors	Cimini (2022); Chebbia et al. (2020)
Board size	BSI	Number of directors on the board.	Khaoula & Moez (2019); Lee & Thong (2022)
Firm profitability	EPR	Earnings before interest and taxes to total assets ratio	Faccio et al. (2020) Khatib & Nour (2021)
Firm size	FSI	Natural logarithm of total assets (in millions of dinars)	Skała & Weill (2018)
Indebtedness	DEB	Total debts / Total assets	Ye et al. (2019); Allioui et al. (2021)
R&D intensity	RDI	R&D expenses divided by annual sales	Chen et al. (2016)

RESULTS AND DISCUSSION

Descriptive Statistics

For all variables, descriptive statistics are included in Table 2. According to the statistics, the average stock return volatility over a period of five years is 41%, with a maximum and minimum of 4.422 and 0.075, respectively. Nevertheless, considering the diversity of the sample studied, it is reasonable to except that RISK exhibits a substantial dispersion with a high standard deviation. Regarding female presence on boards, the proportion of women is about 10.3% of the total number of directors. The average board size is about nine members, and the average return on assets is about 8.2%.

Table 2. Descriptive statistics

Variable	Obs.	Mean	Std	Max	Min
RISK	170	.410	2,025	4.422	.075
FPB	170	.103	.106	5	0
BSI	170	8.797	2.344	12	3
EPR	170	.082	.201	.678	.532
FSI	170	7.917	1.003	9.122	6.715
DEB	170	.412	.225	.806	.119
RDI	170	.030	.024	.090	.000

Multivariate Analyzes

Table 3 shows the correlations between all of the variables. At this stage, we notice that FPB has a negative and significant correlation with the measure of risk used. Without claiming to have reached a firm conclusion, this finding is a priori consistent with the hypothesis formulated and with the findings of other studies using the same measuring indicators (Jizi & Nehme, 2017; Chen & Tong, 2016). FPB also has a strong (p-value 0.0001) correlation with both economic profitability (0.0811) and board size (0.0165). There is a significant correlation between risk and board size in the sample. This finding is consistent with previous research (see, for example, Haider & Fang, 2016; Nakano & Nguyen, 2012). A positive correlation at the 1% confidence level is also reported between risk and return on assets, as well as a significantly positive association between risk and the debt ratio. Finally, and against expectations, there was no significant relationship between risk and the level of R&D investment.

Table 3. Correlations matrix

	1	2	3	4	5	6	7	VIF
1. RISK	1							
2.FPB	-.0760 *	1						1.18
3.BSI	- .0942 ***	.0165 **	1					1.06
4.EPR	.0199 **	.0811 ***	.049	1				1.87
5.FIS	-.015 ***	.0265	.029 **	.068	1			1.40
6.DEB	.0142 *	.0115	.068	.4315 ***	-.050	1		1.08
7.RDI	.0823	.1204 *	-.001	.134 **	-.0458 *	.0153	1	1.95
							M.VIF	1.42

The asterisks *, **, and *** indicate significance at 5%, 1% and, 0.01%, respectively.

Table 3 presents the correlations between all the variables in the study as well as the variance inflation factor (VIF) ranging from 1.06 to 1.95. The average value of the inflation factor is below the conventional value of 10, suggesting the absence of multicollinearity problems.

A regression on panel data was performed to test the hypothesis that the presence of women on the board of directors is negatively associated with the overall risk of the company. In addition, to ensure that the normality assumptions were satisfied, the Durbin-Watson autocorrelation test and the Breusch-Pagan test to check for heteroscedasticity issues were carried out. Finally, The Hausman test is considered in order to decide whether the method of model fixed effects or random effects is applicable. The following hypotheses were examined:

H_0: Consistent estimates of random effects
H_1: Consistent estimates of fixed effects

H_0 is rejected because the level of significance determined by this test is less than 5%. The statistical value of X2 (chi-square) is 7.2614, with a p-value of 0.0000, it is concluded that the fixed effects method produces better estimation.

Table 4. Results of the regression

Variable	Coefficient	t- stat
FPB	**-.0085** **	-2.45
BSI	-.0818 **	-2.66
EPR	.0365	.45
FSI	-.9017 **	-2.47
DEB	.0519 *	2 .46
RDI	.0061 ***	2.49
Intercept	1,970 **	2.36
observations	170	
R^2 (within)	19.82%	
R^2 adjusted	14.48%	
F-statistic	3.55 ***	

Table 4 presents the results of the estimation of model 1 (fixed effects) over the period 2016–2020. Overall firm risk (RISK) is the annualized standard deviation of monthly stock market returns. FPB is the percentage of women on the board. The symbols ***, **, and * indicate significance at the 1, 5, and 10% levels, respectively.

Table 4's findings indicate that the model's explanatory power ($R^2 = 0.1982$) is satisfactory. At the 1% level, Fisher's test has a statistically significant value. The presence of women on the board of directors reduces the firm's risk, as shown by the negative and statistically significant coefficient of the dependent variable (FPB) (Coef. -0.0085; t-stat -2.45). These results support the hypothesis. It also matches the main arguments presented in the theoretical review of the literature. Women are less "adventurous" than men and have an innate aversion to risk. This result joins those obtained in previous empirical research (Lenard et al., 2014; Cheng, 2008). These findings concur also with those of Othmani (2021), who, using a sample of 10 Tunisian banks spanning the years 2005–2018, was able to determine a negative correlation between the number of women on the boards of directors and the Z score used as a proxy for "insolvency" risk. They do not, however, support the findings of Bruna et al. (2019) and Sila et al. (2016), who found no evidence to support the premise that the presence of women on boards is associated with increased risk-taking. In the Tunisian context, these results are in disagreement with those of Loukil and Yousfi (2015), which showed no significant relationship between board gender diversity and the propensity to take strategic or financial risk on a sample of 30 Tunisian-listed firms over the period 1997–2010. One of the likely reasons is that the "false" negative correlation between the two variables would be caused by heterogeneous unobserved factors between firms, which could have an impact on both the board's composition and the firm's risk.

In addition to the impact of gender diversity, a negative correlation between the size of the board and the total risk of the company (at the 5% level) was also found. This supports the risk aversion hypothesis, which contends that large boards prefer to limit leverage since it raises the volatility of equity returns (Wang, 2012). A similar explanation for this is provided by the fact that large boards may result in lengthier decision-making procedures as a result of the need to find compromises, which in turn encourages less hazardous actions. This outcome is consistent with the findings of Nakano and Nguyen (2012), who found that large-board companies had less performance variability and a lower risk of bankruptcy. Another explanation could be found in the arguments put forward by Cheng (2008) and Wang (2012), suggesting that a high number of administrators would prevent boards from functioning properly, thus limiting performance volatility. The bureaucracy and vulnerability to agency issues that characterize large boards can lead to less performance volatility.

Moreover, the risk positively affects the return on assets, as shown by the positive coefficient of the EPR variable. However, this effect is not statistically significant. This finding runs counter to the risk-based logic put forward by Akbas et al. (2017), which argues that risk-taking is not necessarily associated with higher return expectations. Furthermore, a negative correlation was found between firm size and overall risk. This may be because large companies, which benefit from better governance and less information asymmetry, tend to control the volatility of stock returns (To et al., 2019). This negative relationship has also been highlighted by Damanpour (2010), who argues that larger firms have greater control over stock price fluctuations.

The coefficient of the "DEB" variable is positive and is statistically significant at the 10% confidence level. This result confirms the close link between the volatility of stock returns and the leverage effect, suggesting that the volatility of returns represents a risk hindering the ability of the company to finance itself with debt (Ahmed & Hla, 2019). Finally, R&D intensity expenditure presents a positive and significant coefficient, indicating the existence of an association between the volatility of stock market returns and the innovation effort. One of the explanations for this association could be found in the arguments put forward by Mazzucato and Tancioni (2013). The authors emphasized that financial markets are predicted to react to signals supplied by companies about their potential for future growth through R&D spending and innovative behavior.

CONCLUSION

This study sought to determine how gender diversity on corporate boards of directors affected total risk. It was possible to demonstrate the existence of a statistically significant negative relationship between the percentage of women on boards of directors and the volatility of their stock returns by using a regression on panel data pertaining to a sample of Tunisian companies listed on the Tunis Stock Exchange (BVMT) from 2016 to 2020. A lower variability in stock market return is correlated with a larger representation of women on the board. These findings imply that a more equitable representation of women might improve financial performance by reducing risk. This is in accordance with the theory of social identity, which stipulates that identity (of the female group in particular) could influence managerial behavior, particularly in terms of risk-taking. Our work adds to the body of literature that studies the effects of having women in decision-making positions. We offer more proof that gender-based disparities in corporate governance have significant effects on risk management and corporate performance.

Likewise, they support the arguments of the agency's theory, which states that women exercise greater control and participate actively in conflict resolution. The potential explanations for this negative effect would lie not only in the crucial role played by women on boards of directors to ensure better risk oversight, and a reduction in agency costs, but also in the risk aversion generally observed among women (Eckel & Grossman, 2008). The findings also corroborate the agency's hypothesis, which contends that women are more in charge of and actively engage in conflict resolution. In addition to the critical role played by women on boards of directors to ensure better risk oversight and a reduction in agency costs, the potential explanations for this detrimental effect would also include the risk aversion typically observed among women (Eckel & Grossman, 2008). The findings contribute to enriching the debate about this issue, especially given that they use data collected from an Arab-Muslim country where women's personal and social status is often seen differently from that of women in Western countries. These findings are from a nation where the development of governance structures is still in its early stages. However, they affirm that in nations where directorships continue to be controlled by men and where social culture, norms, and religion still hinder gender equality; the presence of women on these boards could improve these processes.

However, it must be noted that, even though our findings are in line with a body of literature that maintains that gender diversity and risk-taking are related (Faccio et al., 2016; Loukil & Yousfi, 2016; Perryman et al., 2016), they are at odds with those of other empirical studies (Bruna et al., 2019), which deny the existence of such a relationship. Thus, this should lead us to consider the role of contingent variables that could play a moderating and/or mediating role in this relationship, such as cultural differences, organizational visibility, or inter-industry differences. On the other hand, reverse causality is likely to exist and merits consideration, meaning that low-risk companies might intentionally choose more female directors (De Cabo et al., 2012). It would therefore be interesting to address endogeneity issues in future research. This research also has several limitations. First, by focusing our survey only on large companies, the results cannot be generalized. Extending the sample to small and medium-sized enterprises would make it possible to give more robustness to the results observed. The second limitation is linked to the overall risk measure, since stock market volatility may not capture all the risks incurred by the company. Finally, the impact of the presence of women may not be immediate: considering a lag effect (by introducing lagged variables in the econometric model) would probably be interesting because the appointment of women may take time to observe its impact.

REFERENCES

Abobakr, MG, & Elgiziry, K. (2016). The effect of board characteristics and ownership structure on the corporate financial leverage. *Accounting and Finance research, 5*(1), 1-14.

Adams, R. B., & Funk, P. (2012). Beyond the glass ceiling: Does gender matter? *Management Science*, *58*(2), 219–235. doi:10.1287/mnsc.1110.1452

Ahmed, Z., & Hla, D. T. (2019). Stock return volatility and capital structure measures of nonfinancial firms in a dynamic panel model: Evidence from Pakistan. *International Journal of Finance & Economics*, *24*(1), 604–628. doi:10.1002/ijfe.1682

Akbas, F., Jiang, C., & Koch, P. D. (2017). The trend in firm profitability and the cross-section of stock returns. *The Accounting Review*, *92*(5), 1–32. doi:10.2308/accr-51708

Allioui, A., Habba, B., & El Azizi, T. B. (2021). Women's Leadership and Pragmatism Incidences on Performance of Listed Family-Owned Firms in the Cultural Context of Arab Countries. *International Journal of Financial Research, 12*(3), 251. doi:10.5430/ijfr.v12n3p251

Asteriou, D., & Bashmakova, Y. (2013). Assessing the impact of oil returns on emerging stock markets: A panel data approach for ten Central and Eastern European Countries. *Energy Economics*, *38*, 204–211. doi:10.1016/j.eneco.2013.02.011

Becker, G. S. (1985). Human capital, effort, and the sexual division of labor. *Journal of Labor Economics*, *3*(1, Part 2), S33–S58. doi:10.1086/298075

Berger, A. N., Kick, T., & Schaeck, K. (2014). Executive board composition and bank risk taking. *Journal of Corporate Finance*, *28*, 48–65. doi:10.1016/j.jcorpfin.2013.11.006

Bernile, G., Bhagwat, V., & Yonker, S. (2018). Board diversity, firm risk, and corporate policies. *Journal of Financial Economics*, *127*(3), 588–612. doi:10.1016/j.jfineco.2017.12.009

Bodie, Z., Kane, A., & Miller, A. J. (2014). *Investment* (10th ed.). McGraw-Hill Education.

Boubakri, N., Cosset, J. C., & Saffar, W. (2013). The role of state and foreign owners in corporate risk-taking: Evidence from privatization. *Journal of Financial Economics*, *108*(3), 641–658. doi:10.1016/j.jfineco.2012.12.007

Boudreaux, K. J. (1973). 'Managerialism and Risk-Return Performance. *Southern Economic Journal*, *39*(3), 366–372. doi:10.2307/1056402

Bruna, M. G., Dang, R., Scotto, M. J., & Ammari, A. (2019). Does board gender diversity affect firm risk-taking? Evidence from the French stock market. *The Journal of Management and Governance*, *23*(4), 915–938. doi:10.100710997-019-09473-1

Chebbia, K., Aliedanb, M. M., & Mohammed, A. (2020). Women on the Board and Environmental Sustainability Reporting: Evidence from France. *International Journal of Innovation. Creativity and Change*, *14*(11), 231–258.

Chen, L. H., Gramlich, J., & Houser, K. A. (2019). The effects of board gender diversity on a firm's risk strategies. *Accounting and Finance*, *59*(2), 991–1031. doi:10.1111/acfi.12283

Chen, S., Ni, X., & Tong, J. Y. (2016). Gender diversity in the boardroom and risk management: A case of R&D investment. *Journal of Business Ethics*, *136*(3), 599–621. doi:10.100710551-014-2528-6

Cheng, S. (2008). Board size and the variability of corporate performance. *Journal of Financial Economics*, *87*(1), 157–176. doi:10.1016/j.jfineco.2006.10.006

Cimini, R. (2022). The effect of female presence on corporate boards of directors on the value relevance of accounting amounts: Empirical evidence from the European Union. *Journal of International Financial Management & Accounting*, *33*(1), 134–153. doi:10.1111/jifm.12138

Cox, L. A. Jr. (2008). Why risk is not variance: An expository note. *Risk Analysis: An International Journal*, *28*(4), 925–928. doi:10.1111/j.1539-6924.2008.01062.x PMID:18554271

Croson, R., & Gneezy, U. (2009). Gender differences in preferences. *Journal of Economic Literature*, *47*(2), 448–474. doi:10.1257/jel.47.2.448

Daily, C. M., & Dalton, D. R. (2003). Women in the boardroom: A business imperative. *The Journal of Business Strategy*, *24*(5), 8–10. doi:10.1108/jbs.2003.28824eaf.002

Damanpour, F. (2010). An integration of research findings of effects of firm size and market competition on product and process innovations. *British Journal of Management*, *21*(4), 996–1010. doi:10.1111/j.1467-8551.2009.00628.x

Đặng, R., Houanti, L. H., Reddy, K., & Simioni, M. (2020). Does board gender diversity influence firm profitability? A control function approach. *Economic Modelling*, *90*, 168–181. doi:10.1016/j.econmod.2020.05.009

De Cabo, R. M., Gimeno, R., & Nieto, M. J. (2012). Gender diversity on European banks' boards of directors. *Journal of Business Ethics*, *109*(2), 145–162. doi:10.100710551-011-1112-6

Eckel, C. C., & Grossman, P. J. (2008). Differences in the economic decisions of men and women: Experimental evidence. Handbook of experimental economics results, 1, 509-519.

Faccio, M., Marchica, M.-T., & Mura, R. (2016). CEO gender, corporate risk-taking, and the efficiency of capital allocation. *Journal of Corporate Finance*, *39*(August), 193–209. doi:10.1016/j.jcorpfin.2016.02.008

Farag, H., & Mallin, C. (2017). Board diversity and financial fragility: Evidence from Europeanbanks. *International Review of Financial Analysis*, *49*, 98–112. doi:10.1016/j.irfa.2016.12.002

Ferreira, D. (2010). Board diversity. Corporate governance: A synthesis of theory, research, and practice, *USA: John Wiley & Sons. Inc*, *225*, 241.

Firmansyah, A., Utami, W., Umar, H., & Mulyani, S. D. (2020). Do Derivative Instruments Increase Firm Risk for Indonesia Non-Financial Companies*?* *International Journal of Business. Economics and Management*, *7*(2), 81–95.

Fischer, E. M., Reuber, A. R., & Dyke, L. S. (1993). A theoretical overview and extension of research on sex, gender, and entrepreneurship. *Journal of Business Venturing*, *8*(2), 151–168. doi:10.1016/0883-9026(93)90017-Y

Haider, J., & Fang, H. X. (2016). Board size, ownership concentration and future firm risk. *Chinese Management Studies*, *10*(4), 692–709. doi:10.1108/CMS-05-2016-0094

Hambrick, D. C., & Mason, P. A. (1984). Upper echelons: The organization as a reflection of its top managers. *Academy of Management Review*, *9*(2), 193–206. doi:10.2307/258434

Heflin, F., Kolev, K. S., & Whipple, B. C. (2022). The risk-relevance of non-GAAP earnings. *Baruch College Zicklin School of Business Research Paper*, 01.

Hillman, A. J., & Dalziel, T. (2003). Boards of directors and firm performance: Integrating agency and resource dependence perspectives. *Academy of Management Review*, *28*(3), 383–396. doi:10.2307/30040728

Hillman, A. J., Shropshire, C., & Cannella, A. A. Jr. (2007). Organizational predictors of women on corporate boards. *Academy of Management Journal*, *50*(4), 941–952. doi:10.5465/amj.2007.26279222

Hinz, R. P., McCarthy, D. D., & Turner, J. A. (1996). *Are Women Conservative Investors? Gender Differences in Participant Directed Pension Investments*. Wharton School Pension Research Council, University of Pennsylvania.

Hoang, T. T., Nguyen, C. V., & Van Tran, H. T. (2019). Are female CEOs more risk averse than male counterparts? Evidence from Vietnam. *Economic Analysis and Policy*, *63*, 57–74. doi:10.1016/j.eap.2019.05.001

Hutchinson, M., Mack, J., & Plastow, K. (2015). Who selects the 'right' directors? An examination of the association between board selection, gender diversity and outcomes. *Accounting and Finance*, *55*(4), 1071–1103. doi:10.1111/acfi.12082

Ibrahim, N., Angelidis, J., & Tomic, I. M. (2009). Managers' attitudes toward codes of ethics: Are there gender differences? *Journal of Business Ethics*, *90*(3), 343–353. doi:10.100710551-010-0428-y

Jensen, M. C., & Meckling, W. H. (1976). Theory of the firm: Managerial behavior, agency costs and ownership structure. *Journal of Financial Economics*, *3*(4), 305–360. doi:10.1016/0304-405X(76)90026-X

Jeong, S. H., & Harrison, D. A. (2017). Glass breaking, strategy making, and value creating: Meta-analytic outcomes of women as CEOs and TMT members. *Academy of Management Journal*, *60*(4), 1219–1252. doi:10.5465/amj.2014.0716

Jizi, M. I., & Nehme, R. (2017). Board gender diversity and firms' equity risk. *Equality, Diversity and Inclusion*, *36*(7), 590–606. doi:10.1108/EDI-02-2017-0044

Jung, S., Repetti, T., Chatfield, H. K. G., Dalbor, M., & Chatfield, R. (2019). Internationalization and accounting-based risk in the restaurant industry. *Journal of Hospitality and Tourism Management*, *41*, 148–155. doi:10.1016/j.jhtm.2019.11.001

Khan, W. A., & Vieito, J. P. (2013). CEO gender and firm performance. *Journal of Economics and Business*, *67*, 55–66. doi:10.1016/j.jeconbus.2013.01.003

Khaoula, F., & Moez, D. (2019). The moderating effect of the board of directors on firm value and tax planning: Evidence from European listed firms. *Borsa Istanbul Review*, *19*(4), 331–343. doi:10.1016/j.bir.2019.07.005

Khatib, S. F., & Nour, A. N. I. (2021). The impact of corporate governance on firm performance during the COVID-19 pandemic: Evidence from Malaysia. *Journal of Asian Finance, Economics and Business, 8*(2), 0943-0952.

Knyazeva, A., Knyazeva, D., & Naveen, L. (2021). Diversity on Corporate Boards. *Annual Review of Financial Economics*, *13*(1), 301–320. doi:10.1146/annurev-financial-101520-065559

Lee, K. W., & Thong, T. Y. (2022). Board gender diversity, firm performance and corporate financial distress risk: international evidence from tourism industry. *Equality, Diversity and Inclusion: An International Journal*, (ahead-of-print).

Lenard, M. J., Yu, B., York, E. A., & Wu, S. (2014). Impact of board gender diversity on firm risk. *Managerial Finance*, *40*(8), 787–803. doi:10.1108/MF-06-2013-0164

Li, Y., & Zeng, Y. (2019). The impact of top executive gender on asset prices: Evidence from stock price crash risk. *Journal of Corporate Finance*, *58*, 528–550. doi:10.1016/j.jcorpfin.2019.07.005

Loukil, N., & Yousfi, O. (2016). Does gender diversity on corporate boards increase risk-taking? *Canadian Journal of Administrative Sciences*, *33*(1), 66–81. doi:10.1002/cjas.1326

Mathew, S., Ibrahim, S., & Archbold, S. (2016). Board attributes that increase firm risk-evidence from the UK. *Corporate Governance: The international journal of business in society, 16* (2), 233-258.

Mazzucato, M., & Tancioni, M. (2012). R&D, patents and stock return volatility. *Journal of Evolutionary Economics*, *22*(4), 811–832. doi:10.100700191-012-0289-x

Menicucci, E., & Paolucci, G. (2020). Does gender diversity matter for risk-taking? Evidence from Italian financial institutions. *African Journal of Business Management*, *14*(10), 324–334. doi:10.5897/AJBM2020.9089

Mirza, S. S., Majeed, M. A., & Ahsan, T. (2020). Board gender diversity, competitive pressure and investment efficiency in Chinese private firms. *Eurasian Business Review*, *10*(3), 417–440. doi:10.100740821-019-00138-5

Nadeem, M., Suleman, T., & Ahmed, A. (2019). Women on boards, firm risk and the profitability nexus: Does gender diversity moderate the risk and return relationship? *International Review of Economics & Finance*, *64*, 427–442. doi:10.1016/j.iref.2019.08.007

Nakano, M., & Nguyen, P. (2012). Board size and corporate risk taking: Further evidence from Japan. *Corporate Governance*, *20*(4), 369–387. doi:10.1111/j.1467-8683.2012.00924.x

Nathaniel, F., Ernawati, E., & Mahadwartha, P. A. (2019). The effect of board gender diversity on firm risk. *In 16th International Symposium on Management (INSYMA 2019)* (Vol. 308, pp. 44-47). Atlantis Press. 10.2991/insyma-19.2019.12

Ntim, C. G., & Soobaroyen, T. (2013). Corporate governance and performance in socially responsible corporations: New empirical insights from a Neo - Institutional framework. *Corporate Governance*, *21*(5), 468–494. doi:10.1111/corg.12026

Othmani, H. (2021). Does board gender diversity matter in the banking sector? Evidence from Tunisia. *African Development Review*, *33*(1), 14–24. doi:10.1111/1467-8268.12487

Perryman, A. A., Fernando, G. D., & Tripathy, A. (2016). Do gender differences persist? An examination of gender diversity on firm performance, risk, and executive compensation. *Journal of Business Research*, *69*(2), 579–586. doi:10.1016/j.jbusres.2015.05.013

Pfeffer, J., & Salancik, G. R. (2003). *The external control of organizations: A resource dependence perspective*. Stanford University Press.

Rossi, F., & Cebula, R. J. (2015). Does the board of directors affect the extent of corporate R&D? Evidence from Italian listed companies. *Economic Bulletin*, *35*(4), 2567–2580.

Saeed, A., Belghitar, Y., & Yousaf, A. (2016). Firm-level determinants of gender diversity in the boardrooms: Evidence from some emerging markets. *International Business Review*, *25*(5), 1076–1088. doi:10.1016/j.ibusrev.2016.01.002

Seebeck, A., & Vetter, J. (2021). Not Just a Gender Numbers Game: How Board Gender Diversity Affects Corporate Risk Disclosure. *Journal of Business Ethics*, *177*(2), 395–420. doi:10.100710551-020-04690-3

Shropshire, C., Peterson, S., Bartels, A. L., Amanatullah, E. T., & Lee, P. M. (2021). Are Female CEOs Really More Risk Averse? Examining Economic Downturn and Other-Orientation. *Journal of Leadership & Organizational Studies*, *28*(2), 185–206. doi:10.1177/1548051821997404

Sila, V., Gonzalez, A., & Hagendorff, J. (2016). Women on board: Does boardroom gender diversity affect firm risk? *Journal of Corporate Finance*, *36*, 26–53. doi:10.1016/j.jcorpfin.2015.10.003

Skała, D., & Weill, L. (2018). Does CEO gender matter for bank risk? *Economic Systems*, *42*(1), 64–74. doi:10.1016/j.ecosys.2017.08.005

Tajfel, H. (1974). Social identity and intergroup behaviour. *Social Sciences Information. Information Sur les Sciences Sociales*, *13*(2), 65–93. doi:10.1177/053901847401300204

Talavera, O., Yin, S., & Zhang, M. (2018). Age diversity, directors' personal values, and bank performance. *International Review of Financial Analysis*, *55*, 60–79. doi:10.1016/j.irfa.2017.10.007

To, A. T., Suzuki, Y., Vuong, B. N., Tran, Q. T., & Do, K. (2019). Foreign Ownership and Stock Return Volatility in Vietnam: The Destabilizing Role of Firm Size. *Organizations and Markets in Emerging Economies*, *10*(2), 356–377. doi:10.15388/omee.2019.10.18

Wang, C. J. (2012). Board size and firm risk-taking. *Review of Quantitative Finance and Accounting*, *38*(4), 519–542. doi:10.100711156-011-0241-4

Watson, J., & Robinson, S. (2003). Adjusting for risk in comparing the performances of male-and female-controlled SMEs. *Journal of Business Venturing*, *18*(6), 773–788. doi:10.1016/S0883-9026(02)00128-3

Xia, H., Tan, Q., & Bai, J. (2018). Corruption and technological innovation in private small-medium scale companies: Does female top management play a role? *Sustainability*, *10*(7), 2252. doi:10.3390u10072252

Yang, P., Riepe, J., Moser, K., Pull, K., & Terjesen, S. (2019). Women directors, firm performance, and firm risk: A causal perspective. *The Leadership Quarterly*, *30*(5), 101297. doi:10.1016/j.leaqua.2019.05.004

Ye, D., Deng, J., Liu, Y., Szewczyk, S. H., & Chen, X. (2019). Does board gender diversity increase dividend payouts? Analysis of global evidence. *Journal of Corporate Finance*, *58*, 1–26. doi:10.1016/j.jcorpfin.2019.04.002

Yu, B., Lenard, M. J., York, E. A., & Wu, S. (2017). Female leadership in banking and bank risk. *Academy of Accounting and Financial Studies Journal*, *21*(3), 1–19.

Zhou, G. (2019). Financial distress prevention in China: Does gender of board of directors matter? *Journal of Applied Finance and Banking*, *9*(6), 127–153.

ENDNOTE

1 BoardEx. (2021). *Global gender diversity analysis women on boards*. BoardEx.

Chapter 7
Assessment of Gender Diversity on Banking Performance in Nepal:
Evidence From Binary Logit Estimation

Sushma Adhikari
Quest International College, Pokhara University, Nepal

Udaya Raj Paudel
Quest International College, Pokhara University, Nepal

Niranjan Devkota
Kathmandu Model College, Tribhuvan University, Kathmandu, Nepal

Krishna Dhakal
Quest International College, Pokhara University, Nepal

Devid Kumar Basyal
Quest International College, Pokhara University, Nepal

Ranjana Koirala
KIST Medical College and Teaching Hospital, Tribhuvan University, Lalitpur, Canada

Sahadeb Upretee
Central Washington University, USA

Seeprata Parajuli
Mahalaxmi Bikas Bank Limited, Kathmandu, Nepal

ABSTRACT

This chapter aims to assess the role of gender diversity on banking performance in Kathmandu Valley. The study adopted descriptive approach. Respondents were sampled from employees of a commercial banks in Kathmandu Valley. Simple random sampling techniques was used to select 300 employees. The questionnaire was used for data collection. Descriptive statistics, correlation, regression, pre-estimation, post-estimation techniques within binary logistic model were used for

DOI: 10.4018/978-1-6684-5981-2.ch007

data analysis. The study found that gender diversity has positive significant influence on enhancing banking performance. Gender diverse teams could help organization enhance creativity in its practice and increase its performance level. This study concluded that gender diversity has been one of the important issues in the world, and enhancing it could result higher productivity and higher performance of an organization. Hence, the chapter recommends that there should be inclusive climate in the workplace and policies supporting work-life balance should be forwarded.

1. INTRODUCTION

The connection between gender diversity and firm performance has been the subject of exploration for over three decades now (Joshi, 2017). Gender diversity achieves more broad perspectives, various types of information and contemplations inside an affiliation and results in unparalleled basic reasoning and essential initiative (Richard, Kirby, & Chadwick, 2013). With respect to encouraging gender diversity as a feature of their working environment procedure, private area firms are regularly left to depend on past experiences, speculations and recounted assertions (Joshi, 2017). Worldwide, women have less entryway for monetary investment than men, less admittance to key and high-level training, more vital prosperity and dangers, and less political portrayal (Estes and Hosseini, 1988). Women's don't take an interest in the worldwide economy similarly as men do (Kochhar & Jain-chandra, 2017). As per McKinsey overall foundation also gauges that a situation where women achieved total gender equality with men could yield worldwide by more than one-quarter comparative with a the same old situation (Joshi, 2017). Exploration on gender and business morals recommends that women's are more moral than men in attitudes and practices (Putnam, 1979; Althalathini, 2022). Associations in which number of female heads are more in number, perform better regarding corporate administration and monetary execution (Omri & Boukattaya, 2018).

Gender diversity is seen as abusing reasonable remarkable credits just as capacities among male and female which could be of acceptable upper hand to the firm (Hassan, 2018). Moreover pioneers of gender diversity, proposes that gender diverse firms will in general acquire the bit of leeway (Ahmad et. al., 2021), for example, lessening cost through lower speeds of turnover and non-appearance when contrasted with firm with less gender diverse teams. The public authority should establish an amiable climate for making a strong work market for women's and they should be advanced through a few data campaigns (ILO, 2005). Next could be encouraging an atmosphere of consideration in the working environment for which firm ought to have formal projects and quantifiable targets and actualize viable variety the board strategies (US Department of Commerce, 2000). Moreover extending the proof base on gender diversity across all hierarchical levels could be other arrangement where firms should screen and assess measurements to keep tabs on women development from section to administration, just as information identifying with the status of women representatives in a few positions relating to variety the board and incorporation, is to be gathered in an occasional premise and made accessible for straightforward analyses (Noland, Moran, & Kotschwar, 2016).

Thus, gender diversity is a source of intangible and socially complex resources that helps a firm to gain sustained competitive advantage in the market (Sabir et al., 2019; Wijekoon, 2021). Such intangible and socially complex resources as obtained from gender diversity are market insight, creativity and innovation, and improved problem-solving that employees will be equipped with (Ali, Kulik, & Metz, 2009). Furthermore, a gender-diverse team can surely produce high quality decisions because male and female bring different ideas and perspectives leading to varied alternatives (Salas, 1995; Wu et. al., 2022). The negative effects of diversity might also continue to unfavorably influence workers even intensify. The increment minority representation (e.g. women) may be seen as a power threat by the majority (e.g. men). Thus, increased competition and struggle would strengthen in-group out-group dynamics further bringing the performance down (Ali, Kulik, & Metz, 2009). Gender diversity has been a center of research among many researcher as it's a burning issue prevailing in any nation that could impact a firm's performance in both positive and negative manner (Nakagawa, 2015). Despite having several social organizations to protect and ensure gender equality among the nations, still we can find women in the world are back in social, economic and political spheres (Baral, 2017; Sabir et al., 2019).

As per the several studies conducted, various gender diversity related issues and findings has been appeared to existence. Likewise, gender diversity offers ascend to relational clash. Gender, similar to age and race, is an impermeable attribute and hard to change. Contrasts in impermeable attributes for the most part lead to more grounded in-gathering/out-bunch inclinations advancing sentiments of hatred, outrage, and disappointment and eventually relational clash (Mellahi & Johnson, 2000). Women don't approach administration. Women's are regularly prohibited from managerial places of power and initiative because of generalizations, which have been built by watching 'non-managerial' populations at large (Estes & Hosseini, 1988). As we have been already aware with the fact that women still are so backward in the sectors of development as compared to men (European Commission, 2018). Though there has been some improvements regarding the participation of women in several affairs of developmental sector, still it's not up to the mark (Alghamdi et. al., 2022). So for this, women at the very first needs to be empowered through several means, they should be well recognized by the nation and should be given equal rights and opportunities as men. Companies in order to help ensure equality among male and female, should promote company as a diversity friendly and acknowledge the benefits both male and female could together contribute so as to improve firm's performance (International Finance Corporation, 2016).

Looking towards the Nepalese context, status of the women is not encouraging especially in rural areas (Paper, 1999). Rural areas are still backward in the gender issue where people don't simply want to agree with the modern thought of creating gender equality and equity particularly for the freedom of the women in every spheres of their life equally as male members (Bhadra & Shah, 2007; Navumau, 2021). Despite Nepalese women participation in service sectors, still in some areas they are suffering from double discrimination of social backwardness as well as gender inequality (Asian Development Bank, 2016). Out of total working-age women, only 8.5 million are in labor force (Perez-Arce, 2021) who are either employed or are in search of employment, and only 2.6 million from the total women labor force are employed, according to the report (CBS, 2009). This shows only 22.5 percent of working age women are employed in Nepal according to the National Labor Force Survey 2017-18. Therefore the role of women in the local developmental contexts, in several areas of country is particularly down and out in light of the fact that the word gender isn't seen fittingly in our general public (Baral, 2017).

Regarding banking sector, it is one of the leading organizations in terms of employment opportunities and female participation in Nepal (Bhandari et al., 2021; Devkota et al., 2021). Plathora of research have been conducted to identify several aspects of banking performance in the past days (Rai et al., 2019; Tandukar et al., 2020; Parajuli et al., 2020; Shrestha et al., 2020; Shrestha et al., 2021; Paudel et al., 2021; Paudel et al., 2022; Devkota et al 2022a; Devkota et al., 2022b). Among them, only few researches have been discussing gender related issues such as Nepal & Lertjanyakit (2019), Devkota et al. (2022a). However, the gender issues are not well covered in both the studies. Thus, this study tries to gain insight regarding gender diversity on banking performance in Kathmandu valley exploring what role gender diversity has on banking performance, present status of gender diversity on banking performance in valley, factors that led to affect gender diversity on banking performance in Kathmandu valley.

Second section of this study includes literature review, followed by methods used in third section. Fourth section discusses results and finally fifth section concludes the study.

2. LITERATURE REVIEW

Among economically active population, 56.63% are male and 43.37% are female (Ongena, 2003). Compared to female, male working population is at a highest number in banking sector. Banking sector is however influenced by gender discrimination. In banking sector, there are no female officers at a higher position (Alhalwachi, 2021). Women's participation is found to be much lower than that of men and it's because of their lower educational attainments and slow rise in literacy rate. Women's position is very much undermined in both education and employment because every decision making positions are being controlled and also dominated by male (Pant, 2016). However, today's business stated that they focus on diverse workforce as they possess varied skills and competencies as they are the source of creativity and innovation. However the basic leadership attributes of males and females in a 'non-administrative' population in which most of people have not experienced formal management education are stood out from an 'managerial' population of potential and real managers who have embraced such education (Triana et. al., 2021; Johnson & Powell, 1994).

Gender diversity can be a positive resource for organizations, taking into consideration the utilization of progressively assorted information and human ranges of abilities (Won et. al., 2021; Bénavidès et al., 1984; Johnson & Powell, 1994). Numerous investigations have shown that there are striking contrasts between the male and female work force, some have in the opposite demonstrated that there are no differences in their efficiency. Feminine gender is progressively turning into the "motor of financial development". When contrasted with men, women in the western nations have a superior possibility of succeeding and exceeding expectations in organizations because of their better execution (Egbuwe & Nwinee, 2019). On an expert level, women supervisors who have arrived at top administration positions can execute the same number of men administrators as far as the usage of clear and feasible destinations (Westcott, 2021). Females surpassed males in scores on giving data, advancing glad relations, being responsive to thoughts, empowering exertion, appearing - concern, and being mindful. Males outperformed females on scores of predominance, coordinating discussions, and hostility (Alpha & Vincent, 2011). The latest data show that only 560 out of 2500 employees are female in Nepal bank limited. Similarly, 190 out of 1373 in Nepal Rastra Bank, 506 out of 2019 in Rastriya Banijaya Bank, 60 out of 256 in Everest Bank, 21 out of 100 in Lumbini Bank are female employees (Tulaadhar, 2018). The Banking and monetary associations have extended in various portions of Nepal and number of taught females are expanding significantly. In spite of having increment number of females on the banking and financial organization, the number is more yet negligible than male. So it is important to direct an exploration to learn about the status of female workers on banking and financial sector of Nepal (Paper, 1999). Moreover, National Labor Force Survey 2017-18 declared that only few odds of working-age women in Nepal are employed. Despite Nepalese women's engagement in service sectors, they nevertheless face double discrimination in some places due to social backwardness and gender inequality. Rural regions are still behind the times when it comes to gender issues, with individuals unable to accept the modern concept of gender equality and parity (Asian Development Bank, 2016; CBS, 2009).

Both male and female officially instructed administrators can contribute similarly to the authoritative choice procedure (Mugaddam, 2021). Future research ought to react all the more completely to difficulties that measures customarily utilized in gender look into reflect male-determined measures. More noteworthy consideration ought to be given to the improvement of measures that suitably speak to the two circles of gender (Carter, Williams, & Reynolds, 1997; Johnson & Powell, 1994). Planned change approach ought to be utilized to systematically oversee diversity, by creating and executing and planned change-corporate decent variety technique (Beniflah & Veloz, 2021). Organizations ought to execute their social reengineering endeavors to move people and the hierarchical culture along the diversity continuum from the conditions of recognizing and esteeming diversity to the ideal condition of overseeing diversity (Nasir & Morgan, 2017). Furthermore, this examination ought to be stretched out to incorporate other visible aspects of cultural diversity, for example, race and age. At long last, diversity was analyzed distinctly at the management group level. Future research should address this issue in regards to surveying diversity independently into three levels of management. Comparative center ought to be set at firm wide and industry levels of examination (Dwyer et al., 2003).

Status of Gender Diversity in Banks of Nepal

As indicated by the Census 2001, women include 50.05% percent of the aggregate population of Nepal. In any case, women in Nepal are most certainly not homogeneous (Adhikari et al., 2004). Due to environmental and socio-cultural diversity, intersectionalities influence the imperatives and chances of women as far as the nature, class, caste/ ethnicity and the development region (Sengupta & Harris, 2022). The male centric nature of the Nepalese society is a solid factor propagating gender uniqueness in the general public including instruction, destitution and absence of dynamic interest in basic leadership and approach making. These elements are straightforwardly or in a roundabout way interrelated with monetary variables. Poverty, gender disparity, customary conviction, absence of mindfulness and support in basic leadership are solid disadvantages of women for the contribution in economic activities (Baral, 2017).

The banking and financial organization have extended in the various pieces of Nepal and the quantity of instructed females is expanding significantly. In spite of this the association of female workers and their status is pitiable in these associations(Law, 2017). So it is obligatory to direct an exploration to learn about the status of female workers of banking and financial sector of Nepal. There is a segregation made in work task for male and female representatives, female worker are not engaged with the basic leadership process. Likewise they are not taking part in various exercises effectively. Simultaneously social issue, gender biases, monetary issue are additionally some serious issues identified with female representative (Banihani et al., 2013).

Eventual fate of country relies on its financial improvement. Bank and financial organizations assume an imperative job in the financial advancement of each nation. Foundation, extension and improvement of banks and financial organization are a challenge for each country (Barston, 2019). On other hand, the cooperation of female workers in these associations is negligible, regardless of whether it is the approach making procedures of banks and financial organizations or in their operating.

3. RESEARCH METHODOLOGY

Theoretical and Conceptual Debate

In today's scenario there is a demand for a diverse people that may be in terms of gender, race, ethnicity etc. Male and female together could help organization gain a better way for its development because they possess different traits and attributes and thus they need to be equal politically, economically and socially (Hillman & Radel, 2021). For this study, several scholars have attempted to link their opinion. The very first theory is Theory of Representative Bureaucracy holds that ''aloof portrayal", or how much an organization utilizes people of varying measurement establishments, will prompt dynamic portrayal, or the mission for approaches reflecting the interests and needs of those individuals (Bradbury & Kellough, 2008). Likewise, the consequent theory is Feminist theory that has dependably been associated with review the social world to such an extent that lights up the powers that make and bolster lopsidedness, abuse, and wretchedness, and in doing everything considered, impels the voyage for correspondence and worth. Feminism is a theory that male and female should be proportionate strategically, fiscally and socially (Gram et. al., 2021). Moreover, symbolic interaction theory handles that people make their social reality by means of day by day connections, in this way; they consider gender to be a segment of individual execution. Gender assumes a job so as to shape all relationship of individuals in everyday life (Aksan, Kisac, Aydin, & Demirbuken, 2009). Next comes Contingency theory which prescribe that gender diversity impacts at the organization level is reliant upon, that is, facilitated by, the alliance's irreplaceable bearing, the different leveled culture where it stays, and furthermore the multivariate correspondence among two or three factor (Dwyer et al., 2003). Petrocelli et al. (2003) presents a conflict theory that says, a society is a battle for power among social gatherings (like women versus men) that go after exceptional assets and it is difficult for female to transcend male, as transcendent gain the standards for ground and opportunity in the all-inclusive community eyes.

The study assumes that its essence to understand the factors influencing gender diversity on banking performances. Gender diversity goes about as a driver of innovations at firm level. Innovation that reveals new ways to development will just spring from high-performing, sexual orientation various groups that boost the intensity of various sentiments, viewpoints and social references. Gender diversity cultivates inventiveness and produces increasingly proficient arrangements (Teruel & Agustí, 2017). Likewise, gender diversity in a business cultivates imagination by giving required aptitudes, information in the activity of business and remembering both male and female for the undertakings of business guarantees uniformity by and by and prompts progressively skillful business. Both men and women of a different race, culture and age should be given equal open entryways for their improvement (Nwokolo et. al., 2022). There is an unquestionable necessity to have a gender diversity in any business to make a productive business (David & Ely, 2005). The essential persuasion that unfurls the "diversity – performance" connection sways between the point of view of social order (perceivable properties, for example, age, sex and racioethnicity) versus enlightening/practical diversity (character, information, values) points of view (Van Knippenberg & Sitkin, 2013). Whereas the last point of view stresses diversity of surface (age, sex, ethnicity) and practical (residency, instructive foundation, aptitude) characteristics expands execution, the previous social order point of view fights that diversity builds the expense of gathering the executives because of the insider/outside elements of social gatherings (Tajfel, 1978). Put gruffly, different groups may hamper execution due to expanded expenses of coordination and arrangement between profoundly various individuals, while heterogeneous groups beat their increasingly homogeneous counterparts because of the more fluctuated assets and better-quality basic leadership accessible (Van Knippenberg & Sitkin, 2013).

Gender diversity leads to short term and long term consequences (Yarram & Adapa, 2021). The short term consequences are classified as effective, cognitive and symbolic. Effective includes factors like, role conflict, role ambiguity and perceived discrimination, whereas cognitive includes factors such as, innovation, number and quality of ideas and range of perspective. Similarly symbolic includes, behavior of low level employees. The long term consequences are classified as Individual, group and organizational. The factors on an individual level includes abseenteism, turnover and performance whereas in a group level, the factors are turnover and performance (Labre & Lauzier, 2021). Similary in an organizational level, the factors includes performance and strategic changes. Here, the dependent variable is banking performance and independent variable is gender diversity which consists of several factors under it such as age, marital status, education, training and development, workplace, competencies and so on. These all factors have a great impact on banking performance that will either positively or negatively impact its overall operational performances. These days diversity isn't just a human issue yet has become a hierarchical issue both inside and outside organization. Those organizations who have figured out how to oversee gender diversity have received rewards from it as far as maintenance of gifted workforce, improved gathering execution, better reaction to changing commercial center and diminish turnover cost (Barbosa & Cabral-Cardoso, 2010). Additionally, female on the top brings educational and social advantages, enhances conduct showed by supervisors and inspires women in the center administration (Dezso & Ross, 2012).

Empirical Framework

For empirical analysis of the study, binary logistic model was selected to identify the significant variables that determine the role of gender diversity and banking performances. The model is given as Pr(Y = C/Xi) = F (Xiβ). Where, Y is the response generated as outcome for attitude level of community that is coded as 0 = less aware, 1= Moderate aware and 2 = High aware; F is the standard logistic cumulative function; X is the set of independent variables.

$$PYi > j = \frac{\exp\left(x_i\beta - k_j\right)}{1+[\exp\left(x_i\beta - k_j\right)}$$,, j = 1, 2… M-1, which implies

$$P\left(Y_i = 1\right) = 1 - \frac{\exp\left(x_i\beta - k_j\right)}{1+\left[\exp\left(x_i\beta - k_j\right)\right]}$$

$$P\left(Y_i = j\right) = \frac{\exp\left(x_i\beta - k_{j-1}\right)}{1+\left[\exp\left(x_i\beta - k_{j-1}\right)\right]} - \frac{\exp\left(x_i\beta - k_j\right)}{1+\left[\exp\left(x_i\beta - k_j\right)\right]},$$ j = 2 , … . . M - 1,implying

$$P\left(Y_i = M\right) = \frac{\exp\left(x_i\beta - k_{m-1}\right)}{1+\left[\exp\left(x_i\beta - k_{m-1}\right)\right]}$$

In the case of M=2, these equations simplify to

$$P(Y=O)=\frac{1}{1+\left[\exp\left(Z_i-k_i\right)\right]}$$

$$P(Y=1)=\frac{1}{1+\left[\exp\left(Z_i-k_2\right)\right]}-\frac{1}{1+\left[\exp\left(Z_i-k_1\right)\right]}$$

Hence, Williams (2016) stated that utilizing the estimation of Z and the assumed logistic distribution of the aggravation term, the ordered logit model can be utilized to assess the likelihood that the unobserved variable Y* falls inside the different edge limits. The empirical specification can be seen as below:

$$Y=\alpha+\beta 1X1+\beta 2X2+\beta 3X3+\beta 4X4+\beta 5X5+\beta 6X6+\beta 7X7+\beta 8X8+\beta 9X9+e$$

Where Y = dependent variable, X_1-X_9 = independent variables and e refers error term.

The performance measurement used in this study are age, marital status, training and development, education, workplace, motivation of employees, satisfaction level of employees, competency level and it is believed to give positive relationship with gender diversity as depicted in table 1.

Table 1. Variables and expected sign of variables

Variable	Description	Value	Expected sign
Dependent Variable			
Banking performance		1=yes 0= otherwise	
Independent Variable			
Age	Age of respondent	in years	±
Sex	Sex of the respondents	1= Male, 0 = Otherwise	±
Marital_ status	Marital status of respondent	1= Married 0= otherwise	±
Training _and_ development	Training and development program received by respondent	1= yes 0= otherwise	+
Work_ experience	Total employee experience year	In category	+
Motivation	Motivation level of respondent	1= yes 0= otherwise	+
Satisfaction	Satisfaction level of respondent	1= yes 0= otherwise	+

Variables Definition and Hypotheses Formulation

This study consist dependent and independent variables. Banking performance is the dependent variable whereas age, sex, marital_status, training_and_development, work_experience, motivation and satisfaction are the independent variables. The variables are explained below:

Age: According to Al-Baidhani (2015), age group does affect the performance of the banking industry. From his research the majority age group affecting the banking performance was 25-35 then the other age group. That means a predominant number of respondents are youngsters.

H_{01}: Age has no significant relationship with banking performance.

Marital status: Jailaxmi and Gautam (2017), used this variable so as to know the impact of marital status on the banking performance and concluded that female who are married are not able to work more properly as they had to balance both personal and professional life.

H_{02}: Marital status has no significant relationship with banking performance.

Training and development: Sharma and Taneja (2018), states that training programs is one of the factor that can offered the targeted potential employees so that they can work with greater efficiency and effectiveness.

H_{03}: Training and development has no significant relationship with banking performance.

Work experience: Malik et al. (2022) argues that experienced employees have better knowledge on the several areas due to their work exposure which impacts their overall understanding of their work and leads to improved operation. So, the period of working experience does affect the performance of an organization to a great extent.

H_{04}: Work experience has no significant relationship with banking performance.

Education: According to Cooke et al. (2019) there is strong relationship between the education that an employee does possess and the overall performance of banking industry. Higher the level of education, higher will be the skills, knowledge and abilities to make an organization successful.

$\mathbf{H_{05}}$: Education has no significant relationship with banking performance.

Workplace environment: According to Nanzushi (2015), in case of improper workplace for employees to work, that will affect their performance in a negative manner. Similarly, if there is positive workplace to work in for employees, they will give their best efforts and performance so as to deliver best result for an organization therefore, leading an organization towards a high performer organization.

$\mathbf{H_{06}}$: Workplace has no significant relationship with banking performance.

Motivation: According to Bao & Nizam (2015), there is a positive and significant relationship between motivation and with performance of employees and ultimately with the organizational performance. Thus, motivation is a key that can be used that can extract best results out of the employee.

$\mathbf{H_{07}}$: Motivation has no significant relationship with banking performance.

Satisfaction: Inuwa (2016) argues that, dissatisfaction is believed to be one of the major factors that will certainly de motivate and demoralize employee in the working area which can result to lower productivity and therefore leading to lower the organization performance as a whole. So, it is essence that employees are well satisfied and are willing to work for an organization so that it contributes to higher productivity and desired performance.

$\mathbf{H_{08}}$: Satisfaction has no significant relationship with banking performance.

Competencies: Hawi et al. (2015) believed that there is positive relationship among competencies including skills, knowledge's and abilities of employees and the overall performance of an industry. Higher the degree of competency, higher will be the organizational performance.

$\mathbf{H_{09}}$: Competencies has no significant relationship with banking performance.

Access to resources: According to Truyens et al. (2016), there is positive and significant relationship among employees gaining access to necessary resources and their performance at work that will ultimately affect organization performance in a positive manner.

$\mathbf{H_{10}}$: Access to resources has no significant relationship with banking performance.

Study Area

Kathmandu valley of Nepal is chosen for the study area. Nepal has 77 districts, and from the 77 district, 3 districts include in Kathmandu valley (Kathmandu, Bhaktapur and Lalitpur) situated in province 3 were taken for the study area of this research (Kutu et al., 2023). The geographic coordinates of Kathmandu valley are: latitudes 27°32"13" and 27°49"10" north and longitudes 85°11"31" and 85°31"38" E (Paudel et al, 2020; Tandukar et al., 2020). The total population of Kathmandu is 1,442,271which has the largest population than another district. This study was emerging issue of most of the banking sector of Nepal because there are both males and females working in a particular organization which would surely impact the banking performance to a great extent. There are many financial institutions but we select only 27 commercial banks of Nepal. The Kathmandu valley was suitable area for research because it has a largest population of Nepal.

Figure 1. Study area

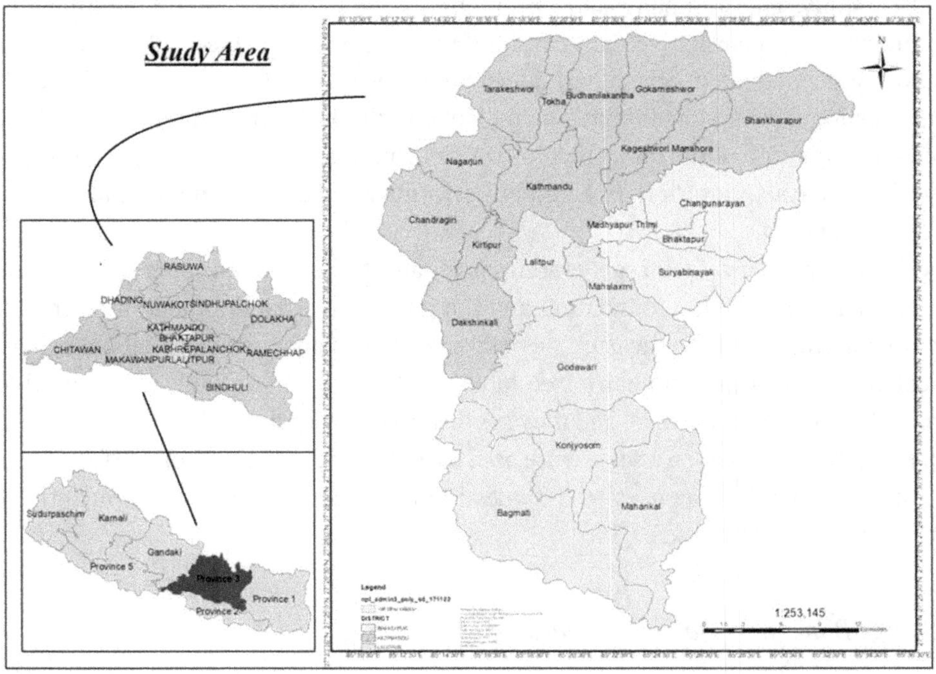

Study Population and Sample Size Determination

As highlighted before the study was conducted in Kathmandu valley of Nepal. The target populations were banking employees who are responsible for the overall performance of bank. A probability sampling was used for the survey and within that simple random sampling was used to collect data. The sampling unit in the study was the bank's employees. To work out the sample size $n_0= z^2 pq/e^2$ (Micky Olutende, Wisiuba Bukhala, & Wesonga, 2018) has been used.

Where, N_0= sample size required for study, Standard tabulated for level of significance (z) = 1.96, p= prevalence or proportion of an event%= 0.50 (More et. al, 2012). So, P= 0.5 and q= 1-p, = 0.5. Allowable error that can be tolerated (e) = 6%. So, total population for the study = (1.96)2 ×0.5×0.5/ $(0.06)^2$ = 266.78, Non-response error 6%, i.e. 266.78*6/100 = 16.00. Thus, sample size taken for study was (266.78+16.00) = 282.78(≈283).

Research Instrument

In this study, Questionnaire and observation were used as research instruments. In order to get quantitative data from individual customers, the banks customers' survey was conducted. Structured questionnaire was used for this study. However, the questionnaire was maintained using Kobo toolbox. After the preparation of the questionnaire, 5% of the total sample size determination was taken as pre- test. For the data analysis, descriptive, banking performance index and inferential method were carried out.

As the primary factor generating profitability from their operations, bank performance is also the foundation and the goal of any banking activity (Ammar & Boughrara, 2019). To measure the banking performance index, researchers have created the set of questionnaire (see table 4). A variety of variables were used to gauge banking performance, and they are discussed accordingly. Then, two of these three aspects are rated on a scale from poor to high, depending on their performance. Each respondent's responses to the question are first computed independently in order to create the index.

Table 2. Banking performance index

Range	Decision
75%-100%	Highly Performance
50%-75%	Moderately Performance
Less than 50%	Low Performance

Source: Field Survey

Result

Socio- Demographic Analysis

300 respondents were interviewed in each of the three districts; Kathmandu, Lalitpur and Bhaktapur. There were altogether 49.50 percent male and 50.50 percent female respondents which indicates that there are equal number of male and female employees in banks of Kathmandu valley which can be said as there is gender equality in terms of hiring employees in banks. Most (65.67%) of the respondents hold masters' degree among which 38.67% are male and 27% are female. It indicates that majority of the respondents are well educated. Similarly, majority of respondents belongs to age group below 30 i.e. 64.78% and majority (37%) of the employers of the banks holds work experience of more than 3 years.

Banking Performance Index Based on Gender

Banking performance index is presented in this section which shows performance of an organization. While analyzing performance of banking organization it was revealed out of total respondents, 11.67 percent were fewer performing employees, 85 percent were moderately performing and only 3.33 percent were high performing employees. Figure 2 shows the performance of organization based on sex. This indicates that majority of the respondents are moderately performing in the organization.

Figure 2. Performance of organization based on sex

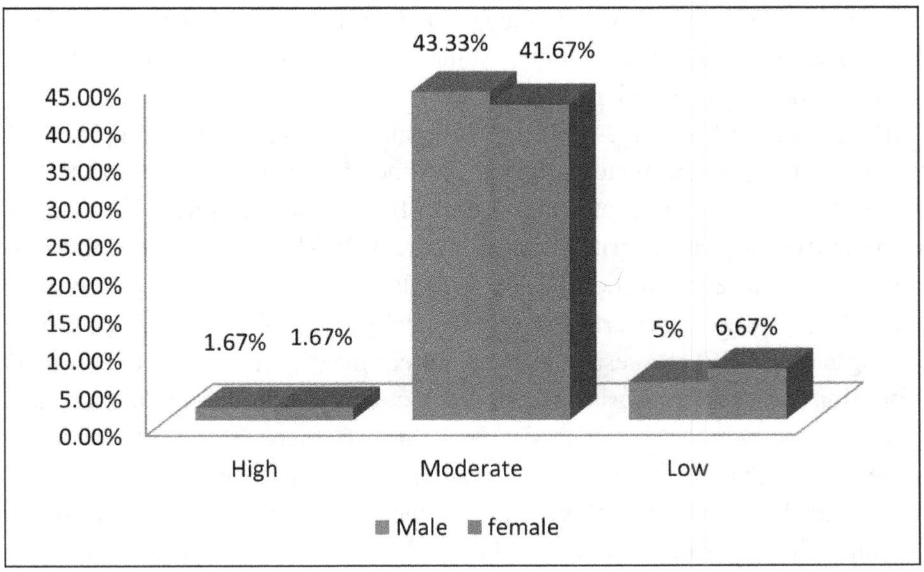

Likewise, this study further revealed that 1.67 percent male and female were high performer respectively. 43.33 percent male were moderate performer and 41.67 percent female were performing moderately. Similarly, 5 percent male were performing to their lowest level and 6.67 percent female were least performer. This study shows that based on banking performance male employees were found to be performing quite well in comparison to female employees.

Pre and Post Estimation Test

Under Pre-estimation we perform specification error, goodness of fit and another diagnostic test. Specification error is done to find out whether the variable or assumptions of statistical model is correct or not (Fornell, 1992). Similarly, goodness of fit is a statistical hypothesis test to see how well sample data *fit* a distribution from a population with a normal distribution (Gupta & Chen, 2001). The Stata command linktest can be used to detect a specification error so as to find if the model is properly specified, one should not be able to find any additional predictors that are statistically significant except by chance (Cheruiyot, 2017). Here, researcher came to know that _hat value is statistically insignificant and _hatsq value is not statistically significant. The _hat value is 0.350 and _hatsq value is 0.661. So, we can conclude that we have chosen few meaningful predictors and the few variables are wrong or have errors and few of them are correct. To be a goodness of fit, the predicted frequency and observed frequency should match closely, and that the more closely they match, the better the fit. When performed goodness of fit, the result obtained for model is Prob > chi2 = 0.8446. In order to be goodness of fit, p-value should be greater than 5% i.e. 0.05 and so we can say that there is a goodness of fit in our models. This helps to determine goodness of fit. We also look towards many other model fit criteria and found the value of Cronbach alpha is 0.983 which is higher than 0.7, so its excellent.

Studies argued that cross-sectional data analysis involves two problems: the heteroscedasticity in the error term and multicollinearity among explanatory variables. To overcome this Variance inflation factor (VIF) Test was performed to deal with the problem of multicollinearity (Tamura et al., 2019). The VIF estimates how much the variance of a regression coefficient is inflated due to multicollinearity in the model. So, we need to perform heteroscedasticity and multicollinearity. Variance inflating factor (VIF) is a test to assess multicollinearity in our regression model (Thompson et al., 2017). Variance inflating factor as per the calculation for model is 1.19 and we know that if VIF is greater than 10, there exist multicollinearity. So, we can say that there is no multicollinearity in the data set. Heteroscedasticity occurs when there is a large difference among the sizes of observation. It is important to identify the Heteroscedasticity as the results will be ruined when running the regression analysis. To understand our data set, we perform heteroscedasticity test. Looking towards hettest, the result appeared for model is prob>Chi2 =0.0000. The assumptions show that there is presence of heteroscedasticity if the value is less than 0.05. So, there is presence of heteroscedasticity in case of model. Hence, we performed robust standard error test to correct the mentioned problem.

Logistic Regression

The Binary Logistic Regression has been used to acquire inferential output for this study. In final regression, the overall of model shows fit as its probability value is less than 5%, and the value of McFadden R^2 is obtained 12.79% which is comparatively good for logistic analysis. The final results generated from the regression are presented in table 3.

Table 3. Final regression

	(1)	(2)	(3)
VARIABLES	**Logit coeff**	**Odds ratio**	**Marginal effects**
Organization performance			
Age	-0.0935	0.911	-0.00126
	(0.115)	(0.105)	(0.00171)
Sex	0.876	2.401	0.0118
	(1.071)	(2.571)	(0.0154)
Maritalstatus	-3.051***	0.0473***	-0.0411*
	(1.087)	(0.0514)	(0.0217)
training_and_development	5.017**	151.0**	0.0675
	(2.497)	(377.1)	(0.0416)
Work_Experience	-1.548	0.213	-0.0208
	(2.642)	(0.562)	(0.0340)
Motivation	3.250***	25.80***	0.0438**
	(1.143)	(29.48)	(0.0179)
Satisfaction	0.600	1.821	0.00807
	(0.890)	(1.622)	(0.0111)
Constant	1.344	3.834	
	(4.234)	(16.23)	
Observations	300	300	300

Robust standard errors in parentheses
*** p<0.01, ** p<0.05, * p<0.1

Table 3 shows that there are three significant variables namely, marital status, training & development and motivation having p-value less than 5%. Now we can say that increase in the number of either married or unmarried people, the odds of being increment in organization performance decreases by a factor of 3.051. Similarly, if there is increase in training & development opportunities for employees, the odds of enhancing performance of organization increase by 5.017times. Again, increase in motivation level of employees, the odds of improving organizational performance increases by 3.250 times. Talking about coefficient in logit model, there are three significant variables that are marital status, training & development and motivation having p-value less than 0.05 i.e. 5%. Talking about marital status, if there is increment in married or unmarried employees, and then the probability of enhancing organizational performance gets increased by 0.0473 units. Similarly, if employees given training & development increases by 1 unit, then the probability of enhancing organizational performance is increased by 151.0 units. Also, if the motivation for employees increases by 1 unit, then the probability of improving organizational performance increases by 25.80 units.

Marginal effects are a useful way to describe the average effect of changes in explanatory variables on the change in the probability of outcomes in logistic regression and other nonlinear models. In marginal effects, we have two significant variables, which are marital status and motivation respectively. The results show a marginal effect of marital status, or the effect for an infinitely small change in marital status is -0.041. This indicates that the organizational performance decreases by 0.041 with a marginal change in marital status. Also, the result shows a marginal effect of motivation is 0.043 which indicates that organizational performance will be enhanced by 0.043 with a marginal change in motivation. The coefficients of -0.041 for marital status and 0.043 for motivation represents changes on probability scale ranging from 0 to 1.

From the analysis it is clear that, gender diversity is not just about ensuring fair representation of men and women in teams but also the diversity spurs innovation and higher-order problem-solving (Joshi, 2017). Firms should foster the right climate of inclusion to leverage gender diversity towards better firm performance. It was found that almost 58.53% respondents are highly concerned regarding gender diversity as they believe that gender diversity brings numerous benefits to an organization like enhanced reputation of an organization, increased innovation, good working conditions and many more. Therefore organizations are ready to accept gender diversity inclusion at the workplace as it provides several benefits to an organization (Bibi, 2016). Also almost 99% of respondents have agreed on the fact that they are treated fairly in their workplace. Likewise, most of the respondents think motivating employees and making them competent enough would result higher performance of a banking organization (Nakagawa, 2015). Similarly, employees were not facing any sorts of gender issues in their job and working environment and also very few of them believe that there could be administrative barriers so as to maintaining gender diversity. There are several employees who are still fighting for the equality at the workplace and that has created a barrier for an organization to gain higher performances (Stojanovic et. al., 2020). 91% respondents believed that building an inclusive workplace could be one of the best managerial solutions for enhancing gender diversity in an organization. Organizations have been forwarding these steps so as to minimized the gender bias in an organization and support gender diversity or equality at a workplace so that they can work properly and be effective in their practice (Pham & Thesis, 2017).

CONCLUSION AND RECOMMENDATIONS

This research aims to find the current prospects of gender diversity role on banking performance inside the Kathmandu valley. However, gender diversity is one of the major issues in today's context and it helps to bring creativity and innovation in an organization through diverse ideas, processes and much more, such matter must extend beyond regulation and must permeate into the culture and genetic code of the organizations. Therefore, it must be accepted in spirit and should not just be a matter of compliance for tick box mechanism for mere tokenism. There is not just a need to examine the gender diversity but also one should have a deeper understanding of the impact of diversity and inclusion of the women on the several sectors. There is also a need to bring more competent women on boards so as to analyze the real impact on the financial performance of an organization.

In the context of Nepal, the role of gender diversity does have a positive impact on banking performance because today women along with men have been able to handle every affairs of an organization with their creative ideas and increased performance level. Many studies have shown that companies with more women in senior leadership roles are more likely to have better results. There has been relatively low percentages of females on boards of directors and top and middle-level executive management positions in several banks, increasing such percentages might lead to better bank performance and will broaden the range of managerial skills on the board and add more managerial perspectives, including a tendency for more conservativeness in decision-making, more caring for social issues and for the needs of multiple groups of stakeholders. There are various reasons for gender inequality or diversity in Nepal. Firstly, the women themselves are not allowed to attain higher education and are still fighting for equal education in the country. Secondly, the government has not guaranteed equal rights for female in several areas especially in rural and backward community. Also, women are not allotted enough places in several areas of development in a nation. However, the organizations have been trying to create a climate of inclusion in their workplace so as to create gender diversity in an organization.

Based on the findings and conclusion of the study following recommendations are kept forward (i) fostering a climate of inclusion in the workplace (ii) creating a supportive labor market for women (iii) strengthening policies that support work-family balance (iv) expanding the evidence base on gender diversity across all organizational levels and (v) promoting private-sector engagement in designing and implementing policies.

Contribution of the Study

Gender related subject is a burning issue in any country at a present context so this might create interest in general public to gain enough learning about it. Therefore, this paper makes a number of theoretical and practical contributions. Despite the lack of literature on the subject, there are theoretical implications on how to increase the visibility of gender diversity in literature. It makes a theoretical contribution by providing a summary of gender diversity policies and by giving the current literature greater structure. The study was made more thorough by reviewing a variety of literature on gender diversity and concepts related to it by a number of writers. Thus, findings will help various researchers, government, professionals, policy makers and other stakeholders who are willing to conduct research on similar field relating to gender diversity. Lastly, this study can help society and country to understand gender diversity with a clear picture and make them maintain gender equality in terms of several dimensions.

Limitations of the Study

This study discovered that there are several banks in the Kathmandu valley that have fair gender policies and employees that experience gender equality in the workplace. Due to the short time frame, the research only includes the main survey; however, the secondary data survey may be used to examine the improvement in employee and banking performance. Further research may be done in other regions as well because this study was only done in the Kathmandu Valley, allowing for a more comprehensive analysis of how gender diversity improves banking efficiency. Some of the variables chosen and included in the study may not have effectively suited their purposes because the conceptual framework was being examined for the first time.

REFERENCES

Adhikari, B., Di Falco, S., & Lovett, J. C. (2004). Household characteristics and forest dependency: Evidence from common property forest management in Nepal. *Ecological Economics*, *48*(2), 245–257. doi:10.1016/j.ecolecon.2003.08.008

Ahmad, Z., Azam, N., Nasir, Y., & Khan, U. (2021). Impact of gender differences on leadership: An investigation of moderating impact of gender-based biasness. [BBE]. *Bulletin of Business and Economics*, *10*(4), 151–166.

Aksan, N., Kısac, B., Aydın, M., & Demirbuken, S. (2009). Symbolic interaction theory. *Procedia: Social and Behavioral Sciences*, *1*(1), 902–904. doi:10.1016/j.sbspro.2009.01.160

Al-Baidhani, P. (2013). The effects of corporate governance on bank performance: Evidence from the Arabian Peninsula. *Ahmed, The Effects of Corporate Governance on Bank Performance: Evidence from the Arabian Peninsula.*

Alghamdi, A. K. H., Alsaadi, R. K., Alwadey, A. A., & Najdi, E. A. (2022). Saudi Arabia's vision 2030's compatibility with women and children's contributions to national development. *Interchange*, *53*(2), 1–22. doi:10.100710780-021-09451-3

Alhalwachi, L. F., & Mordi, C. (2021). Gender inequality barriers and solutions to senior management positions: perspectives on women in Bahraini banking sector. *Journal of Sustainable Finance & Investment*, 1-22.

Ali, M., Kulik, C. T., & Metz, I. (2009). The impact of gender diversity on performance in services and manufacturing organizations. *Academy of Management 2009 Annual Meeting: Green Management Matters.* AOM.

Alpha, A., & Vincent, S. (2011). Gender differences in organizational strategy execution: A comparative study between female and male managers in obstacle management. *African Journal of Marketing Management*, *3*(7), 149–167. https://ssrn.com/abstract=2084456%5Cnhttp://www.academicjournals.org/AJMM

Althalathini, D., Al-Dajani, H., & Apostolopoulos, N. (2022). The impact of Islamic feminism in empowering women's entrepreneurship in conflict zones: Evidence from Afghanistan, Iraq and Palestine. *Journal of Business Ethics*, *178*(1), 39–55. doi:10.100710551-021-04818-z

Ammar, N., & Boughrara, A. (2019). The impact of revenue diversification on bank profitability and risk: Evidence from MENA banking industry. *Macroeconomics and Finance in Emerging Market Economies*, *12*(1), 36–70. doi:10.1080/17520843.2018.1535513

Asian Development Bank. (2016). Gender equality results case study: Nepal Gender Equality and Empowerment of Women Project. ADB. https://www.adb.org/sites/default/files/publication/185563/nepal-gender-equality-and-empowerment-women-project.pdf

Banihani, M., Lewis, P., & Syed, J. (2013). Is work engagement gendered? *Gender in Management*, *28*(7), 400–423. doi:10.1108/GM-01-2013-0005

Bank and Financial Institution Act, Nepal. (2017). *Bank and Financial Institution Act, 2073* BFIN. https://www.nrb.org.np/contents/uploads/2019/12/Bank_And_Financial_Instituion_Act_2017_-_English_Version_20190311-1.pdf

Bao, C., & Nizam, D. I. (2015). the Impact of Motivation on Employee Performance in the Electronics Industry in China. *International Journal of Accounting and Business Management*, *3*(2), 29–45. doi:10.24924/ijabm/2015.11/v3.iss2/29.45

Baral, B. (2017). Gender development perspective: A contemporary review in global and Nepalese context. *Geographical Journal of Nepal*, *10*, 141–152. doi:10.3126/gjn.v10i0.17395

Baral, B. (2017). Gender development perspective: A contemporary review in global and Nepalese context. *Geographical Journal of Nepal*, *10*, 141–152. doi:10.3126/gjn.v10i0.17395

Barbosa, I., & Cabral-Cardoso, C. (2010). Equality and diversity rhetoric: One size fits all? Globalization and the Portuguese context. *Equality, Diversity and Inclusion*, *29*(1), 97–112. doi:10.1108/02610151011019237

Barston, R. P. (2019). *Modern diplomacy*. Routledge. doi:10.4324/9781351270090

Bénavidès, J., Guilloux, F., Allam, D. E., Uzan, A., Mizoule, J., Renault, C., Dubroeucq, M. C., Guérémy, C., & Le Fur, G. (1984). Opposite effects of an agonist, R05-4864, and an antagonist, PK 11195, of the peripheral type benzodiazepine binding sites on audiogenic seizures in DBA/2J mice. *Life Sciences*, *34*(26), 2613–2620. doi:10.1016/0024-3205(84)90048-1 PMID:6330481

Beniflah, J., & Veloz, J. (2021). Building a multicultural organisation: A conceptual model for organisational change in the 21st century. *Journal of Cultural Marketing Strategy*, *5*(2), 153–168.

Bhadra, C., & Shah, M. T. (2007). Nepal: Country gender profile. *Report prepared for JICA*.

Bhandari, U., Yadav, S., Devkota, N., Paudel, U. R., Rajbhandari, S., & Karki, D. (2021). Private and public bank consumers' preference in Kathmandu Valley: Evidence from customers' satisfaction index. *International Research Journal of Science, Technology. Education and Management*, *1*(1), 67–78.

Bibi, N. (2016). Role of gender diversity in organizational effectiveness and its implications. *International Review of Management and Marketing*, *6*(4), 80–85.

Bradbury, M. D., & Kellough, J. E. (2008). Representative bureaucracy: Exploring the potential for active representation in local government. *Journal of Public Administration: Research and Theory*, *18*(4), 697–714. doi:10.1093/jopart/mum033

Carter, N. M., Williams, M., & Reynolds, P. D. (1997). Discontinuance among new firms in retail: The influence of initial resources, strategy, and gender. *Journal of Business Venturing*, *12*(2), 125–145. doi:10.1016/S0883-9026(96)00033-X

CBS. (2009). Report on the Nepal labour force survey 2008. *Statistical report*. 244.

Cheruiyot, K. J. (2017). Determinants of technical efficiency in Kenyan manufacturing sector. *African Development Review*, *29*(1), 44–55. doi:10.1111/1467-8268.12237

Cooke, F. L., Cooper, B., Bartram, T., Wang, J., & Mei, H. (2019). Mapping the relationships between high-performance work systems, employee resilience and engagement: A study of the banking industry in China. *International Journal of Human Resource Management*, *30*(8), 1239–1260. doi:10.1080/09585192.2015.1137618

David, T., & Ely, R. (2005). Making Differences Matter: A new paradigm for managing diversity. *Harvard Business Review on Women in Business, 74*(5), 125–157. https://pdfs.semanticscholar.org/9112/a3e0ebfb74d1418d078093bd4429ffb6bd90.pdf

Devkota, N., Adhikari, S., Parajuli, S., Bhandari, U., & Poudel, U. R. (2022a). Employees Perception on Gender diversity on banking performance in Kathmandu valley: Status, Challenges and Way-forward. *Qubahan Academic Journal*, *2*(1), 1–7. doi:10.48161/qaj.v2n1a87

Devkota, N., Paudel, U. R., & Khanal, G. (2021). Is Current Understanding Adequate for Green Banking Practices in Nepal: A Lesson Learned. In Handbook of Research on Climate Change and the Sustainable Financial Sector (pp. 84-98). IGI Global. doi:10.4018/978-1-7998-7967-1.ch006

Devkota, N., Rai, R., Khanal, G., Padda, I. U. H., Paudel, U. R., Parajuli, S., & Bhandari, U. (2022b). Customer Perception and Awareness of Green Banking Practices: An Alternative Strategy of Environmental Sustainability. In Disruptive Technologies and Eco-Innovation for Sustainable Development (pp. 20-41). IGI Global.

Dezsö, C. L., & Ross, D. G. (2012). Does female representation in top management improve firm performance? A panel data investigation. *Strategic Management Journal*, *33*(9), 1072–1089. doi:10.1002mj.1955

Dwyer, S., Richard, O. C., & Chadwick, K. (2003). Gender diversity in management and firm performance: The influence of growth orientation and organizational culture. *Journal of Business Research*, *56*(12), 1009–1019. doi:10.1016/S0148-2963(01)00329-0

Egbuwe, T. I., & Nwinee, B. F. (2019). Gender Impact on Execution of Business Strategy for Effective Economic Performance in Nigeria. *International Journal of Science and Business*, *3*(3), 141–150.

Estes, R., & Hosseini, J. (1988). The gender gap on wall street: An empirical analysis of confidence in investment decision making. *The Journal of Psychology*, *122*(6), 577–590. doi:10.1080/00223980.1988.9915532

European Commission. (2018). *2018 Report on equality between women and men in the EU*. EC. doi:10.2838/21655

Fornell, C., & Yi, Y. (1992). Assumptions of the two-step approach to latent variable modeling. *Sociological Methods & Research*, *20*(3), 291–320. doi:10.1177/0049124192020003001

Gram, L., Granados, R., Krockow, E. M., Daruwalla, N., & Osrin, D. (2021). Modelling collective action to change social norms around domestic violence: Social dilemmas and the role of altruism. *Humanities and social sciences communications*, *8*(1), 1-15.

Gupta, A. K., & Chen, T. (2001). Goodness-of-fit tests for the skew-normal distribution. *Communications in Statistics. Simulation and Computation*, *30*(4), 907–930. doi:10.1081/SAC-100107788

Hassan, Z. (2018). IMpact of gender diversity on indian firm's financial performance. *International Journal of Management, Accounting and Economics, 5*(5).

Hawi, R., Alkhodary, D., & Hashem, T. (2015). Managerial competencies and organizations performance. *International Journal of Management Sciences*, *5*(11), 723–735.

Hillman, W., & Radel, K. (2021). The social, cultural, economic and political strategies extending women's territory by encroaching on patriarchal embeddedness in tourism in Nepal. *Journal of Sustainable Tourism*, 1–22.

ILO. (2005). *Youth: Pathways to decent work.* ILO. http://www.ilo.org/youthmakingithappen/Resources/01.html%5Cn papers2://publication/uuid/CC56FB32-F1EE-47AF-BF14-72722C4E6008

International Finance Corporation. (2016). *Working with Smallholders: A Handbook for Firms Building Sustainable Supply Chains.* World Bank.

Inuwa, M. (2016). Job satisfaction and employee performance: An empirical approach. *The Millennium University Journal, 1*(1), 90–103. doi:10.58908/tmuj.v1i1.10

Jailaxmi & Gautam, A. (2017). Work life balance of bank employees as related to age, gender and marital status. *International journal of management, and business studies, 7*(1), 44-46.

Johnson, J. E., & Powell, P. L. (1994). Decision making, risk and gender: Are managers different? *British Journal of Management, 5*(2), 123–138. doi:10.1111/j.1467-8551.1994.tb00073.x

Joshi, R. (2017). Does Gender Diversity Improve Firm Performance? Evidence from India. *Undp.*

Kochhar, K., & Jain-chandra, S. (2017). *Women, work, and economic growth: Leveling the playing field.* e-Library. https://www.elibrary.imf.org/doc/IMF071/23146-9781513516103/23146-9781513516103/Other_formats/Source_PDF/23146-9781475579062.pdf?redirect=true

Kutu, S., Devkota, N., Upretee, S., Paudel, U. R., & Dhakal, K. (2023). Commercial Bank Readiness for Adoption of Marketing 4.0: Evidence From Nepal. In Marketing and Advertising in the Online-to-Offline (O2O) World (pp. 247-266). IGI Global.

Labre, J. F., & Lauzier, M. (2021). Studying the influences of organizational learning on turnover intentions, absenteeism, and organizational performance among employees working in a French-Canadian hospital. *International Journal of Training Research, 19*(1), 1–20. doi:10.1080/14480220.2020.1864439

Malik, A., Budhwar, P., Patel, C., & Srikanth, N. R. (2022). May the bots be with you! Delivering HR cost-effectiveness and individualised employee experiences in an MNE. *International Journal of Human Resource Management*, *33*(6), 1148–1178. doi:10.1080/09585192.2020.1859582

Mellahi, K., & Johnson, M. (2000). Does it pay to be a first mover in e. commerce? The case of Amazon. com. *Management Decision*, *38*(7), 445–452. doi:10.1108/00251740010373458

Micky Olutende, O., Wisiuba Bukhala, P., & Wesonga, B. (2018). Exercise Prescription: Practices of Healthcare Professionals in Hospital Setting, Kenya. *Journal of Physical Activity Research*, *3*(1), 47–54. doi:10.12691/jpar-3-1-8

Mugaddam, A. (2021). Language shift and gender in Dilling, Sudan: Who leads the process?. *Journal of Arts and Humanities*, *10*(03), 01-13.

Nakagawa, Y. (2015). The gender diversity firm performance relationship by industry type, working hours, and inclusiveness: An empirical study of Japanese firms. [JDM]. *Journal of Diversity Management*, *10*(1), 61–78.

Nanzushi, C. (2015). *The effect of workplace environment on employee performance in the mobile telecommunication firms in Nairobi city county* [Doctoral dissertation, University of Nairobi].

Nasir, M. A., & Morgan, J. (2018). The unit root problem: Affinities between ergodicity and stationarity, its practical contradictions for central bank policy, and some consideration of alternatives. *Journal of Post Keynesian Economics*, *41*(3), 339–363. doi:10.1080/01603477.2017.1387060

Navumau, V., & Matveieva, O. (2021). The gender dimension of the 2020 Belarusian protest: Does female engagement contribute to the establishment of gender equality? *New perspectives*, *29*(3), 230-248.

Nepal, J., & Lertjanyakit, H. (2019). Impact of Gender Based Discrimination on Employee Performance in Case of Nepalese Commercial Banks. *Nepalese Journal of Management Science and Research*, *2*(1), 21–30.

Noland, M., Moran, T., & Kotschwar, B. R. (2016). Is gender diversity profitable? Evidence from a Global Survey. SSRN *Electronic Journal*, (March 2019). doi:10.2139/ssrn.2729348

Nwokolo, O. O., Coombs, A. A., Eltzschig, H. K., & Butterworth, J. F. IV. (2022). Diversity and inclusion in anesthesiology. *Anesthesia and Analgesia*, *134*(6), 1166–117. doi:10.1213/ANE.0000000000005941 PMID:35130194

Omri, A., & Boukattaya, S. (2018). Gender diversity and firm performance: Evidence from French boardrooms. *EuroMed J. of Management*, *2*(4), 356. doi:10.1504/EMJM.2018.096456

Ongena, S. (2003). Working Paper Series. *RE:view*, *85*(6). doi:10.20955/r.85.67

Pant, B. (2016). *Financial Inclusion in Nepal: Policy Review and Prescriptions.* 1–18. NRB. https://nrb.org.np/ecorev/articles/2.pdf

Parajuli, S., Paudel, U. R., & Devkota, N. (2020). Banking communications: A perceptual study of customer relations. *South Asian Journal of Social Studies and Economics*, *8*(3), 23–34. doi:10.9734ajsse/2020/v8i330212

Paudel, U. R., & Devkota, N. (2022). Assimilation of Communication Deviance in Customer and Banker Appraisals of Commercial Banks in Kathmandu, Nepal. In Innovative Economic, Social, and Environmental Practices for Progressing Future Sustainability (pp. 1-17). IGI Global.

Paudel, U. R., Parajuli, S., Devkota, N., & Mahapatra, S. K. (2020). What determines customers' perception of banking communication? An empirical evidence from commercial banks of Nepal. *Global Economy Journal*, *20*(04), 1–21. doi:10.1142/S2194565920500190

Paudel, U. R., Tamrakar, L., Devkota, N., Maga, S. R., & Parajuli, S. (2021). Promoting Effective Managerial Communication on Banking Sector in Kathmandu Valley: Cross Sectional Analysis. *International Research Journal of Management Science*, *6*(1), 110–127. doi:10.3126/irjms.v6i1.42352

Perez-Arce, F., & Prados, M. J. (2021). The decline in the US labor force participation rate: A literature review. *Journal of Economic Surveys*, *35*(2), 615–652. doi:10.1111/joes.12402

Pham, T., & Thesis, D. (2017). Gender Diversity Management Policies.

Putnam, L. L. (1979). Women in Management: Leadership Theories, Research Results, and Future Directions. *Annual Meeting of the Central States Speech Association.*

Rai, R., Kharel, S., Devkota, N., & Paudel, U. R. (2019). Customers perception on green banking practices: A desk. *The Journal of Economic Concerns*, *10*(1), 82–95.

Richard, O. C., Kirby, S. L., & Chadwick, K. (2013). The impact of racial and gender diversity in management on financial performance: How participative strategy making features can unleash a diversity advantage. *International Journal of Human Resource Management*, *24*(13), 2571–2582. doi:10.1080/09585192.2012.744335

Sabir, F. S., Maqsood, Z., Tariq, W., & Devkota, N. (2019). Does happiness at work lead to organisation citizenship behaviour with mediating role of organisation learning capacity? A gender perspective study of educational institutes in Sialkot, Pakistan. *International Journal of Work Organisation and Emotion*, *10*(4), 281–296. doi:10.1504/IJWOE.2019.106891

Sengupta, M., & Harris, L. M. (2022). Interrogating differences: Intersectionality and participatory livelihood development in the upland forest of Tripura (Northeast India). *Geoforum*, *130*, 59–68. doi:10.1016/j.geoforum.2022.02.002

Sharma, S., & Taneja, M. (2018). The effect of training on employee performance. *International Journal of Recent Technology and Engineering*, *7*(4), 6–13.

Shrestha, E., Devkota, N., Paudel, U. R., & Parajuli, S. (2021). Post-merger Employee Satisfaction in Commercial Banks of Nepal: Findings from Employee Satisfaction Index. *Journal of Business and Social Sciences Research*, *6*(1), 45–62. doi:10.3126/jbssr.v6i1.38128

Shrestha, S., Devkota, N., Paudel, U., Bhandari, U., & Parajuli, S. (2020). Bankers' Communication Know-how: An Analysis from Commercial Banks of Kathmandu valley. *Quest Journal of Management and Social Sciences*, *2*(1), 80–99. doi:10.3126/qjmss.v2i1.29023

Singh, V., & Point, S. (2006). (Re)presentations of gender and ethnicity in diversity statements on European company Websites. *Journal of Business Ethics*, *68*(4), 363–379. doi:10.100710551-006-9028-2

Stojanovic, A., Milosevic, I., Arsic, S., Urosevic, S., & Mihajlovic, I. (2020). Corporate social responsibility as a determinant of employee loyalty and business performance. *Journal of Competitiveness*, *12*(2), 149–166. doi:10.7441/joc.2020.02.09

Tajfel, H. E. (1978). Differentiation between social groups: Studies in the social psychology of intergroup relations. *Academic Press*, *1*(1), 1-10.

Tamura, R., Kobayashi, K., Takano, Y., Miyashiro, R., Nakata, K., & Matsui, T. (2019). Mixed integer quadratic optimization formulations for eliminating multicollinearity based on variance inflation factor. *Journal of Global Optimization*, *73*(2), 431–446. doi:10.100710898-018-0713-3

Tandukar, H., Devkota, N., Khanal, G., Padda, I. U. H., Paudel, U. R., Bhandari, U., Adhikari, K., & Parajuli, S. (2020). An empirical study in Nepalese commercial bank's performances on green banking: An analysis from the perspective of bankers. *Quest Journal of Management and Social Sciences*, *3*(1), 49–62. doi:10.3126/qjmss.v3i1.37591

Teruel, M., & Agustí, S.-B. (2017). The link between gender diversity and innovation: What is the role of firm size? *International Review of Entrepreneurship, 15*(3), 319–340.

Thompson, C. G., Kim, R. S., Aloe, A. M., & Becker, B. J. (2017). Extracting the variance inflation factor and other multicollinearity diagnostics from typical regression results. *Basic and Applied Social Psychology, 39*(2), 81–90. doi:10.1080/01973533.2016.1277529

Triana, M. D. C., Gu, P., Chapa, O., Richard, O., & Colella, A. (2021). Sixty years of discrimination and diversity research in human resource management: A review with suggestions for future research directions. *Human Resource Management, 60*(1), 145–204. doi:10.1002/hrm.22052

Truyens, J., De Bosscher, V., & Sotiriadou, P. (2016). An analysis of countries' organizational resources, capacities, and resource configurations in athletics. *Journal of Sport Management, 30*(5), 566–585. doi:10.1123/jsm.2015-0368

Truyens, J., De Bosscher, V., & Sotiriadou, P. (2016). An analysis of countries' organizational resources, capacities, and resource configurations in athletics. *Journal of Sport Management, 30*(5), 566–585. doi:10.1123/jsm.2015-0368

Tulaadhar, J. K. (2018). *Status of female employees in banking sector of Nepal: a case study of Kailali district* [Doctoral dissertation].

US Department of Commerce. (2000). Best practices in achieving workforce diversity. USDC.

Van Knippenberg, D., & Sitkin, S. B. (2013). A critical assessment of charismatic—transformational leadership research: Back to the drawing board? *The Academy of Management Annals, 7*(1), 1–60. doi:10.5465/19416520.2013.759433

Westcott, M. (2021). Women specialist managers in Australia–Where are we now? Where to next? *The Journal of Industrial Relations, 63*(4), 501–521. doi:10.1177/00221856211001913

Wijekoon, A., Salunke, S., & Athaide, G. A. (2021). Customer heterogeneity and innovation-based competitive strategy: A review, synthesis, and research agenda. *Journal of Product Innovation Management, 38*(3), 315–333. doi:10.1111/jpim.12576

Won, D., Hwang, B. G., & Chng, S. J. (2021). Assessing the effects of workforce diversity on project productivity performance for sustainable workplace in the construction industry. *Sustainable Development, 29*(2), 398–418. doi:10.1002d.2155

Wu, J., Richard, O. C., Triana, M. D. C., & Zhang, X. (2022). The performance impact of gender diversity in the top management team and board of directors: A multiteam systems approach. *Human Resource Management*, *61*(2), 157–180. doi:10.1002/hrm.22086

Yarram, S. R., & Adapa, S. (2021). Board gender diversity and corporate social responsibility: Is there a case for critical mass?. *Journal of cleaner production*, 278, 123z319.

APPENDIX

Questionnaire

Table 4. Banking performance

Particulars	Yes	No
A. Employee satisfaction		
i) I enjoy my organization's culture.		
ii) My organization offers adequate opportunities for promotion & career development.		
iii) I feel valued for your contributions.		
iv) I feel my job responsibilities are clearly defined.		
v) I feel my job utilizes my skills and abilities as it could.		
B. Working environment		
i) Organization is dedicated to diversity and inclusiveness		
ii) Understand how my work impact organizational goals		
iii) satisfied with the culture of my work place		
iv) Organization's fiscal well-being is stable		
v) Organization has a safe working environment		
C. Training & advancement opportunities		
i) Opportunities for improving professional skills		
ii) Organization is conducting training programs frequently		
iii) Training and development have helped you to improve your work efficiency		
iv) Training help to increase the motivation level of employees		
v) promotion opportunities for capable people		
D. Employee motivation		
i) My level of motivation affects my performance.		
ii) I am satisfied with the incentive provided by the organization.		
iii) My salary is favorable as compared to other brands.		
iv) There is considerable opportunities for growth and career development.		
v) There is high degree of autonomy provided in decision making and other practices.		
E. Competence		
i) Ability to adapt a situation or to solve a problem in a new way, openness of a mind for new situation, solution and ideas.		
ii) Ability to analyze problems and situations in a critical and logical manner.		
iii) I believe my personal development would benefit from using a competency management styles.		
iv) Possess enough skills and knowledge to make right decisions for organization.		
v) Able to solve problems effectively and efficiently.		

Chapter 8
Between Pay and Performance: A Perspective on Wage Inequality in the Accounting Profession

Ana Lucas
Universidade Europeia, Portugal

Ivo Dias
Universidade Europeia, Portugal

Carla Gomes da Costa
Universidade Europeia, Portugal

ABSTRACT

Gender discrimination in the employment market is a sensitive issue that has been the subject of numerous studies and, in particular, of profuse political action on the part of governments and international institutions to eradicate it. Although gender discrimination issues are manifested in multiple dimensions, this study focuses on gender wage discrimination in the socio-professional group of certified accountants in Portugal. The ongoing process of feminization in the profession, starting in the last decade, justifies a first study on the issue of gender wage discrimination in a profession traditionally exercised by men and with little research in this domain. The application of a survey, with 751 validated observations, is the base for the empirical component of this study. In addition to wage issues, academic qualifications, time in the profession, age, and working conditions were considered as variables for analysis. The conclusions obtained point to a lesser wage for women concerning men in all the variables considered.

DOI: 10.4018/978-1-6684-5981-2.ch008

INTRODUCTION

The reflection on gender issues is not new but is still relevant. Despite the existence of some positive changes, inequalities persist, being expressed in wage differences among the same professionals according to gender.

As one of the most ancient forms of inequalities related to discrimination, being a woman involves a set of characteristics forming gender stereotypes and prejudices socially embedded, that have been reproduced across generations.

Women's discrimination as a social problem with socio-economic consequences must be seen as a political agenda issue. Changing gender attitudes by preventing any form of discrimination is to inhibit social contexts where inequalities replication and justification are built.

Despite specific and justified differences in wages according to different abilities, and appraised performance, there are major and unjustified wage differences according to gender. Additionally, gender segregation is also noticed in vertical promotion, despite merit.

The Accounting Profession (AP) has been dominated by men until 2010 in Portugal. Since then, it has been noticed an increase in women's enrolment in the Professional Order, surpassing men. However, wage differences and social prestige remain different between men and women.

In this context, this study addressed the following research question: "To what extent is there evidence of gender discrimination (GD) under the bias of remuneration among Certified Accountants (CAs) in Portugal?". To answer this question, a survey was conducted with Portuguese CAs, analyzing the wage differences based on gender, but also concerning the professionals' academic degrees, age, time of profession, and job situation.

Findings showed that no matter the perspective, men earn more than women. And, even worse, this discrepancy exists in all age groups, meaning, there is no evidence that the new generations will change the situation. So, as gender inequalities are currently still a reality in the AP in Portugal, it is necessary and urgent that employers take measures to ensure equal pay, bearing in mind that wages must vary according to competencies and skills, not according to gender.

Moreover, the study also presents some recommendations, based on previous literature, that allows employers to adopt preventive and corrective measures regarding the gender wage gap.

In summary, this empirical study contributes to the research on the wage gap based on gender, confirming its existence in a profession marked by a feminization process. The study results also contribute to highlighting some practical implications to the business area, such as the presentation of some employers' measures to counter the wage gap based on gender.

After this introduction, the chapter will follow with a literature review on the following issues: a historical background on gender inequality (GI), the socioeconomic consequences of GI and GD, the stigma of being a woman through wage discrimination, the gender wage gap in the AP and tools for employers to narrow or eliminate gender pay gaps. The study then follows the presentation of the research question, hypotheses, and methodology. At last, the study presents the findings and its conclusions.

Gender Inequality (GI): Historical Background

As a sensitive topic to address in the Western world, GI is still a form of discrimination between human beings based initially on biological characteristics dictated by birth, among other sociocultural determinants. The understanding of how the gestation of a boy or a girl will conditionate their form of treatment, education, and future life opportunities has been explained by the ancestral sexual division of labor.

Even if this sexual division of labor has historically been analyzed stereotypically, as some alternative interpretations try to point out (Gurven & Hill, 2009; Panter-Brick, 2002). However, the dominant explanation of the sexual division of labor, based on psychophysical and psychobiological characteristics of a determined anthropogenesis, conceives and justifies a set of factors as differentiating gender roles.

The understanding of the human species' evolution from an eminently biological and reproductive basis designed the role of women reserved to the home, to the gestation of children, and their care. Men were responsible for the conquest and protection of their territory and the survival of their families, in the role of warrior and hunter.

Despite all the revolutions throughout history, struggling for fundamental rights of freedom of expression, (such as the vote, emancipation in the face of autonomous decision-making not dependent on a man, father, or husband, the right to sexual expression, and the right to choose or not to choose motherhood), being a woman is still a stigma in many societies - a condemnation at birth to the detriment of a future different from what is expected and convenient for women (Sobczack, 2018). With an identity built based on her psychobiology, being a mother, a caretaker, and concerned for the common good, her future is conditioned by the impossibility to risk leaving social normality, conceived for a woman. Another way of understanding gender inequality as something that inhibits women's choices as something internalized is the importance given to the context, for example at the company level. Women may have similar expectations in choosing a given top position, but the context needs to be enabling (Fernandez-Mateo & Kaplan, 2018). The sexual division of labor has been the basis for the foundation of western modern societies based on nuclear families (Sear, 2021), in which roles justify the experience of reproductive sexuality, by the definition of well-defined parental roles – mothers holding their main social role as children's caregivers and fathers holding their labor positions to support their families. Gender has been an essential social category more prevalent than others explaining socioeconomic inequalities.

Based on differences between men and women according to physical, psychological, and emotional traits, there has been developed several beliefs, attitudes, and behaviors leading to justified discrimination throughout history. Being a woman may also appear associated with other types of inequalities responsible for attributing greater discrimination, such as the categories of poverty, low education, race, and age (Ndinda & Ndhlovu, 2018).

From Gender Inequality (GI) to Gender Discrimination (GD): Socioeconomic Consequences

GD, like any form of discrimination, is based on a perceived inequality based on a set of characteristics. These characteristics, understood as differences between social categories, inherent to disparities in the social status held, generate discrimination against to whom has a weaker status. In this way, perceived, accepted, and justified inequality follows its course historically, being reproduced throughout generations until it becomes institutionalized as an unquestionable or barely questionable truth. When this set of less positive or even negative characteristics is internalized by the weakened social category, by accepting this stigma it ends up being the one that reproduces this prejudice even without being aware of it.

Even though the inequalities are the result of social construction reproduced through generations, they have been responsible for social and economic women's fragility (Kulich & Chipeaux, 2019). Despite some improvements in women's status due to education levels and better work opportunities, there was a remarkable change in women's stereotypes related to work being seen as more competent in the last decades (Eagly et al., 2020).

The fight against GI is not a women's cause, but a cause for the dignity of the human being and the respect and social integration of the individual, regardless of his or her characteristics, in a democratic society that stands for equality and freedom. Therefore, it is urgent to question not only the individual but also the socio-economic consequences of not fully women's participation in society in all its forms. Nevertheless, women have lower labor force participation, lower remuneration, and fewer career promotion, thus increasing poverty and endangering the welfare of children (Pignatti, 2020).

The gender gap must be seen as a global problem involving society, not only women or families. Instead of trying to change women's behavior and attitudes to resemble men in the workplace, there is a structural change to be made – changing the contexts responsible for the reproduction of women's disadvantage (Kossek et al., 2017).

Being a Woman: Reproducing the Stigma Through Wage Discrimination (WD)

The existence, consistency, and permanence of a set of stereotypes and social gender prejudices continue to covertly justify the observed differences in remuneration. There is a set of characteristics that are difficult to attribute to women in a positive way, such as superior cognitive skills or physical fragility as an unavoidable attribute, and the impossibility to meet certain demands due to being the home guardian. Despite the increase in the level of education and proven track record in the market, there is still a set of perceptions in the minds of decision-makers that inhibit change and decision-making and the option for a woman of childbearing age.

We realize the dimension of the problem when we see that discrimination is not only made by men but also by women – as the Queen Bee Syndrome example (Sobczack, 2018). These aspects have justified (in countries considered as "developed countries") giving up on motherhood at fertile age (which biologically are ages associated with fertility) or opting for late motherhood (which limits fertility due to female biology).

Regarding the wage gap in which there is a female pay penalty, it has been shown that in organizations adopting diversity goals, there is a female pay premium to high potential women (Leslie et al., 2017). Among the different forms of GD, the wage gap is one of the most studied (Blau & Kahn, 2017; Hardies et al., 2021; Shoham & Lee, 2018). Many studies have been carried out on the topic in the USA and Europe, including several meta-analyses (Chantreuil & Lebon, 2015; Stanley & Jarrell, 1998; Weichselbaumer & Winter-Ebmer, 2006). Wage disparity is visible in all countries, regardless of their level of development, hence also in Europe (Bilan et al., 2020; European Commission, 2020).

Naturally, different salaries are paid to employees with different abilities, such as cognitive skills, years of schooling, professional experience, seniority, or who perform functions with different characteristics. However, salary differences based on gender, race, or religion can no longer be considered acceptable (Figueiredo & Botelho, 2013). The fact that wage differentials between men and women are not justified in terms of labor productivity is generally known as gender WD *(Del Río* et al., 2011).

WD is thus defined as arbitrary treatment, not based on merit or performance criteria, that violates the principle of "equal pay for equal work" (Coleman, 2003; Del Río et al., 2011; Irfan et al., 2021).

Generally, the gender pay gap is the difference between the average earnings of men and women, usually reported as the ratio of earnings between men and women or as an actual wage gap (Moreno et al., 2021), or as the percentage of male earnings. In the European Union, this difference is measured as the relative difference in the average gross hourly wage between women and men (Danaj, 2016).

Despite increases in the participation rate of women in the labor market and the level of education, there is a pay gap between men and women. Women remain underrepresented in top management positions – vertical sex segregation, the "glass ceiling" (Albrecht et al., 2003; Arulampalam et al., 2007) and overrepresented in certain types of jobs – horizontal sex segregation, "glass walls" (Baldwin et al., 2001; Boraas & Rodgers III, 2003; Neuman & Oaxaca, 2004; Ransom & Oaxaca, 2005) – and sectors (industrial sexual segregation) (Blau & Winkler, 2018; England, 2010; Marques & Ferreira, 2015; Tonoyan et al., 2020).

Previous studies refer that several factors have been pointed out for gender WD (Danaj, 2016) and are associated with lower availability for work, long periods of absence from the labor market, and more frequently the interruption of their careers (Bertrand et al., 2010; R. L. Oaxaca & Ransom, 1994), periods of maternity leave or family support (Ferrant et al., 2014; Iversen & Rosenbluth, 2011), as well as situations of reduced hours and flexible working hours (Blau & Kahn, 2017) or part-time jobs (Addison et al., 2020; Figueiredo & Botelho, 2013).

In a way, this salary disparity results from rules, procedures, and management practices in a business context (Bilan et al., 2020; Irfan et al., 2021), making it difficult to include and promote diversity, with a negative impact on organizational commitment and performance (Cornwell et al., 2017; Gomez & Bernet, 2019), as well as generating reputational risks (Ugarte & Rubery, 2021), which amplifies when is extrapolated to a macro context.

There are many examples in which this disparity in income between genders has been measured, noting that it affects different age groups and different functions and sectors of activity. Likewise, different methodologies are used to seek to find explanations, either for the causes of these disparities or for the impacts on gender social inequality issues (Shoham & Lee, 2018).

The first studies on WD follow the traditional approach and were carried out by Oaxaca (1973) and by Blinder (1973). According to these authors, every gender wage gap can be broken down into two components (Weichselbaumer & Winter-Ebmer, 2006): the explained component, generally called the "endowment effect" or "productivity effect", which is based on differences in productivity (Blau & Kahn, 2017; Hardies et al., 2021; Jung & Choi, 2017; R. L. Oaxaca & Ransom, 1994); and the unexplained "discrimination effect", based on evident GD.

Because this wage disparity has profound economic impacts in terms of increasing inequality, generating gender differences in terms of poverty (Miller & Vagins,

2019), and contributing to an inefficient distribution of resources (Figueiredo & Botelho, 2013), equal treatment of women has become a global social issue and therefore wage discrimination is a matter of political and social concern. To define adequate policies, it is important to produce rigorous estimates of discrimination (Galego & Pereira, 2010).

The imposition of gender quotas or gender parity in the highest positions has been replacing the laws of equal opportunities and equal treatment, which prevailed on political agendas, and it is expected that the rise of more women to top positions have a direct impact on female employment and wages (Cardoso & Winter-Ebmer, 2010).

Although there is, in global terms, a significant improvement concerning the average distance from gender parity, the issues related to economic participation and opportunities, where WD is included, do not present such satisfactory average results, expanding the time horizon in which the global gender gap will be eliminated (WEF, 2022). Current longitudinal studies, such as the European Communication Monitor, confirm that there is a significant and permanent WG in this field, even in the most industrialized countries in Europe (Moreno et al., 2021; Zerfass et al., 2020).

Since 1957, the principle of equal pay between men and women for equal work or work of equal value has been enshrined in European treaties, however, despite successive directives and recommendations, wage differences remain and are the basis of the European Strategy for Equality of Gender 2020-2025 (Denis & Julián, 2022). According to 2020 data, the unadjusted WG between men and women in the EU was 13% (16.4% in 2012), with different realities among the Member States (Figure 1), with Portugal presenting a lower value: 11.4% (EUROSTAT, 2022).

Figure 1. Gender pay gap (2020)
Source: EUROSTAT (2022).

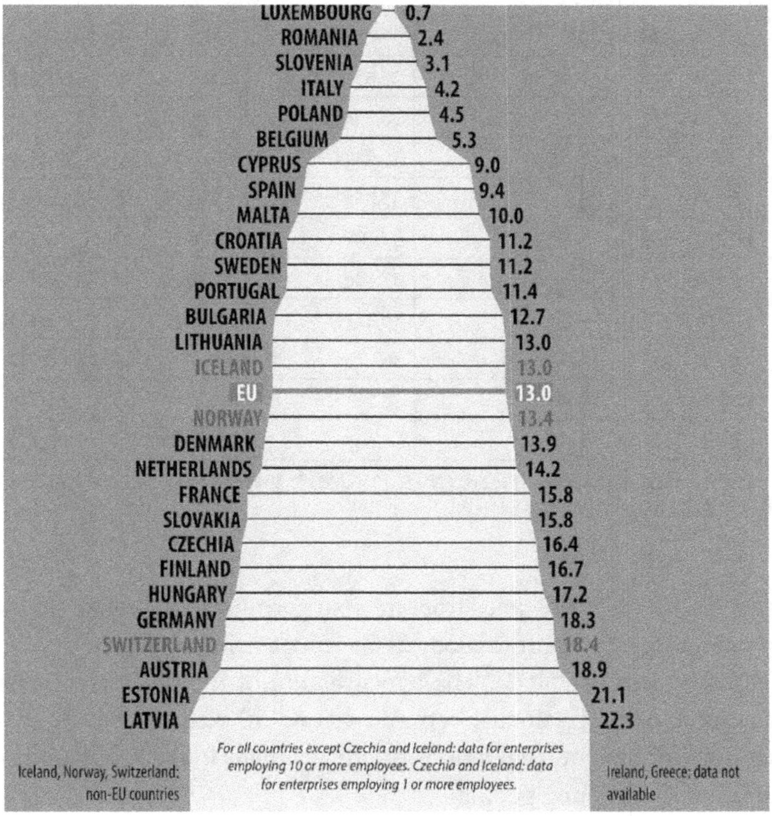

Successive studies carried out in Portugal show that the salary differences between men and women seem to have been decreasing slowly and steadily. At higher salary levels the salary differences seem to be increasing, despite the significant investment in education made by women and their high involvement in the labor market (González et al., 2009).

Gender Wage Gap (GWG) in the Accounting Profession (AP)

Accounting has traditionally been a male-dominated profession, but it changed in 2010 in Portugal. At least in quantitative terms, when women enrolled in the Professional Order outnumbered men (Santos, 2017). From that year on, the percentage of women has been steadily increasing compared to the number of men, and by the end of 2021, women already accounted for almost 54% of total Portuguese CAs (Table 1).

Table 1. Evolution of the number of CAs by gender

Year	Men		Women		Total
	Number	%	Number	%	
2012	35,799	49.28	36,851	50.72	72,650
2013	36,611	48.92	38,233	51.08	74,844
2014	34,866	48.54	36,959	51.46	71,825
2015	34,410	48.02	37,255	51.98	71,665
2016	33,868	47.72	37,107	52.28	70,975
2017	33,323	47.30	37,120	52.70	70,443
2018	32,504	46.89	36,821	53.11	69,325
2019	32,011	46.63	36,631	53.37	68,642
2020	31,687	46.41	36,591	53.59	68,278
2021	31,433	46.14	36,687	53.86	68,120

Source. Ordem dos Contabilistas Certificados (2015, 2016, 2017, 2018, 2019, 2020, 2021); Ordem dos Técnicos Oficiais de Contas (2013, 2014).

The analysis of gender by age structure also permits us to realize the evolution of the feminization of the profession, as in recent generations there is a greater percentage of women (Table 2). The age structure of the profession also reveals a greater number of professionals between 40 and 50 years old, with about 44%. There are, however, several generations of professionals in the profession, showing a continuous entry of young people.

Table 2. Number of CAs by gender in 2021

Age Group	Men		Women		Total
	Number	%	Number	%	
<30	526	27.38	1,395	72.62	1,921
≥30 e < 40	1,981	31.09	4,390	68.91	6,371
≥40 e < 50	10,952	36.53	19,032	63.47	29,984
≥50 e < 60	7,602	47.68	8,342	52.32	15,944
≥60	10,372	74.62	3,528	25.38	13,900
Total	31,433	46.14	36,687	53.86	68,120

Source. Report and Accounts of the Ordem dos Contabilistas Certificados (2021).

Throughout its history, the AP had several advances and setbacks. The designation itself attributed to AP has evolved, as well as the importance associated with their responsibilities. The reforms implemented by Marquis of Pombal, starting in 1755, are of paramount importance for accounting and its professionals. For the first time in the history of Portugal, the AP and access to the profession were regulated. However, from that time to the present, the importance given by legislators to accounting and its professionals has varied greatly.

Officially, the AP was only recognized in 1963. Since that date, the accountant has been a professional with great responsibilities, not only at an accounting level but also tax, since he/she represents his/hers client before the Tax Authority. However, the great impulse in professional recognition and regulation took place only during the 1990s (Gonçalves et al., 2014). Indeed, the first regulation of the profession appeared in 1995, with the Statute of Official Accountants (Estatuto Dos Técnicos Oficiais de Contas, 1995).

Currently, and since 2015, it is the Statute of the Order of Certified Accountants (OCA[1]) (Estatuto Da Ordem Dos Contabilistas Certificados, 2015) that regulates several important aspects of the profession, including the access conditions, the legal responsibilities, and how the activity is carried out. Only the professionals enrolled in the Order can use the professional title of CAs, as well as exercise the profession.

Along with some personal conditions, related to ethics, enrolment in the OCA must follow some conditions: to possess the academic qualifications of a bachelor's degree or higher, in the areas of accounting, management, economics, business sciences, or taxation; to attend a curricular or professional internship; and to obtain approval in an exam, to be organized and carried out by the Order.

At last, the certified activity can be carried out: on its account; as members of a society of professionals; as public workers; or within the scope of the provision of an individual employment contract. In all of these situations, the CA is personally and directly responsible for the accounting and tax compliance of the entities to which it assumes this responsibility.

According to the Law and the regulation of the profession, none of the previous conditions refers to any differences related to the professional's gender, so, at least in theory, the condition that equal work corresponds to identical working conditions is fulfilled. However, according to previous studies (Júnior et al., 2015; Santos, 2017), the profession in Portugal also presents a gender wage gap. The challenges faced by women have been the subject of much research, especially international ones.

Yet, research on gender in accounting is still not enough (Khalifa & Kirkham, 2009; Lehman, 2012). GI despite having been reduced in recent years, is still far from being overcome. Indeed, CAs seem to be no exception to this reality. Therefore, the importance of the explicit introduction of this problem in accounting studies, questioning sexist notions of competence, commitment, practice, and even what it means to be an accountant, as a way of breaking the cycle of the perpetuation of these notions and the imbalance of power (Khalifa & Kirkham, 2009).

Moreover, according to the studies of Júnior et al. (2015) and Santos (2017), even with the growing number of women in the profession, institutionalized inequality seems to be maintained in the AP, with a lack of gender equity in terms of monetary gain and social prestige. Additionally, it was identified that women working in the accounting area are subject to lower wages than men. Furthermore, women's professional practice is directed to the areas of execution, with the management assigned to men.

To Narrow or Eliminate Gender Pay Gaps: Tools for Employers

Although some authors, such as Smith (2012), consider that the elimination of the wage differential between men and women has been processed exclusively in the production of hard legislation and recourse to the formal participation of the social partners, there were no significant results.

In the case of Portugal, in some studies carried out (Casaca, 2022a, 2022b) a growing intervention of these social actors is defended, along with the reinforcement of the role of the State, namely through public policies, which recognize the need for an integrated legislative instrument, ensure remuneration transparency and effectiveness of the law (Casaca, 2022b).

The aforementioned integrated legislative instrument would allow the different measures that promote equal pay between men and women to be implemented in an articulated and coherent way, mitigating the limitations of measures taken individually, reaching relevant topics such as, for example, achieving equal participation of women and men in paid and unpaid domestic and care work (Casaca, 2022b).

Concerning remuneration transparency, it is up to the State to oblige companies to present information on remuneration in a more disaggregated way, to allow a more effective analysis of gender wage discrimination (Casaca, 2022b). Finally, concerning ensuring effective compliance with the law, in addition to the State, as an employer, it should be an example to be followed, it must monitor the application by companies of diagnostic procedures and intervention in the elimination of practices of gender wage discrimination (Casaca, 2022b).

On the other hand, the data available for Portugal, namely those verified for the pre-pandemic period, suggest that factors such as age, seniority, and level of education continue to explain the wage differential between men and women (Casaca, 2022a). The existence of human capital management practices in a business context that enhance the maintenance of gender wage discrimination requires measures to effectively promote equality in these practices.

Among the factors identified as explaining the unfavorable pay differential for women, we find horizontal gender segregation, the allocation of women and men to different levels of qualification, gender stereotypes, the lower values earned by productivity or attendance bonuses, compared to the men, the bias due to gender stereotypes about the social roles of women and men, both in the methods and practices of evaluating the components of functions, as well as in the criteria for measuring productivity, as well as the fact that women are more affected by the precariousness of the contractual ties, job insecurity, and part-time work (Casaca, 2022a).

Also, for the specific case of Portugal, the International Labor Organization (Organização Internacional do Trabalho, 2021) identified, based on the contributions of the social partners, a set of action proposals, which follow different, but complementary, axes of intervention: social dialogue; public policy; awareness, training, and knowledge; and transparency of company information.

This philosophy of action is in line with the proposals by Oelz et al. (2013): promoting awareness of the gender pay gap; broadening knowledge of the equal pay - equal value principle; making equal pay a national policy objective; adopting and enforcing appropriate legislation; promoting objective job evaluation; assessing progress; and adopt measures as needed.

Research Question and Hypotheses

In line with the literature, it seems significant to find out if the gender wage gap exists also in the accountant profession in Portugal. So, in this context, the following question arises: To what extent is there evidence of GD under the bias of remuneration among CAs in Portugal?

Methodology

Rendering to previous studies (Júnior et al., 2015; Santos, 2017) the AP is no exception to the wage gap based on gender, but they noticed the need for more empirical studies to prove this reality. Accordingly, empirical studies should analyze this situation considering not only the perception of respondents but concrete data, such as differences in earnings based on gender in general and academic degrees and age in particular.

Following this gap in the literature, this paper consists of an empirical study on the participation of CAs working in Portugal. As presented before, the research question is: "To what extent is there evidence of GD under the bias of remuneration among CAs in Portugal?".

To answer this question, a survey was carried out, based on a questionnaire answered by almost 1,000 accounting professionals. It was considered only CAs' answers, so the sample was reduced to 751 observations (Table 3).

Table 3. Sample characterization

Age Group	Men		Women		Total
	Number	%	Number	%	
<30	27	27.3	72	72.7	99
≥30 and < 40	67	40.6	98	59.4	165
≥40 and < 50	127	43.5	165	56.5	292
≥50 and < 60	43	39.8	65	60.2	108
≥60	65	74.7	22	25.3	87
Total	329	43.8	422	56.2	751

Source. Own preparation.

The questionnaire was applied in a training program to about 3,000 accountants and also through direct contact with about 2,500 accountants on LinkedIn. The answer rate was about 17.5%. As there are 70,443 members registered with the OCC on December 31st, 2017, the sample obtained represents 1.07% of these.

The questionnaire administration strategy involved convenience sampling since all CAs were equally likely to respond to the questionnaire if they were present at the training or were contacted via LinkedIn (Hill & Hill, 2016).

However, to assess the representativeness of the sample, the statistical test was applied in which, for a universe of 70,443 CAs and a sample of 751 respondents, we have, for a confidence level of 95%, a margin of error of 3.56%. This means that by changing the sample within the same universe, the result of the investigation carried out may vary by 3.56%. The proportion of men and women in the profession by age group and the proportion of CAs by the district of residence were also analyzed.

From the characterization of the proportion of men and women by age group, it is considered that both genders are representative, as well as all age groups, in a convenience sampling strategy. As from the characterization by proportion by the district of residence, it is considered that generically and in a convenience sampling strategy, the sample is representative of the population.

Answers to seven of the questionnaire questions were central. Two of these questions were on characterization: gender and age. The other five questions were to identify the earnings, the academic degree, the time of profession, and the job situation.

The respondents chose one of the earnings groups per month: < 500 USD (1); 501 USD - 1,000 USD (2); 1,001 USD - 1,500 USD (3); 1,501 USD - 2,000 USD (4); 2,001 USD - 2,500 USD (5); and > 2,500 USD (6). The considered academic degrees were: undergraduate; graduate; bachelor's; master's; and Ph.D. The time of profession was converted into periods from 0 to 5 years, 5 to 10, and so on. The job situation was to identify one of four situations: self-employed; as a member of a professional society; as a public servant; or as an employee.

The primary data obtained allowed a quantitative and descriptive analysis, through graphs and Box-Plot diagrams, considering aspects related to the following correlations between gender and wage: academic degrees, age, time of profession, and job situation.

FINDINGS/RESULTS

After the presentation of the methodology, this chapter now exposes its main findings, which will allow answering the research question. They exhibit the relationship between earnings by gender and academic degree, age group, time of profession, and job situation. All findings present the real sample used in each one, as the n.a. answers were not considered, and they differ from one analysis to another.

Earnings in the Accounting Profession (AP) by Gender

This first section presents a general result regarding wage groups according to gender. It explores if there are differences in the earnings level between men and women.

To analyze the earnings by gender, it was quantified that the number of men and women in each earning group was converted into a percentage (Table 4). The study excluded a total of 41 answers that did not inform on wage group.

Table 4. Sample characterization

Wage Group	Men		Women		Total
	Number	%	Number	%	
< 500 USD	9	45.0	11	55.0	20
501 USD - 1,000 USD	65	30.4	149	69.6	214
1,001 USD - 1,500 USD	99	40.4	146	59.6	245
1,501 USD - 2,000 USD	52	51.0	50	49.0	102
2,001 USD - 2,500 USD	34	63.0	20	37.0	54
> 2,500 USD	52	69.3	23	30.7	75
n.a.	18	43.9	23	56.1	41
Total	329	43.8	422	56.2	751

Source. Own preparation.

Then, it was used a column chart. The findings presented in Figure 2 are clear: most CAs earn between 501 USD per month and 1,500 USD. Concerning gender differences, as earnings increase, men are in a higher percentage. Indeed, more women are earning less, until 1,500 USD per month, but as earnings increase, from 1,501 USD monthly on, there are more men than women.

Figure 2. Wage group by gender
Source. Own preparation.

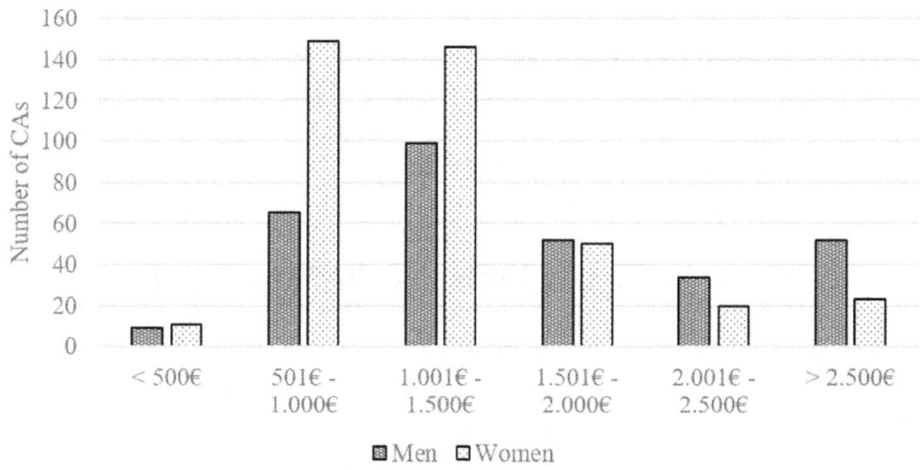

Earnings by Gender and Academic Degree

This section aims to examine whether is a gender wage gap concerning academic degrees.

To explore the earnings by gender and academic degree, it was quantified that the number of men and women with each academic degree was converted into a percentage (Table 5). The study excluded a total of 12 answers that did not express the academic degree.

Table 5. Sample characterization

Academic Degree	Men		Women		Total
	Number	%	Number	%	
Undergraduate	30	65.2	16	34.8	46
Bachelor	40	53.3	35	46.7	75
Graduate	208	41.3	296	58.7	504
Master	41	38.7	65	61.3	106
Ph.D	3	37.5	5	62.5	8
n.a.	7	58.3	5	41.7	12
Total	329	43.8	422	56.2	751

Source. Own preparation.

Then, it was used the Box-Plot graph (Figure 3). Through Box-Plot it is possible to observe how the variables are distributed concerning data homogeneity, central tendency values, maximum and minimum values, and outliers if any (Pestana & Gageiro, 2014). With this graph, it turns clear that there is a trend to higher earnings in men than in women in all academic degrees.

Figure 3. Earnings by gender and academic degree
Source. Own preparation.

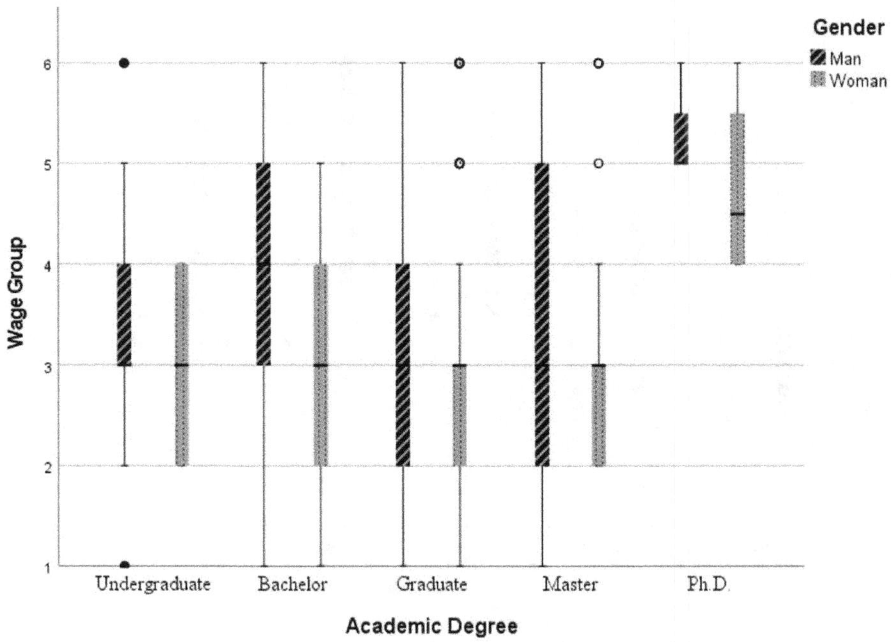

Earnings by Gender and Age Group

This section aims to examine whether the gender earnings gap is common to all generations.

To explore the earnings by gender and age group, it was quantified the number of men and women in each age group was converted into a percentage (Table 3). Then, it was used the Box-Plot graph (Figure 4). Through Box-Plot it is possible to observe how the variables are distributed concerning data homogeneity, central tendency values, maximum and minimum values, and outliers if any (Pestana & Gageiro, 2014).

In the youngest age group, up to 30 years old, women earn less than men. It seems at first glance that it is equal for both genders. However, a close observation notices that the wage group for men is up to 1,500 USD-2,000 USD, and for women is up to 1,000 USD-1,500 USD. In the other four age groups, from 30 years old on, clearly, men are earning more than women.

In short, there is a trend for higher earnings in men than in women in all age groups.

Figure 4. Earnings by gender and age group
Source. Own preparation.

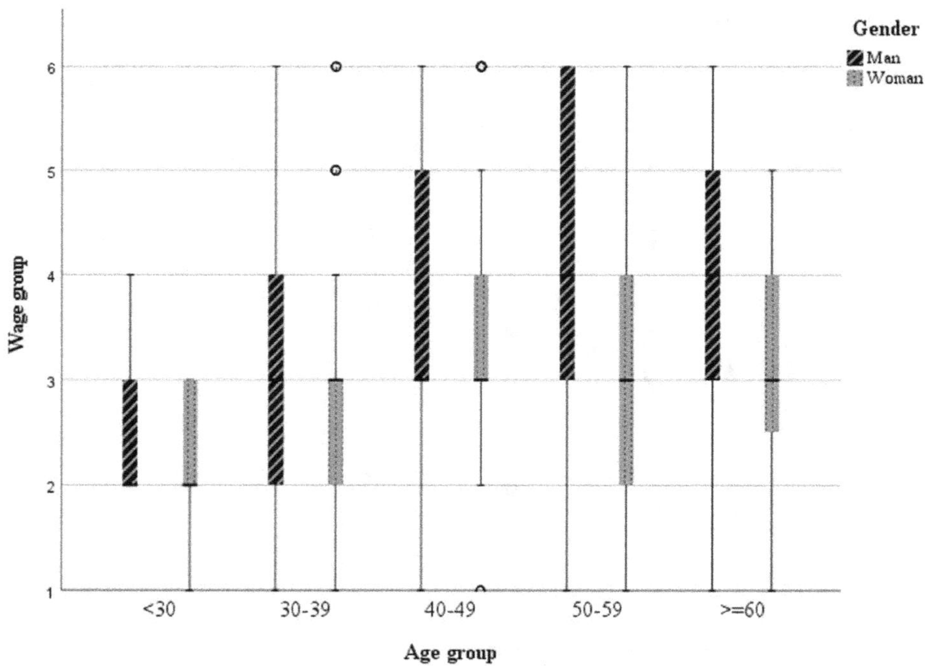

Earnings by Gender and Time of Profession

This section aims to compare how the time of profession influences, or not, the CAs' wage based on gender.

To analyze the wage by gender and time of profession, it was quantified that the number of men and women in the time of profession group was converted into a percentage (Table 6). The study excluded a total of 122 answers that did not provide this information.

Table 6. Sample characterization

Time of Profession (Years)	Men		Women		Total
	Number	%	Number	%	
<5	51	31.7	110	68.3	161
≥5 and < 10	47	48.5	50	51.5	97
≥10 and < 15	24	48.0	26	52.0	50
≥15 and < 20	67	46.5	77	53.5	144
≥20 and < 25	42	44.7	52	55.3	94
≥25 and < 30	15	33.3	30	66.7	45
≥30 and < 35	12	60.0	8	40.0	20
≥35 and < 40	14	77.8	4	22.2	18
n.a.	57	46.7	65	53.3	122
Total	329	43.8	422	56.2	751

Source. Own preparation.

Using a Box-Plot graph (Figure 5) and except for CAs under five years and from 15 to 19 years of profession, all groups show indubitably higher wages for men than for women.

In short, there is a trend to higher earnings in men than in women also based on time of profession.

Figure 5. Earnings by gender and time of profession
Source. Own preparation.

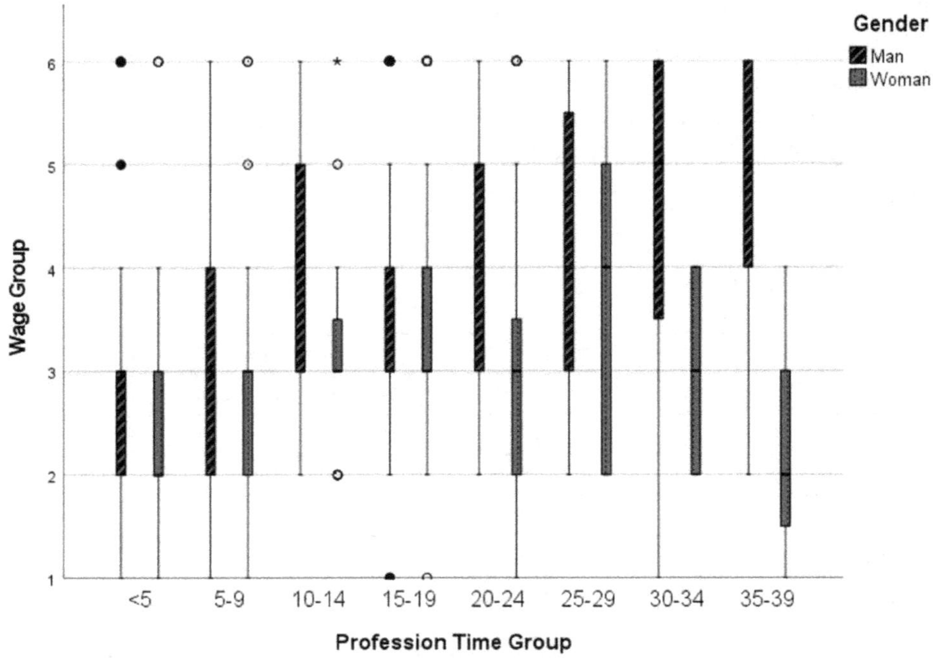

Earnings by Gender and Job Situation

This section aims to compare how men and women exercise their professional activity, and how it influences their wages based on gender.

To analyze the job situation by gender, it was quantified that the number of men and women in each situation was converted into a percentage (Table 7). The study excluded a total of 79 answers that did not inform on the job situation.

Table 7. Sample characterization

Job Situation	Men		Women		Total
	Number	%	Number	%	
Employee	182	38.4	292	61.6	474
Members of a professional society	57	55.9	45	44.1	102
Public servants	5	45.5	6	54.5	11
Self-employed	54	63.5	31	36.5	85
n.a.	31	39.2	48	60.8	79
Total	329	43.8	422	56.2	751

Source. Own preparation.

Then, it was also used a Box-Plot graph (Figure 6). It allows observing that it is a profession that is practiced in all ways possible, and both genders practice all forms. However, in the more usual way, women (61.6%) tend to work more as an employee than men (38.4%).

Concerning to CAs' wages, those professionals earn more as employees, as members of a professional society, and as public servants, but in all categories, men tend to be more well-paid than women.

Figure 6. Earnings by gender and job situation
Source. Own preparation.

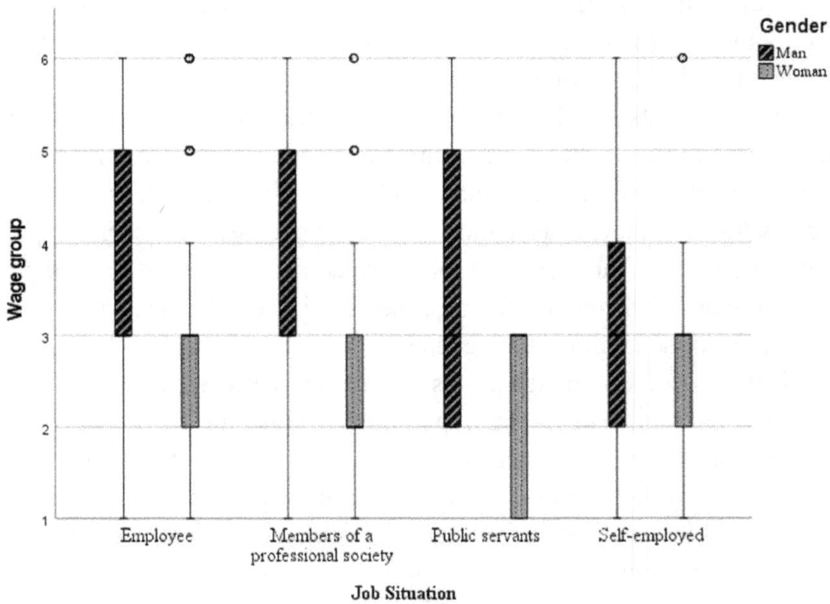

CONCLUSION

With some setbacks, the trend, particularly in Europe, has been to reduce the gender wage gap (Bilan et al., 2020; European Commission, 2020), but it remains an unavoidable reality, despite the goals set out in the European Strategy for Equality of Gender (Denis & Julián, 2022; EUROSTAT, 2022; Moreno et al., 2021; Zerfass et al., 2020).

As the AP is in a feminization process, as well as many other professions, there is a phenomenon that embodies several symbolic barriers that make it impossible for women to obtain better organizational conditions, namely equal wages to men.

Many articles suggest an interest in empirical research on this topic. Thus, this study consisted of an empirical study of the Portuguese AP, to understand if there were different wage conditions, as the profession exercise itself implies no difference if it is done by a man or a woman. It analyzed the relationship between earnings by gender and academic degree, age group, time of profession, and job situation.

Results are conclusive on the research question. The study findings show that as it comes to wages, there are more women in the lowest earnings group and, as the earnings increase, the percentage of men is higher. This situation is similar in all age groups, which makes the situation more serious. The wage gap in CAs is, indeed, a reality in Portugal.

To mitigate this issue, there are tools for employers and the State already previously studied. The State should make equal pay a national policy objective, demanding greater remuneration transparency, by obliging companies to present information on remuneration in a more disaggregated way. As for employers, measures like promoting objective job evaluation and assessing progress would certainly reduce the gender wage gap in their companies.

This study's results should, however, be carefully analyzed. Even is possible to conclude that in the studied context there is a gender wage gap, there are some limitations to be aware of. Mainly, the sample is very small, as despite having 751 valid observations, it represents about 1.5% of the professional order members.

Future empirical research on this topic is welcome, as it brings forward pressure to make sure that for identical functions, the working conditions, and particularly wages, are indeed identical for both genders.

Historically a male-dominated profession, being a certified accountant has been a professional goal for many women, particularly since the last decade when the number of women in the profession has surpassed the number of men. As a qualified profession, it opens opportunities for women to occupy positions in their careers that allow access to higher levels of remuneration, as well as to develop business projects led by them. In this sense, future replication of the study will allow an assessment of whether salary parity will be achieved.

In short, GI is currently still a reality in the AP in Portugal. And, if no action is taken to the contrary, the tendency is to maintain this situation.

REFERENCES

Addison, J. T., Chen, L., & Ozturk, O. D. (2020). Occupational skill mismatch: Differences by gender and Cohort. *Industrial & Labor Relations Review*, *73*(3), 730–767. doi:10.1177/0019793919873864

Albrecht, J., Björklund, A., & Vroman, S. (2003). Is there a glass ceiling in Sweden? *Journal of Labor Economics*, *21*(1), 145–177. doi:10.1086/344126

Arulampalam, W., Booth, A. L., & Bryan, M. L. (2007). Is there a glass ceiling over Europe? Exploring the gender pay gap across the wage distribution. *Industrial & Labor Relations Review*, *60*(2), 163–186. doi:10.1177/001979390706000201

Baldwin, M. L., Butler, R. J., & Johnson, W. G. (2001). A hierarchical theory of occupational segregation and wage discrimination. *Economic Inquiry*, *39*(1), 94–110. doi:10.1093/ei/39.1.94

Bertrand, M., Goldin, C., & Katz, L. F. (2010). Dynamics of the gender gap for young professionals in the financial and corporate sectors. *American Economic Journal. Applied Economics*, *2*(3), 228–255. doi:10.1257/app.2.3.228

Bilan, Y., Mishchuk, H., Samoliuk, N., & Mishchuk, V. (2020). Gender discrimination and its links with compensations and benefits practices in enterprises. *Entrepreneurial Business and Economics Review*, *8*(3), 189–203. doi:10.15678/EBER.2020.080311

Blau, F. D., & Kahn, L. M. (2017). The gender wage gap: Extent, trends, and explanations. *Journal of Economic Literature*, *55*(3), 789–865. doi:10.1257/jel.20160995

Blau, F. D., & Winkler, A. E. (2018). *The Economics of Women, Men, and Work* (8th ed.). Oxford University Press.

Blinder, A. S. (1973). Wage discrimination: Reduced form and structural estimates. *The Journal of Human Resources*, *8*(4), 436–455. doi:10.2307/144855

Boraas, S., & Rodgers, W. M. III. (2003). How does gender play a role in the earnings gap-an update. *Monthly Labor Review*, *126*, 9.

Cardoso, A. R., & Winter-Ebmer, R. (2010). Female-led firms and gender wage policies. *Industrial & Labor Relations Review*, *64*(1), 143–163. doi:10.1177/001979391006400107

Casaca, S. F. (2022a). *Os benefícios sociais e económicos da igualdade remuneratória entre mulheres e homens: Economic Case.* https://genderpaygap-elimination.pt/wp-content/uploads/2022/03/Economic-Case_new.pdf

Casaca, S. F. (2022b). *Os benefícios sociais e económicos da igualdade remuneratória entre mulheres e homens: Policy Brief.* https://genderpaygapelimination.pt/wp-content/uploads/2022/03/Policy-Brief_act.pdf

Chantreuil, F., & Lebon, I. (2015). Gender contribution to income inequality. *Economics Letters*, *133*, 27–30. doi:10.1016/j.econlet.2015.05.009

Coleman, M. G. (2003). Job skill and black male wage discrimination. *Social Science Quarterly*, *84*(4), 892–906. doi:10.1046/j.0038-4941.2003.08404007.x

Cornwell, C., Rivera, J., & Schmutte, I. M. (2017). Wage discrimination when identity is subjective evidence from changes in employer-reported race. *The Journal of Human Resources*, *52*(3), 719–755. doi:10.3368/jhr.52.3.0815-7340R1

Danaj, E. (2016). Gender Wage Gap. Encyclopedia of Family Studies, 1–3.

Del Río, C., Gradín, C., & Cantó, O. (2011). The measurement of gender wage discrimination: The distributional approach revisited. *The Journal of Economic Inequality*, *9*(1), 57–86. doi:10.100710888-010-9130-7

Denis, L., & Julián, M. P. (2022). *Gender pay gaps in the European Union—A statistical analysis*. Publications Office of the European Union.

dos Técnicos Oficiais de Contas, O. (2013). *Relatório e contas 2013*. https://pt.calameo.com/read/000324981fbf34e2f6fe4

dos Técnicos Oficiais de Contas, O. (2014). *Relatório e contas 2014*. https://pt.calameo.com/read/000324981a5991de0c4c9

Eagly, A. H., Nater, C., Miller, D. I., Kaufmann, M., & Sczesny, S. (2020). Gender stereotypes have changed: A cross-temporal meta-analysis of US public opinion polls from 1946 to 2018. *The American Psychologist*, *75*(3), 301–315. doi:10.1037/amp0000494 PMID:31318237

England, P. (2010). The gender revolution: Uneven and stalled. *Gender & Society*, *24*(2), 149–166. doi:10.1177/0891243210361475

Estatuto da Ordem dos Contabilistas Certificados, no. Lei n.º 139/2015, de 7 de setembro, Ordem dos Contabilistas Certificados (2015). https://www.occ.pt/fotos/editor2/dr7setembroocc.pdf

Estatuto dos Técnicos Oficiais de Contas, no. Decreto-Lei 265/95, de 17 de Outubro, Ministério das Finanças, Diário da República n.º 240/1995, Série I-A de 1995-10-17 (1995).

European Commission. (2020). *A Union of Equality: Gender Equality Strategy 2020-2025*. Brussels, COM(2020) 152 final.

EUROSTAT. (2022). *Gender pay gap in the EU down to 13.0%*. https://ec.europa.eu/eurostat/en/web/products-eurostat-news/-/edn-20220307-2

Fernandez-Mateo, I., & Kaplan, S. (2018). Gender and organization science: Introduction to a virtual special issue. *Organization Science*, *29*(6), 1229–1236. doi:10.1287/orsc.2018.1249

Ferrant, G., Pesando, L. M., & Nowacka, K. (2014). *Unpaid Care Work: The missing link in the analysis of gender gaps in labour outcomes. In Boulogne Billancourt.* OECD Development Center.

Figueiredo, M. da C., & Botelho, M. (2013). Decomposition of the gender wage gap in Portugal, 1998–2007: The evidence of gender discrimination. *Portuguese Journal of Social Science*, *12*(3), 287–315. doi:10.1386/pjss.12.3.287_1

Galego, A., & Pereira, J. (2010). Evidence On Gender Wage Discrimination In Portugal: Parametric And Semi-Parametric Approaches. *Review of Income and Wealth*, *56*(4), 651–666. doi:10.1111/j.1475-4991.2010.00413.x

Gomez, L., & Bernet, P. (2019). Diversity improves performance and outcomes. *Journal of the National Medical Association*, *111*(4), 383–392. doi:10.1016/j.jnma.2019.01.006 PMID:30765101

Gonçalves, C., Gonçalves, G., & Sequeira, L. (2014). *A Profissão de Técnico Oficial de Contas—Enquadramento normativo*. VidaEconómica.

González, P., Santos, L. D., & Santos, M. C. (2009). Education and gender wage differentials in Portugal: What can we learn from an age cohort analysis? *Education Economics*, *17*(2), 263–278. doi:10.1080/09645290802628437

Gurven, M., & Hill, K. (2009). Why do men hunt? A reevaluation of "man the hunter" and the sexual division of labor. *Current Anthropology*, *50*(1), 51–74. doi:10.1086/595620 PMID:19579355

Hardies, K., Lennox, C., & Li, B. (2021). Gender discrimination? Evidence from the Belgian public accounting profession. *Contemporary Accounting Research, 38*(3), 1509–1541. doi:10.1111/1911-3846.12667

Irfan, M., Bhatti, O. K., & Malik, R. K. (2021). Impact of Compensation on Inclusive Organizations. *Compensation and Benefits Review, 53*(3), 103–129. doi:10.1177/0886368720971922

Iversen, T., & Rosenbluth, F. M. (2011). *Explaining Occupational Gender Inequality: Hours Regulation and Statistical Discrimination*. APSA 2011 Annual Meeting Paper.

Jung, J. H., & Choi, K.-S. (2017). Gender Discrimination and Worker Selectivity: A Comparison of the Self-employed and Wage Earners. *Global Economic Review, 46*(3), 251–270. doi:10.1080/1226508X.2017.1305284

Júnior, L. C. L., da Silveira, N. S. P., & Santini, R. B. (2015). A feminização da área contábil: Um estudo qualitativo básico. *Revista de Educação e Pesquisa Em Contabilidade (REPeC), 9*(1).

Khalifa, R., & Kirkham, L. (2009). Gender. In The Routledge Companion to Accounting History. Routledge.

Kossek, E. E., Su, R., & Wu, L. (2017). "Opting out" or "pushed out"? Integrating perspectives on women's career equality for gender inclusion and interventions. *Journal of Management, 43*(1), 228–254. doi:10.1177/0149206316671582

Kulich, C., & Chipeaux, M. (2019). Gender inequality in economic resources. In *The social psychology of inequality* (pp. 35–51). Springer. doi:10.1007/978-3-030-28856-3_3

Lehman, C. (2012). We've come a long way! Maybe! Re-imagining gender and accounting. *Accounting, Auditing & Accountability Journal, 25*(2), 256–294. doi:10.1108/09513571211198764

Leslie, L. M., Manchester, C. F., & Dahm, P. C. (2017). Why and when does the gender gap reverse? Diversity goals and the pay premium for high potential women. *Academy of Management Journal, 60*(2), 402–432. doi:10.5465/amj.2015.0195

Marques, T. de M. G., & Ferreira, C. M. (2015). Mulheres na gestão de topo: A problemática do gap de gênero e salarial. *Revista Ibero Americana de Estratégia, 14*(1), 43–59. doi:10.5585/riae.v14i1.2150

Miller, K., & Vagins, D. (2019). *The simple truth about the gender pay gap*. American Association of University Women.

Moreno, Á., Khalil, N., & Tench, R. (2021). Enemy at the (house) gates: Permanence of gender discrimination in public relations career promotion in Latin America. *Communicatio Socialis*, *34*(3), 169–183.

Ndinda, C., & Ndhlovu, T. P. (2018). Gender, poverty and inequality: Exploration from a transformative perspective. *Journal of International Women's Studies*, *19*(5), 1–12.

Neuman, S., & Oaxaca, R. L. (2004). Wage decompositions with selectivity-corrected wage equations: A methodological note. *The Journal of Economic Inequality*, *2*(1), 3–10. doi:10.1023/B:JOEI.0000028395.38694.4b

Oaxaca, R. (1973). Male-female wage differentials in urban labor markets. *International Economic Review*, *14*(3), 693–709. doi:10.2307/2525981

Oaxaca, R. L., & Ransom, M. R. (1994). On discrimination and the decomposition of wage differentials. *Journal of Econometrics*, *61*(1), 5–21. doi:10.1016/0304-4076(94)90074-4

Oelz, M., Olney, S., & Tomei, M. (2013). *Equal pay: An introductory guide*. Academic Press.

Ordem dos Contabilistas, C. (2015). *Relatório e contas 2015*. https://www.occ.pt/fotos/editor2/rc2015d.pdf

Ordem dos Contabilistas, C. (2016). *Relatório e contas 2016*. https://www.occ.pt/fotos/editor2/rc2016_b.pdf

Ordem dos Contabilistas, C. (2017). *Relatório e contas 2017*. https://pt.calameo.com/read/00032498147b319bfa1f4

Ordem dos Contabilistas, C. (2018). *Relatório e contas 2018*. https://pt.calameo.com/read/00032498177cb91926b08

Ordem dos Contabilistas, C. (2019). *Relatório e contas 2019*. https://www.occ.pt/news/DIversos/RC2019.pdf

Ordem dos Contabilistas, C. (2020). *Relatório e contas 2020*. https://pt.calameo.com/read/000324981c94bf0cad338

Ordem dos Contabilistas, C. (2021). *Relatório e contas 2021*. https://www.occ.pt/news/Documentos/RC2021.pdf

Organização Internacional do Trabalho. (2021). *Estudo sobre a diferença salarial entre homens e mulheres em Portugal.* https://www.ilo.org/lisbon/publica%C3%A7%C3%B5es/WCMS_836143/lang--pt/index.htm

Panter-Brick, C. (2002). Sexual division of labor: Energetic and evolutionary scenarios. *American Journal of Human Biology, 14*(5), 627–640. doi:10.1002/ajhb.10074 PMID:12203817

Pestana, M. H., & Gageiro, J. N. (2014). *Análise de Dados para Ciências Sociais, A complementaridade do SPSS*. Edições Sílabo.

Pignatti, N. (2020). Encouraging women's labor force participation in transition countries. *IZA World of Labor: Evidence-Based Policy Making*. Advance online publication. doi:10.15185/izawol.264.v2

Ransom, M., & Oaxaca, R. L. (2005). Intrafirm mobility and sex differences in pay. *Industrial & Labor Relations Review, 58*(2), 219–237. doi:10.1177/001979390505800203

Santos, C. (2017, Maio). A mulher profissional. *Revista Contabilista - Ordem Dos Contabilistas Certificados, 206*, Article 206.

Sear, R. (2021). The male breadwinner nuclear family is not the 'traditional' human family, and promotion of this myth may have adverse health consequences. *Philosophical Transactions of the Royal Society B, 376*(1827).

Shoham, A., & Lee, S. M. (2018). The causal impact of grammatical gender marking on gender wage inequality and country income inequality. *Business & Society, 57*(6), 1216–1251. doi:10.1177/0007650317696231

Smith, M. (2012). Social regulation of the gender pay gap in the EU. *European Journal of Industrial Relations, 18*(4), 365–380. doi:10.1177/0959680112465931

Sobczack, A. (2018). The Queen Bee Syndrome. The paradox of women discrimination on the labour market. *Journal of Gender and Power, 9*(1), 51–61. doi:10.14746/jgp.2018.9.005

Stanley, T. D., & Jarrell, S. B. (1998). Gender wage discrimination bias? A meta-regression analysis. *The Journal of Human Resources, 33*(4), 947–973. doi:10.2307/146404

Tonoyan, V., Strohmeyer, R., & Jennings, J. E. (2020). Gender gaps in perceived start-up ease: Implications of sex-based labor market segregation for entrepreneurship across 22 European countries. *Administrative Science Quarterly*, *65*(1), 181–225. doi:10.1177/0001839219835867

Ugarte, S. M., & Rubery, J. (2021). Gender pay equity: Exploring the impact of formal, consistent and transparent human resource management practices and information. *Human Resource Management Journal*, *31*(1), 242–258. doi:10.1111/1748-8583.12296

WEF. (2022). *Global Gender Gap Report 2022—Insight Report*. https://www3.weforum.org/docs/WEF_GGGR_2022.pdf

Weichselbaumer, D., & Winter-Ebmer, R. (2006). Rhetoric in economic research: The case of gender wage differentials. *Industrial Relations*, *45*(3), 416–436. doi:10.1111/j.1468-232X.2006.00431.x

Zerfass, A., Verhoeven, P., Moreno, Á., Tench, R., & Verčič, D. (2020). *European Communication Monitor 2020: Ethical Challenges, Gender Issues, Cyber Security, and Competence Gaps in Strategic Communication: Results of a Survey in 44 Countries*. EUPRERA-European Public Relations Education and Research Association.

KEY TERMS AND DEFINITIONS

Accounting Profession: A regulated profession in which professionals must be mandatorily registered in the Certified Accountants Association, being exclusively assigned the use of this professional title, as well as the exercise of the respective profession. Its main functions are to plan, organize and coordinate the accounting of entities subject to income taxes that have or must have regularly organized accounting, respecting the legal rules and accounting principles in force, to assume responsibility for the technical regularity, in the accounting and tax areas, of the referred entities, and to sign, together with the legal representative of the entities referred to, the respective tax returns.

Feminization of Accounting Profession: A phenomenon of changing a profession that was historically exercised by males to be currently performed mostly by females and with a tendency to increase the discrepancy between the genders, with the female gender currently much higher in number than the male gender.

Gender Discrimination: Any act of disadvantaging a person solely based on their gender, in the personal or professional sphere, without considering other aspects.

Gender Inequality: Unequal treatment of people based on gender, by considering psycho-physiological factors and social roles that normally place women at a disadvantage compared to men.

Gender Pay Gap: An indicator that measures salary discrimination, in terms of gender, that does not result from differences in the function performed, performance, skills possessed, professional experience, or seniority, that is, from objective factors, but from practices based on prejudice or discriminatory management practices based on the employee's gender.

ENDNOTE

1 Ordem Dos Contabilistas Certificados – OCC, in Portuguese.

Chapter 9
Woman Entrepreneurship in Creative Crafts:
The Case of "Benim Küçük Atölyem"

Burak Erkut
Doğu Akdeniz Üniversitesi, Cyprus

Hüseyin Karşılı
Bahçeşehir Cyprus University, Cyprus

ABSTRACT

This chapter focuses on a specific case of woman entrepreneurship – creative crafts. After being considered a dead industry, the creative crafts industry is going through a phase of comeback, where anti-commercialism, localism, and sub-cultural identification all drive the revival of this industry. The aim of this chapter is to understand the "how" and the "why" of women's entrepreneurship engaging in the creative crafts industry. For this purpose, the authors utilize a qualitative research approach combining observatory research, literature review, and interviews to highlight the decision of a woman entrepreneur to become active in the creative crafts industry and to understand how she is performing this duty – in particular, how she creates a unique work-life balance with the help of her husband and her family.

INTRODUCTION

Economic and social conditions shape business opportunities, and these opportunities can be equivalently situated in high technology industries as well as traditional ones. Currently, crafts industry is going through a phase of revival, not only because of

DOI: 10.4018/978-1-6684-5981-2.ch009

economic conditions but also due to social phenomena such as anti-commercialism, localism and sub-cultural identification (Jakob, 2013). Despite this ongoing phenomenon of the revival of the crafts industry, little has been done in business research to define or explore the "how" and "why" behind entrepreneurship in creative crafts. Some attempts to define crafts industry were done both by researchers and policy-makers alike, but little consensus has been reached on what one can define as "crafts" (Jakob, 2013). For example, (Adamson, 2009) defines crafts as "the application of skill and material-based knowledge to relatively small-scale production" (p. 3), whereas (U.S. Bureau of Labor Statistics, 2021) defines craft artists as those who "create or reproduce handmade objects for sale and exhibition using a variety of techniques, such as welding, weaving, pottery, and needlecraft". Despite these definition attempts, crafts, especially creative crafts are understood in a very limited, one-sided way as research is primarily focusing on the manual skills necessary for crafts (Sennett, 2008).

In order to overcome this shortcoming in research, a new stream of research from entrepreneurial studies started to focus on the transformative role of crafts entrepreneurs and what *else* is required for becoming a crafts entrepreneur in creative industries other than manual skills (Floris et al., 2020; Jakob, 2013; Katre, 2020; Marques et al., 2019; Phillipov, 2016; Ratten, 2022b, 2022a; Smagina & Ludviga, 2021; Thurnell-Read, 2021; Toker & Erkut, 2022). In this sense, research highlights the process of becoming a craft entrepreneur as a complex phenomenon, being at the crossroads of utilizing knowledge from different disciplines management, creativity, arts, and economics. This chapter focuses on a specific case of creative crafts entrepreneurship to focus on *why* an entrepreneur decides for becoming a creative crafts entrepreneur and *how* she is performing it. The research is a qualitative one, combining observatory research with a literature review and interviews to explore the phenomenon of creative crafts entrepreneurship. The rest of the chapter is organized as follows: First, the authors provide a review of the recent literature from the field of entrepreneurship research. Next, the authors describe their methodology. Afterwards, the authors present their findings and discuss them. Finally, a conclusion is provided, which also gives an overview of the limitations of this study together with suggesting some potential avenues for future research.

BACKGROUND

Creative crafts activities are as old as humankind, but they only recently went through a phase of revival, which came unexpected due to the general belief that crafts industry was considered dead or marginalized after the Industrial Revolution (Yang et al., 2021). (Ratten, 2022a) describes the crafts industry as a bridge of cultural traditions connecting artistic talent and economic activity, hence, it simultaneously fulfills two goals – contributing to the cultural scene of a country as well as to its economic development. Being active in the crafts industry goes through entrepreneurship, as the focal person handcrafts tangible items embodying their imagination and creativity. Whereas some of the basic materials being used in the crafts industry may be same, what distinguishes one artisan product from another is the creative design processes which differs from one artisan entrepreneur to another and which involves an aesthetic component (Ratten, 2022a). In this sense, the crafts industry can be characterized with highly differentiated products, where the focal artisan's unique imagination and creativity are the main sources of differentiation. Recent literature describes artisan entrepreneurs as the opposite of mass production, somehow like the entrepreneurial image the young Schumpeter had in his mind (also known as Schumpeter Mark I), focusing on the creation of new combinations, running a one-person-show, starting from the creative design process, and continuing with manufacturing and sales, being the sole responsible person for these processes (reference needed).

Nevertheless, academic research on the topic of crafts industry and entrepreneurial activities in this industry is limited (Phillipov, 2016; Ratten, 2022b). This may be also because artisans had a difficult relationship with commercialization, as commercialization and aesthetic creativity does not always have a straightforward relationship. Another possible reason is that academic research on entrepreneurship has its traditional domain in high technology start-ups or corporate entrepreneurship, and only recently started to view innovation within traditions (Floris et al., 2020). Nevertheless, (Toker & Erkut, 2022) notice that in the last two years there is a growing interest from former white-collar workers to give up their regular jobs and switch to entrepreneurial activities which are mainly in the traditional crafts sector, but in a different way: They are innovating and creating novelties using traditions and customs, interpreting the local culture in their own creative ways. A similar trend has also been identified by (Jakob, 2013) after the global economic recession. Usually, the most recent revival of the crafts industry is described as the third wave, which is mainly associated with "the current rise of fragmented consumer cultures and the increasing significance of handmade labour processes and the symbolic qualities of products" (Yang et al., 2021) (p. 547). With regard to innovating in creative crafts industries, (Naidu et al., 2014) identify eight factors that have significant impact. These are adding value to products, a unique design, development of novelties, distinctive cultural touch, technology use (especially advanced), experience and ability of owner to follow new trends and use of good quality raw materials. Similarly, (Marques et al., 2019) focus on the nature of innovation in traditional crafts industry, and identify that those entrepreneurs active in traditional crafts industry aim to keep the local culture and local traditions alive through innovations.

One of the particularly interesting issues in creative crafts entrepreneurship is the role played by interdisciplinarity. In this case, the contribution by (McAra & McHattie, 2020) provides an interesting insight. The authors report from a pop-up studio that brought together 22 Malaysian students of six distinctive indigenous craft pathways which are otherwise taught discrete from each other, leaving little space for interdisciplinary work. Through the pop-up studio, the intervention enabled an interdisciplinary interaction across these indigenous craft pathways to provide fertile grounds for innovation. Through the intervention, participating students could shift their creativity approach to offer a more interdisciplinary approach towards innovation. In this sense, creative crafts entrepreneurship differs from traditional crafts in the pure artistic sense, as traditional crafts may be separate from each other, whereas creative crafts entrepreneurship may offer space for innovating by means of creating new combinations of existing traditional craft pathways.

Entrepreneurship in the crafts industry therefore differs from entrepreneurship in other industries primarily because the focal entrepreneurs are mainly driven by their creativity, aesthetic perspective, and artisan talent instead of a mere commercialization focus (Smagina & Ludviga, 2021). Whereas creativity is an important asset for entrepreneurship regardless of the industry, in case of crafts industry it is interpreted in a different way since in case of high technology entrepreneurship creativity is used for solving problems to close a market gap. In case of crafts industry, creativity is the point of departure to create a unique, artisan artefact which may nevertheless have a commercial value. Even though there are different approaches to frame entrepreneurship in crafts industry, recent research indicates that it should be treated and explored as a separate category in entrepreneurship research, in opposition to familiar, yet different cases of cultural entrepreneurship or low technology entrepreneurship (Smagina & Ludviga, 2021). Furthermore, (Ratten, 2022a) indicates that artisan businesses are unique in their character, and therefore, each artisan business should be analyzed on a case-by-case basis instead of relying on generalized assumptions.

METHODOLOGY

The main aim of this research is to explore the phenomenon of creative crafts entrepreneurship and its underlying mechanisms in case of a single-person creative crafts entrepreneur. In the previous section, state-of-the-art literature was analyzed to identify that entrepreneurship in creative crafts industry is unique, and no generalization is hitherto possible since each case may reflect different findings. In addition, since research in this field is not advanced, the "how" and the "why" of creative crafts entrepreneurship still needs to be highlighted. Hence, the research questions that are going to be explored are:

- Why is a single-person creative crafts entrepreneur engaging in creative crafts entrepreneurship?
- How is a single-person creative crafts entrepreneur engaging in creative crafts entrepreneurship?

This research utilizes a qualitative research design by focusing on a combination of interviews and an observational study. According to the methodological contribution by (Bøllingtoft, 2007), observational studies can add new aspects and perspectives to entrepreneurship research by adding depth to the *why* and *how* of entrepreneurship. In this context, North Cyprus is selected as the place of observation due to its long history of crafts. North Cyprus is traditionally a place of crafts industries since the conquest of the Cyprus Island by the Ottoman Empire, following the Turkish population's movement from mainland Türkiye to Cyprus who were mainly craftsmen. First, both authors visited various crafts bazaars in North Cyprus to get to know the crafts industry. Consequently, the observational study was conducted in July-August 2021, over a duration of two weeks, with a local creative crafts entrepreneur. From the continuum of observer roles presented by (Bøllingtoft, 2007), the author chose a complete insider role by means of the "participant as observer" approach, with which the author participated in the entrepreneurial activities of the focal artisan entrepreneur. In this sense, while the author got an active role in the activities, his identity was also known to the entrepreneur and her family, all of them being aware of the research purpose. In addition, a literature review was conducted, and interviews were conducted with 7 family members of Gülçin and one customer of hers (8 interviews in total, 4 female and 4 male). All interviews were conducted in Turkish, and recorded by a digital recording app. All interviewees were aware of the recording and approved it. In addition, authors took notes during the interviews. In this sense, the approach followed a triangulation procedure. During the interview processes, an interview guide accompanied the researchers which contained questions and general topics of interest related to the research questions. The researchers concurrently conducted and analyzed interviews to get an overview of the explorative character of the phenomenon and the related research questions.

FINDINGS AND DISCUSSION

Findings

The observatory research took place in July-August 2021 in the home of the entrepreneur and in her mother's home by one of the authors (Burak Erkut). The entrepreneur's name is Gülçin Uluçınar. She was born in 1989 and holds a bachelor's degree in pre-school teaching. She started her career as a pre-school teacher in a private school and gave birth to her first child in February 2016. After the end of her pregnancy leave, she found the atmosphere of her working place not particularly friendly for a person who recently gave birth and decided to resign. Back then, she started a new entrepreneurial activity that she named "Benim Küçük Atölyem" (translated as "My Little Atelier"), in which she focused on creating different kinds of ornaments made from felt, which is a traditional material used in Cyprus. As a source of inspiration, she initially followed other people on Instagram who created ornaments using felt, but later on became more independent from existing models of ornaments and created her own designs for purposes such as child birthdays, engagement parties, weddings, new year celebrations and further special occasions. She created an Instagram page, through which she could interact with her current and potential customers, receive orders, and keep her followers updated with new products. In addition, she could also utilize the network of her family and friends for further orders, as well as further orders from people living in her village and the neighboring villages. In July 2019, she gave birth to her second child, and her enterprise went through a creative break. Despite her husband Rıfat's support and an increasing demand for her products, she needed this creative break both for taking care of her newly born daughter and for analyzing new trends such as 3D printing and epoxy printing. This creative break went until July 2021, when she accepted an order of designing scented stones for a wedding party. The order was made for 400 ornaments – scented stones in the form of starfish.

This was the moment when the authors got involved in the observational part of the research. Gülçin knew one of the authors from his previous study (Toker & Erkut, 2022) and allowed him to become a "participant as observer" in her everyday work. The initial interview made with Gülçin focused on why she chose to become a creative crafts entrepreneur. Gülçin mainly emphasized that this was in fact a necessity-driven type of entrepreneurial activity, as it started in a period when she resigned from her former job. Even though she managed to keep up with her entrepreneurial activity after she got her current job, back then, she could not keep up with the work-life balance of her previous job and wanted to be more independent, taking care of her newly born baby, but at the same time having an income that was based on her talent. She was always keen on handicrafts and found the local culture of Cyprus particularly nurturing and inspiring. Despite the necessity-driven entrepreneurial approach, she did not want to randomly choose her field of action but wanted to make something in line with her talent and skills. Since she has always been talented with handcrafting items, this was a greenfield for her. Indeed, her point of departure was only a small step compared to what she has learned after she started her entrepreneurial activity – this was, on the first line, either inspiring from present models or completely creating new models of ornaments out of the traditional material felt, but later also included handcrafting ornaments out of materials that she did not previously use in her everyday life, such as scented stones or epoxy. Therefore, even though her customers are always open for new ideas regarding ornaments, and there was a clear market gap, her approach was necessity-driven, but did not require a big learning experience at the beginning. This was also a finding that was confirmed by further interviews with her family members, who all stated that her resignation was a decisive moment to be financially independent and at the same time more flexible to take care of her newly born baby. In addition, the interviewed family members stated that there were family members from previous generations who were especially talented with handcrafting items, therefore, Gülçin could easily observe these family members in her everyday life and could gain her talent of handcrafting at an early age. Furthermore, interviews with family members also highlighted that the beginnings of Gülçin's entrepreneurial activity did not require her to learn new skills. This only came afterwards, once she decided to completely create and design new ornaments for special purposes, and when she stopped restricting herself with felt only. This was partially unintentional, because her reputation led her to get new orders from new customers who already asked her e.g., to design an ornament for their wedding with coffee beans. Through this way, she learned to work with new types of material and to enhance her knowledge of handcrafting. Nevertheless, this was not solely a process of learning to work with new materials or create new designs, as interviews with further family members suggest. On the contrary, she also learned how to professionally use an Instagram and a Facebook page for her entrepreneurial activity, to make attractive photographs of her handcrafted ornaments, to select marketing slogans for individual items, and to interact with current or potential customers through social media. This latter point was also something that Gülçin mentioned, indicating that her entrepreneurial activity of designing ornaments was there to make special days of her customers unforgettable. This was something she could offer with her imagination and her creativity, and it was in fact a stronger motivation than mere profit-making despite the necessity-driven point of departure for her entrepreneurial activity. Her family members, who have been interviewed, also indicated that despite making a profit, she frequently invested her profits in learning to work with new materials or learning to create new items using existing materials. Even though her customers approve a specific design for their own purpose, to reach this point, she requires a lot of experimentation and trial-and-error with different materials to offer them solid alternatives. In this sense, they do not see the backstage of her entrepreneurial activity, the creative phase, but are merely confronted with ready-made suggestions. In fact, the trial-and-error based approach requires some investment as well, therefore, she uses one part of her earnings to reinvest in this experimentation phase.

A creative design phase was the first phase of the project. Gülçin already imagined some models in her mind, which she discussed together with the author, she drew them on paper as a point of departure. Out of the models she drew, she evaluated potential ones together with the author which would be most suitable for the wedding party of the customer. After this creative design phase, some of the models have been suggested to the customer, who decided for the model that was a scented stone in the form of a blue starfish with golden glossing on its top, together with a relevant scent resembling a sea breeze, as the wedding party had the concept of sea. In this sense, the creative part of the entrepreneurial process was not merely deciding on the object, but also on its appearance and scent. Afterwards, she started with planning the details of the scented stones, which were to be handcrafted. The next issue was to get the raw materials to handcraft the scented stones – the raw materials that needed to be purchased were a white powder, a specific dye, some glossing as well as the essential oil. One can easily find some suppliers of these raw materials, but the competition is not very big, therefore, Gülçin and similar entrepreneurs are rather price-takers in this setup. She mentioned that even though she knows her suppliers personally, they too are price-takers as raw materials are imported and not manufactured in Cyprus. Gülçin already owned silicon molds in the shape of starfish, which were also necessary. Since she was well informed about the raw material prices, she could easily make a price suggestion to the customer, which is mainly covering the cost she paid for the raw materials plus a mark-up for her own entrepreneurial effort. For the scented stones to be handcrafted, she and the author first had to put the powder, water, the essential oil into a large bowl to mix it well. Usually, powder and water need to be mixed with a certain ratio to make the dough consistent. In addition, the mixing of these ingredients had to be slow and should be performed with hand and not with a hand mixer, to avoid bubbles endangering the consistency of the dough. In addition, they had to work with smaller quantities, since the mixture could quickly turn into solid, and it is not advisable to work with a big quantity of ingredients once, but instead, work with smaller quantities for multiple times. In addition, she did not have enough silicon molds, so the entire process of mixing the ingredients, creating the dough, putting into silicon molds, letting it dry and finally removing it carefully from silicon molds had to be repeated multiple times.

During this process, the author first observed how she was measuring the amount of ingredients necessary for the dough, how she was mixing, and occasionally helped her to mix the ingredients. Later, the author could become more confident in mixing, and she allowed him to do it on his own. This was in a way like cooking a dish but required very precise amounts of ingredients as well as paying attention to small details such as stirring slowly to avoid bubbles. On the contrary, the process of putting the dough into the silicon molds was simpler than removing the dried scented stone out of the silicon mold without damaging it – which, of course, required some time to dry even though the summer weather in Cyprus is hot enough. Therefore, the time needed for the activity varied depending on the stage. This means that during the handcrafting of the dough more time was required, and the entrepreneur and the author were more active in comparison to waiting for the scented stones to dry. In this sense, after many rounds of repeating the same process, they finally finished the making of the scented stones.

The next step in the entrepreneurial activity of Gülçin was to package the ornaments with blue tulle, and to staple the wedding party details on it with a small piece of paper. For this purpose, Gülçin gathered her family members (her husband, her cousin, her mother, her two sisters, their husbands) in her mother's home. There was a task division since the starting point of the day: Gülçin, her cousin, her mother, and her sisters should package the ornaments, the author should cut the printed A4 paper into pieces, and Gülçin's husband should take care of the kids, together with the husbands of the other two sisters. As a small incentive, there was watermelon, hellim (traditional Cyprus cheese) and coffee for everyone. This was again a repetitive duty, the author had to pay extra attention to cut the paper into small pieces of square forms, every piece should be stapled to the packaged ornaments. Packaging the ornaments with tulle was rather a difficult duty, as the author has observed, since there was a single, very big piece of tulle that had to be cut in the same dimension for every ornament. Nevertheless, Gülçin, her cousin, her mother, and her sisters were already experienced with this type of packaging from helping Gülçin in the past with similar orders.

Gülçin, her family and the author could not finish everything at once; instead, they were making small breaks either for drinking coffee, eating hellim and watermelon or simply paying attention to kids. Apart from Gülçin's two kids, her two sisters also had three kids, therefore, the place was anything but silent. Even though it was a big relief that the three men were taking care of the kids, it was natural that the kids were sometimes coming to the working station and asking questions, showing their toys or trying to see what Gülçin and others were doing. In these cases, they were also making breaks because their duties were requiring a lot of attention. However, this was not a frequent case, since the three men knew quite well how to entertain the kids. In addition to the toys that they brought along, there was a television with internet connectivity, so they could easily go to YouTube or similar platforms to show kids cartoons or other programs that would be of interest for them. Hence, there was an interesting work-life balance thanks to the support of her family: One part helping her with packaging, the other part helping her with her kids, whereas she could focus on her duty to pack the ornaments. The entire process took them around two days to finish. The delivery to the customer occurred right after finishing the packaging of the ornaments. A brief interview with Gülçin's customer indicated that the customer chose to work with Gülçin because she values authentic goods, not mass-produced ones, designed for specific purposes and with a certain perspective of aesthetics.

Discussion

The entire process, the creative phase, the handcrafting phase and the packaging phase, not only required patience, but also a number of skills that are not obviously related with entrepreneurship. One skill that is central is a basic understanding of the chemistry of materials, since one requires the correct proportions of the raw materials to prepare the dough, one requires the correct speed of stirring so that the dough is prepared in a consistent way, and one needs to handle the dough with care when pouring it into the silicon molds as well as when taking it out of the same molds. It is also important to practice packaging, for example, cutting the right amount of tulle, making sure that the package is consistent, and cutting the paper tags in a proper way. On the other hand, one also requires a good understanding of public relations both online and offline, since the main channel of interaction with customers is the social media presence. From there onwards, one can initiate a dialogue in a constructive way to receive the order and make sure that the order comes in line with the expectations of the customers. Even for those who knows Gülçin well, like her friends or her villagers, need to get an idea of how her products look like to initiate their order; therefore, also they need to have a good look at the social media presence of her entrepreneurial activity. This also requires a dialogue between the entrepreneur and the customer and needs to be managed in an efficient way for recurrent sales and/or word-of-mouth marketing.

These skills indicate that the focal creative crafts entrepreneur needed to work in an interdisciplinary way, similar to what has been proposed in the study of (McAra & McHattie, 2020). Even though Gülçin's way of working interdisciplinary differs from the context described in (McAra & McHattie, 2020), it nevertheless offers a different creative mindset to start with. Also, with regard to the interviews being conducted, the authors could identify that Gülçin's family members described her very often as a "multi-talented individual", who is able to grasp new information from hitherto separated fields such as chemistry and marketing. In this sense, the focal creative crafts entrepreneur certainly requires handcrafting skills, but also skills that are coming from the domain of other disciplines. Despite the help coming from her family members, the most important phase in her entrepreneurial action, namely the design phase, occurs without the help of any family members – only in her own creative mindset. This means that she is able to bring together her skills, capabilities and perceptions of different disciplines in a unique framework to progress with innovation. This is in line with the findings of (Smagina & Ludviga, 2021) who emphasize that the focus of creative crafts entrepreneurs is on creativity and not primarily on mere profit-making, which is also the case with Gülçin. Despite her initial objective of starting her entrepreneurial activity as a necessity-driven approach, she uses her talent, her creative mindset, and her skills to progress with uniquely designed ornaments. In addition to the design phase, also the selection of the relevant raw materials is not a mere spot exchange process, but rather a long-term relationship with a trusted supplier to ensure the best achievable quality. Comparing this evidence with factors that influence innovation in a crafts-artisan setup by (Naidu et al., 2014), one can identify that the emphasis on the use of good quality raw materials is an important factor of influence in Gülçin's entrepreneurial activity. In addition, the basic raw materials are re-interpreted with emphasis to their usage in a wedding party, and with an interpretative, creative framework of Gülçin's mindset, hence, leading to the factor of adding value and creating unique design in the framework of (Naidu et al., 2014).

In addition, there are some skills which are obviously related with entrepreneurship, which are observed to be necessary during the entire entrepreneurial process. The first one is associated with creativity, which is considered as an important asset for entrepreneurial activity. Being creative in the sense of an artisan crafts entrepreneur indicates that the entrepreneur can imagine new combinations or new meanings in original ways and translate these into entrepreneurial action by means of the creation of novel artefacts. In case of Gülçin, her main asset is her imagination, which she utilizes to create new combinations of existing basic materials. After all, the silicon molds, the white powder for the creation of scented stones, as well as the essence oil all exist in separate forms; what she does with her creativity is to imagine an object that can fit well within the concept and the imagination of her customer, that has a unique combination of color, scent, appearance, and presentation (the latter through packaging).

The second one is associated with risk-taking behavior. Even though this is not her only job, as she is a pre-school teacher in a private school, she is investing her money, her time, and her efforts in this entrepreneurial activity. This means she is taking a risk, and any possible obstacle in front of an on-time and correct delivery of the order indicates that she would pay this with her reputation. This is a serious risk given she is not engaging in mass production but using her creativity, imagination, and entrepreneurial skills to create something unique that will fit the needs of her customer.

The third one is associated with managing people and raw materials in a way that resembles the duty of an operations manager. Even though raw materials can be bought from different suppliers, they are usually imported input goods, therefore, suppliers put a mark-up on the costs to sell it to entrepreneurs like Gülçin, who in turn puts another mark-up on this price to sell it to the end customer. Important in this context is to check out for the best quality of materials at the most affordable price, but also to engage in a long-term relationship with the supplier, since this may result in the advantage of the entrepreneur: If not in case of a price discount, then in case of becoming a priority customer for the supplier. Hence, if the supplier brings a restricted number of raw materials and there is excess demand, the supplier can choose to sell it to the priority customer. In addition, managing people is required as the ornaments must be packaged in the same way, and there should be no visible differences between any of the 400 ornaments. This requires a good degree of concentration, but also a good level of understanding of how the final product should look like. In addition, there needs to be incentives for those who are helping her. Since it is her family, she does not pay them in cash, but offers coffee, watermelon and hellim in exchange for their efforts. Especially during hot summer months, watermelon and hellim is a good combination to overcome heat and is highly prepared among locals in Cyprus. Therefore, this offer can give them a sense of refreshment and can compensate for their efforts. Managing people also goes through creating an atmosphere of a work-life balance for the entrepreneur. In this case, Gülçin's husband Rıfat together with her two sisters' husbands Hasan and Mustafa play a pivotal role, since they are the ones who take care of the kids during the entire entrepreneurial process.

Altogether, these three identified skills imply that creative crafts entrepreneurship is more than having manual skills, which is in line with the criticism of (Sennett, 2008). In addition, the implication by (Hofland-Mol & Poortvliet, 2019) suggests that manual skills are only one part of the big picture, the other part being the entrepreneurial part. As a consequence, the creative crafts domain does not imply a mere artistic activity but rather an intersection of artistic activity with entrepreneurial skills and capabilities. This was most clearly seen in the observed case, and as such, the entrepreneur in the observed case was not *less* entrepreneurially active and/or talented than entrepreneurs in other industries, e.g., high technology or services. Nevertheless, public perception of creative crafts entrepreneurs is mainly based on the craftmanship and not on the entrepreneurial activity itself. This may be problematic because of a number of reasons. Firstly, this misperception may make potential crafts workers have the impression that no entrepreneurial skills or knowledge is necessary to engage in creative crafts entrepreneurship, which may have consequences such as higher failure rates. Second, this misperception may also be problematic regarding the role assigned to the creative crafts entrepreneurship by the society. If the society does not see the necessary skills and capabilities for creative crafts entrepreneurship, the activity may be simply seen as a non-profit or a pure artistic activity, and as such, may influence both the willingness-to-pay for the handcrafted items of creative crafts entrepreneurs, and legitimizing any potential policy interventions to support this industry, e.g., with support schemes financed by taxpayers.

In addition to the above-mentioned misperception, another issue that has been identified in the explored case was that the creative crafts entrepreneurs were offering differentiated goods, but their number was greater than the suppliers for the raw materials, a contradiction to the phenomenon identified by (Jakob, 2013). Jakob's observation of the creative crafts industry was that the growth in the creative crafts industry was mainly due to craft support activities such as raw materials or marketing support, but not because of the increase in handcrafted items. In other words, it was the craft support activities which was competitive, but not the creative crafts activities themselves. Here, the authors observed a different situation: Many small creative crafts entrepreneurs offering differentiated goods, but only few suppliers for the raw materials necessary for the handcrafting of these differentiated goods. An implication for this situation is that the suppliers may overcharge creative crafts entrepreneurs because of their oligopolistic nature in comparison to the competitive nature of the creative crafts entrepreneurs. Nevertheless, this observation of creative crafts entrepreneurs being active in a competitive market should not imply that they are all producing similar goods – on the contrary, they offer differentiated goods reflecting their own perception of aesthetics, their own imagination and creative mindset. As Gülçin's customer also suggested, it is not hard to order ready-made scented stones from big ventures focusing on mass production, but this would not be as meaningful as specially designed scented stones for her most special day. This is in line with the findings of (Yang et al., 2021), as creative crafts entrepreneurship is not a mere repetition of mass-produced items in small scale, but rather, using a creative mindset to design unique items and give meaning to these that goes beyond their material value. In this setup, it was also important to note that the aesthetic component was visible throughout the entire process, as such, confirming the findings by (Ratten, 2022a) stating that creative crafts entrepreneurship involves an aesthetic approach in the design process.

LIMITATIONS

Regarding limitations, the authors aim to emphasize that this is a single case, qualitatively analyzed using observation, and does not aim to offer a generalized perspective on crafts entrepreneurship. As stated in the literature review, and in line with the observations of (Ratten, 2022a), a case-by-case approach is necessary to explore the phenomenon of creative crafts entrepreneurship, since each case of creative crafts entrepreneurship may be different regarding its "how" and "why". Despite the criticism towards observation as an explorative method, the approach introduced a triangulation method to observation by connecting the findings with interviews on the one hand, and a literature review on the other.

FUTURE RESEARCH DIRECTIONS

The research objective was within the framework of critical realism (Bøllingtoft, 2007), as the authors aimed to observe the underlying mechanisms that can explain the "how" and "why" of creative crafts entrepreneurship. This means there is room for future research, as creative crafts entrepreneurship is still a new topic in entrepreneurship research despite crafts industry being as old as mankind. On the one hand, this chapter calls for future explorations of individual or multiple cases of creative crafts entrepreneurs. On the other hand, the chapter can serve as the basis for more systematic research towards capturing patterns in creative crafts entrepreneurship.

CONCLUSION

The financial commitment of the creative industries is estimated according to the two points of view: Gross Domestic Product (GDP) and number of workers. The developing financial effect of creative industries has become increasingly clearer in the past few years, also in North Cyprus which was the geographical location of observation. Despite that in North Cyprus the term "creative crafts enterprises" as well as the capability of these enterprises for job creation and financial improvement is notable for decades, characterizing creative industries is something rather new. Empirical evidence features the way that organizations run by innovative substance makers business people and inventive specialist organizations business visionaries have a more prominent effect and potential for financial development than inventive experience suppliers' business people and inventive unique makers business people (Bujor & Avasilcai, 2014). This is because of the way that the former two make/produce and infrequently own intellectual property that can be imitated with the reason to financial development, while the latter two normally offer fewer open doors for public financial development, known as craftsman based rather than industrialized, as also stated by (Bujor & Avasilcai, 2014). The illustrated case here offers insights into the creative crafts entrepreneurship, especially focusing on the "why" and "how" of it. The "why" is primarily answered by a duality of two notions: Necessity and talent. Even though Gülçin started her entrepreneurial activity as a necessity-driven approach, her main competitive advantage is her talent, her creative mindset, and her abilities to engage in handcrafting, public relations, marketing, purchasing, and managing all under the same roof. The "how" is primarily answered by a duality of two notions: A very creative, individualistic phase for designing unique ornaments, followed by a very organized manufacturing phase, involving the management of raw materials, and people who help the entrepreneur. This resembles the case of an individual ambidextrous entrepreneur, who combines creative entrepreneurial behavior with capabilities to turn resources into outputs in an efficient way (Volery et al., 2015).

ACKNOWLEDGMENT

First and foremost, we would like to thank our dear wives Bügem Kırgın and Gülden Karşılı who guided us in starting this project. They provided us with important advice and helped us go through difficult periods. Their motivation and support contributed tremendously to the successful completion of the project. Furthermore, we dedicate our work to Melin Karşılı and Nisan Türkan Erkut. Melin is Hüseyin Karşılı's daughter and she was born during the writing phase of this chapter on 26 January 2022, whereas Nisan Türkan is Burak Erkut's daughter and she was born during the proofreading of this chapter on 7 March 2023.

REFERENCES

Adamson, G. (2009). *The Craft Reader*. Bloomsbury Visual Arts.

Bøllingtoft, A. (2007). A critical realist approach to quality in observation studies. In H. Neergaard & J. Ulhøi (Eds.), *Handbook of Qualitative Research Methods in Entrepreneurship* (pp. 406–433). Edward Elgar. doi:10.4337/9781847204387.00027

Bujor, A., & Avasilcai, S. (2014). Creative Entrepreneurship in Europe: A Framework of Analysis. *Annals of the Oradea University, 1*(1), 151–156. doi:10.15660/AUOFMTE.2014-1.2960

Floris, M., Dettori, A., & Dessi, C. (2020). Innovation within tradition: Interesting insights from two small family bakeries. *Piccola Impresa/Small Business, 1*, 70–92.

Hofland-Mol, M., & Poortvliet, M. (2019). Crafts in the Netherlands: From an Economic to a Value-Based Perspective. In A. Mignosa & P. Kotipalli (Eds.), *A Cultural Economic Analysis of Craft* (pp. 129–142). Springer International Publishing. doi:10.1007/978-3-030-02164-1_11

Jakob, D. (2013). Crafting your way out of the recession? New craft entrepreneurs and the global economic downturn. *Cambridge Journal of Regions, Economy and Society*, *6*(1), 127–140. doi:10.1093/cjres/rss022

Katre, A. (2020). Self-Directed Learning on the Runway to Crafts Entrepreneurship. *Artivate: A Journal of Entrepreneurship in the Arts, 9*(2). doi:10.34053/artivate.9.2.119

Marques, C. S., Santos, G., Ratten, V., & Barros, A. B. (2019). Innovation as a booster of rural artisan entrepreneurship: A case study of black pottery. *International Journal of Entrepreneurial Behaviour & Research*, *25*(4), 753–772. doi:10.1108/IJEBR-02-2018-0104

McAra, M., & McHattie, L.-S. (2020). Crafting Futures: Inspiring Interdisciplinary Innovation with Young Craft Artisans in Malaysia. *Pages on Arts and Design*, *18*, 306–328.

Naidu, S., Chand, A., & Southgate, P. (2014). Determinants of innovation in the handicraft industry of Fiji and Tonga: An empirical analysis from a tourism perspective. *Journal of Enterprising Communities: People and Places in the Global Economy*, *8*(4), 318–330. doi:10.1108/JEC-11-2013-0033

Phillipov, M. (2016). Using media to promote artisan food and beverages: Insights from the television industry. *British Food Journal*, *118*(3), 588–602. doi:10.1108/BFJ-06-2015-0219

Ratten, V. (2022a). Artisan entrepreneurship in Indonesia. In V. Ratten (Ed.), *Entrepreneurship in Indonesia* (pp. 14–31). Routledge.

Ratten, V. (2022b). Food artisan entrepreneurship in Indonesia. In *Entrepreneurship in Indonesia* (pp. 32–44). Routledge.

Sennett, R. (2008). *The Craftsman*. Yale University Process.

Smagina, A., & Ludviga, I. (2021). *What is Crafts Entrepreneurship? The Development of its Definition Through Entrepreneurs` and Consumers` Perceptions*. doi:10.22616/REEP.2021.14.045

Thurnell-Read, T. (2021). Kindred spirits: Doing family through craft entrepreneurship. *The Sociological Review*, *69*(1), 37–52. doi:10.1177/0038026120916131

Toker, B., & Erkut, B. (2022). Old Roots into New Trees: Artisan Entrepreneurship in Cyprus. In R. Boateng, S. L. Boateng, & T. Anning-Dorson (Eds.), *Delivering Distinctive Value in Emerging Economies: Efficient and Sustainably Responsible Perspectives from Management Researchers and Practitioners*. Routledge. doi:10.4324/9781003152217-7

U.S. Bureau of Labor Statistics. (2021, March 31). *27-1012 Craft Artists*. Occupational Employment and Wage Statistics.

Volery, T., Mueller, S., & von Siemens, B. (2015). Entrepreneur ambidexterity: A study of entrepreneur behaviours and competencies in growth-oriented small and medium-sized enterprises. *International Small Business Journal: Researching Entrepreneurship*, *33*(2), 109–129. doi:10.1177/0266242613484777

Yang, X., Xu, H., & Ni, S. (2021). The creative renewal of a craft cluster: The role of materiality and mobility in cluster evolution. *Regional Studies*, *55*(3), 546–555. doi:10.1080/00343404.2020.1802417

ADDITIONAL READING

Aisyah, S., Musa, C. I., & Ramli, A. (2017). Effect of Characteristics and Entrepreneurial Orientation towards Entrepreneurship Competence and Crafts and Arts Small and Medium Enterprises Business Performance in Makassar. *International Review of Management and Marketing*, *7*(2), 166–173.

Bellér-Hann, I. (1998). Crafts, entrepreneurship and gendered economic relations in Southern Xinjiang in the era of 'socialist commodity economy''.'. *Central Asian Survey*, *17*(4), 701–718. doi:10.1080/02634939808401064

Katre, A. (2020). Self-Directed Learning on the Runway to Crafts Entrepreneurship: Achieving Product–Market Fit through Learning Cycles with Self-Management and Self-Control. *Artivate*, *9*(2), 45–62. doi:10.1353/artv.2020.0013

Ona, J. G., & Solis, L. S. L. (2017). Challenges and opportunities for the development and promotion of Ibaloy crafts as tourism products. *International Journal of Culture, Tourism and Hospitality Research*, *11*(4), 593–607. doi:10.1108/IJCTHR-11-2016-0112

Ratten, V. (2022). *Entrepreneurship in Creative Crafts*. Routledge. doi:10.4324/9781003267225

Roostika, R., Wahyuningsihb, T., & Haryono, S. (2015). Destination Competitiveness Analysis for Creative Crafts Industries in Bantul Yogyakarta Indonesia. *Journal of Corporate Governance, Insurance, and Risk Management*, *2*(3), 16–33. doi:10.56578/jcgirm020302

Sarmento, M., Amorim, M., Dias, M. F., & Madaleno, M. (2019). Product Innovation in the Crafts Sector. *Technology Transfer and Entrepreneurship*, *5*(2), 100–109. doi:10.2174/2213809906666181218111649

KEY TERMS AND DEFINITIONS

Creative Crafts: An embodiment of human creativity in the form of functional or utilitarian products.

Creativity: An individual's ability to interpret the world in different, novel ways.

Entrepreneurship: The application of skills such as taking initiative, intuitive decision-making, networking, identification of opportunities, creatively solving problems, strategic thinking, and personal effectiveness in order to create a new venture by launching a new product or a new service.

Necessity-Driven Entrepreneurship: A type of entrepreneurial activity in which the individual starts up his/her own venture for the sake of generating income, e.g., after losing his/her job. In this instance, the aim of the activity is survival.

Oligopoly: A market form that is based on a small number of producers.

Product Differentiation: Developing and launching a product that differs from other products in the same industry by means of its properties.

Schumpeterian Types of Innovation: Joseph Alois Schumpeter described five different ways of innovating; these are (1) introducing a new or an improved product or service, (2) introducing a new process, (3) shaping a new market, (4) identifying a new raw material, and (5) creating new types of industrial organization.

Chapter 10
From Struggle to Strength: Gender Parity in Top-Level Leadership

Subrata Kumar Ray
Prabhu Jagatbandhu College, India

Sutapa Ray
Prabhu Jagatbandhu College, India

Asim Kumar Karmakar
School of Professional Studies, Netaji Subhas Open University, India

ABSTRACT

Gender inequality has always been an issue of concern. Leaders in business and government make significant and far-reaching decisions influencing many facets of society. But relatively few of these powerful positions are held by women. This chapter explores gender in leadership by focusing on the difficulties women experience in attaining and being seen as effective in top leadership positions. This chapter highlights the COVID-19 effects on management decision and gender discrimination. In this regard, this chapter takes into account the gender-differential impact of COVID-19 in relation to the response strategies, challenges, and policies at the management level and also in the global labour market. Next the chapter focuses on the most important cause of this gender disparity in management levels of empowerment of women's economic positions. This chapter is dedicated to the goal of getting rid of gender disparity and attaining a just society based on ethical norms and principles of working conditions of women in the management as well as global labour markets.

DOI: 10.4018/978-1-6684-5981-2.ch010

INTRODUCTION

Gender inequality has always been an issue of concern. The main reason behind this is attributed to the preponderance of men in positions of power. In a patriarchal society it has always been men who have dominated and exploited the women. When men and women are treated differently gender inequality arises. It is a matter of common observation that men and women perform the same tasks which require application of same skills, knowledge and experience for which men are given higher remuneration than their female counterparts. This is unethical discrimination of women emerges when women is paid low in comparison with men.. This is an issue of gender ethics which needs to be rectified.

If we look at the history of human development we will see that woman has been as important as man. In fact the development of a nation depends to a large extent on the status, employment and work performed by women in the society. Without the participation of women in national activities, the social, political, or economic progress of a country will be stagnated. Women constitute half of the human population. Contributing two-thirds of world's work hours, she earns only one-third of the total income and owns less than one-tenth of the world's resources. This shows that the status of women is in a pathetic condition and this is more so in a country like India. Gender inequality is a stark reality facing us despite the efforts of social reformers trying to eradicate this inequality since generations now(Pawer 2020). This chapter endeavors to show the traverse the path of women leaders from the struggle to strength in contributing to gender parity in the society infested with gross inequality. Besides, this chapter, along with other things explores gender in leadership by focusing on the difficulties women experience in attaining and being seen as effective in top leadership positions.

Women Empowerment

Empowerment has become a popular term. By the 1980s empowerment was being advocated as a necessary ingredient for challenging and transforming unequal political, economic and social structure. It was regarded as a weapon for the weak—best wielded through participatory, grassroots community based activities. However, empowerment has many meanings and by the mid-1990s, some mainstream development agencies had begun to adopt the term, while mainstream institutions and their practitioners for the most part envision empowerment as a means for enhancing efficiency and productivity within the status quo rather than as a mechanism for social transformation. These debates and perspectives have influenced (and been influenced by) development theorists and practitioners concerned with women, gender and development as well. An initial focus on integrating women into development in the 1970s, shifted to a concern with gender and gender relations in the late 1980s (Moser, 1993; Parpart et al., 2000). However, some activists and theorists from the South, and a few from the North, began to recognize the limitations of even this advance. They began to argue that women would never develop unless they are empowered to challenge patriachy and global inequality. Gita sen and Caren Crown introduced the term in their landmark book, Development, Crises and Alternative Visions (1987). They offered a new vision of empowerment rooted in a commitment to collective action growing out of the lived experiences of women (and men) in the South, as well as a concern for political and economic inequality. While utopian in tone, the book calls for a collective vision, a set of strategies and new method for mobilizing political will, empowering women (and poor men) and transforming society. The authors put considerable faith in the transformative potential of 'political mobilization, legal changes, consciousness raising, and popular education'(p.187).

Writing on empowerment and gender as an approach to development has continued to emerge in the alternative development literature, especially from the South. In 1994, for example, Srilatha Batliwala considered empowerment as 'the process of challenging existing power relations and of gaining greater control over the sources of power' (1994: 130).Thus, while acknowledging the need to improve the lives of grassroots women, Batliwala insists that women's empowerment requires transformative political action as well.

Naila Kabeer (1994) also insists on the centrality of empowerment for the struggle to achieve gender equality. She criticizes the liberal and Marxist emphasis on power over resources., institutions and decision-making, and adds emphasis on power as ability to control discussions/discourses and agenda. Like Batliwala, she emphasizes collective, grass roots participatory action--- power to work with others 'to control resources, determine agendas and to make decisions ' (Kabeer 1994: 229). More concerned with action than theory, she continues to explore practical, measurable way to empower women (Kabeer, 1999).

Bringing a broader analytical perspective to the analysis of gender and empowerment, Jo Rowlands (1997) argues that' empowerment is more than participation in decision-making; it is personal, relational and collective. She recognizes that empowerment is not just a gender issue, but a development issue affecting women and men. She remains convinced that the key to empowerment lies in mobilizing marginalized people, especially women. She cautions, however, that empowerment is a process rather than an end product, neither easily defined nor measured. At the same time, she believes that there is a core to the empowerment process… which consists of increases in self-confidence and self-esteem (1997: 129-30).

Sustainable development of a nation is impossible without women's empowerment and gender equality. Consequently, it is asserted that gender equality is both a human rights issue and a precondition for, and indicator of, sustainable development. It is also affirmed that gender disparity is prevalent across the cultures of the world and that without serious steps to tackle it, sustainable development cannot be achieved. Furthermore, it is rightly believed that to create a just and sustainable world and to enhance women's roles in sustaining their families and communities, achieving gender equality is paramount. On the other hand, if gender equality is not maintained, it will retard the country's development.

Disparity in Top Leadership Positions

There is an astounding gender gap in top leadership positions across all countries in the world. The genesis of this gap lies in various factors which we have tried to identify here. Unless these are understood in depth, these barriers may be overcome and consequently gender bias may be reduced.

Firstly, women have to face the criticism of going against their basic nature whenever they assume a position of power and leadership. Ambition and aggression in men is considered to be their innate characteristics whereas in case of women they are criticized as pushy, selfish, abrasive, aggressive and deceitful. It is extremely unfair that the same personality traits are considered positive traits in case of men and negative traits in case of women. Aggression is a valued leadership quality in men and a negative quality in women which becomes a hindrance in their path of growth. This leads to a prejudice that women are either not ambitious enough to be leaders or are too aggressive leaders. Women are seen struggling to develop a variety of leadership that reconciles the dichotomy between their feminine traits and the opposing leadership qualities. It is a tricky situation to strike a balance between these two extreme poles. One who is able to do so comes out as a powerful leader who changes the society for the better.

Secondly, women leaders are frequently criticized for being easily swayed by other people's opinions rather than following their own judgments regarding various issues on which strict decisions need to be taken. A successful leader must be impartial, decisive, confident and exemplary.

Thirdly, women are often criticized that they are not enough authoritative in performing their leadership responsibilities. They are considered to be weak and indecisive when it comes to taking tough administrative measures and policy decisions. Their preference for collaborative and participative leadership gives an impression that they are not fit for leading by example. Consequently women leaders are not generally taken seriously.

Fourthly, women are the primary caregivers in society. In the family it is expected that she will be the one to sacrifice her career for taking care of members of the family. Even outside the family whenever an elderly kin is sick or in trouble it is the woman who is expected to rush to provide service to the person in need.

Fifthly, sex discrimination is a huge hindrance in the path of women aspiring for top leadership positions. Discriminatory attitudes are often embedded in inaccurate facts about women's actual capacity to shoulder the responsibilities of top leadership positions.

Sixthly, women are a target of sexual harassment at workplace and become victims of male sexual assaults. Sexual harassment is a big hindrance in the path of women struggling to empower herself and achieve top leadership positions. Sexual harassment at workplace demoralizes women and creates an environment of intimidation as they feel hesitant to report cases for fear of being further victimized

Last but not the least, we would like to highlight the problem of mentoring in case of women aspiring for top leadership positions. Since very few women reach the top, there is a dearth of successful female role models and mentors. Behind every successful person there is a mentor who guides the younger aspiring people working hard to climb up the ladder to the top leadership positions. A mentor is someone who gives advice and support to a less experienced person and influences his personal and professional growth.

The way out of this vicious circle of men making male leaders is to foster unity among women to combat institutional norms which have been excluding women throughout generations. Women have to be more aware and conscious about mentoring junior women to reach the topmost leadership positions. An alternative approach has to be developed which will attempt to counter the traditional style of leadership involving competitive, patriarchal, and individualistic values that are intrinsic to the hierarchical process highlighting men as leaders.

COVID-19: Effects on Management Decision and Gender Disparity

With the advent of Covid-19 the situation seems to have worsened and put women under considerable stress. They continued to carry the burden of care during the pandemic, increasing the gender gap which was already disproportionally high in normal times. The women work-force has been ethically wronged since generations. During the pandemic the women were subjected to forced sexual activities which resulted in higher birth rates. This proved to be harmful for the economy. Both inside the household as well as outside, the women are tortured and are ethically highly wronged.

This seems to be a gross violation of ethical norms and principles. But the situation was not like this in the ancient vedic ages. However,cross different countries (some developed and some developing countries) various strategies have been adopted to effectively tackle the problem of gender disparity in the top level leadership and the labour market. We enumerate some of the measures below:

Education and Women Empowerment

Education is milestone of women empowerment as only the educated women can play a very dominant role in the economic development of our country as well as in becoming informed citizens, parents, and family members. Therefore educating the women" is the most powerful tool that can bring change of position of women in society bringing reduction in inequalities and functions as a means of improving their status within the family. Education implies not only gaining knowledge but also transforming that knowledge into application through vocational training and skill development.

Major efforts to achieve gender equality should be linked to the economic empowerment of women's economic positions, ensuring not only equal rights for men and women, but also equal benefits from economic activities. Women empowerment is the answer here. Empowerment is a multi-dimensional process, which should enable women to realize their full identity and power in all spheres of life

Sustainable development of a nation in parity with with the SDGs is impossible without women's empowerment and gender equality. Consequently, it is asserted that gender equality is both a human rights issue and a precondition for, and indicator of, sustainable development. It is also affirmed that gender disparity is prevalent across the cultures of the world and that without serious steps to tackle it, sustainable development cannot be achieved. Furthermore, it is rightly believed that to create a just and sustainable world and to enhance women's roles in sustaining their families and communities, achieving gender equality is paramount. On the other hand, if gender equality is not maintained, it will retard the country's development.

Therefore, without the equal inclusion of women in all areas of development initiatives, sustainable development cannot be achieved. For example, women's entrepreneurship should be encouraged at all levels. The Self-help groups have given women the much needed socio-economic boost to attain financial independence. But the ground reality in case of Bangladesh in the face of rigid Muslim Laws, social restrictions on women, the position and status of women are slightly increased. The ground reality seems to be far from the projected statistics. The amendment in the Indian Constitution initiated by the then Prime Minister of India, Shri Rajiv Gandhi, to introduce 33% reservations for female candidates in the Panchayat Elections, has definitely made a place for women in the political scenario of the nation but in reality women have not actually been given any political powers. The men dictate them and dominate the political decisions in a pseudo form. Women assume the chair but are mere puppets in the hands of their male counterparts (Jha & Mishra, 2020).

The increasing vulnerable situations of India's women, particularly of its women's workers is confirmed by the Global Gender gap Report published by the World Economic Forum (WEF) in 2017. The report looks at the four components: economic participation, educational attainment, health status, and political empowerment. In three of the four indicators, India ranks in the bottom half of the table. For example, in terms of economic empowerment of women, India ranked 139 out of 144 countries, and in terms of health and survival it ranked 141 out of 144 countries. Even in educational attainment, a factor hyped by the government as a major achievement, the country only ranked 112 out of 144 countries the only indicator where it ranked in the top top-20 was political empowerment. Because of this, the overall position of India improved slightly, but the country still ranked a poor 180 amongst 144 countries as far as gender was concerned (World Economic Forum, 2017).

Women Leaders in the Global Scenario

The world has been battered by multiple crises in the recent years, including a global pandemic that has infected tens of millions, cost more than 1.5 million lives, and devastated almost every nation's economy. But according to a study by the Centre for Economic Policy Research (CEPR) and the World Economic Forum (WEF), countries led by women had "systematically and significantly better" outcomes related to COVID-19, which were the result of "proactive and coordinated policy responses" such as earlier lockdowns. This fact is something to be pondered upon. In this section we highlight which women have offered models of creative, thoughtful and decisive leadership. Whether guiding a nation with a steady hand or rising up against injustice, these leaders offer glimpses of how to make progress in the most difficult of circumstances.

First, we may mention the name of Prime Minister of New Zealand, Jacinda Ardern. She has been highly appreciated for leading one of the world's most successful coronavirus responses. Jacinda Ardern and her Labour party won a landslide victory in October's election. Angela Merkel, chancellor of Germany has been acknowledged as a great leader Third, we talk of Kamala Harris, US Vice-president elect.

We can also talk of some leaders/ women activists from India who have created a difference to the world by their inspirational lives and works. Indian women have always been a symbol of beauty, strength, and intelligence. Today the success of Indian women in various walks of life has proved that they have earned this reputation very well. We may mention the name of Medha Patekar, Kiran Bedi, Laxmi Agarwal, Aruna Roy, Sunitha Krisnan, Arundhati Roy, Kriti Bharti, Vandana Shiva, Manasi Pradhan, and Saraswathi Gora.

In this context we may lay down certain indicators of women empowerment and gender parity by following which the goal of eradicating disparity may be achieved. They are as follows:

- Participation in crucial decision-making processes
- Extent of sharing domestic work by men
- Extent to which a woman takes control of her reproductive functions and decides on family size
- Extent to which a woman is able to decide how and where she will spend her earnings
- Feelings of pride and value in her work
- Self-confidence and self-esteem
- Ability to prevent violence against her or others (Segalo & Fine, 2020)

At the community and organizational level the indicators of empowerment are:

- Existence of women's organizations
- Allocation of funds to women and women's projects
- Increased number of women leaders at village, district, state and national levels
- Involvement of women in the design, development and application of technology
- Participation in community programmes, politics, and arts
- Exercising her legal rights when required

Concluding Observations: The Roadmap to Gender Parity

Women are still significantly underrepresented at all levels of management. And on top of this, women continue to have a worse day-to-day experience at work. To bring about radical change, companies need to invest deeply in all aspects of diversity, equity, and inclusion. This starts with taking bold steps to ensure that women of diverse identities are well represented. Companies also need to create a culture that fully leverages the benefits of diversity—one in which women, and all employees, feel comfortable bringing their unique ideas, perspectives, and experiences to the table. When women are respected and their contributions are valued, they are more likely to be happy in their jobs and to feel connected to their coworkers.

First, they need to put more practices in place to ensure promotions are equitable. Companies are currently taking more steps to reduce bias in hiring, and they need to apply that same rigor to the performance review process.

Women's day-to-day experiences are shaped primarily by their interactions with managers and colleagues, which means that deep cultural change is possible only if all employees are empowered to be part of the solution. This starts with raising awareness. Employees need to understand the barriers that women face—particularly women with traditionally marginalized identities—and the benefits of a more inclusive culture. Companies can promote awareness by sharing data on the experiences of women in their organizations, bringing in thought-provoking speakers, and encouraging employees to openly share their experience and ideas. For employees to move from awareness to action, training is an important step. The number of employees who receive training on bias, antiracism, and ally ship is on the rise. Companies need to take bolder steps to encourage participation, such as offering incentives or making training mandatory. They should also invest in ongoing employee education; it takes consistent reinforcement to reshape deep-rooted biases and change behavior, so a one-and-done approach to training is not enough. And companies need to be sure that they are incorporating the new ideas and tools from training into everyday processes, too. For example, before hiring and promotion processes begin, companies can send out reminders about how bias can influence evaluations; research shows that this simple practice can improve outcomes for women and other people from underrepresented groups. Finally, companies should clearly communicate what is expected of employees and what it means to have an inclusive culture. Building this thinking into company values is a good place to start, but organizations would benefit from articulating the specific behaviors and actions that promote inclusion.

Companies can make their workplaces more inclusive. Senior leaders also play a key role in ensuring that such initiatives are appropriately resourced across their organizations. This is just another reason why it is critically important to hold leaders accountable for progress in this area and to formalize this accountability.

From the above discussions what comes is that to get rid of gender disparity and attaining a Just Society based on ethical norms and principles of working conditions of women in the management in line with the advancement of global labour markets is urgently called for.

REFERENCES

Batliwala, S. (1994). The Meaning of Women's Empowerment: New Concepts from Action. In G. Sen, A. German, & L. C. Chen (Eds.), *Population Policies Reconsidered: Health, Empowerments and Rights*. Harvard University Press.

Jha, P., Kumar, A., & Yamini Mishra, Y. (2020). Labouring Women: Issues and Challenges in Contemporary India. Orient Blackswan.

Kabeer, N. (1994). *Reversed realities: Gender Hierarchies in Development Thought*. Verso.

Kabeer, N. (1999). Resources, agency, achievements: Reflections on the measurement of women's empowerment. *Development and Change*, *30*(3), 435–464. doi:10.1111/1467-7660.00125

Karmakar, A. K., & Bagchi, P. (2022). Gender Inequality, Women Empowerment and Public Action in India. In S. Maiti, T. Gupta, & D. Sharma (Eds.), *Economic Growth, Development and Social Challenges in the New Normal* (pp. 85–99). Kunal Books.

Moser, C. (1993). *Gender Planning and Development: Theory, Practice and Training*. Routledge.

Pawer, A. S. (2020). *Agony of the Indian Women*. Dattsons.

Rowlands, J. (1997). *Questioning Empowerment: Working with Women in Honduras*. Oxam Publications. doi:10.3362/9780855988364

Segalo, P., & Fine, M. (2020). Underlying conditions of gender-based violence—Decolonial feminism meets epistemic ignorance: Critical transnational conversations. *Social and Personality Psychology Compass*, *14*(10), 1–10. doi:10.1111pc3.12568

Sen, G., & Crown, C (1987). *Development, Crises and Alternative Visions: Third World Women's Perspectives*. Monthly Review Press.

World Economic Forum. (2017). *The Global Gender Gap Report*. WEF.

Chapter 11
Tearing the Veil of Hegemonies:
The Emancipatory Power of Accounting for Entrepreneurial Women in the Amazon

Juliene do Socorro e Silva Pereira
Federal University of Pará, Brazil

Àleff dos Santos Santana
Federal University of Pará, Brazil

Adriana Rodrigues Silva
Polytechnic Institute of Santarém, Portugal

Rui Manuel da Costa Robalo
Polytechnic Institute of Santarém, Portugal

ABSTRACT

This study aims to examine how the emancipatory power of accounting enables ruptures of hegemonies in the context of entrepreneurial women in the Amazon. The research applied the personal testimony method with the participation of four entrepreneurial women with an accounting background. The data were collected through interviews. The results show that entrepreneurial women in the Amazon faced work environments with prejudice, devaluation, discredited capacity, and harassment. However, this scenario has been undergoing changes brought about by female entrepreneurship and, above all, accounting. The evidence indicates that the emancipatory power of accounting can provide a break with socially produced hegemonies, enabling the personal, professional, and financial independence of the women. Thus, the contribution of this study lies in the verification of the use of accounting to deconstruct prejudiced and chauvinistic social structures, reflecting positively on society and organizations.

DOI: 10.4018/978-1-6684-5981-2.ch011

INTRODUCTION

Since the constitution of the former civil societies, men have attributed characteristics capable of identifying them as a superior being, mainly due to the historically associated idea of him being the family protector and defender of collective interests (Lugarinho, 2013). Men have also attributed the power of commercialization and market movement. However, this scenario has been undergoing changes, given the struggle and incorporation of women into these activities (Monteiro & Souza, 2007).

Nevertheless, female entrepreneurship has been the most contemporary means of manifestation of these changes (Nogueira et al., 2013; Dornelas, 2012). Female entrepreneurship is capable of transforming conceptions into opportunities (Dornelas, 2012), enabling the placement of many women in the labour market (Nogueira et al., 2013) and allowing for growth, benefits, and job generation for other women, becoming a positive cycle in societies (Monteiro & Souza, 2007).

In Amazon, entrepreneurial women create employment and income for the female public (Queiroz, 2013). Furthermore, entrepreneurship in the Amazon encourages family groups (Filion, 1999), as well as provokes a persistent search to preserve and develop sustainability in the context in which these women are inserted (Gomes, 2021). In this scenario, accounting can play a fundamental role, essentially in aiding the rupture of socially constructed paradigms (Sampaio et al., 2017).

The conventional purpose of accounting has not undergone significant changes over time. Its function remains to provide helpful information for economic decisions (Iudícibus, 2021). Nevertheless, accounting cannot be isolated from the social processes that take place both internally and externally in organizations (Mellemvik, Monsen & Olson, 1988). Thus, the broadening of the meaning of accounting has allowed contemporary research to present its emancipatory potential, that is, paradigmatic and situational changes that can be realized through accounting (Gallhofer & Haslam, 2017; Gallhofer, Haslam & Yonekura, 2015).

When relating accounting as an emancipation tool for entrepreneurial women, this area of knowledge stands out for the study of minorities in a social environment (Gallhofer & Haslam, 2017). Since hegemonies, double working day and the prejudiced practice continue strengthening barriers in disadvantage of women (Bruschini & Lombardi, 2002), accounting may be able to show society a new social view, enabling freedom, opportunity, among other factors (Haslam, 2016; Jonathan, 2005). Hegemonies are sustained in the economic, political, cultural, and ideological domains of dominant groups and vulnerable individuals (Fairclough, 2016). These constructs negatively affect diversity and the guarantee of fundamental rights (Ferreira, 1986). Therefore, instruments are needed to help minorities overcome these obstacles (Gallhofer & Haslam, 2017; Ferreira,1986).

Although there is research on accounting as a mechanism of social transformation (Gallhofer & Haslam, 2019; Sampaio et al., 2017), there is still a need in the specialized literature for studies that demonstrate the emancipatory power of accounting in remote regions and with minority groups (Gallhofer & Haslam; 2019; Queiroz, 2013; Filion, 1999), such as that of active entrepreneurial women in the Amazon. To fill the existing gap in the literature, this study aims to examine how the emancipatory power of accounting enables ruptures of hegemonies in the context of entrepreneurial women in the Amazon. To this end, the research method used was oral reporting in the mode of personal testimony. Four entrepreneurial women with a degree in accounting and ventures located in the Amazon region participated in this study.

The contribution of this research consists of the evidencing of accounting, together with feminist entrepreneurship, as a tool capable of supporting the disruption of prejudiced and chauvinistic social structures, providing freedom and equality among the actors of society. That is, the exercise of the emancipatory power of accounting to positively modify social and organizational environments.

THEORETICAL FRAMEWORK

Female Entrepreneurship

Entrepreneurship has been gaining wide national and international prominence, presenting relevance in the 1990s, but peaking between 2000 and 2010 (Dornelas, 2012). In 2019, the Global Entrepreneurship Monitor showed that the total entrepreneurship rate in Brazil was 38.7%, i.e., it estimated that 53.4 million Brazilians are developing some entrepreneurial activity (Gem, 2020). By the year 2020, due to the crisis caused by the covid-19 pandemic, the Brazilian Micro and Small Business Support Service (Sebrae) estimates that the entrepreneurship rate will grow by 25%, an increase caused by the groups most affected by unemployment, such as women (Sebrae, 2020).

Some authors (e.g., Baron & Shane, 2007; Dornelas, 2012; Sarkar, 2010) define entrepreneurship as innovative ideas that enable the production of social benefits and improvements. For Dornelas (2012) entrepreneurship is the involvement of people and processes that together can transform ideas into opportunities. In turn, Sarkar (2010) states that entrepreneurial activities are processes of creation and/or expansion of businesses that are innovative or are born from verified opportunities. Baron and Shane (2007) conceptualize entrepreneurship as the involvement of recognizing the opportunity to create something new, not being necessary the formation of a new service or product.

When we seek the application of this concept in women's entrepreneurial activities, the literature on female entrepreneurship demonstrates limitations and does not clearly portray the information on the subject, nor with due protagonist to the cases involved (Kobeissi, 2010). The lack of access to the concept of female entrepreneurship makes women fit broadly into the definition of "entrepreneur", with no differences between men and women entrepreneurs (Strobino & Teixeira, 2014). Nevertheless, women have been asserting themselves in the labour market, thus referring to a great interest from the public sector, as well as from academic institutions, on the phenomenon of female entrepreneurship. This interest is justified because women are standing out in leadership positions, conquering more spaces in organizations, and obtaining recognition for the functions developed (Nogueira et al., 2013).

In Brazil, Sebrae (2020) highlights that in the last two years the proportion of entrepreneurial women has grown, reaching 45% of entrepreneurs. In addition, these women are categorized as "heads of household," that is, entrepreneurial activity has given these women the position of main source of income for their families, surpassing the conditions of their spouses. Currently, there are approximately 9.3 million Brazilian women in charge of an enterprise, corresponding to 34% of all business owners in the country.

On the other hand, the devaluation of women and their low salaries have been associated with the mistaken image of women as dependent and obliged to work only in the domestic sphere (Bruschini and Lombardi, 2002). However, breaking this paradigm has imposed a double role on women, that is, a double working day. For Jablonski (1996), a double working day is the accumulation of tasks that generates problems, conflicts, and stress for women. The conflict between work and family is related to three dimensions: excessive time spent at work; tension (anxiety, depression, and irritability); and behaviour, linked to self-confidence and objectivity (Greenhaus & Beutell,1985). Even so, many women decide to become entrepreneurs in search of flexible schedules, developing skills to manage these challenges (Gomes et al., 2009; Shelton, 2006; Quental & Wetzel, 2002).

As for business expansion, entrepreneurial women seek to grow in different ways compared to men, as they are more conservative and their planning, growth, and decision-making take place on an individual basis (Irme, 2019). Moreover, entrepreneurial women face difficulties in obtaining financial resources (Irme, 2019; Robb & Watson, 2012), with restrictions on access to credit (Irme, 2019; Julien et al., 2012), with social prejudice (Julien et al., 2012), with the lack of government policy and incentive aimed at female entrepreneurs (Gem, 2020; Sebrae, 2018), and with conflicts in work and family relationships (Mari et al., 2016).

The defining traces of the female public who are in the direction of their own business persist over the years. Thus, for Buttner and More (1997) there are three fundamental factors in the profile of entrepreneurial women: (i) self-determination, autonomy, and freedom; (ii) control of their destiny; and (iii) barriers related to the professional development of these women. Furthermore, entrepreneurial women seek autonomy, flexible working hours, a break from paradigms, freedom, and equal rights.

Even with the development of women in the labour market, gender inequalities (Abramo, 2004) or discrimination (Abramo, 2015) have not been reduced, nor women have had access to the more important hierarchical positions (Sebrae, 2018). Moreover, women also face problems related to low wage expectations. Although they mostly possess the highest levels of education than men assigned to similar positions, women end up receiving less for their labour (Dieese, 2021; Blau, 1998). According to Madalozzo (2011), investment difficulties are also generated by the prejudice that companies create by preferring men as CEO (Chief Executive Officer), believing that they are more rational in business. The environments in organizations based on assumptions of male superiority collaborate with the emergence of the glass ceiling phenomenon, characterized by the imposition of invisible barriers that hinder the professional advancement of women (Santos et al., 2014). The analysis developed by Botelho et al. (2008) shows that the difficulties faced by women are directly related to the cultural and social paradigms reflected in the professional environment.

However, the economic, political, cultural, and social instabilities of the 19th and 20th centuries allowed women to compete for better positions and for professions previously linked only to the male figure (Schweitzer, 2008). Sebrae's expectation is that the group of Brazilian women will soon reach 49% of the economically active population, as women began to be part of the decision-making processes of organizations, as well as to produce and manage their own businesses (Souza et al., 2016). Regarding the management of their own businesses, female entrepreneurship has been contributing to overcoming professional barriers faced by women (Nogueira et al., 2013), not in the sense of growth within organizations, but in the constitution of their own ventures that place them in prominent positions.

Hegemony and Entrepreneurial Woman in Amazon

Ferreira (1986) argues that hegemony is an idealization of supremacy, i.e., superiority of one people over the other, as for example, may be male over female. Completing this thought, Fairclough (2016) highlights that hegemony can arise from economic, political, cultural, and ideological domains. The major variables of hegemony, primarily when it comes to minorities, genders, and sexes, is against equality, being this defended by social paradigms (Fairclough, 2016; Ferreira,1986).

When assessing the hegemony related to female entrepreneurship, the gender revolution brings women greater recognition of their capacity related to their rights, leaving behind inferiority and submission (Mussak, 2004). More recently, women have become more independent and owners of their own destinies and choices (Marchesnay & Machado, 2012).

When dealing with entrepreneurial women in the Amazon, it is essential to highlight the use of sustainable resources in the region's businesses (Rodrigues, 2020). In agreement, Ferreira et al. (2020) emphasizes that women in the Amazon have a conservative relationship, because besides being able to take inputs and income for their own enjoyment and that of their family, they have an effective host that goes further than the work. It is totally feasible to evaluate the benefits for environmental conservation, local income generation and the relevant participation in sustainable development (Gomes, 2021).

When analysing the work developed by Queiroz (2013), one of the few works referring to entrepreneurship in the Amazon, the results obtained were that the women initially undertook entrepreneurship out of necessity and felt overburdened and guilty for not knowing how to manage their tasks with their children. As time went by, these women began to leave the informal economy and start up business because of opportunity. When they assessed their capabilities and determination, they opted to innovate in some business fields, always mindful of the vision of independence, positive thoughts that ended up encouraging their families and the ability of women to generate employment and income opportunities for other women.

In the Amazon, family incentive is common, which ends up reaching a network of family members interested in the most varied fields. Filion (1999) argues that the individuals who are most likely to become entrepreneurs are those who already have an entrepreneur in the family, since they use this family member as an example. By relating women to the action of entrepreneurship and their educational role, they can contribute directly to the entrepreneurial knowledge of their children and family members.

There are convergent points among women in the most varied regions, such as the duplicity of roles, hegemony and androcentrism, and patriarchy. Nevertheless, women are standing out thanks to their productive strength and income generation (Queiroz, 2013). The quest for gender equity goes far beyond economic, political, legal, and general participation requirements, and it is also a quest for equity in rights (Cruz, 2012). By achieving equity and breaking inequalities, patriarchal precepts and paradigms are broken (Andrade, 2008).

In the business environment, accounting can be a useful tool to help break oppressive structures (Gallhofer & Haslam, 2009), aiming to contribute to human emancipation and social change (Gallhofer & Haslam, 2004, 2002, 1996). This is because accounting is a tool that can be useful for conducting a critical analysis of social relations, influencing and encouraging discussions; highlighting the dialogue on exploitation, inequality and violence suffered by individuals; uncovering and transforming situations that violate human rights (Gallhofer & Haslam, 1996); and overcoming the assumptions of positivist rationality that subjects consciousness and human actions to the imperative of universal laws (Menezes & Santiago, 2014). This potential of accounting characterizes it as emancipatory.

Emancipatory Accounting

Emancipatory accounting may be a branch of social accounting, becoming a new target in social and critical research (Gray et al., 2013). This is because the new social accounting is used to refer to broad concepts of accounting, making analogies to the most varied issues that are correlated, especially to environmental and sustainability reports, regional diversities, gender inequalities and others (Braga & Paulani, 2020). Within this logic, social accounting is pointed out as important and indispensable for emancipatory accounting, because it offers perspectives of critical studies focused on different contexts of society (Gallhofer & Haslam, 2004).

According to Haslam (2016), emancipation needs to be observed to move accounting in relation to the possibilities of identities, interests, and projects, in terms of positioning these in an evolving activity. The relationship between accounting and emancipation needs to be visualised as an identity, that is, one that can ascertain the most varied environments and the wide range of individuals, making this a movement that tends to be in constant progress, considering that emancipatory accounting aims to recognise minorities such as women, indigenous people, oppressed classes, and genders (Haslam, 2016). Emancipatory accounting mainly aims at shedding prejudice and implementing justice, equality, freedom, and various forms of emancipation from social and/or organisational issues (Haslam, 2016; Silva, 2016).

Gallhofer and Haslam (1997), almost twenty-five years ago, had already highlighted the need for research on emancipatory accounting for minorities, the oppressed, women and indigenous people. Then, Gallhofer and Haslam (2017) pointed out that if one were to survey the entire landscape of accounting discourse, one would find relatively little research on emancipatory accounting, or accounting that can be seen to generate emancipation. This is true even in academic papers focused on critical and interdisciplinary research. Therefore, there is still a high need for critical research in accounting that exposes more possibilities for studies that are essential for both accounting and the emancipation it causes (Gallhofer & Haslam, 2019).

Accounting comes from a range of logical information and therefore needs to be better scrutinised to address social improvements (Haslam, 2016). The accounting information needs better exploration so that accounting is indeed emancipatory and reaches as many people as possible. Emancipation from the accounting perspective aims to enforce justice, equality, well-being and be a tool to break major social paradigms (Sampaio et al., 2017). In addition, it can enable the moral development of the individuals (Martins & Branco, 2001).

Scholars such as Sampaio et al. (2017) bring an approach to accounting capable of promoting and ensuring well-being, equality, social justice, and freedom. For these authors, thinking about emancipation is also to associate it with education. This is because, access to knowledge allows human beings to travel a path towards personal, professional, and spiritual growth. From this perspective, the authors observed the potential of accounting as a tool that is able to promote the emancipation of women when they assume proactive roles in society, benefiting from this tool in conducting the economic and financial life of the family and of their own businesses, obtaining for themselves the freedom to exercise a trade or to conquer the recognition of also being an important part for the social, economic and political composition of a society.

METHODOLOGY

Method

To meet the objective proposed in this study, a qualitative research approach was adopted, applying the oral report method - sub-classification "personal testimony". This method is based on oral narratives of individuals' experiences, as human agents of social participation (Kosminsky, 1986). It differs from life history because it enables the direct observation of the investigated phenomenon and consequently, with a shorter analysis time lapse and more in-depth information (Queiroz, 1983). In this research, the use of this method provides an understanding of the presence of women in the social context of entrepreneurship, limited to the specific period of their trajectories.

Additionally, the exploratory research method was applied. Exploratory research was used because of the particularities of the phenomenon since emancipatory accounting can contemplate multiple approaches. The method allows increasing knowledge in several aspects of the object of study (Oliveira, 2011), which in this case focuses on the emancipatory power of accounting in the context of female entrepreneurship.

Procedures for Choosing Participants

When qualitative exploratory research is applied, a small group of case studies should be chosen (Oliveira, 2011). The parameters must respect the minimum limit of four case studies and the maximum of ten, to avoid the lack of information or the accumulation of non-essential data that may divert the focus of the discussion of the findings (Eisenhardt, 1989).

This study included the participation of four cases of female entrepreneurs who own diversified businesses in the Amazon region. To select the participants, the researchers used social networks. Searches were conducted for profiles of women publicly declared to be entrepreneurs, with an academic degree in accounting and with their economic activities located in the Amazon region. The entrepreneurial women found in the searches were invited to participate in the study. Of the invitations made, four women agreed to collaborate with the study on a voluntary basis.

Data Collection

Data were collected through semi-structured interviews conducted in June and July 2020. Based on the specialized literature on emancipatory accounting and female entrepreneurship used as a theoretical reference, a script of questions was created to meet the aim of this research.

The questions were divided into two groups of analysis. In the first group of analysis, we highlight accounting in female entrepreneurship with the purpose of understanding the reasons for the choice of accounting by entrepreneurial women in the Amazon, and how they apply accounting knowledge in their businesses. Also, in the first group of analysis, we highlighted the organizational difficulties and the strategies used by the interviewees to overcome them before graduating in accounting. In the second group of analysis, we highlighted accounting as an emancipatory instrument for entrepreneurial women in the Amazon, aiming mainly to reveal how accounting can be applied to overcome personal and professional barriers, as well as to break social paradigms. We emphasized that before these two groups of analysis, personal questioning was conducted to understand more about the interviewed entrepreneurial women and their ventures. Table 1 shows the interview script of the study used within each group of analysis.

As the research was applied during the pandemic crisis of the covid-19 pandemic, all safety procedures recommended by the World Health Organization were respected. The interviews took place via videoconferences and the Terms of Free and Informed Consent were sent to the e-mail addresses of the participants who signed them. The return of these Terms also occurred electronically. It is noteworthy that the interviews were recorded. Each interview lasted an average of 50 minutes. The recordings were transcribed and totalled 24 pages.

Table 1. Interview script for each group of analysis

Groups of Analysis	Question	Purpose
Accounting in female entrepreneurship	Why did you choose accounting training?	To understand the reasons for the choice of accounting by entrepreneurial women in the Amazon
	How did accounting lead you to choose entrepreneurship?	To understand how accounting awakens the desire for entrepreneurship in Amazonian women
	How do you apply accounting in your entrepreneurial activity?	To point out the role of accounting in the entrepreneurial activity of Amazonian women
	Before accounting and entrepreneurship, simply because you are a woman, what difficulties have you experienced or witnessed in an organisational environment?	To know the environment of organisational difficulties faced by women in the Amazon, before accounting training and entrepreneurship
	Before accounting and entrepreneurship, how did you overcome your limitations (financial, for example)?	To know the strategies used by women in the Amazon to overcome their limitations, before accounting and entrepreneurship
Accounting as an emancipatory tool for entrepreneurial women in the Amazon	How has accounting helped you to overcome professional barriers?	To identify the role of accounting in overcoming professional barriers for entrepreneurial women in the Amazon
	Has accounting in your business provided any social equality and/or equality of competition in the marketplace? In what way?	To know the means that accounting provides social and/or market equality for entrepreneurial women in the Amazon
	After accounting in your business, were there significant changes in family dependency?	To know the changes that accounting can generate in the family dependency of entrepreneurial women in the Amazon
	Do you believe that accounting has added social value for you and your business? Why do you think so?	To understand how accounting adds social value to entrepreneurial women in the Amazon

Data Analysis

To analyse the data and discuss the results, we used the content analysis technique. This technique is adopted to describe and interpret the content of all types of documents and texts (Moraes, 1999).

As for the operationalisation of the technique, we performed a clipping of the material used (Oliveira, 2011). The texts were separated according to the content addressed, to allow us the selection of the contents directly related to emancipatory accounting and female entrepreneurship. After the selection, the content was presented in a form that met the objective of this study.

However, so that the methodological technique was not limited to the description of the data, interpretations were also made (Moraes, 1999). Thus, from the reading, it was sought to understand their meanings. The interpretation related the conceptions found in the exploratory phase of the material with the theoretical framework and the findings, thus reaching the conclusions of this research.

DESCRIPTION OF THE DATA

This section is divided into two subsections. The first subsection presents the reports of entrepreneurs related to accounting in female entrepreneurship. Then, in the second subsection, we address the reports related to accounting as an instrument of emancipation and rupture of hegemonies of entrepreneurial women in the Amazon.

4.1 Accounting in Female Entrepreneurship

Women represent strength and resilience both in accounting and in female entrepreneurship. There are several reasons that can lead women to decide for training in accounting. For instance, it can be by opportunity and affinity. In the case of entrepreneur 1, she reported: "I had the opportunity to work as an accounting assistant in a small company years ago, I didn't even know accounting… when I started working, I started to like it, the management part and the organization part, the control, the analysis too, I started to love accounting and I went looking for the course".

Other reasons may be knowledge and financial security, as entrepreneur 2 highlights: "Accounting allows us this knowledge of how the business works. So, as I always liked to be an entrepreneur, selling clothes. . . . I wanted something that would give me security, a knowledgeable basis so that I could do it and, among my search, I chose accounting because it is a more complete area, because it gives me numbers, information so that I can make decisions, so I chose accounting". Furthermore, some of the entrepreneurial women interviewed found themselves being influenced by market options and by known people that led them to accounting.

Accounting brought solutions to solve business-related issues, as Entrepreneur 1 points out: "We sold regional sweets; and we took and sold them, and what we received we did not invest in the company, we ended up spending. So, accounting came to innovate entrepreneurship within our company. We innovated with new initiatives, so today, through accounting, we inserted entrepreneurship and the company is having a positive result".

However, accounting can be influential in entrepreneurial knowledge. For example, entrepreneur 3 argues that: "Accounting did not wake me up, but it gave me broader views on entrepreneurship". Joining accounting and entrepreneurship can be more advantageous when related to independence, as it happens in the case of entrepreneur 4. She states that: "Teachers always encouraged accountants not to be only employees. They always said that accountants would have their own business, so, they motivated me to have my own business".

Exploring how entrepreneurial women use their accounting knowledge in their ventures, entrepreneur 4 reveals that: "Relating to this part of entrepreneurship, first is knowing how to do your cash flow and knowing how to handle working capital, we apply this. This accounting knowledge becomes much easier when you become an entrepreneur, because it is much easier for you to identify. . . . So, all this you can absorb and put into practice". Entrepreneur 1 adds: "Accounting knowledge, I started to add managerial skills, so now, I manage the company using the knowledge acquired in accounting."

Entrepreneur 2 uses accounting as an answering tool for other entrepreneurs. She states as follows: "So, as I bring business solutions to other entrepreneurs, I take it as the solution to difficulties (referring to accounting), because we are able to analyse most of the difficulties of entrepreneurs in Brazil...and the main objective of accounting is to generate concrete information, so that users can make better decisions based on accounting indicatives."

It is important to highlight that many women experience difficulties over the years in organizational environments. In this research it was possible to identify some of these difficulties. Within the organizations, there was harassment and attitudes embedded in the patriarchal context, as narrated by Entrepreneur 3: "There is the issue that they always think that men are more competent than women. I also suffered harassment, harassment from my former boss. So, we couldn't say anything, because I worked there and needed to, what did I do? I played blind (referring to pretending not to see the issue). He asked me to dinner, to go out and I played dumb, because it was the job that paid my bills every month. . . . It is worth mentioning that when I got there, I was the one who had to do things, sweep the room, clean the tables. While the men arrived and sat down to work. Today, I can see why things are coming up, but at the time it was something common, a domestic work developed in my workplace."

Accounting knowledge, together with entrepreneurship, proved to be transformative for the women interviewed and their families. Entrepreneur 2 highlights: "Before accounting, I confess that it was quite difficult, because I came from a humble family that faced many difficulties. The way I dealt with this (financial resources), was a somewhat desperate way, everything was disorganized. When accounting came in, my purchasing power grew, and so has that of my family."

Accounting and entrepreneurship, besides allowing overcoming barriers, brought female empowerment to the women interviewed. Entrepreneur 2 describes: "It is a profession that empowers women, because until then it was a profession made for men, right? Women have a differential, women accountants have a differential to men accountants, it is something women have, and men do not have, which is the ability to observe. So, accounting itself is a profession that needs much greater observation, because of the numbers, the analysis and all this is very important."

Entrepreneur 4 adds: "Accounting is still seen as predominantly a male profession, although in the course we see that the room has more women than men. But, in the active market, in the business sector where I work, dealing with businessmen, we deal a lot with the men and then we see that accounting comes to break this barrier, in my life it broke. . . . Accounting has given me trips, knowledge, accounting helped me to enter a world that is still dominated by men. The social issue has already happened, I arrive in a work environment and start to stand out, some men doubt my competence for fear of having their positions lost to a woman."

In the same vein, Entrepreneur 3 emphasizes the relevance of accounting knowledge and how she was able to overcome barriers within the venture: "It is an extremely important profession for any type of venture. After I had my venture, I saw people saying that accountant was too expensive. Today, I see how important it is to have good accounting, even more after this pandemic. What I saw of desperate friends. . . . Accounting provided a very good quality of life to my business."

Accounting for the Rupture of Hegemonies in the Context of Entrepreneurial Women in the Amazon

When evaluating the overcoming of professional barriers in the context studied, it is emphasized that higher education ends up enabling other opportunities and visions (how women start to be socially seen), apart from attributing them capacity and knowledge. In this sense, entrepreneur 1 highlights: "Before I graduated people looked at me in a certain way, and from the moment I graduated they looked me totally different, so, people seem to start seeing and valuing you. . . . They start to believe in your potential and, before that, they didn't give me proper credibility, as if you didn't have the capacity of what you say or do."

Entrepreneur 4 believes that accounting can still be seen as a totally male area and, by having the insertion of women, demystifies this barrier of homogeneity. This entrepreneurial woman emphasizes: "Many times, we are even surprised, because a man always expects another man to talk about management and business, when you come across a woman you break this barrier, and realize that women are also capable, accounting helped in this breaking of the entrepreneurial mentality within the business". This fact was also perceived by entrepreneur 2 who reinforced the empowerment of women and the overcoming of barriers because of accounting.

When analysing the entrepreneurial context in conjunction with accounting, female entrepreneurs reveal that by using the correct tools, helps solve problems and provides quick and effective solutions. Furthermore, they highlight the importance of accounting for ventures, especially in the covid-19 pandemic scenario.

In this research, it was possible to identify feelings of discomfort regarding the perception of social equality, since wage differences and prejudice are still 'extremely normal' in certain participants' contexts. Thus, Entrepreneur 2 highlights: "Social equality, it is not yet a reality, we still live the wage gap issue, there is still a very big prejudice in the workplace for being a woman. . . . I realize that I have made a difference, that a few years from now I believe that the next generations will not face, I believe that I am part of a generation that is promising, that is starting to conquer spaces."

In turn, some entrepreneurs reveal that accounting has enabled knowledge and highlight in the development of the activities provided, as narrated by Entrepreneur 4: "Accounting has given me greater respect. . . . I work with several cultural bands in the State and now, in the pandemic, this factor of being an entrepreneur made people look at me differently. So, there is this more respectful behaviour, because besides being an entrepreneur, I am an accountant. My business has grown a lot, because I am in a new neighbourhood and that has gained market share."

For Entrepreneur 3, accounting brought social equality and the capacity to challenge in several situations. She evidenced that: "The fact of being a woman, an entrepreneur, where you have a higher education and can apply what you know within your business, this will give you an absurd differential." Entrepreneur 1 also emphasizes that by using accounting as a management tool, it was possible to obtain the capacity to acquire social equality.

The participants agree that accounting has generated financial and family independence, in addition to reversing previously pre-defined roles. Entrepreneur 1 emphasizes: "I used to study and had other domestic services. Nowadays, we have a company and I'm the one who started going out to deal with the company's affairs. . . . So, I spend most of the time away and my husband stays with my son. What I did before, he is the one who does it. . . . Before, we had the man working outside and the woman doing the house services. With my training, there was an inversion of roles, I went to the street, and he stayed at home. Accounting provided me with this. . . . From the moment I started dealing with accounting, I became independent."

For entrepreneur 2, accounting enabled the ascension, as well as a better quality of life. She highlights: "The question of ascension is real, of having a social ascension. . . . The question of change of standard of living, things that were very scarce before in my childhood, such as food resources, entertainment, clothing, goods, property, utensils and when I entered the market, I had a rise. So, we were able to have another level, leisure, travel, buy the things we want, eat better, live better, have a better quality, a better standard of life, which is thanks to accounting. You start to grow in the area, your family also grows together, and one thing that is unanimous is the family's growth as a whole."

Moreover, these changes cause a family incentive, causing the family to become independent. Entrepreneur 3 clarifies this as follows: "The company, it grew a lot, it allowed me independence, but also family independence, my sister also acquired financial independence…my father also, after I started to be an entrepreneur, my father also became an entrepreneur, today he has his own business, it ended up touching the whole family."

When relating accounting and entrepreneurship with social value, one perceives greater visibility, opportunities, innovation, and profitability. For instance, Entrepreneur 1 states: "Accounting gave me visibility, both in actions, in operations, in sales. . . . At the end, we want to have a return, a social value, we really appreciate social issues within the company…it makes all the difference. So, we try to impact someone's life with our attitudes, for example, we try to change from plastic to recyclable paper bags. We try to adjust so that we can interfere positively in people's lives and in the environment. We believe that when a company is socially responsible, it stands out. And in the social aspect, it has given me independence."

The social value is attributed to the knowledge that Accounting causes, as well as the capacity to impact on the lives of entrepreneurs and on the paths of the ventures. Entrepreneur 2 reveals: "The social value of accounting for me, today… is the impact that accounting causes. . . . Because accounting has a strong social impact, because when you apply the accounting principles, everything we learned in college, when it is applied within the business, there is a growth, an evolution within the company, within the business. . . . The applicability of accounting within my business, it generates a whole social benefit that I understand as an accountant. I can transmit this to my clients, to other businesses, this is my venture. It's to undertake and help other entrepreneurs to understand the objective of the social field, the objective that accounting has in the scenario, which is not just to make a profit, it's not just to sell or make money, it's to generate social wealth, expansion, so that other families can rise socially and have a better quality of life. The principles and teachings are very strong, the accounting knowledge has a very strong social value, it changes as behaviours change, as society moves, as the economy moves." Furthermore, entrepreneur 4 believes that the social value added by accounting is also directed towards empowerment and influencing other women.

Accounting and entrepreneurship allowed for the disruption of social paradigms in the context of the interviewed women, bringing significant changes such as knowledge and the multiplicity of developing intellectual roles. In this sense, Entrepreneur 1 reports: "Before I used to work in the operational sector, nowadays I have moved on to the occupational sector. I used to do repetitive work and many times in history women are placed in indifferent positions. Now we can see that this has decreased, women have gained prominence, being able to develop mental work and a variety of services. . . . Nowadays, I have many responsibilities, I can flip through a process and analyse it, I know how to do it, I have the skills to do it and people started to give me this responsibility, because they believe in my ability to develop it well. . . . Accounting brought me this, the power I have today."

Entrepreneur 3 believes that there were changes in the work environment, especially regarding professional growth. According to her: "Since it is still a male environment, so when I entered and saw that there is a market and that I could have the ability, I could dominate the market and make a difference, it was through accounting. In addition, there is the knowledge and the power to influence other women, because I see that other women mirror what I do. . . . Although I am in a male environment, the feminine touch, the woman…ends up bringing a lightness into this market, which helps to have and build this equity, because there is no way that women can be equal to men, by nature, we are not equal, both have different characteristics. So, I believe that there is room for everyone if there is equity."

Lastly, Entrepreneur 4 highlights how the functionality of joining accounting and entrepreneurship enabled the venture to add benefits. She narrates: "Through knowledge…so, theory leads to perfection in practice, but it is the day-to-day that makes you improve and perfect yourself. At first, nothing is easy, but with time you gain experience and there is this aggregation of social values, for sure. If it wasn't for accounting, perhaps my business wouldn't have been so successful. As all theory needs practice, accounting showed me entrepreneurship and made it work."

DISCUSSION OF RESULTS

The purpose of this study was to analyse how the emancipatory power of accounting enables hegemonic ruptures in the context of entrepreneurial women in the Amazon. The data allow us to show that the female entrepreneurs investigated achieved their emancipation through the accounting and entrepreneurship, given that there were significant role reversals within their homes and businesses. Participants became independent, seeking to stand out in the marketplace to exist gender equity.

The findings confirm the results evidenced in the research of Bruschini and Lombardi (2002). The authors highlight the devaluation of the female audience and the low salaries that result from the image of women that is used and devalued, linking them to work only in the domestic sphere. In other words, in the sphere where they work, women are subject to chauvinist actions and conducts, having to resist paradigms related to gender issues.

Moreover, women need to disengage from their personal issues to assume their duties (unlike most men), tensions that generate difficulties and conflicts such as stress (Jablonski, 1996). When assessing these conflicts, their causes, and the difficulties, it is known that these impair the professional and personal development of women within their daily attributions (Abramo, 2007). Despite the social evolution and the post-modern period, women still face social difficulties related to hegemonies.

Mussak (2004) reveals that the existence of hegemony in entrepreneurship caused the revolution of the sexes, highlighting the female audience before their businesses. Nogueira et al. (2013) indicate that the presence of women in the labour market has become increasingly noticeable, a circumstance linked to the impacts and the differences that the female audience has been promoting in society. In entrepreneurship, the important role of women in the execution of their tasks has provided for them the achievement of leadership positions, recognition, and prominence (Nogueira et al., 2013). Inclusively, Irme (2019) exposes that the growth of female entrepreneurship tends to last longer, because women's way of entrepreneurship is different, as women are less aggressive, talkative and take care regarding the decisions made, leveraging their careers, and preserving the continuity of the business. The results of this study validate the observations of Nogueira et al. (2013) and Irme (2019), since the women interviewed stand out for their features and professional performance.

The interviewees' reports corroborate Buttner and More's (1997) statement that the entrepreneurial woman has a profile that seeks to break paradigms, autonomy, freedom, and equal rights. To materialize their quests, the participants in this research made use of their knowledge derived from accounting. Knowledge of accounting enabled the recognition and development of the women interviewed in their professional environments. This is because accounting, in its emancipatory nature, has as its main objective the detachment of social paradigms, the sense of justice, equality and freedom, in addition to seeking to solve social and organizational problems (Haslam, 2016, Gallhofer & Haslam, 2017). Thus, the interviewees attribute their important entrepreneurial achievements to accounting, highlighting accounting as an emancipatory tool in their lives. For the entrepreneurial women interviewed, accounting not only allowed them to tear the veil of submission (hegemonies), but to gain prominence, freedom, knowledge, recognition, and capacity to pursue their activities.

CONCLUDING REMARKS

Hegemonies are practices that create the environment of superiority in society, affecting vulnerable groups such as women. The female group faces social paradigms that impose obstacles to their personal and professional development. The specialized literature shows that this scenario has been changing, being able to transform the scenario of remote regions with conservative traditions, such as the Amazon.

Factors such as entrepreneurship and accounting knowledge may be directly related to these positive modifications in women's lives. Given this understanding, this study analysed whether the emancipatory power of accounting enables hegemonic ruptures in the context of entrepreneurial women in the Amazon. The research included the participation of four women who provided personal testimonials through interviews.

The results show that the female entrepreneurs participating in the study, before their professional performance in entrepreneurship and their training in accounting, experienced personal and professional challenges of prejudice, devaluation, discredit in their capacity and even harassment. However, this environment was impacted by the emancipation supported by accounting.

Female entrepreneurship played an essential role in the emancipatory process of entrepreneurial women in the Amazon. However, the participants in this study emphasized and attributed to accounting the reason for the improvement of their personal and professional living conditions and, above all, the acquisition of financial independence. Therefore, there is evidence that accounting knowledge provides, through its emancipatory power, the breaking of socially constructed hegemonies, for example, such as the idea encouraged in the Amazon that women should be subjected to their partners' wills (popularly known as the veil of marriage).

This research contributes with evidence of the social nature of accounting, together with feminist entrepreneurship, highlighting them as a tool capable of supporting the disruption of prejudiced and chauvinistic social structures, and freedom and equality among the actors in society. We emphasize that the findings of this research are restricted to the interviewees' perceptions and that no comparisons between personal statements and facts recorded in documents may be made. Future studies are recommended to investigate the exercise of the emancipatory power of accounting by other social groups in overcoming paradigms related to race, gender, and sexuality of individuals. Furthermore, it is suggested that new studies compare the reality of women entrepreneurs in the Amazon with other regions of Brazil or contexts of adversity such as the COVID-19 pandemic crisis.

REFERENCES

Abramo, L. (2004). Perspectiva de gênero e raça nas políticas públicas. *Mercado de Trabalho: Conjuntura e Análise*, *25*(11), 17–21.

Abramo, L. (2015). *Uma década de promoção do trabalho decente no Brasil: uma estratégia de ação baseada no diálogo social*. Organização Internacional do Trabalho. Disponível em: https://www.ilo.org/wcmsp5/groups/public/---americas/---ro-lima/---ilo-brasilia/documents/publication/wcms_467352.pdf

Abramo, L. W. (2007). *A Inserção da mulher no mercado de trabalho: uma força de trabalho secundária*. Tese de Doutorado em Sociologia, Universidade de São Paulo.

Andrade, J. (2008). *O Turismo Científico na Amazônia: Um estudo das oportunidades, necessidades e potencialidades para a cidade de Manaus*. Manaus: Dissertação de Pós-Graduação em Ciências Ambientais e Florestais, Universidade Federal do Amazonas.

Baron, R. A., & Shane, S. A. (2007). *Empreendedorismo: uma visão do processo*. Cengage Learning.

Blau, D. (1998). The Well-Being of American Women: 1970-1995. *Journal of Economic Literature*, *36*(1), 112–165.

Botelho, L. L. R., Schons, C. C. J., Vieira, B., & Cunha, C. J. C. A. (2008). *Desafios gerenciais das mulheres empreendedoras: como exercer a liderança em espaços de identidade masculina? O caso da alpha tecnologia*. Disponível em: https://www.researchgate.net/profile/Cristiano-Cunha/publication/38320124_Desafios_gerenciais_das_mulheres_empreendedoras_como_exercer_a_lideranca_em_espacos_de_identidade_masculina_O_caso_da_Alpha_Tecnologia/links/0c96051abdbc542fb4000000/Desafios-gerenciais-das-mulheres-empreendedoras-como-exercer-a-lideranca-em-espacos-de-identidade-masculina-O-caso-da-Alpha-Tecnologia.pdf

Braga, M. B., & Paulani, L. M. (2020). *A nova contabilidade social: uma introdução à macro economia*. Saraiva.

Bruschini, C., & Lombardi, M. R. (2002). Instruídas e trabalhadeiras: Trabalho feminino no final do século XX. *Cadernos Pagu*, *17*(18), 157–196. doi:10.1590/S0104-83332002000100007

Buttner, E. H., & Moore, D. P. (1997). Women's organizational exodus to entrepreneurship: Self-reported motivations and correlates with success. *Journal of Small Business Management*, *35*, 34–46.

Cruz, M. H. S. (2012). *Mapeando diferenças de gênero no ensino superior da Universidade Federal de Sergipe*. São Cristóvão: Editora UFS.

Dieese - Departamento Intersindical de Estatística e Estudos Socioeconômicos. (2021). *Especial Mulheres - A inserção das mulheres no mercado de trabalho (Brasil e Regiões).* Disponível em: https://www.dieese.org.br/outraspublicacoes/2021/graficosMulheresBrasilRegioes2021.html

Dornelas, J. (2012). Empreendedorismo: transformando ideias em negócios (6th ed.). São Paulo: Editora Atlas.

Eisenhardt, K. M. (1989). Building theories from case study research. *Academy of Management Review*, *14*(4), 532–550. doi:10.2307/258557

Ferreira, A. B. D. H. (1986). *Novo dicionário da língua portuguesa*. Editora Nova Fronteira.

Ferreira, G. T. C., Kaetsu, P. T., & Cunha, C. L. (2020). Empreendedorismo na Amazônia brasileira: Uma revisão sistemática da literatura. *Humanidades & Inovação*, *7*(16), 443–455.

Filion, L. J. (1999). Empreendedorismo: Empreendedores e proprietários-gerentes de pequenos negócios. *Revista ADM*, *34*(2), 5–28.

Gallhofer, S., & Haslam, J. (1996). Accounting/art and the emancipatory project: Some reflections. *Accounting, Auditing & Accountability Journal*, *9*(5), 23–44. doi:10.1108/09513579610151944

Gallhofer, S., & Haslam, J. (1997). Beyond accounting: The possibilities of accounting and "critical" accounting research. *Critical Perspectives on Accounting*, *8*(1-2), 71–95. doi:10.1006/cpac.1996.0087

Gallhofer, S., & Haslam, J. (2002). Accounting and emancipation: some critical interventions. Routledge.

Gallhofer, S., & Haslam, J. (2004). Reply to critique of "accounting and emancipation: some critical interventions.. Emerald Group Publishing Limited.

Gallhofer, S., & Haslam, J. (2009). *Emancipation*. Routledge.

Gallhofer, S., & Haslam, J. (2017). Critical theory. Routledge.

Gallhofer, S., & Haslam, J. (2019). Some reflections on the construct of emancipatory accounting: Shifting meaning and the possibilities of a new pragmatism. *Critical Perspectives on Accounting*, *63*, 1–19. doi:10.1016/j.cpa.2017.01.004

Gallhofer, S., Haslam, J., & Yonekura, A. (2015). Accounting as differentiated universal for emancipatory praxis: Accounting delineation and mobilisation for emancipation(s) recognising democracy and difference. *Accounting, Auditing & Accountability Journal, 28*(5), 846–874. doi:10.1108/AAAJ-08-2013-1451

Gem - Global Entrepreneurship Monitor Empreendedorismo no Brasil: 2019. (2020). *Coordenação de Simara Maria de Souza Silveira Greco; diversos autores*. Curitiba: IBQP.

Gomes, A. F., Santana, W. G. P., & Araújo, U. P. (2009). Empreendedorismo feminino: o estado-da-arte. In XXXIII Encontro da Anpad (pp. 1–16). São Paulo.

Gomes, A. S. (2021). A história da contabilidade e a evolução da mulher: Empoderamento e crescimento profissional feminino. *Revista de Estudos Interdisciplinares do Vale do Araguaia, 4*(2), 1–16.

Gray, R., Dillard, J., & Spence, C. (2013). Pesquisa em contabilidade social como se o mundo importasse um ensaio sobre postalgia e um novo absurdismo. *Revista de Contabilidade e Organizações, 7*(17), 119–133. doi:10.11606/rco.v7i17.59345

Greenhaus, J. H., & Beutell, N. J. (1985). Sources of conflict between work and family roles. *Academy of Management Review, 10*(1), 76–88. doi:10.2307/258214

Haslam, J. (2016). Informings for control and emancipatory interests in accounting: new reflections on the intellectual emancipation of accounting and the possibilities of emancipatory accountings. In J. Haslam & P. Sikka (Eds.), *Pioneers of Critical Accounting: A Celebration of the Life of Tony Lowe* (pp. 143–161). Palgrave Macmillan. doi:10.1057/978-1-137-54212-0_8

IRME - Instituto Rede Mulher Empreendedora. (2019). *Pesquisa "Empreendedorismo no Brasil: um recorte de gênero nos negócios"*. Disponível em: https://materiais.rme.net.br/empreendedorismo-no-brasil-um-recorte-de-genero

Iudícibus, S. (2021). *Teoria da Contabilidade*. Atlas.

Jablonski, B. (1996). Papéis conjugais: conflito e transição. *Relação amorosa, casamento, separação e terapia de casal, 1*(1), 113-123.

Jonathan, E. G. (2005). Mulheres empreendedoras: Medos, conquistas e qualidade de vida. *Psicologia em Estudo, 10*(3), 373–382. doi:10.1590/S1413-73722005000300005

Julien, P. A., Marchesnay, M., & Machado, H. V. (2012). Interdisciplinaridade da pesquisa em empreendedorismo e em PME: Por uma teoria empreendedora que contemple diferenças culturais. *Gestão & Planejamento, 11*(2), 355–368.

Kobeissi, N. (2010). Gender factors and female entrepreneurship: iInternational evidence and policy implications. *Journal of International Entrepreneurship*, *8*(1), 1–35. doi:10.100710843-010-0045-y

Kosminsky, E. (1986). Pesquisas qualitativas: A utilização da técnica de histórias de vida e de depoimentos pessoais em sociologia. *Ciencia e Cultura*, *38*(1), 30–36.

Lugarinho, M. C. (2013). Masculinidade e colonialismo: em direção ao "homem novo" (subsídios para os estudos de gênero e para os estudos pós-coloniais no contexto de língua portuguesa). *Revista do Núcleo de Estudos de Literatura Portuguesa e Africana (NEPA) da UFF, 5*(10), 15-38.

Madalozzo, R. (2011). CEOs e composição do conselho de administração: A falta de identificação pode ser motivo para existência de teto de vidro para mulheres no Brasil? *Revista de Administração Contemporânea*, *15*(1), 126–137. doi:10.1590/S1415-65552011000100008

Mari, M., Poggesi, S., & De Vita, L. (2016). Family embeddedness and business performance: Evidences from women-owned firms. *Management Decision*, *54*(2), 476–500. doi:10.1108/MD-07-2014-0453

Martins, L. C., & Branco, A. U. (2001). Desenvolvimento moral: Considerações teóricas a partir de uma abordagem sociocultural construtivista. *Psicologia: Teoria e Pesquisa (Brasília)*, *17*(2), 169–176. doi:10.1590/S0102-37722001000200009

Mellemvik, F., Monsen, N., & Olson, O. (1988). Functions of accounting - a discussion. *Scandinavian Journal of Management*, *4*(3-4), 101–119. doi:10.1016/0956-5221(88)90003-6

Menezes, M. G. D., & Santiago, M. E. (2014). Contribuição do pensamento de Paulo Freire para o paradigma curricular crítico-emancipatório. *Pro-Posições*, *25*(3), 45–62. doi:10.1590/0103-7307201407503

Monteiro, C. F. D. S., & Souza, I. E. D. O. (2007). Vivência da violência conjugal: Fatos do cotidiano. *Texto & Contexto Enfermagem*, *16*(1), 26–31. doi:10.1590/S0104-07072007000100003

Moraes, R. (1999). Análise de conteúdo. *Review of Education*, *22*(37), 7–32.

Mussak, E. (2004). O entusiasmo do empreendedor. *Vencer*, *56*(1), 98.

Nogueira, M., Alvarez, C., & Urbano, D. (2013). Socio-cultural factors and female entrepreneurship. *The International Entrepreneurship and Management Journal*, *9*(2), 183–197. doi:10.100711365-013-0251-x

Oliveira, M. (2011). *Metodologia Científica: um manual para a realização de pesquisas em administração.* UFG. Disponível em: https://files.cercomp.ufg.br/weby/up/567/o/Manual_de_metodologia_cientifica_-_Prof_Maxwell.pdf

Queiroz, J. L. A. P. (2013). *Trajetória de vida e trabalho das mulheres empreendedoras de Boa Vista, Roraima: avanços e vitórias. Dissertação de Mestrado.* Universidade Federal do Amazonas.

Queiroz, M. I. P. (1991). *Variações sobre a técnica de gravador no registro da informação viva.* T.A. Queiroz.

Quental, C., & Wetzel, U. (2002). Equilíbrio trabalho-vida e empreendedorismo: a experiência das mulheres brasileiras. Encontro Nacional da Associação Nacional de Pós-Graduação e Pesquisa em Administração (EnANPAD), 26.

Robb, A. M., & Watson, J. (2012). Gender differences in firm performance: Evidence from new ventures in the United States. *Journal of Business Venturing, 27*(5), 544–558. doi:10.1016/j.jbusvent.2011.10.002

Rodrigues, H. E. (2020). *Empreendedorismo feminino no meio rural paraense: estudo com agricultoras familiares em municípios do Baixo Tocantins. Dissertação de Mestrado.* Universidade Federal Rural da Amazônia.

Sampaio, E. S., Gomes, D. R. R., & Porte, M. S. (2017). História da contabilidade e o gênero feminino: O caso Anna Jansen, a rainha do maranhão (Sec. XIX). *Revista Española de Historia de la Contabilidad, 14*(26), 59–89. doi:10.26784/issn.1886-1881.v14i26.306

Santos, C. M. M., Tanure, B., & Carvalho Neto, A. M. (2014). Mulheres executivas brasileiras: oO teto de vidro em questão. *Revista Administração em Diálogo, 16*(3), 56–75.

Sarkar, S. (2010). *Empreendedorismo e inovação.* Forte da Casa: Escolar Editora.

Schweitzer, S. (2008). As mulheres e o acesso às profissões superiores: uma comparação européia, séculos XIX e XX. In Mercado de trabalho e gênero: comparações internacionais. Rio de Janeiro: Editora FGV.

Sebrae - Serviço Brasileiro de Apoio às Micro e Pequenas Empresas. (2018). *Os desafios da mulher empreendedora.* Disponível em: https://www.sebrae.com.br/sites/PortalSebrae/artigos/os-desa fios-da-mulher-empreendedora,e74ab85844cb5510VgnVCM1000004c0 0210aRCRD

Sebrae - Serviço Brasileiro de Apoio às Micro e Pequenas Empresas. (2020). *Brasil deve atingir marca histórica de empreendedorismo em 2020.* Disponível em: https://www.agenciasebrae.com.br/sites/asn/uf/NA/brasil-deve-atingir-marca-historica-de-empreendedorismo-em-2020,d9c76d10f3e92710VgnVCM1000004c00210aRCRD

Shelton, L. M. (2006). Female entrepreneurs, work–family conflict, and venture performance: nNew insights into the work–family interface. *Journal of Small Business Management*, *44*(2), 285–297. doi:10.1111/j.1540-627X.2006.00168.x

Silva, S. M. C. D. (2016). *Tetos de vitrais: gênero e raça na contabilidade no Brasil. Tese de Doutorado*. Universidade de São Paulo.

Souza, M. B., Trindade, F. M., Freire, R., & Lyra, F. R. L. R. (2016). Potencial empreendedor de empresárias do setor turístico de Florianópolis (SC). *Revista Alcance*, *23*(4), 455–474.

Strobino, M. R. D. C., & Teixeira, R. M. (2014). Empreendedorismo feminino e o conflito trabalho-família: Estudo de multicasos no setor de comércio de material de construção da cidade de Curitiba. *Revista ADM*, *49*(1), 59–76.

Chapter 12
Dealing With Mavericks in the Workplace

Lucinda Blue
Johnson C. Smith University, USA

ABSTRACT

The purpose of this chapter is to emphasize how Black women must illustrate skills in corporate America, medium to small businesses, non-profits, academia, politics, healthcare, etc. to obtain leadership status. They have invested much time in their education and their work life. They have crafted their leadership skills, taken calculated risks, and proved to have the abilities to "lead by example" in different disciplines. However, formal and informal leadership is not all accommodating and accepting; it comes with headaches, frustrations, and politically motivated intentions, and Black women must maneuver through the ups and downs. Everyone does not want them "at the table." They have broken the "glass ceiling" in some professions, but there are mavericks, who stir up trouble to get the Black woman to retreat. This chapter will highlight three techniques and graphically show responses how Black women can navigate to be successful in their chosen professions.

INTRODUCTION

A well-known Black female leader once said, "I didn't learn to be quiet when I had an opinion. The reason they knew who I was is because I told them" (Williams, 2019). This quote was stated by Ursula Burns, former Xerox Chairman and CEO from 2009 to 2017. In 2018, she was appointed the Executive Chairman of VEON, where she served until 2020. Why highlight someone like Ursula Burns? She is a trailblazer who has been portrayed as "a transformational leader in business, as well

DOI: 10.4018/978-1-6684-5981-2.ch012

as an articulate, proactive, and a radical thinker" (The Newsroom, 2013). Many describe her leadership style as transformational because she has been known to listen, respond cautiously, pay attention to details, and seek buy-in from her direct team. Ursula Burns served on the board of directors for various American companies, such as Exxon Mobil, Nestlé, Uber, American Express, Waystar, Diageo, and Datto, Inc.

Her leadership story continues through her various networking and service projects. Ursula Burns has said that growing up, she had to "face-to-face with racism or sexism" (Ignatius, 2021), so she learned to be numb to it, which caused her to be more effective and professional in the workplace.

Another torchbearer is Thasunda Brown Duckett of TIAA. On September 7, 2021, she was the keynote speaker during a webinar. She spoke about her leadership journey and how her humble beginnings brought her to this place and time in Corporate America. She learned how to persevere as Chief Executive Officer of Chase Consumer Banking. Using her finance and marketing education, she was previously the Director of Emerging Markets at Fannie Mae, "where she led the implementation of national strategies designed to increase homeownership among Black and Hispanic Americans" (WBC, 2021). During the webinar she also spoke of her strong support of the third annual TIAA HBCU Early Career Insights Program (TIAA, 2021) and her commitment to "pay it forward". She is passionate about helping others understand the wealth gap and how to understand, empower, and engage with education and career success. Through her formal and informal leadership styles, she has her trials and tribulation. She often speaks of optimism and positivity, but mavericks "sneak into the room", and confusion happens. However, Thasunda Brown Duckett has remained steadfast with energy, commitment, and gratitude to serve in this capacity.

More Black leaders could be spotlighted, but for the purpose of this writing, one more Fortune 500 leader has been recognized and that is Rosalind Brewer of Walgreens Boots Alliance. With her appointment to this position in March 2021, it made her the third Black woman serving as a CEO for a Fortune 500 company. She has served in other notable leadership positions, such as Starbucks, Sam's Club, Walmart, and Kimberly-Clark. Rosalind Brewer spoke at Spelman College, her alma mater's May commencement ceremony, May 2021. She mentioned that she had been discounted after being given assignments that others did not want. She felt that she had ranked as a failure before she had a chance to accomplish the tasks, but through it all, she believed in perseverance. She said, "No matter how high we fly, we still hit the glass dome constructed by our biased culture" (Guynn, 2019). *USA Today* referred to her as "one of corporate America's most prominent women and black female executives. Brewer has been noted a "Highly Powerful Woman" by both Forbes and Fortune magazines (Durbin, 2021).

How did these Black women reach this plateau? What leadership skills do they possess? Were they born with these leadership skills, or did they learn these skills by observing, studying, and practicing? Also, it is obvious that there has been a willingness and desire of others in authority to recognize, advocate, and provide opportunities for these Black women to work through their SWOT analysis (strengths-weaknesses-opportunities-threats). However, the mavericks' goals are to cause doubt, confusion, and unnecessary conversation. See Appendix 1; it shows a sample of an individual assessment that anyone in leadership can complete in determining the SWOT analysis.

Mavericks are often viewed in the negative context; however, the Collins Dictionary defines the word maverick as "a person of independent or unorthodox views" (Collins Dictionary, 2021). Regardless of the negative or positive context, the maverick must be addressed for the good of the organization.

The chapter aims to address the mavericks in the workplace by highlighting leaders, discussing their leadership styles, and identifying and explaining three (3) workable techniques that can be considered and utilized in the workplace. Peter Drucker, known as the Father of Modern Management, once said that "employees are hired but people report to work" (Blue, 2015). So, Burns, Duckett, and Brewer are definitely leading by example to embrace those in the organization who understand and share the vision to obtain and maintain the employees who focus on thriving through economic critics, such as the COVID-19 pandemic uncertainty, social injustice, global warming concerns, mental health awareness, and everyday issues.

BACKGROUND

Ability to influence. Self-awareness. Showing empathy. Potential to delegate. Power. Integrity. Effective communication. These are some of the significant characteristics of leadership. Valarie Johnson (2019) entitled a manuscript called, "Black Women are Natural Born Leaders Quotes from the Great Harriet Tubman Journal". Johnson captured Harriet Tubman's leadership style in an amazing way by reliving her life story from 1820 to 1913; Harriet Tubman's "excellence, her confidence, and her legacy" have been recognized in Johnson's publication. Even though Harriet Tubman was not plagued with mavericks in the workplace, she had to deal with mavericks who did not share her unconventional vision of being freed and freeing others. She was brutally abused by slaveholders to emancipate herself, and she risked her life repeatedly to liberate others. In her role as the Underground Railroad, she liberated approximately 70 people prior to the Civil War, and she assisted many others with her knowledge of safe spaces and escape routes. "I never ran my train off the track and I never lost a passenger," she later said of her experience (Johnson, 2019). She lived a life committed to freedom and dignity for all people. Valarie Johnson (2019) has used her "enthusiasm and creativity to teach and inspire others to use their own unique strengths, talents and abilities to live the life of their dreams."

"Realizing that it's not right to judge others. Seek understanding of others, but first, know thyself!" (Blue, 2015) can definitely be said of those Black women who paved the way to achieve leadership status. Instead of believing what mavericks think, it is apparent that leaders must be aware of the mavericks' behavior and know that they can cause problems for everyone. Note the following inspirational quotations by Black women in history:

"I leave you love. I leave you hope. I leave you the challenge of developing confidence in one another. I leave you respect for the use of power. I leave you faith. I leave you racial dignity." – Mary McLeod Bethune, founder of Bethune-Cookman University, founder the National Council of Negro Women, an educator, a national civil rights pioneer, activist, one of the founders of the United Negro College Fund (Bethue-Cookman, 2021).

"Pay me Friday when you get paid. Then we both can start the new week with a good attitude of keeping our promises and helping somebody else." – Ada Bowen, small community store owner from South Carolina in the early 1970s. (J. Carstarphen, personal communication, November 26, 2021).

"Do not desire to fit in. Desire to oblige yourselves to lead." - Gwendolyn Brooks, author and poet. In 1968, she was awarded the poet laureate recognition Illinois ("Gwendolyn Brooks", poetsorg, n.d.).

"If they don't give you a seat at the table, bring a folding chair." – Shirley Chisholm, who was the first Black Congresswoman. She was also the first Black woman to announce the Democratic Party's presidential bid in !972 (Chisholm, 2010).

"There are not many of us African American Sister Presidents, and those of us who are in this field do not have an easy time of it. Why the story goes that one Black woman college president died and went to hell, and it was two weeks before she realized that she wasn't still on the job." – Johnnetta B. Cole, who is an educator, the first Black woman president of Spelman College, a Historically Black Colleges and Universities, and after leaving that position, she was president of Bennett College from 2002 to 2007. She now serves as president of During 2009–2017 she was Director of the Smithsonian Institution's National Museum of African Art (Cole, 2011).

"When I liberate myself, I liberate others. If you don't speak out ain't nobody going to speak out for you." – Fannie Lou Hamer, who was an American voting and women's rights activist, community organizer, and a leader in the civil rights movement (Fannie, n.d.).

"Charlotte needed a consistent leadership…foundation for the future…live able city…challenges by living in a growing city." – Vi Lyles, Major of Charlotte, NC

(2017 – Present). Prior to being elected as mayor, Lyles worked as a consulting director by assisting non-for-profit governmental organizations at the Lee Institute and Flynn Health Holt Leadership company ("Vi Lyles," 2019).

"The most common way people give up their power is by thinking they don't have any." – Alice Walker, who was an American novelist, short story writer, poet, and social activist. In 1982, she became the first African-American woman to win the Pulitzer Prize for Fiction (White, 2005).

"Don't sit down and wait for the opportunities to come. Get up and make them." – Madam C.J. Walker, who was a Black woman entrepreneur, philanthropist, and political and social activist. The Guinness Book of World Records has her listed as the first female self-made millionaire in America (Biography.com, 2018).

"To bring about change, you must not be afraid to take the first step. We will fail when we fail to try." – Rosa Parks, who is known as Black woman activist in the civil rights movement and her historical role in the Montgomery bus boycott. She has been recognized by the United States Congress as "the first lady of civil rights" and "the mother of the freedom movement" (McGuire, 2012).

Each of these Black women portrays a profound message of formal and informal leadership. There are hundreds of Black women who are represented in Corporate America, medium to small businesses, non-profits, academia, politics, healthcare, etc. They stand on the shoulders of those before them, and they all realize that leadership is not the designated title; it is the expertise, outcomes, and accomplishments that go with it. The mavericks attempt to put "cataracts" on the lens that focuses on the overall goals and objectives. These leaders and others tend to set principles, such as, 1) providing a thorough strategic plan that aligns with the respective organization; 2) using authenticity in goal setting and prioritizing, accordingly; 3) measuring accomplishments and gauging the timeline; and 4) very careful not to micromanage (Guynn, 2021). Also, when dealing with mavericks, leaders must acknowledge and "own" their mistakes. If they don't, mavericks will have a "field day" in ridiculing and maliciously publicizing the Black woman's unintentional mistakes.

To study other Black women in leadership and how they have dealt with mavericks, respond to the following questions:

1. What is the vision that the maverick has for himself or herself for the designated organization?
2. How can a maverick attract the qualified employees?
3. If a maverick is portrayed as being tenacious, how can that be a positive characteristic?
4. How can mavericks in today's organizations (of all kinds) be competitive for the benefit of everyone?

5. What are some challenges that mavericks encounter when communicating with others? (Blue, 2015)

There are other questions that can be asked and discussed. Black women must constantly collaborate, stay committed, and communicate, but we can always practice the fish philosophy. Lundin (2000) and his co-authors speak of the fish philosophy as a simple, innovative, and practical technique that works for any leader. It has been said that 85% of employees dislike their job, so the medthods of the fish philosophy have shown that work productivity improves. These techniques are:

1. Be Present
2. Choose Your Attitude
3. Make Their Day
4. Play

Now, it is not practical that all Black women leaders can interact with all employees every day. However, through adequate delegation, communication (verbal and written), visiting the work site, when possible, etc., can be "a remarkable way to boost morale and improve results" in all organizations. "As we value various cultures and accept differences as well as similarities, we can cultivate the talents and expertise of the disenchanted, inspire the disengaged, and strive for inclusiveness in the world" (Blue, 2015).

MAIN FOCUS OF THE CHAPTER

Issues, Controversies, Problems

Confronting the Problem

Even though Black women in leadership continue to progress, this type of recognition is still underway. "Women still only make up 8.2% of Fortune 500 CEOs, with women of color making up 1.2%, CBS News reported" (Essence, 2021). The emphasis is on the Black women's approach to illustrate leadership skills in a diverse culture, but they must demonstrate knowledge, confidence, and resilience.

The Black women's leadership style must be firm, clear, direct, and polite. The emphasis is on "polite" because sometimes it may appear to be too controlling for other cultures to comprehend the intent. Formal and informal leadership is not all accommodating and accepting. It comes with headaches, frustrations, and politically motivated calculations, and Black women must maneuver through the ups and downs. Mavericks appear in the workplace unannounced, and Black women must be equipped to work through the situations from the beginning to the end. Mavericks can be handled in a professional way to not disturb the teamwork that is necessary in a workplace. The leader must develop individual scoreboards to analyze the SWOT Analysis and to create a motivated workplace, so that those who are toxic will be encouraged to change or they will eventually "give up" and leave. Mavericks have the propensity to derail the positive progress of Black women by sabotaging the goals and objectives by demonstrating a negative focus. See the Appendix 2: The Employment Engagement Model. This model can help the leader connect to the employees, preferably associates and team members, to gain buy-in to reach goals and objectives.

Black women in leadership can utilize several techniques to combat the proposed confusion. Three (3) techniques and examples can be used by Black women to navigate in their chosen professions. One technique is leadership as a metacognitive variable; like other variables, it enables one to "think" about their "thinking". According to Hocking (1979), leaders should lead so people will want to follow. If leaders don't want mavericks to consume their workspace, Hocking said, "The only way I know to avoid criticism is to say nothing, do nothing, and be nothing" (Hocking, 1979). Hubbard (2021) made a similar comment even though he was not talking about Black women, but he was speaking about leaders in general. Dealing with mavericks should make Black women stronger, just like Ursula Burns stated that she had become "numb". This strong will and numbness will make the Black woman less distracted and more focused on the business at hand.

Another technique for Black women in leadership can be called emotional intelligence (often referred to as EQ). Black women must express themselves clearly and concisely, so others do not see them as angry, jealous, or afraid. They must have the ability to control their emotions and acquire the ability to perceive and manage others' emotions. This technique can be learned with practice by working with others collaboratively to minimize or remove confusion and negativity (Green, 2021).

Lastly but certainly not least, the third technique can be called resilience. The Oxford Dictionary defines resilience as "the capacity to recover quickly from difficulties" (Oxford Dictionary, 2022). Recalling the Black women highlighted in this writing demonstrates the resilience that they amplified by enduring and being successful in their accomplishments. They coupled opportunity with networking and connections to make a positive impact on society. The Gallup Poll (2021) shows that Black Women rank the lowest in percentage compared to White women and Hispanic women with the following statement: "I have the same opportunities for advancement as everyone else".

Black Women – 27%
White Women – 36%
Hispanic Women – 33%

Thus, including women of color in the decision-making position is still low, but progress is definitely being made. With more leadership exposure, EQ, and resilience, more Black women will continue to be role models to minimize the glass ceiling practices, biases, and discrimination (Gallup Poll, 2021).

Mavericks Don't Listen

Who are the mavericks? How do they look? Can they be identified in the workplace? Do they have a tattoo or some noticeable marking on their forehead? The answer is not simple, but there are some behaviors that can be observed. Mavericks talk too much. They constantly criticize and frenetically get others to be pessimistic about everything that the leader is attempting to accomplish. They dismiss the idea that leadership is a relationship. When they attempt to outwardly discriminate on the basis of race, creed, and color, then they develop resistance to the truth, especially if the leader is a Black woman.

Mavericks are energetic and "come to work every day" to make a statement. If they could only engage in the devil's advocate to speak out on opposing or unpopular issues, then they could help everyone see the broader view on a topic. Consequently, they tend to generate confusion when they oppose a situation, conversation, or work activity. They are the catalysts behind the chaos. However, if their intent is to "stir up trouble" in the organization, they compromise the leader's goal to create a "relationship between those to aspire to lead and those who choose to follow" (Kouzes & Posner, 2007).

According to Locker and Kaczmarek (2001), mavericks can enhance their listening skills by practicing the following behaviors:

- Pay attention
- Focus on the leader and other team members in a generous way
- Avoid making assumptions
- Listen for feelings as well as facts

Mavericks can listen if they choose to "be present" in body and mind.

In short, mavericks could be good listeners and be projective and empathic if they want to improve the organization as a whole and be supportive of the leader. There are some listening assessments that leadership can utilize for self-help and for the organization, as whole.

Black women leaders can “teach” mavericks how to be great communicators and be positive for the organization. Jeff (2021) has identified (5) ways to become a better listener. They are:

1. Choose to be intentionally present

Today, nearly everyone has a smartphone, and no one really talks to each other. On average, each of these users spends about 3 hours and 43 minutes each day on their mobile devices. It can be difficult not to look at your phone to check a message or comment on a Facebook status you just posted. If you want to be a better listener, turn off your phone or silence it. Eliminate distractions and focus on the person talking. If you can’t meet in person and are talking to someone on the phone, don’t be tempted to check your email on your monitor or you will lose focus. Remember that you can only listen intently when you’re not distracted.

2. Become an Other-minded listener

When it comes to being a good listener, it’s better to be interested than interesting. To do this, be quick to listen and slow to speak and learn to ask open ended questions. Seeking first to understand instead of to be understood will create a safe environment for the other person to feel heard and valued. By becoming genuinely interested in the other person’s perspective, you help the other person trust you and share honestly what they believe and why they believe it. Who knows — you might be able to learn a thing or two from a different point of view.

3. Be empathetic and never judge

Listening is an act of empathy as you try to see a situation through another person’s eyes and understand how they’re feeling. You can’t do this when you’re judging them as they’re talking. Remember that people will open up more when you’re not judging them. Extend respect, compassion, grace, and forgiveness to the degree that you would like it extended to you.

4. Show that you’re actually listening

To be a better listener, show the other person that you’re actually listening to them. Your body language shows how attentive you are to the other person. Make eye contact. Lean forward and learn to nod, especially when you give out suggestions, as that would encourage the other person to talk more. Avoid thinking about what you will say next in your response to them.

5. Don't talk while the other person is still talking

One rule of thumb: Wait for the other person to finish talking before commenting or asking a question. It can be rude to stop the person mid-sentence because you need to talk. Also — when you don't understand, don't hesitate to ask them to repeat what they have just said. If possible, you can also consider repeating what they have said to ensure that you have fully understood it." ("5 ways to become a better listener," 2021)

Preconceptions and Biases

Wouldn't it be professional for mavericks to think positive about how to improve the organization instead of having preconceptions and biases? They should put their energy into improving the organization. According to Halstead (2018), he said "For example, I may know you to be a person who has no experience in this area, therefore, it's hard to listen to you because I don't think you know what you're talking about."

Mavericks are not good at doing things for the right reasons. It is perceived that leadership can be lonely, so Black women, especially, must handle much of the stress and heavy lifting in solidarity. When mavericks express criticism, Black women must realize that everybody will not give a helping hand or kind words. Therefore, the end result is communication among the mavericks and the leadership to attempt to find the root cause of the conflict.

To survive in the business world or leadership, Black women leaders must know their network of advocates. They cannot be blindsided by those who pretend to be supportive. Wilson (2021) states that "it is impossible to become a great leader unless learning how to survive sabotage." Black women leaders must learn how to spot possible sabotage before it is visibly apparent. They must protect themselves from unphysical attacks that compromise integrity and reputation, so seeing these acts before they occur is essential. According to Wilson (2021), there are four horsemen (agents) of sabotage. They are jealousy, lying, arrogance, and seduction. Jealousy was highlighted in a survey that was completed by Black women leaders. In the survey, it did not show that these Black women surveyed were concerned about jealousy, but they must not ignore it! In this instance, jealousy was only ranked at 9%, along with imposter syndrome. Black women leaders must build a culture that demonstrates their confidence in their strategic outcomes and not fear of success, their energy and girt in their results and not complacency, and their education and expertise and not self-doubt.

SOLUTIONS AND RECOMMENDATIONS

Black women in leadership are pressured to do their job with excellence and preciseness. These leaders are considered service leaders who explain why the path needs to be taken, what measures success, and how to celebrate, as needed. They must identify their weaknesses they attempt to correct them. Listed below are some types of leadership weaknesses.

- Separating or standing apart from your team.
- Being overly critical.
- Micromanaging employees.
- Requiring constant contact.
- Acting without integrity.
- Failing to set clear expectations.
- Failing to set clear goals or objectives.
- Providing ineffective feedback ("Initiative One," 2021).

An important technique to help Black women to be more effective in their formal and informal leadership style is McClelland's Needs Theory, which focuses on three (3) recognizable needs that Black women's leadership can embrace to motivate workplace engagement. They are the needs for achievement, affiliation, or power. These needs are closely related to Theory X (dislike work and responsibility) and Theory Y (motivated and inspired to do the best job) Model. See Appendix 3. These motivators are not inherent which are developed through culture and life experiences. Black women have created example after example of their work accomplishments which prove that they are leaders. Compared to white women, they usually don't have advocators to support their accomplishments. They must seek opportunities and believe that they have a fair chance to advance. Thirdly, but not least, is the Five Factor Model, which is used to measure the five major domains. They are N – Negative Emotionality (Neuroticism), E – Extraversion, O – Openness, A – Agreeableness, and C - Consciousness. These domains have been tested and re-tested in academic and research environments and have proved to be superior for explaining the describing personality that is easily translated into different languages and cultures. These leaders can use this model to understand employees in work situations.

These techniques can be studied and analyzed by Black women in leadership as ways to accomplish tasks as they work with diversity, inclusion, and equity. Hilderman (2019) stressed the importance of leaders to build a team that understands their visions, shares their passion, and operates their businesses in their absences. Gill (2011) shares information about the different types of leadership and their effectiveness. Explaining these types can help one to understand the traits one can develop to become an effective leader. As role models, these Black women have accomplished much, and they can influence younger Black women to learn from their triumphs and challenges. Hopefully, this chapter will stimulate discussions about formal and informal leadership styles. Also, it is hoped that this information will motivate Black women to seek leadership positions and empower them in the workplace, academia, and/or civic/political opportunities to enhance the overall dynamics.

Black women were surveyed to obtain the viewpoint of their leadership styles. A total of 165 surveys were distributed with a 27.3% completeness. The questions/statements are as follows:

- Years of leadership experience
- How effective are you as a Black woman (or Woman of Color) in leadership (ranking 1 - lowest and ranking 5 - highest)?
- What is your leadership discipline/occupation?
- What is your most effective leadership characteristic?
- Identify your biggest obstacle in leading others.
- How did you or how are you navigating these obstacles?
- When ranking your leadership style with others (Black women, Women of Color, or other ethnic groups), how do you perceive the fairness of your personal leadership evaluation?

The results speak for themselves. Reviewing the results will generate meaningful discussions about Black women's formal and informal leadership styles. See Appendix 4 for the results of each question/statement. These results will stimulate individual leader reflection or encourage workgroup discussions in various organizations.

The survey consisted of two results that deserve some analyses. They are:

- What is your most effective leadership characteristic?
- Identify your biggest obstacle in leading others.

Black women surveyed rank knowledge and expertise at 17.8% with self-awareness and continue personal development and developing others at 13.1%. The participants also ranked integrity at 12.2%. Realizing that Black women face many obstacles in their leadership positions, the survey showed that participants ranked "not having enough overall support" at 55.6%. This is appalling to some degree but not surprising compared to the other responses to this statement. Consequently, according to the survey, Black women do not have many obstacles in "motivating others" because inherently, they strive to help others succeed.

Therefore, according to Llopis (2014), "Success for a leader is a by-product of themselves and mentors." All leaders take an intentional approach in doing their best for the good of the organization that they lead and present. Gill (2011) states that a successful leader is effective if they think long-term for potential mentoring successors. Obviously, all the Black women leaders spotlighted in the chapter will not be leading forever. Therefore, they must position the organization to move forward by "teaching" and "mentoring" others. There are types and practices of leadership that produce effectiveness and efficiency, and even the maverick can be taught how to be positive and not confrontational and aggressive. Explaining these types can help one understand the traits that must be developed to make one a more effective leader. There are executive assessments that can be purchased to make a more informed hiring, placement, or developmental decisions. Both practical and theoretical insights into current work support the idea that an ability to change or implement changes according to circumstances is the key characteristic of effective leadership (Gill, 2011, p. 38-40).

CONCLUSION

Maxwell (2002) noted that leadership has (5) distinct goals. They are:

1. Define leadership and explore the skills and types,
2. Understand the importance of leadership,
3. Analyze what a leader vs manager can be and cannot be,
4. Expand understanding of leadership models and practices, and
5. Identify and develop personal leadership philosophy and approach.

Maxwell (2002) explains that learning the leadership traits can be a continuous process. Successful learners are also learners; they practice the complicated facets daily by working with individuals.

Leadership is complicated. It has many facets: respect, experience, emotional strength, people skills, discipline, vision, momentum, timing — the list goes on. Leadership is also a process that has four phases of growth, such as:

Phase 1: I don't know what I don't know

Phase 2: I know what I don't know

Phase 3: I grow and know and it starts to show

Phase 4: I simply go because of what I know

Black women can be better leaders because of their history of what others like them have endured and conquered. They develop “girt” through it all. Their leadership positions are not bestowed on them “just because”; they have had to work long hours and years to reach a leadership position. Not surprisingly, the task does not end with the appointment; it begins.

Juggling work and personal life can be hectic, and sometimes the maverick sees that as a way to cause friction in the workplace for the Black woman leader. The maverick can begin to begin rumors that the Black woman leader cannot handle the job at hand, that they have to be absent, that they are not focused on the overall responsibilities, and that they tend to neglect and not delegate properly. That is when the Black woman has to showcase her work skills, advocate for herself, and network to find strong supporters. Kouzes & Posner (2007) emphasize five practices of exemplary leadership; they are 1) Model the way, 2) Inspire, 3) Challenge the process, 4) Enable others to act, and 5) Encourage. Each practice centers around trust. Once the Black woman enters the leadership position and understands the “current state”, then she can listen and act to support the organization, as a whole, along with providing customer service to her internal and external stakeholders.

It is also necessary to constantly assess the people around her, so the Black woman leader must know who the mavericks are. Start each day with vigor and excitement and hope that others will be energized by your positive spirit (Blue, 2015). This attitude should keep the mavericks at “arm’s length”. According to Badaracco (2002), leaders can do their job quietly, can lead boldly, and obtain measurable, positive results by delegating and communicating clearly to resolve tough leadership decisions. They don’t have to be in the public spotlight every day, but they need to be visible to the stakeholders. It is important that they are truly attentive and engaged to understand the total business operation. If they lead with integrity, the mavericks will not have a chance to influence the organization and distract the business.

Multidimensional tasks can be used by the Black woman to deal with difficult employees. These leadership skills can help the Black woman succeed in her formal and informal approach to advance any organization in a better strategic direction. The Black woman must not let disintegration destroy the positive work and lose the cohesion or strong foundation that has been established.

Llopis (2014) in his article entitled, “Leadership Is About Enabling the Full Potential In Others”, indicates that potential leaders in this 21st century must be courageous and ready to accept the challenges and even venture out of the typical ways of doing things. Consequently, these qualities may be the proper response in encouraging others to “buy in” to diversity, equity, and inclusion to promote governance, personal development, guidance, direction, productivity, and success. These new leaders can be strongly motivated by great present-day leaders to enhance women in management and the global labor market.

REFERENCES

ways to become a better listener. (2021). https://christlikedialogue.org/5-ways-to-becoming-a-better-listener/

Badaracco, J. L. Jr. (2002). *Leading Quietly*. Harvard Business School Publishing.

Bethue-Cookman College. (2021). https://www.cookman.edu/history/our-founder.html

Biography.com Editors. (2018, February 28). *Madam C.J. Walker*. Retrieved from https://www.biography.com/inventor/madam-cj-walker

Blue, L. (2015). *Fruitful Inspirations*. Trafford Publishing.

Chisholm, S. (2010). *Unbought and Unbossed: Expanded 40th Anniversary Edition*. Take Root Media.

Cole, J. B. (2011). *Conversations: Straight Talk with America's Sister President. Anchor: Penguin Random*. House.

Collins Dictionary. (2021). *Maverick*. https://www.collinsdictionary.com/us/dictionary/english/maverick

Durbin, D. A. (2021, January 27). Black woman CEO: Walgreens taps Starbucks exec, Roz Brewer, for role. *Usa Today*. www.usatoday.com. https://www.usatoday.com/story/money/business/2021/01/27/black-woman-ceo-walgreens-taps-starbucks-exec-roz-brewer-role/4278423001/

Essence. (2021, June 7). *Two black women CEOs make history on Fortune 500 list*. https://www.essence.com/news/money-career/two-black-women-ceos-make-history-on-fortune-500-list/

Fannie Lou Hamer. (n.d.). National Women's History Museum. https://www.womenshistory.org/education-resources/biographies/fannie-lou-hamer

Ferguson, D. (2021). *How great leaders communicate*. https://globalleadership.org/articles/leading-others/how-great-leaders-communicate-to-create-movement/

Gallup Poll. (2021, March 5). *Lloyd, Camille. Black Women in the Workplace*. Gallup.com

Gill, R. (2011, September). Managing People in Organizations: Integrating the Study of HRM and Leadership. *Harvard Business Review*, *28*(3), 1–40.

Green, S. (2021, October 31). *Emotional Intelligence: Why It's Important. Life and Health Network*. Lifeandhealth.org

Guynn, J. (2019). *Amazon names black Starbucks exec Rosalind Brewer to all-white board in 'barrier-breaking; appointment.* https://www.usatoday.com/story/news/2019/02/04/amazon-names-starbucks-exec-rosalind-brewer-first-black-board-member/2769779002/

Halstead, F. (2018). Leadership skills that inspire incredible results. Career Press, an imprint of Red Wheel Weiser, LLC.

Hilderman, J. (n.d.). *Clone yourself: Build a team that understands your vision, shares your passion, and runs your business for you.* Gauvin, Jacques, OverDrive, Inc.

Hocking, D. (1979). Be a leader people follow. GL Regal, A Division of G/L Publications.

Hubbard, E. (2021). https://quoteinvestigator.com/2015/01/09/say-nothing/

Ignatius, A. (2021, July – August). I'm here because I'm as good as you. *Harvard Business Review*. https://hbr.org/2021/07/im-here-because-im-as-good-as-you

Initiative One. (2021). https://www.initiativeone.com/insights/blog/leadership-challenges/

Johnson, V. (2019). Black women are natural born leaders quotes from the great Harriet Tubman journal. @Coachvalj journals.

Kouzes, J. M., & Posner, B. Z. (2007). The leadership challenge: The most trusted source on becoming a better leader (4th ed.). The Leadership Challenge: A Wiley Brand.

Llopis, G. (2014). *Leadership Is About Enabling the Full Potential In Others*. Retrieved July 29, 2014, from https://www.forbes.com/sites/glennllopis/2014/07/29/leadership-is-about-enabling-the-full-potential-in-others/?sh=791092b76698

Locker, K. O., & Kaczmarek, K. S. (2001). Business communication: Building critical skills. McGraw-Hill Higher Education: A Division of the McGraw-Hill Companies.

Lundin, S. C., Paul, H., & Christensen, J. (2000). Fish! A remarkable way to boost morale and improve results. Hyperon.

Maxwell, J. C. (2002). *Leadership 101*. Thomas Nelson Publishing.

McGuire, D. (2012, December 1). *Opinion: It's time to free Rosa Parks from the bus*. CNN. https://www.cnn.com/2012/12/01/us/opinion-its-time-to-free-rosa-parks-from-the-bus/index.html

Oxford Learners Dictionary. (2021). *Resilience*. https://www.oxfordlearnersdictionaries.com/us/definition/english/resilience

Robinson, E. (2011). Disintegration: The splintering of Black America. Anchor Books: A Division of Random House, Inc.

The Newsroom. (2013). *Video: Xerox Chairman and CEO Ursula Burns discusses leadership and pushing past the status quo*. https://business.wfu.edu/newsroom/video-xerox-chairman-and-ceo-ursula-burns-discusses-leadership-and-pushing-past-the-status-quo/

TIAA. (2021). *Announcing our third annual HBCU early career insights program*. TIAA.

White, E. (2004). *Alice Walker: A Life*. W. W. Norton & Company.

Williams, P. (2019). *Tell them who you are*. https://medium.com/@preslaysa/tell-them-who-you-are-c4ab1a4c0f12

Wilson, B. (2021). *Sabotage: Leadership That Overcomes Betrayal, Theft and Deceit*. Propellor Company.

Women Business Collaborative. (2021). *Women CEOs in America*. https://www.wbcollaborative.org/women_leaders_ceo/thasunda-brown-duckett/

ADDITIONAL READING

Blanchard, K. (2013). *Leadership and the one minute manager*. HarperCollins Publishers.

Burchard, B. (2009). *The Student Leadership Guide* (4th ed.). Morgan James Publishing, LLC.

Favors, J. M. (2019). *Shelter in a Time of Storm: How Black Colleges Fostered Generations of Leadership and Activism*. John Hope Franklin Fund of the University of North Carolina Press. doi:10.5149/northcarolina/9781469648330.001.0001

Gill, R. (2011, September). Managing People in Organizations: Integrating the Study of HRM and Leadership. *Harvard Business Review*, *28*(3), 1–40.

Goleman, D. (1998). *Working with emotional intelligence*. Bantam Books.

Hughes, K. (2019). *5 Leadership Assessment tools You Need to Try*. Retrieved July 10, 2019, from https://www.projectmanager.com/blog/leadership-assessment-tools

Marquet, L. D. (2020). *Leadership Is A Language*. Penguin Random House, LLC.

Maxwell, J. C. (2002). *Leadership 101*. Thomas Nelson Publishing.

Render, S. Jr, & Hanna, H. (2015). *Quantitative Analysis for Management* (12th ed.). Pearson.

Why black women are better leaders. (2021). https://www.forbes.com/sites/paologaudiano/2019/12/02/why-black-women-are-better-leaders/?sh=2d42524e259b

Women are advancing in the workplace but women of color still lag behind. (2021). https://www.brookings.edu/essay/women-are-advancing-in-the-workplace-but-women-of-color-still-lag-behind/

KEY TERMS AND DEFINITIONS

Devil Advocacy: When a person verbally speaks on the opposing position to cause decision for the purpose of examining all possible viewpoints. This is not popular position, it is helps to ensure trust, clarity, and transparency.

Glass Ceiling: An informal or a conversational term used to describe the obstacles that females, especially Women of Color, confront in the workplace in attempting to seek upper management and leadership positions. In 1991, the U.S. Department of Labor established the Glass Ceiling Act that addresses the elimination of invisible barriers for the advancement of women and minorities in all organizations.

Five Factor Model: An assessment of personal traits that are outlined in five dimensions - Extraversion, Agreeableness, Conscientiousness, Neuroticism, and Openness to Experience. Depending on the personal and work life situation the ranking can fluctuate within each dimension.

Strategic Plan: A detailed document that explains step-by-step processes to identity the vision and mission with their goals and objectives. Once the strategic plan is endorsed, then each level of the organization can determine how it impacts progress and how to track key performance indicators.

SWOT Analysis: A technique used by individuals or organizations to assess strengths, weaknesses, opportunities, and threats relating to performance. This analysis can usually make individuals and organizations aware of area to focus to overall personal and professional growth.

Theory X: A theory measuring people's work motivation. It complements Theory Y. Douglas McGregor created these theories in the 1960s while he was working at the MIT Sloan School of Management. This theory assumes that people dislikes work, that they avoid it, and that they lack ambition and initiative.

Theory Y: A theory measuring people's work motivation. It complements Theory X. Douglas McGregor created these theories in the 1960s while he was working at the MIT Sloan School of Management. This theory assumes that people get energize in working through challenges at work. They are self-motivated and self-directed. This sense of enthusiasm makes them empowered in their problem-solving and decision-making.

TIAA: Founded in 1918. Acronym stands for "Teachers Insurance and Annuity Association of America-College Retirement Equities Fund". Formerly named "TIAA-CREF". It is a Fortune 100 financial services organization. In 2020 the company employed over 16,000 employees and had a total equity of over 38B dollars. Thasunda Brown Duckett is its current president and CEO.

Walgreens: Second largest pharmacy store in the United States ranking behind CVS. Its products and services include filling prescriptions, health awareness, wellness products, and photo services. Its holding company is Walgreens Boots Alliance, Inc. which is headquartered in Illinois. Rosalind Brewer, a Black woman, is its current CEO who manages a revenue of over 139B dollars.

XEROX: An American Fortune 500 corporation. Its business is selling print and digital document products and services. It is an international company and is headquartered in Connecticut. It is incorporated in New York. Ursula Burns was its first Black woman CEO from 2009 through 2016.

APPENDIX 1: INDIVIDUAL SWOT ANALYSIS

Table 1.

Strengths	Weaknesses
• What strengths do you provide in the workplace (i.e., technical skills, soft skills, education, and certifications)? • What is your best attribute that you can share in the workplace? • Give an example of the workplace philosophy. • What would your co-workers say about your strength(s)?	• What are some areas to improve in the workplace? • What long-term and short-term formal training is needed? Cost? • What identified weaknesses do not need to be improved at this time? • What would your co-workers say about your weaknesses?
Opportunities	**Threats**
• What are your individual opportunities facing you in the workplace? • Identify at least (3) three business trends that can be looked at on an individual basis.	• Identify at least (3) major obstacles that you encounter in the workplace. • What work advantages do your co-workers have that you don't possess? • What changes are occurring on the job that you are currently handling? • What opportunities or weaknesses do you perceive as threats?

APPENDIX 2: THE EMPLOYMENT ENGAGEMENT MODEL

Figure 1.

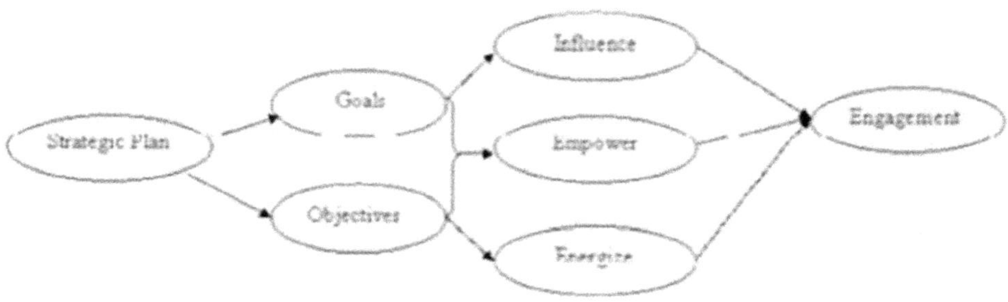

APPENDIX 3: THEORY X AND THEORY Y

Figure 2.
Source: Copyright © 2015 L.B. Blue

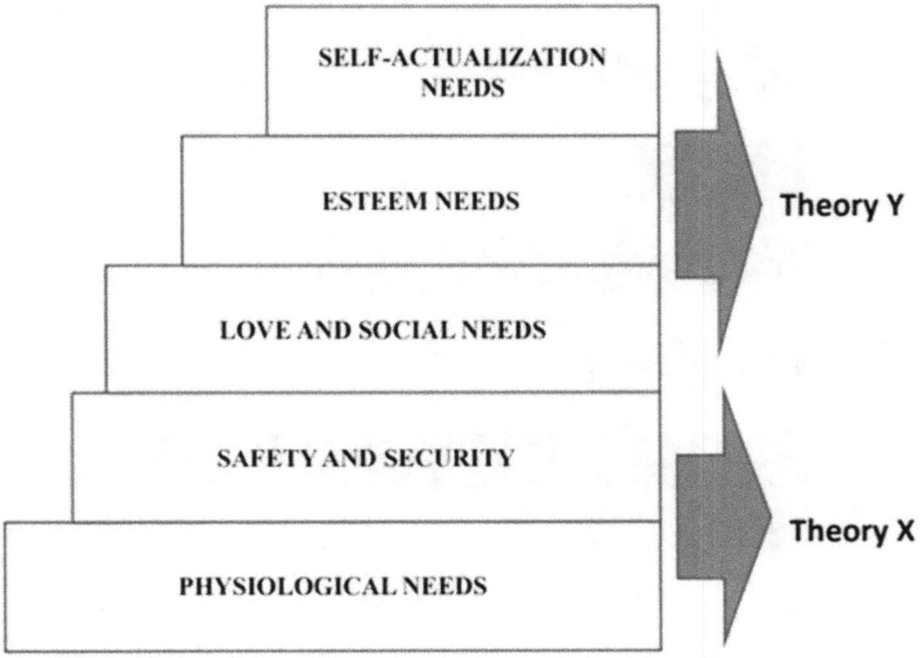

APPENDIX 4: SURVEY RESULTS

Figure 3. Q1 – Years of leadership experience

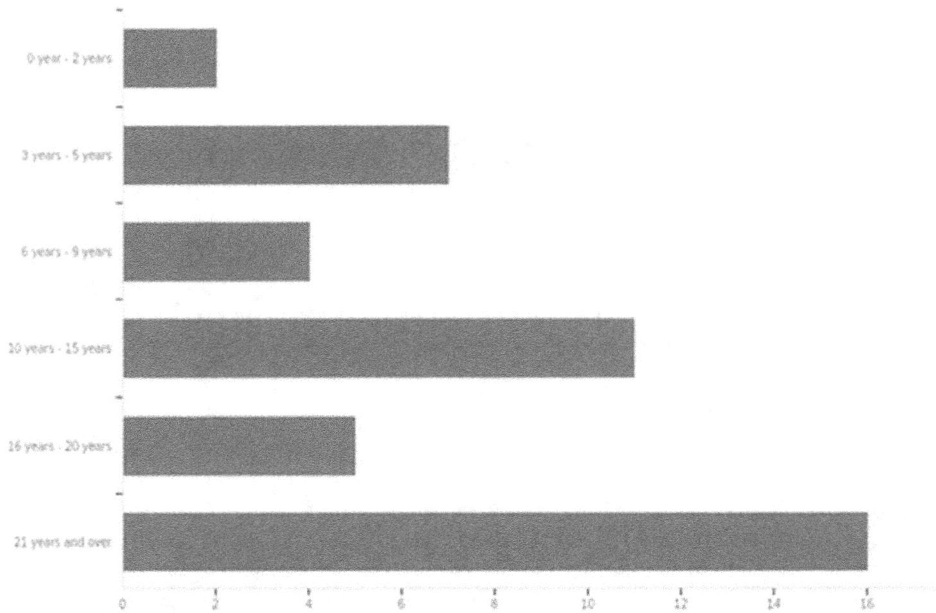

Figure 4. Q2 – How effective are you as a Black woman (or Woman of Color) in leadership (ranking 1 - lowest and ranking 5 - highest)?

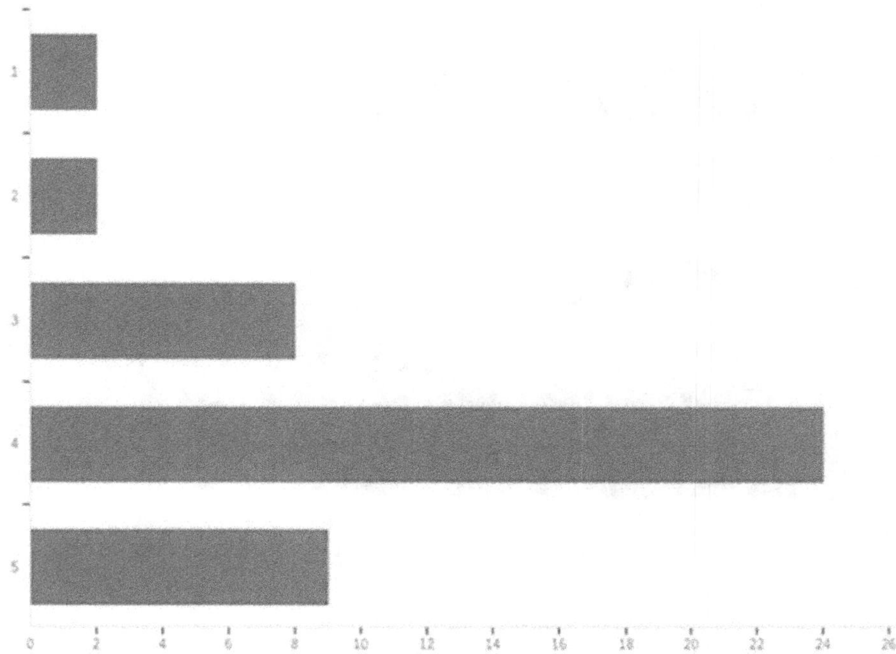

Figure 5. Q3 – What is your leadership discipline/occupation? (Choose one!)

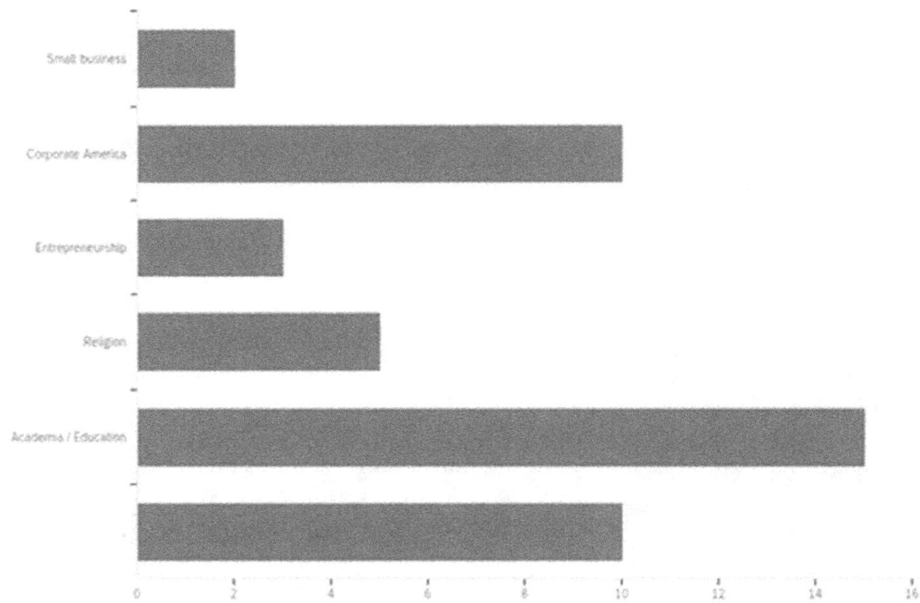

Figure 6. Q4 – What is your most effective leadership characteristic?

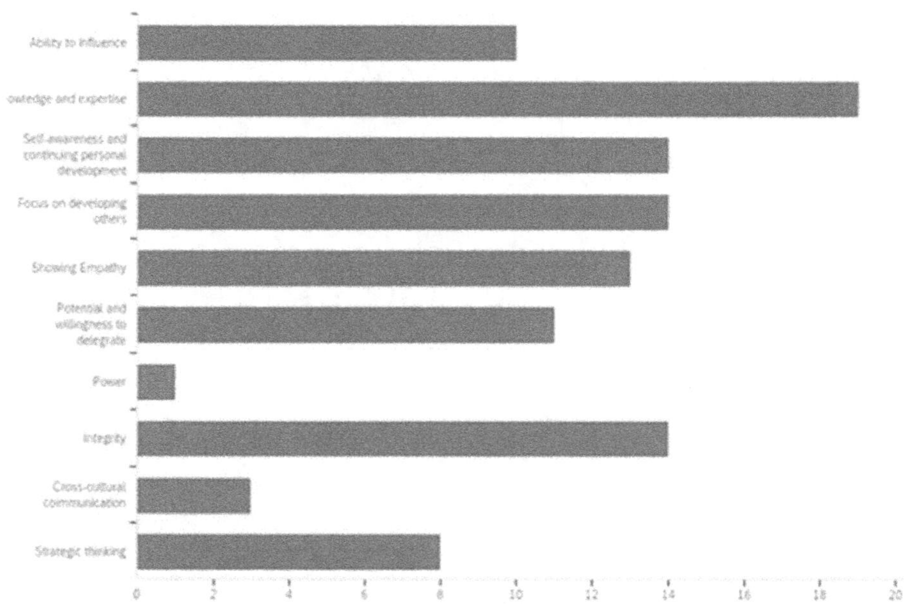

Figure 7. Q5 – Identify your biggest obstacle in leading others

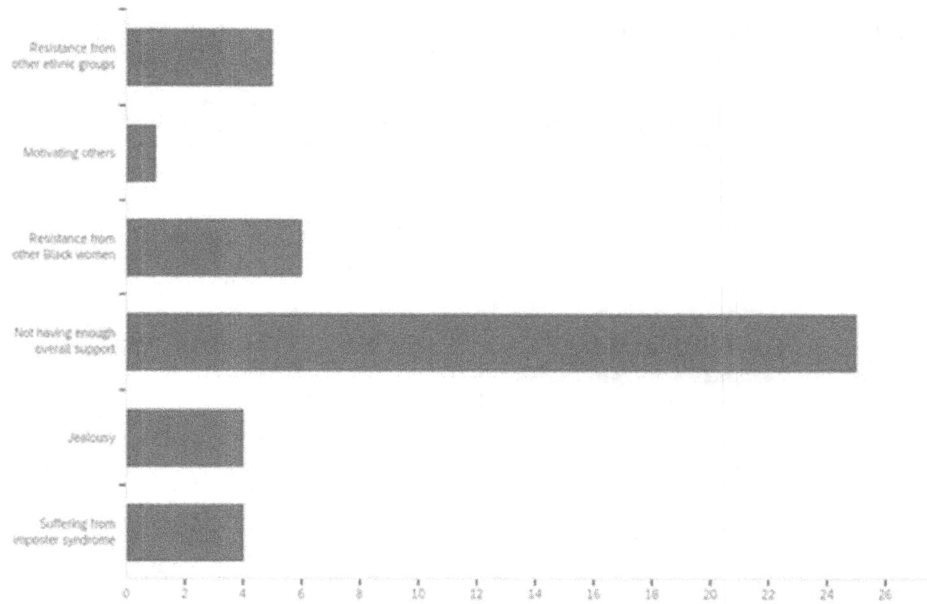

Figure 8. Q7 – How did you or how are you navigating these obstacles?

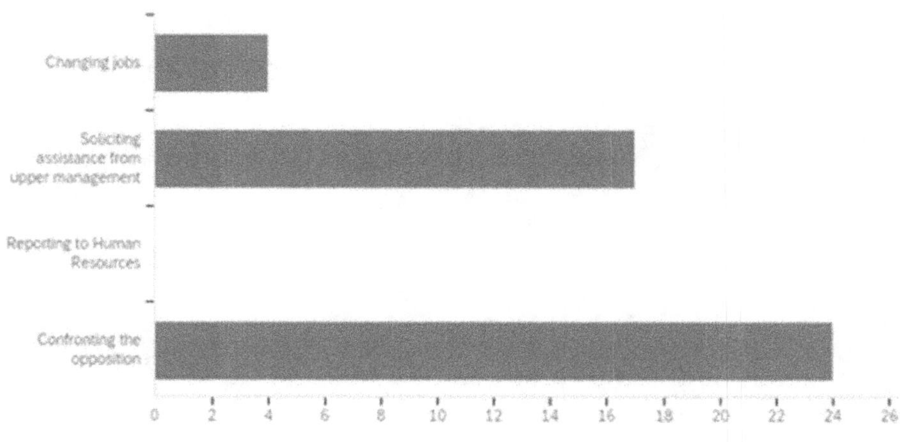

Figure 9. Q8 – When ranking your leadership style with others (Black women, Women of Color, or other ethnic groups), how do you perceive the fairness of your personal leadership evaluation?

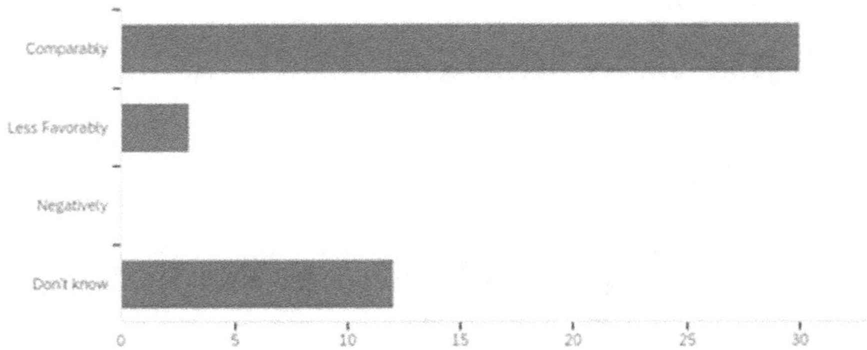

Chapter 13
Breaking the Glass Ceiling:
Oral History of the Professional Trajectories of Women in Public Accounting

Aleff dos Santos Santana
Federal University of Pará, Brazil

Adriana Rodrigues Silva
Polytechnic Institute of Santarém, Portugal

Adelaine Brandão Soares
Federal University of Pará, Brazil

Jessika Jhenniffer da Silva Carvalho
Federal University of Pará, Brazil

Lidiane Nazaré da Silva Dias
Federal University of Pará, Brazil

ABSTRACT

This chapter aims to analyse the professional trajectories of women working in public accounting in light of the glass ceiling phenomenon. The authors applied the oral history method. To this end, they collected testimonies, through semi-structured interviews, with the participation of three public servants of the Directorate of Finance and Accounting (DFC), the largest higher education institution (HEI) in the northern region of Brazil. The results show that the women interviewed do not consider barriers to taking management positions. Despite previous contrary results, it was possible to ascertain that the public servers participating in the study recognise that women are breaking not only the ceiling but the entire organisational structure of public sector glass. This research contributes to broadening and deepening the literary discussion on gender and accounting. Furthermore, by adopting the oral history methodology, this chapter highlights the construction of the identity of the actors, recognising that the past is built according to the needs of the present.

DOI: 10.4018/978-1-6684-5981-2.ch013

INTRODUCTION

Before the world wars, the man was seen as the family's sole provider, while the woman was responsible for maintaining the home and caring for the children (Boniatti et al., 2014). Due to these pre-established roles, women could not perform activities considered male activities. Thus, a separation was created between professions exclusively for women and professions restricted to men (Feitosa & Albuquerque, 2019).

Women assumed an important role outside the home during the two world wars (1914 to 1945). Husbands went off to fight and defend the country and often did not return home, or when they did, they were unable to work. Thus, it fell to women to shoulder their role in industries, in the countryside, and in providing for the family (Schlickmann & Pizarro, 2013).

During the post-war period, the number of women in the labour market increased related to the growth of their education levels. The work environment was biased, and wages were lower than for men. However, despite many challenges, women have always sought to stand out to reach leadership positions previously occupied by a public restricted to men (Araújo & Ribeiro, 2002).

After the social changes of 1930, the labour market changed. Women began to be accepted and to have their work valued. The labour legislation created by the Vargas government provided some equality between men and women regarding the workload, increased the space, and improved the employment conditions of the female public (Marques, 2016). Even with the evolution of trade and labour law, cultural issues led companies to grant positions of higher hierarchy to men, generating prejudice as an obstacle faced by women in these organisations. In addition, the lack of opportunity and the difficulty reconciling the time between domestic and professional tasks led to this impasse (Boniatti et al., 2014).

Prejudice has generated a phenomenon called the glass ceiling. The glass ceiling phenomenon excludes the female audience from the decision-making process in most organisations. Fragility, barriers, and vulnerability in the workplace are some characteristics of this phenomenon associated with women (Rodrigues & Silva, 2015).

In the accounting area, the struggle of women against prejudice and, primarily, against the existence of professional barriers have been the subject of several academic studies (Powell & Butterfield, 1994; Vaz, 2013; Palotti & Freire, 2015; Silva, 2016; Cohen et al., 2018; Oliveira & Woida, 2018; Silva et al., 2018; Arruda & Sá, 2019; Quintero & Castro, 2019). These social clashes of the female public aim for greater appreciation, better positions, salaries, and professional recognition (Lemos Junior, Santini & Silveira, 2015).

However, previous research points to resistance in the public sector, with barriers persisting to reaching hierarchically important positions within government organisations (Abreu & Meirelles, 2012) and lower salaries when women assume roles in the sector's senior management (Unt et al., 2021).

Given the wide disparity in perceptions of the glass ceiling between public accounting and private accounting, Cohen et al. (2020) encourage the development of research focusing on the perceptions of professionals working in public accounting. In addition, studies also reveal the need for deepening the glass ceiling phenomenon, given the rarity of scientific investigations about women in the Brazilian public administration (Barroso, 2015).

In this sense, this chapter analyses the professional trajectories of women working in public accounting, considering the glass ceiling phenomenon. We used the oral history method to collect testimonials, through semi-structured interviews, with the participation of 3 (three) public servants of the Directorate of Finance and Accounting (DFC) of the largest public Higher Education Institution (HEI) in the northern region of Brazil.

This research contributes to broadening and deepening the literary discussion on gender and accounting. The accounting literature highlights the professional path of women accountants to reach management positions and break social paradigms. Regarding gender literature, possible professional limitations in public administration imposed by gender may be minimal in governmental and educational organisations. Moreover, by adopting the oral history methodology, this article expects to contribute, in practical terms, with the encouragement of the adoption of a tool that enables a better understanding of the construction of action strategies and representations of groups or individuals in different societies (Ferreira, 2002).

Conceptual Framework

This section comprises two subsections. The first presents the conceptual approach to the glass ceiling. Consequently, the second highlights the glass ceiling phenomenon in public sector entities.

Glass Ceiling

The under-representation of women in senior positions in the corporate sector was termed the "glass ceiling" by Marilyn Loden at a panel discussion on women's aspirations in 1978. Marilyn Loden, at the time, was an experienced HR professional working in the telecommunications industry (BBC News, 2017). Marilyn presented that the barriers to women's career advancement were cultural and not related to individual characteristics, as suggested by other participants in the panel (BBC News, 2017).

After its emergence, the term glass ceiling was gradually used (Steil, 1997). However, it was in March 1986 that it became popular in the United States, with the publication of the article "The glass ceiling: Why women cannot seem to break the invisible barrier that blocks them from the top jobs", by Carol Hymowitz and Timothy D. Schellhardt, by The Wall Street Journal (Lahiri, Sarkar & Bhargava, 2022). The article presented that despite the more significant insertion of women in the United States labour market, the top executive positions continued to be occupied mainly by men (Hymowitz & Schellhardt, 1986).

The glass ceiling phenomenon demonstrates women's barriers to ascending to higher-level positions (Steil, 1997). This is mainly because of the increased presence of women in the labour market, increasingly occupying space in the social, cultural, professional, and political reality, which traditionally only men occupied. However, Cooper (2010) demonstrates that in history, it is possible to identify the discussion about the differences between the sexes, given that women were perceived as having neither the nature nor the intelligence for the commercial world and were more suited to be companions of men than competitors.

The glass ceiling would collectively harm women, creating barriers blocking individual growth due solely to their gender and not their inability to assume management positions in organisations (Steil, 1997). This phenomenon is characterised "by the lower speed with which women ascend in the career, which results in their underrepresentation in the command positions of organisations and, consequently, in the high spheres of power, prestige, and remuneration" (Vaz, 2013, p.765).

For Meyerson and Fletcher (2000), the glass barriers go beyond the ceiling, as other factors hinder the growth of women as professionals; thus, not only the ceiling but the "walls" and "beams" of the organisational structure of a company would be obstacles to be faced by them. In this sense, it is possible to consider that the glass ceiling phenomenon increases in proportion when viewed in the power relationship regarding the issue of gender inequality, primarily when we consider its use as a form of oppression.

Gender issues present themselves in almost all processes of organisational life, including jokes, metaphors used, administrative policies, body language, and the environment, which show the phenomenon of the glass ceiling intrinsic in organisations (Miranda, 2006). The aspects that characterise the splendour of the glass ceiling in these environments are, for example, discrimination, prejudice, structure and organisational culture, lack of guidance, no flexible schedules, absence of challenging experiences, wage gap, absence of respect, support, and authority, among others (Carneiro, Frare & Gomes, 2022).

However, the conflict between men and women in organisations is often concealed or hidden between the lines of social interaction at work, like more subtle forms of discrimination (Martin, 2000). Both the formal and informal sectors of work present problems of unequal pay between men and women, as well as prejudice regarding the quality of services provided by women (Probst, 2003). The relationship between gender and organisation suggests the existence of entangled networks of relationships in which gender is deeply involved and embedded. It is not just a formal organisational chart but a network of formal and informal relationships that run through the organisation daily (Meyer, 2000). In this sense, organisations must address these conflicts seriously and clearly to combat such discrimination.

In general, organisations have been receptive to women's work. This receptiveness, however, must be carefully assessed because, even with greater openness to the entry of women into organisations in management positions, not all positions are available for them to occupy (Souza & Guimarães, 2000). Even though there are no longer any reserved spaces with definitively defined functions or insurmountable walls between men and women, there is still veiled and disguised segregation in the organisational environment (Belle, 1993). As an example, we highlight maternity leave, which should be recognised as a benefit for both men and women; however, when included in the competitive world of management, it becomes a negative aspect in the evaluation of women (Miranda et al., 2013). This shows that despite the expansion of women in the labour market, they struggle to access certain positions, considering the higher qualification requirement for career advancement.

The glass ceiling phenomenon exists in organisational environments and represents individual-, firm-, and institutional- or societal-level barriers (Pungalia & Cetindamar, 2022). The segregation mechanism reflects the hierarchical relationship, which can be seen in the difference in career opportunities between men and women that prevent professional advancement.

The Glass Ceiling Phenomenon in Public Sector Entities

According to Vaz and Hoffman (2011), in Brazil, women in the public sector work more in the social sectors of direct public administration, such as the Ministry of Culture, Education, Health and the Ministry of Social Security and Assistance. In the areas of economic, infrastructure and administrative missions, the presence of women is incipient.

The 1934 Constitution added equality in selecting people to occupy public posts. The 1934 Constitution established that the choice of human resources for entry into public service has merit as the base, guaranteeing equal pay for those with similar responsibilities. In this sense, the government applies tests or title exams to select the public servant.

Notwithstanding the equal opportunity of access granted to men and women to the different careers in the public sector, the State presents in its staff a pattern of occupational insertion differentiated between the sexes (Cohen et al., 2018). For

Abreu and Meirelles (2012), when the professional ascension of women is analysed, there is more vigorous resistance than in the private sector, considering the barriers to management positions. According to Morais et al. (2006), when questioned about whether there is discrimination against women in the federal civil service, 68% of the respondents indicated that. Among women, the perception of bias is 85%, and among men, it is 57%.

In the public sector, we observe the glass ceiling phenomenon in analysing women's participation in commissioned posts in the senior management and advisory group (known as DAS). There are six DAS levels, i.e., the higher the decision-making level, the higher the post. These positions are designed to perform management, leadership and advisory functions in the direct federal, autonomous and foundational public administration. These positions are generally filled by appointment, are temporary, and can be occupied by career government employees.

The Annual Socioeconomic Report of Women (2022) results showed that women hold 43% of DAS positions. In the last ten years, the number of women in this position has never been higher than that of men, proving that despite considerable advances, women still need to be in superior command positions. The following is a breakdown of the Executive Branch civil servants by gender and level of education (Table 1).

Table 1. Distribution of executive power servers, September 2022

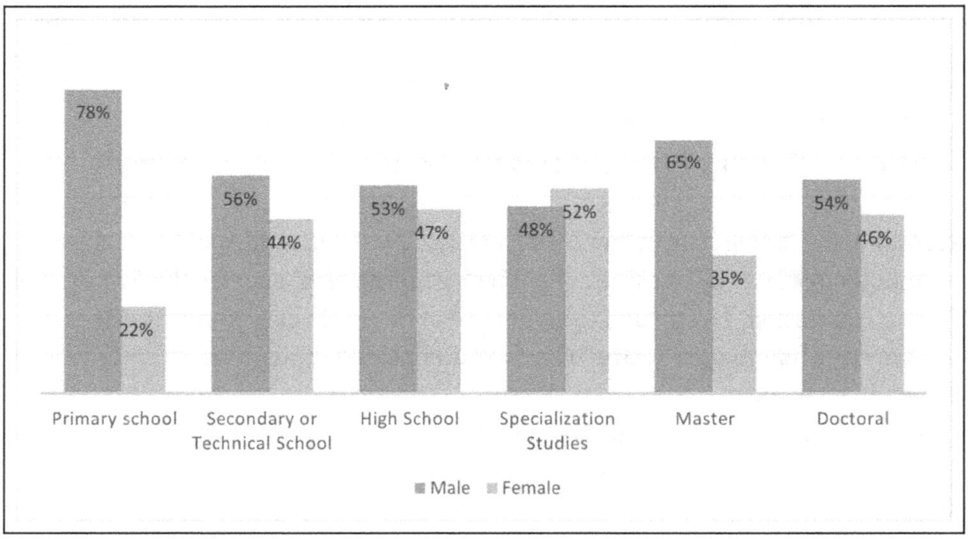

Source: Statistical Panel of Personnel, Federal Public Servants - Gender, 2022.

The literature indicates that the qualification does not explain the gap between women and men in management positions but rather the discriminatory factors, the sexual division of labour that overburdens women and the gender expectations imposed by the socialisation process (Firmino & Silva, 2014). When women prefer not to ascend professionally, it is due to fear of the obstacles and the conflicts that emerge for them to reconcile their professional life with their personal (family) life. Usually, these fears are intensified in positions of command and the most prestigious careers (Vaz, 2013).

Another criticism is the lack of technical, objective, and public criteria for commission positions, which do not require public competition. Vaz (2013, p. 788) highlights:

In the federal public administration, it is precisely for the high command positions—the commissioned posts—that there is no mandatory public competition for hiring public servants. Access to such positions is through appointment, including those who do not career state employees. Thus, there is no guarantee that selection follows technical and universal criteria.

The situation of inequality between women and men, as well as imbalances of ethnic, racial, gender identity, sexual orientation and class among women, as structuring elements of Brazilian society, is necessary to think about how each body can contribute to addressing these inequalities with their actions (Brasil, 2014).

Firmino and Silva (2015) conclude that institutional change is necessary for the labour market, government bodies and society to think about equal opportunities. The authors suggest equalising paternity and maternity leaves, the creation of adequate structures for childcare and quotas for access to committees or executive boards.

METHODOLOGY

This research analyses the professional trajectories of women working in public accounting, considering the glass ceiling phenomenon. To this end, we applied the oral history method from a qualitative perspective. According to Matos and Senna (2011), the oral source allows for new historiographical conceptions and contributes to understanding the investigated object from an experienced dimension. Moreover, the information generated by this research modality has the same validity as the data collected from traditional sources (Perazzo, 2015). Oral history presents some strands of scientific research, among them the production of knowledge through personal trajectories (Gonçalves & Lisboa, 2007).

The justification for using this methodological approach stems from the fact that oral history reveals itself as an alternative and essential instrument in understanding organisational environments (Gomes & Santana, 2010). In this study, the method is used to understand the performance of the female audience in the government-corporate environment, starting from the premise of the persistence of barriers to professional advancement faced by women in the public sector (Abreu & Meirelles, 2012).

The oral history method can be applied as three techniques: Thematic Oral History, Oral Life History and Oral Tradition (Ribeiro & Machado, 2014). This study is focused on a particular point in the trajectories of women working in public accounting - the glass ceiling phenomenon. In this sense, we chose the thematic oral history technique, as it enables the collection of the opinion of a particular audience on a specific theme or subject (Barros, 2005).

Oral history is a method that uses interviews to build knowledge (Freund, 2013). In this sense, women who worked in the Directorate of Finance and Accounting (DFC) of a public Higher Education Institution (HEI) in the City of Belém, Pará State, Brazil, were interviewed. The choice of the governmental organisation of activity in the educational field is based on the demand in the literature (Öge et al., 2014). The option for the referred institution was already motivated by its national recognition as the largest HEI in the northern region of Brazil.

The researchers conducted an on-site visit and invited the civil servants of the DFC to participate in the research. We choose the organisation by convenience. Three women expressed interest in collaborating voluntarily with the present study. The interviews were scheduled, considering the availability and location of the discussion informed by the participants. The testimonies collection took place in Portuguese and followed the pre-defined schedules. In Table 2, we present a brief description of the interviewees.

Table 2. Description of the interviewees

Identification	Education	Position	Years of Service
Public Servant 01	Technical Accountant	Technical Accountant	Between 40 and 45 years
Public Servant 02	Bachelor in Accounting	Administrative Assistant	Between 20 and 25 years
Public Servant 03	Bachelor in Accounting	Accountant	Between 10 and 15 years

Source: Research Data.

Before the interviews began, we explained the purpose research to the participants, and the Informed Consent Form (ICF) was signed by them and given to the researchers. We recorded the interviews individually and transcribed them. Some excerpts of the statements report situations of prejudice experienced by the participants; given this, wishing to preserve their physical and moral integrity, they received unique identification in place of their names, according to Table 2.

The data collection occurred through a semi-structured questionnaire based on the subject's literature. It is worth mentioning that a pre-test was made with one of the participants (chosen randomly) to understand if the questions were straightforward for constructing the reports. The participant approved the information collection instrument of the research.

The questions were created based on the literature on the subject, as well as divided into two groups of analysis: (1) Women in Public Accounting, to identify the work environment and the factors that lead women to the public administration; and (2) The Glass Ceiling Phenomenon, to understand its presence in the state workspace, as well as its change according to the trajectory of each servant. The participants also answered questions to identify personal characteristics (Table 2).

For data treatment, we applied content analysis. We used this technique in three phases of research, according to Campos (2004): (1) pre-exploration phase of the literature, used in the a priori category that helped collect elements for the choice of units of analysis; (2) selection of units of analysis, based on the study objective; (3) categorisation and subcategorisation process, a process built simultaneously with the return to the theoretical body of research. We communicated the findings to readers of the publication to understand how it was expressed in the findings, originating from data in the source language. The research interpreted the message communicated in the source language and transferred it into the target language so that the receiver of the message could understand what was meant (Van Nes et al., 2010).

Data Description

Women in Public Accounting

Women play an essential role in social development and the evolution of public-sector accounting. Several factors lead women to choose to account and, preferably, accounting applied to the public sector. This section presents women's narratives focused on this preference and their trajectory in the area.

The excellent feeling (love) that public accounting provides them (women) is one of the reasons for entering the public career, as mentioned by Public Servant 02 when she said that it was the "passion" that led her to choose public sector accounting.

Public Servant 01 reported that her love for public accounting emerged in her technical course: "Since I took my technical course, I liked public accounting, but more than commercial accounting, industrial accounting, banking accounting, these accounts that I saw, I liked public accounting better".

On the other hand, Public Servant 03 said she chose to work in the public sector. Thus, to achieve this goal, it was necessary to study the subject of public accounting, which was often charged in the competitions she used to take. She said, "I did not choose public accounting; I chose to be a civil servant. I decided at the end of 2007 to study for the civil service exams, and then I focused on my studies. As my position is an accountant and I only took the competitive examination for my position, I focused my study on public accounting because it was a subject that was often required in the competitive examinations for the position I was aiming for".

The respondents stressed the importance of the presence of women in public service. Two participants responded that there is no understanding of unequal distribution between men and women in public administration.

However, Civil Servant 02 believes in the possibility of inequality; she said: "I do not know how to measure it, but in the sectors that I was (referring to the sectors she worked in), there was a balance between men and women. I have been a director of Finance and Accounting (mentions two institutions where she worked), and there were more men than women in the directors of Finance and Accounting forums. In the places where I have worked, there are currently more men than women. Women are not standing out much, and they are accountants too".

This last statement conveys the impression of a primarily male presence in the public sector's top management accounting environment. Women have the same positions and functions as men, but they do not perceive an emphasis on the duties they perform in public administration.

When asked about their perception of women in management positions in the accounting area when they joined the civil service, all of them replied that there were already women occupying management positions at the University. Civil Servant 03 narrated the following: "When I entered the university, which is the body in which I work, the head auditor was a woman, and the public accountant of the body was also a woman. However, the positions of pro-rector and rector were all men. However, I can see that this is growing; we are occupying more space".

Moreover, in the reports of Civil Servant 02, we can also notice the presence of women in management positions in the accounting area; the interviewee said: "There were some. I replaced (mentions the name of a female civil servant) as the accountant in charge; although my position was not as an accountant, my training was. Then she went to auditing, and I stayed in accounting for five years in (mention the name of the institution), after which I went to (mention the name of the institution) as the accountant there".

The interviewees highlighted the lack of respect towards women (currently) and the lack of technical knowledge (when they began their careers) as the main difficulties they faced in exercising their respective positions. Civil Servant 01 said that her problem was related to the operationality of new technologies and accounting systems. Before, she did everything manually, but now she needs to use the computer to develop her work.

In turn, Civil Servant 02 reported that "because I am a woman, many do not respect you; you have to conquer by showing your work and conquer daily. Mainly at (mention the name of the institution), even suffering harassment that made me sad, especially because I chose to go there. Which made me rethink 'did I make the right choice to go there? However, with time, I left with tributes, with a room full of people for my farewell, and I was surprised with this achievement; this is valorisation".

Public Servant 03 highlights the lack of technical knowledge as a factor that hinders the exercise of the position; she said: "The first difficulty I faced was the lack of technical knowledge. The discipline of public accounting was not very well worked during college. I had experience in the private sector, so I worked in an accounting office. I did not know how the accounting routine worked in public service. Moreover, I started even before the standardisation to international standards, the change of the balance sheets in 2015, and the convention to international standards. So, I initially had difficulty understanding how the accounting routine worked in the public service. . . . That was my main difficulty". Corroborating the report, Public Servant 02 comments: "We observe that those who pass the competitions and enter do not have any notion of public accounting, especially the Federal".

To conclude this group of questions, the interviewees were asked to describe their trajectory with public accounting. For Public Servant 01, this trajectory is summed up in the word "hard work" (an expression of dedication to work). In turn, Public Servant 02 describes as follows: "The issue of knowledge is the main one, but also of financial achievements; what I have today would not be possible without public accounting. The appreciation of it and the compatible remuneration. Within this trajectory, I spent ten years out qualifying and training".

Civil Servant 03 described her trajectory: "Public accounting for me has always been very challenging. . . . My experience with public accounting was even in college. I had never interned in a public agency, and I had never worked in a public agency until I decided to study for the competitive examination and join the civil service. . . . Public accounting has evolved a lot, and many things have changed. It is always very challenging because we must always be aware of what is happening; there are many requirements and regulations. Accounting regulations and public service regulations. So, it is always a challenge".

Therefore, one can see that the interviewees chose the civil service because of, firstly, liking the accounting performed in public administration. Moreover, they decided to enter this type of employment, aiming at better working conditions and financial stability. Furthermore, it can be stated that the participants recognised women's occupations in management positions. However, the perception of women's lack of professional prominence in the public sector persists.

Breaking Walls, Beams, and the Glass Ceiling in the Public Sector

This section presents statements related to the glass ceiling phenomenon to describe its presence or absence in public administration, especially in higher education institutions.

When the female respondents were asked about the possibility of prejudice at work because they are women, Public Servant 01 said she had never suffered discrimination. However, the other interviewees claimed to have already suffered this embarrassment.

Civil Servant 03 said she had already suffered prejudice: "I think this is not a characteristic of the civil service; in the civil service, we even manage to notice less of it (referring to prejudice) because salaries are equal. . . . However, I think that women experience this in a general situation. In the private or public sector, we experience these situations of people doubting our capacity because we will have children, or they think that because we have children, we will not be able to cope with the work, and they demand that women do it. I am not a mother, but they demand from women who are mothers that they take care of their children, take care of their jobs, and take care of everything in the same way. Moreover, the woman is charged at home and work as if she needed to care for everything as perfectly as possible".

Civil Servant 02 also claimed to have suffered prejudice in the exercise of public office, describing the following: "The very issue of envy and jealousy. Sometimes people want to get ahead without deserving it. They want to get you out because of the power of your position. What I achieved was not for political but for professional reasons".

The interviewees also spoke of the barriers women face in their work sector. Civil Servant 02 pointed to the lack of opportunity to be heard as the main impasse; she said: "being listened to. In general, regardless of gender, it is about valuing yourself. They think you must stay in a quiet little room without being heard. No, it would help if you made yourself heard and respected. The question of decision is sometimes in our hands to guide our managers. . . . Women suffer a much greater prejudice for being a woman. . . . I believe that, in this trajectory, I arrived at the sense of being heard. I conquered the presence of deans supporting me. For example, it was peculiar at (mention the name of the institution); the rector gave me all the accountants and structured me. There are things that we have to run after. We cannot just accept it. We need to know if that way is the right one so we can go further".

Questioned in the same way, Civil Servant 03 reported: "We always face situations like this. As I said before, if we position ourselves in a particular case, say or give a new idea for a service or are very assertive in what we say, then people doubt they think we are PMS (referring to pre-menstrual tension), for example. If you are powerful in what you want and if you have an idea to propose, and if men, in the vast majority, do not agree with this idea, then they will ask if you are single, they will ask if you have a boyfriend (according to the interviewee, men usually say: go home, relax, go dating). People doubt your capacity. People think that women are more stressed. They believe that women are going crazy. However, we want to take a stand and have a voice. Issues of harassment, too, of men paying you an inappropriate compliment in the middle of a meeting or in the middle of your work to make you feel uncomfortable. The other interviewee said that the courier woman faced was not identified in her workplace due to the time dedicated to her role."

Still, the issue of women in management positions was brought up in another question but is now related to the present time and not the moment of entry into public service. Civil Servant 03 said, "This is changing. Today, here at the university, the Director of Finance is a woman, an extremely competent woman. The head auditor is a woman. We also have pro-rectors, super-competent ones, who are occupying these positions. We still do not have any female deans. This is a challenge for us, an important challenge. However, for all the reasons I mentioned, it is difficult. Society has this prejudice, although here at the University, it is a very plural space. This space welcomes everyone very well and has an exciting space for democratic and women's struggles. I think this is the space we should occupy more, but we still face challenges of this type, as I mentioned, prejudice about whether a woman can reconcile a career with motherhood. . . . However, I also see that we have enormous potential because in post-graduate and undergraduate courses, especially in accounting, the area I worked in, women have always been in the majority and still are today. Some courses are mostly female, so I think it is a space that we should occupy".

Public Servant 01 believes that prejudice makes it impossible for women to occupy management positions. Civil Servant 02 also believes in this difficulty for women. She said: "Because we are women, we are already discriminated against. The issue of who is new, maternity interferes by the time of leave, often losing a function because there are six months from public service, and sometimes it extends longer due to holidays. During this period, someone else took your place. Will it be the same when you return? This makes it a little tricky".

Questions were asked about the space that women have been acquiring in public service. Civil Servant 03 said: "It is a space we should occupy more and more. I am not only talking about executive public service, which is where I work (Ministry of Education). I am mainly talking about the legislative branch. We need representatives in power; I think we need women who discuss causes that are dear to us, like the issue of abortion and the issue of harassment in the workplace".

On the other hand, Public Servant 02 highlights: "Women are advancing a lot. Even because we women, regardless of our training, end up standing out more than men because we run after, the number of those who enter (higher education), I think, is more women; at least the statistics show this. We are often ahead of men". On the other hand, civil servant 01 believes this space generates more training opportunities for women.

Regarding the scenario of women's recognition, we highlight the speech of Civil Servant 03 when she said: "I think that this recognition is much more due to our position, to the struggle of women than necessarily of accountants, of organs. We already see some initiatives from our council, the "Meeting of Accountant Women", there are already some initiatives. However, I see that it is much more a struggle of women as a gender, as a unit. [Our director of Finance at the university is a very competent accountant, a great example for us. Why not a pro-rector? Why not a PhD accountant or dean of the University (mentions the institution's name)? That is what I long for. I still have that dream".

Thus, we can observe by the discourse of the interviews that women, directed to the federal public power and related to education services, have always occupied management positions, as narrated by the participant with the most extended service in the institution. However, barriers have always existed, and the servant's technical difficulties and prejudice are routinely faced by women, as mentioned above.

DISCUSSION

This work aimed to analyse the professional trajectories of women in the field of public accounting in light of the glass ceiling phenomenon. The data allow us to state that women in the accounting and finance department of the investigated HEI since they joined the institution until the day of the present research. Women occupy important positions (leadership) in decision-making and do not have as much difference in the number of women as men.

This result corroborates the study by Powell and Butterfield (1994). The authors found that women in the Senior Executive Service of the Federal Government of the United States of America (USA) do not have so many barriers to assuming management positions. The explanation lies in the particularities of the organisation, which impose equal selection for the most senior positions in public administration. In Brazil, the scenario is the same, given the federal constitution's diligence of the equality obligation (Palotti & Freire, 2015). This fact would justify women's management positions in the institution chosen as a sphere of scientific research.

However, the reports presented by the interviewees confirm the results evidenced in the research of Silva (2016). In other words, in the accounting field, women are subject to predominantly macho statements and conduct, thus revealing the persistence of gender prejudice and the existence of some glass ceilings.

Moreover, women disengage themselves more from personal issues than men, to sum up, the positions of strategic positioning in organisations (Oliveira & Woida, 2018). The data in the previous section prove this type of sacrifice that civil servants make for professional advancement in the public sector. Often, these personal factors serve as a basis for the emergence of discrimination against these women.

When we analyse the presence of the glass ceiling phenomenon in public institutions, the work of Vaz (2013) is essential to understand this relationship between public power and the professional advancement of women. The author highlights that women also have an unfavourable representation in the academic environment, especially regarding the positions of prestige within universities. However, as the interviewees' reports identified, women have shown more relevance in this acting universe. Not only are management positions being occupied by them, but also an increase in the representation of women in the academic environment is perceived. The results of this study show that the congresses of women and their entry into the postgraduate programs understand the growing importance of women to academia.

Firmino and Silva (2015) highlight that the public sector can expose certain assumptions of gender discrimination, opening space for the consequences of these practices in work environments. The evidence of the data shows that the impacts of gender on the career of women during the process of professional growth are the lack of credibility by men and the absence of a more powerful position for the female audience. That is, we can perceive the indications of the consequences pointed out by the authors above, such as the lack of appreciation and the prestige of good results achieved in the position.

Unlike Abreu and Meirelles (2012), in the Brazilian public education sector, the women interviewed do not have as many barriers to professional advancement as in the private sector. Thus, we can affirm that female civil servants are breaking not only the ceiling but the entire glass organisational structure of the public sector and are growing progressively, conquering positions of higher hierarchy. However, traces of gender prejudice are still noted.

CONCLUSION

The present chapter analysed the trajectories of women who work in public accounting, considering the glass ceiling phenomenon. The results show that the women participating in the research chose public service because of, firstly, liking the accounting undertaken in public administration. In addition, they decided to enter this type of employment, aiming at better working conditions and financial stability. The interviewed civil servants acknowledge that women have been occupying management positions, although the perception of the lack of professional prominence of the female public persists.

The results corroborate the research of Abreu and Meirelles (2012). Thus, they present a new vision of the public work environment, at least in the public education service, given that the participants do not have many barriers to professional advancement compared to the private labour market, a fact pointed out in the authors' investigation. This reality allows us to state that the female civil servants interviewed are increasingly breaking the glass ceiling phenomenon and are growing progressively and conquering positions of higher hierarchy, even if traces of gender prejudice are still noted.

Furthermore, on the part of the participants, there is an impression of the recognition of women over the last few years. In this way, actions aimed at the recognition of the work of female civil servants are still a point to be reinforced. They consider that technical knowledge is one of the barriers faced by these women when they enter public service. These obstacles feed the mistrust that prevents the full recognition of women as qualified professionals.

It is noteworthy that the number of servers interviewed is a limitation of the research, given that the present study was applied when many were on break from work, i.e., unavailable to participate. Thus, new perspectives were not addressed in this academic work. In methodological terms, the limitation focuses on the fact that by resorting to memory, oral history depends on the social power of the group that holds it. Memory, represented by the relationship between repetition and remembrance, may carry a value judgment since we do not remember the images of the past as they happened but according to the social forces of the present that act upon us (Ferreira, 2002).

The main contribution of this research is the expansion and deepening of the literary discussion on gender and accounting, which is considered still incipient in academia (Santos, Melo & Batinga, 2021). We also contributed by showing that possible professional limitations in administration imposed by gender can be minimised through external requirements imposed by law and thus promote equal selection for the functions with higher administration hierarchy. It is also emphasised that by using the oral history methodology, we explore the relations between memory and history and place in evidence the construction of the identity of the actors, recognising that the past is constructed according to the needs of the present (Ferreira, 2002). Finally, it is suggested for future research to expand the sample and diversify the federative entities investigated, analysing the state and municipal public administration.

REFERENCES

Abreu, M. A. A., & Meirelles, R. L. (2012). *Mulheres e Homens em Ocupação de DAS na Administração Pública Federal. In Relatório de Pesquisa: Instituto de Pesquisa Econômica Aplicada*. IPEA.

Araújo, V. F., & Ribeiro, E. P. (2002). Diferenciais de Salários por Gênero no Brasil: Uma Análise Regional. *Revista Economica do Nordeste*, *33*(2), 1–22.

Arruda, M. A. R., & Sá, M. A. D. (2019). A Cultura Organizacional e o Fenômeno Teto de Vidro. *Revista FSA*, *16*(4), 261–280. doi:10.12819/2019.16.4.14

Barros, V. M. (2005). O Novo Velho Enfoque da Informação Contábil. *Revista Contabilidade & Finanças*, *16*(38), 102–112. doi:10.1590/S1519-70772005000200009

Barroso, C. (2015). As Mulheres nos Altos Escalões da Administração Pública no Brasil. *Revista do Serviço Público*, *66*(1), 145–159. doi:10.21874/rsp.v66i1.796

Belle, F. (1993). *Executivas: Quais as Diferenças na Diferença?* Editora Atlas.

Boniatti, A. O., Souza Velho, A., Pereira, A., Pereira, B. B., & Oliveira, S. M. (2014). A Evolução da Mulher no Mercado Contábil. *Revista Gestão e Desenvolvimento em Contexto*, *2*(1), 19–27.

Brasil. Constituição da República Federativa do Brasil. (1998/2020). Planalto, Brasília.

Brasil, Ministério do Planejamento. (2022). *Painel Estatístico de Pessoal, distribuição por Gênero, Setembro de 2022*. http://painel.pep.planejamento.gov.br/QvAJAXZfc/opendoc.htm?document=painelpep.qvw&lang=en-US&host=Local&anonymous=true

Campos, C. J. G. (2004). Método de Análise de Conteúdo: Ferramentas para a Análise de Dados Qualitativos no Campo da Saúde. *Revista Brasileira de Enfermagem*, *57*(5), 611–614. doi:10.1590/S0034-71672004000500019 PMID:15997809

Carneiro, L. B., Gomes, D. G., Cruz, A. P. C., & Frare, A. B. (2022). Glass ceiling: A study on the factors of this phenomenon in Brazil from the perception of women managers. *SINERGIA-Revista do Instituto de Ciências Econômicas. Administrativas e Contábeis*, *26*(1), 173–185.

Cohen, J. R., Dalton, D. W., Holder-Webb, L. L., & McMillan, J. J. (2020). An analysis of glass ceiling perceptions in the accounting profession. *Journal of Business Ethics*, *164*(1), 17–38. doi:10.100710551-018-4054-4

Cooper, K. (2010). Accounting by women: Fear, favour and the path to professional recognition for Australian women accountants. *Accounting History*, *15*(3), 309–336. doi:10.1177/1032373210368422

Feitosa, Y. S., & Albuquerque, J. S. (2019). Evolução da Mulher no Mercado de Trabalho. *Business Journal*, *1*(1), 1–17. doi:10.6008/CBPC2674-6433.2019.001.0005

Ferreira, M. D. M. (2002). História, Tempo Presente e História Oral. *Topoi (Rio de Janeiro)*, *3*(5), 314–332. doi:10.1590/2237-101X003006013

Firmino, C. R., & Silva, F. H. E. (2015). *Desigualdades de Gênero no Serviço Público do Poder Executivo Federal. Escola Nacional de Administração Pública*. ENAP.

Freund, A. (2013). História Oral como Processo Gerador de Dados. *Revista Tempos Históricos*, *17*(1), 28–62.

Gonçalves, R. C.; Lima, T. K. (2007). Sobre o Método da História Oral em sua Modalidade Trajetórias de Vida. *Revista Katálysis*, *10*, 83-92.

Lahiri, M. M., Sarkar, S., & Bhargava, M. (2022). A brief history of 'glass ceiling': The past, present & the future. *Academy of Marketing Studies Journal*, *26*(6), 1–5.

Lemos, L. C. Junior, Santini, R. B., & Silveira, N. S. P. (2015). A Feminização da Área Contábil: Um Estudo Qualitativo Básico. *Revista de Educação e Pesquisa em Contabilidade*, *1*(1), 64–83.

Marques, T. C. N. (2016). A regulação do trabalho feminino em um sistema político masculino, Brasil: 1932-1943. *Estudos Históricos (Rio de Janeiro)*, *29*(59), 667-686.

Matos, J. S., & Machado, A. F. (2006). Diferencial de Rendimentos por Cor e Sexo no Brasil (1987-2001). *Revista Economica*, *8*(1), 5–27.

Matos, J. S., & Senna, A. K. (2011). História Oral como Fonte: Problemas e Métodos. *Revista Historiæ*, *2*(1), 95–108.

Meyerson, D. E., & Fletcher, J. K. (2000). A Modest Manifest for Shattering the Glass Ceiling. *Harvard Business Review*, *78*(1), 127–136.

Miranda, A. R. A., Cappelle, M. C. A., Fonseca, F. P., Mafra, F. L. N., & Moreira, L. B. (2013). O Exercício da Gerência Universitária por Docentes Mulheres. *Revista Pretexto*, *14*(1), 106–123.

Miranda, L. C. (2006). *A Percepção da Mulher no Mercado de Trabalho: Emprego, Carreira ou Vocação*. Faculdade IBMEC.

Morais, J. G., Oliveira, C. G., Campos, K. R. S., Viana, G. M., & Fernandes, M. L. R. (2006). Gênero, Raça e Competências de Direção no Serviço Público Federal. *Cadernos Enap*, *36*(1), 1–69.

Öge, S., Karasoy, A., & Kara, Ö. (2014). A research on glass ceiling syndrome career barriers of women academics. *International Journal of Economics and Management Engineering*, *8*(9), 3019–3028.

Oliveira, B. B., & Woida, L. M. (2018). O Fenômeno *Glass Ceiling* e o Acesso à Informação: Estudo sobre Barreiras Invisíveis Impostas às Mulheres no Trabalho. *Revista de Filosofia Temática*, *3*(1), 61–75.

Palotti, P., & Freire, A. (2015). *Perfil, Composição e Remuneração dos Servidores Públicos Federais: Trajetória Recente e Tendências Observadas. Cadernos ENAP, 42*.

Perazzo, P. F. (2015). Narrativas Orais de Histórias de Vida. *Revista Comunicação & Inovação*, *16*(30), 121–131.

Powell, G. N., & Butterfield, A. (1994). Investigating the "Glass Ceiling" Phenomenon: An Empirical Study of Actual Promotions to Top Management. *Academy of Management Journal*, *37*(1), 68–86. doi:10.2307/256770

Pugalia, S., & Cetindamar, D. (2022). Insights on the glass ceiling for immigrant women entrepreneurs in the technology sector. *International Journal of Gender and Entrepreneurship*, *14*(1), 44–68. doi:10.1108/IJGE-10-2020-0169

Ribeiro, M. C., & Machado, A. L. (2014). O Uso do Método História Oral nas Pesquisas Qualitativas: Contribuições para a Temática do Cuidado em Saúde Mental. *Estudos e Pesquisas em Psicologia*, *14*(2), 578–591. doi:10.12957/epp.2014.12562

Rodrigues, S. C., & Silva, G. R. (2015). A Liderança Feminina no Mercado de Trabalho. *Revista Digital de Administração*, *1*(4), 1–12.

Santos, M. A., Melo, M. C. D. O. L., & Batinga, G. L. (2021). Representatividade da Mulher Contadora em Escritórios de Contabilidade e a Desigualdade de Gênero na Prática Contábil: Uma Questão ainda em Debate? *Sociedade. Contabilidade e Gestão*, *16*(1), 148–163. doi:10.21446cg_ufrj.v0i0.30679

Schlickmann, E., & Pizarro, D. (2013). A Evolução da Mulher no Trabalho: Uma Abordagem sob a Ótica da Liderança. *Revista Borges*, *3*(1), 70–89.

Silva, S. M. C. (2016). *Tetos de Vitrais: Gênero e Raça na Contabilidade no Brasil*. Tese de Doutorado, Faculdade de Economia, Administração e Contabilidade, Universidade de São Paulo.

Steil, A. V. (1997). Organizações, Gênero e Posição Hierárquica - Compreendendo o Fenômeno do Teto de Vidro. *Revista ADM*, *32*(3), 62–69.

Unt, M., Rokicka, M., Täht, K., & Roosalu, T. (2021). "Glass Ceiling" and "Sticky Floor" in Estonian Public and Private Sectors. In *Gendering Post-Soviet Space* (pp. 195–209). Springer. doi:10.1007/978-981-15-9358-1_9

Van Nes, F., Abma, T., Jonsson, H., & Deeg, D. (2010). Language differences in qualitative research: Is meaning lost in translation? *European Journal of Ageing*, *7*(4), 313–316. doi:10.100710433-010-0168-y PMID:21212820

Vaz, D. V. (2013). O Teto de Vidro nas Organizações Públicas: Evidências para o Brasil. *Economia e Sociedade*, *49*(3), 765–790. doi:10.1590/S0104-06182013000300007

Vaz, D. V., & Hoffmann, R. (2011). Segregação Ocupacional por Sexo no Setor Público Brasileiro no Período 1995 e 2008. *Revista da ABET*, *10*(1), 120–141.

APPENDIX

Table 3. Interview script

Unit of Analysis	Questions	Purpose
Description of Participants	What is your full name?	To present the profile of the research participants.
	How old are you?	
	What is your background?	
	What position do you hold in the Public Administration?	
	How many years have you been part of the civil service?	
Women in Public Accounting	What factors led you to choose public accounting?	To identify the work environment and the factors that drive women into public administration.
	When you joined the civil service was the number of women in accounting higher or lower than the number of men? Has this scenario changed?	
	When you joined the public service did women in your sector have leading positions?	
	What difficulties have you faced in the exercise of your office?	
	How would you describe your experience with public accounting?	
Glass Ceiling in the Public Sector	As a woman have you ever suffered prejudice from the opposite sex or even from other women in the function that you develop?	To understand the presence of the glass ceiling phenomenon in the state workspace, as well as its change according to the trajectory of each participant.
	What are the main barriers faced by women in your sector for being female?	
	Do you believe that it is still more difficult for women to reach management positions in the institution you work for? Why do you think so?	
	What do you have to say about the space that women have been acquiring in public service?	
	Comparing the scenario at the time you entered public service and the present day, do you perceive an appreciation of the value of women as professionals in public accounting?	

Compilation of References

ways to become a better listener. (2021). https://christlikedialogue.org/5-ways-to-becoming-a-better-listener/?gclid=Cj0KCQiAqbyNBhC2ARIsALDwAsA4YDsGMThvuAGkQozUeizkYsUREYMvjBDpqem8I65Mf-dZfxyFSAoaAjNrEALw_wcB

Abad, D., Lucas-Pérez, M. E., Minguez-Vera, A., & Yagüe, J. (2017). Does gender diversity on corporate boards reduce information asymmetry in equity markets? *BRQ Business Research Quarterly*, *20*(3), 192–205. doi:10.1016/j.brq.2017.04.001

Abobakr, MG, & Elgiziry, K. (2016). The effect of board characteristics and ownership structure on the corporate financial leverage. *Accounting and Finance research, 5*(1), 1-14.

Abramo, L. (2015). *Uma década de promoção do trabalho decente no Brasil: uma estratégia de ação baseada no diálogo social*. Organização Internacional do Trabalho. Disponível em: https://www.ilo.org/wcmsp5/groups/public/---americas/---ro-lima/---ilo-brasilia/documents/publication/wcms_467352.pdf

Abramo, L. (2004). Perspectiva de gênero e raça nas políticas públicas. *Mercado de Trabalho: Conjuntura e Análise*, *25*(11), 17–21.

Abramo, L. W. (2007). *A Inserção da mulher no mercado de trabalho: uma força de trabalho secundária*. Tese de Doutorado em Sociologia, Universidade de São Paulo.

Abreu, M. A. A., & Meirelles, R. L. (2012). *Mulheres e Homens em Ocupação de DAS na Administração Pública Federal. In Relatório de Pesquisa: Instituto de Pesquisa Econômica Aplicada*. IPEA.

Adamson, G. (2009). *The Craft Reader*. Bloomsbury Visual Arts.

Adams, R. B., & Funk, P. (2012). Beyond the glass ceiling: Does gender matter? *Management Science*, *58*(2), 219–235. doi:10.1287/mnsc.1110.1452

Adams, R., & Ferreira, D. (2009). Women in the boardroom and their impact on governance and performance. *Journal of Financial Economics*, *94*(2), 291–309. doi:10.1016/j.jfineco.2008.10.007

Addison, J. T., Chen, L., & Ozturk, O. D. (2020). Occupational skill mismatch: Differences by gender and Cohort. *Industrial & Labor Relations Review*, *73*(3), 730–767. doi:10.1177/0019793919873864

Adhikari, B., Di Falco, S., & Lovett, J. C. (2004). Household characteristics and forest dependency: Evidence from common property forest management in Nepal. *Ecological Economics*, *48*(2), 245–257. doi:10.1016/j.ecolecon.2003.08.008

Adusei, M., & Obeng, E. Y. T. (2019). Board gender diversity and the capital structure of microfinance institutions: A global analysis. *The Quarterly Review of Economics and Finance*, *71*, 258–269. doi:10.1016/j.qref.2018.09.006

Ahmadi, A., Nakaa, N., & Bouri, A. (2018). Chief executive officer attributes, board structures, gender diversity and firm performance among French CAC 40 listed firms. *Research in International Business and Finance*, *44*, 218–226. doi:10.1016/j.ribaf.2017.07.083

Ahmad, Z., Azam, N., Nasir, Y., & Khan, U. (2021). Impact of gender differences on leadership: An investigation of moderating impact of gender-based biasness. [BBE]. *Bulletin of Business and Economics*, *10*(4), 151–166.

Ahmed, Z., & Hla, D. T. (2019). Stock return volatility and capital structure measures of nonfinancial firms in a dynamic panel model: Evidence from Pakistan. *International Journal of Finance & Economics*, *24*(1), 604–628. doi:10.1002/ijfe.1682

Ahrens, P., & Scheele, A. (2022). Game-Changers for Gender Equality in Germany's Labour Market? Corporate Board Quotas, Pay Transparency and Temporary Part-Time Work. *German Politics*, *31*(1), 157–176. doi:10.1080/09644008.2021.1984428

Akbas, F., Jiang, C., & Koch, P. D. (2017). The trend in firm profitability and the cross-section of stock returns. *The Accounting Review*, *92*(5), 1–32. doi:10.2308/accr-51708

Aksan, N., Kısac, B., Aydın, M., & Demirbuken, S. (2009). Symbolic interaction theory. *Procedia: Social and Behavioral Sciences*, *1*(1), 902–904. doi:10.1016/j.sbspro.2009.01.160

Aksnes, D. W., & Sivertsen, G. A. (2019). Criteria-based assessment of the coverage of Scopus and Web of Science. *Journal of Data and Information Science*, *4*(1), 1–21. doi:10.2478/jdis-2019-0001

Al-Baidhani, P. (2013). The effects of corporate governance on bank performance: Evidence from the Arabian Peninsula. *Ahmed, The Effects of Corporate Governance on Bank Performance: Evidence from the Arabian Peninsula.*

Albrecht, J., Björklund, A., & Vroman, S. (2003). Is there a glass ceiling in Sweden? *Journal of Labor Economics*, *21*(1), 145–177. doi:10.1086/344126

Alghamdi, A. K. H., Alsaadi, R. K., Alwadey, A. A., & Najdi, E. A. (2022). Saudi Arabia's vision 2030's compatibility with women and children's contributions to national development. *Interchange*, *53*(2), 1–22. doi:10.100710780-021-09451-3

Al-Haddad, S., & Kotnour, T. (2015). Integrating the organizational change literature: A model for successful change. *Journal of Organizational Change Management*, *28*(2), 234–262. doi:10.1108/JOCM-11-2013-0215

Alhalwachi, L. F., & Mordi, C. (2021). Gender inequality barriers and solutions to senior management positions: perspectives on women in Bahraini banking sector. *Journal of Sustainable Finance & Investment*, 1-22.

Ali, M., Kulik, C. T., & Metz, I. (2009). The impact of gender diversity on performance in services and manufacturing organizations. *Academy of Management 2009 Annual Meeting: Green Management Matters*. AOM.

Allioui, A., Habba, B., & El Azizi, T. B. (2021). Women's Leadership and Pragmatism Incidences on Performance of Listed Family-Owned Firms in the Cultural Context of Arab Countries. *International Journal of Financial Research*, *12*(3), 251. doi:10.5430/ijfr.v12n3p251

Alpha, A., & Vincent, S. (2011). Gender differences in organizational strategy execution: A comparative study between female and male managers in obstacle management. *African Journal of Marketing Management*, *3*(7), 149–167. https://ssrn.com/abstract=2084456%5Cnhttp://www.academicjournals.org/AJMM

Althalathini, D., Al-Dajani, H., & Apostolopoulos, N. (2022). The impact of Islamic feminism in empowering women's entrepreneurship in conflict zones: Evidence from Afghanistan, Iraq and Palestine. *Journal of Business Ethics*, *178*(1), 39–55. doi:10.100710551-021-04818-z

Alves, P., Couto, E. B., & Francisco, P. M. (2015). Board of directors' composition and capital structure. *Research in International Business and Finance*, *35*, 1–32. doi:10.1016/j.ribaf.2015.03.005

Ammar, N., & Boughrara, A. (2019). The impact of revenue diversification on bank profitability and risk: Evidence from MENA banking industry. *Macroeconomics and Finance in Emerging Market Economies*, *12*(1), 36–70. doi:10.1080/17520843.2018.1535513

Andrade, J. (2008). *O Turismo Científico na Amazônia: Um estudo das oportunidades, necessidades e potencialidades para a cidade de Manaus*. Manaus: Dissertação de Pós-Graduação em Ciências Ambientais e Florestais, Universidade Federal do Amazonas.

Ang, J. (1991). Small business uniqueness & the theory of financial management. *Journal of Small Business Finance*, *1*(1), 1–13. doi:10.57229/2373-1761.1108

Araújo, V. F., & Ribeiro, E. P. (2002). Diferenciais de Salários por Gênero no Brasil: Uma Análise Regional. *Revista Economica do Nordeste*, *33*(2), 1–22.

Arioglu, E. (2020). Female board members: The effect of director affiliation. *Gender in Management*, *35*(2), 225–254. doi:10.1108/GM-05-2019-0080

Arnold, M. G. (2018). Sustainability value creation in frugal contexts to foster Sustainable Development Goals. *Business Strategy & Development*, *1*(4), 265–275. doi:10.1002/bsd2.36

Arruda, M. A. R., & Sá, M. A. D. (2019). A Cultura Organizacional e o Fenômeno Teto de Vidro. *Revista FSA*, *16*(4), 261–280. doi:10.12819/2019.16.4.14

Arulampalam, W., Booth, A. L., & Bryan, M. L. (2007). Is there a glass ceiling over Europe? Exploring the gender pay gap across the wage distribution. *Industrial & Labor Relations Review*, *60*(2), 163–186. doi:10.1177/001979390706000201

Asian Development Bank. (2016). Gender equality results case study: Nepal Gender Equality and Empowerment of Women Project. ADB. https://www.adb.org/sites/default/files/publication/185563/nepal-gender-equality-and-empowerment-women-project.pdf

Asteriou, D., & Bashmakova, Y. (2013). Assessing the impact of oil returns on emerging stock markets: A panel data approach for ten Central and Eastern European Countries. *Energy Economics*, *38*, 204–211. doi:10.1016/j.eneco.2013.02.011

Atena, F., & Tiron-Tudor, A. (2020). Gender as a dimension of inequality in accounting organizations and developmental HR strategies. *Administrative Sciences*, *10*(1), 1–24. doi:10.3390/admsci10010001

Badaracco, J. L. Jr. (2002). *Leading Quietly*. Harvard Business School Publishing.

Baixauli-Soler, J. S., Lucas-Perez, M. E., Martin-Ugedo, J. F., Minguez-Vera, A., & Sanchez-Marin, G. (2016). Executive directors' compensation and monitoring: The influence of gender diversity on Spanish boards. *Journal of Business Economics and Management*, *17*(6), 1133–1154. doi:10.3846/16111699.2014.969767

Baldwin, M. L., Butler, R. J., & Johnson, W. G. (2001). A hierarchical theory of occupational segregation and wage discrimination. *Economic Inquiry*, *39*(1), 94–110. doi:10.1093/ei/39.1.94

Banihani, M., Lewis, P., & Syed, J. (2013). Is work engagement gendered? *Gender in Management*, *28*(7), 400–423. doi:10.1108/GM-01-2013-0005

Bank and Financial Institution Act, Nepal. (2017). *Bank and Financial Institution Act, 2073* BFIN. https://www.nrb.org.np/contents/uploads/2019/12/Bank_And_Financial_Instituion_Act_2017_-_English_Version_20190311-1.pdf

Bao, C., & Nizam, D. I. (2015). the Impact of Motivation on Employee Performance in the Electronics Industry in China. *International Journal of Accounting and Business Management*, *3*(2), 29–45. doi:10.24924/ijabm/2015.11/v3.iss2/29.45

Baral, B. (2017). Gender development perspective: A contemporary review in global and Nepalese context. *Geographical Journal of Nepal*, *10*, 141–152. doi:10.3126/gjn.v10i0.17395

Barberis, N., & Thaler, R. (2003). A survey of behavioral finance. In G. M. Constantinides, M. Harris, & R. M. Stulz (Eds.), *Handbook of the Economics of Finance* (Vol. 1, pp. 1053–1128). Elsevier Science B.V.

Barbosa, I., & Cabral-Cardoso, C. (2010). Equality and diversity rhetoric: One size fits all? Globalization and the Portuguese context. *Equality, Diversity and Inclusion*, *29*(1), 97–112. doi:10.1108/02610151011019237

Barclay, M. J., & Smith, C. W. Jr. (1995). The maturity structure of corporate debt. *The Journal of Finance*, *50*(2), 609–631. doi:10.1111/j.1540-6261.1995.tb04797.x

Baron, R. A., & Shane, S. A. (2007). *Empreendedorismo: uma visão do processo*. Cengage Learning.

Barroso, C. (2015). As Mulheres nos Altos Escalões da Administração Pública no Brasil. *Revista do Serviço Público*, *66*(1), 145–159. doi:10.21874/rsp.v66i1.796

Barros, V. M. (2005). O Novo Velho Enfoque da Informação Contábil. *Revista Contabilidade & Finanças*, *16*(38), 102–112. doi:10.1590/S1519-70772005000200009

Barston, R. P. (2019). *Modern diplomacy*. Routledge. doi:10.4324/9781351270090

Batliwala, S. (1994). The Meaning of Women's Empowerment: New Concepts from Action. In G. Sen, A. German, & L. C. Chen (Eds.), *Population Policies Reconsidered: Health, Empowerments and Rights*. Harvard University Press.

Baumann-Pauly, D., Scherer, A. G., & Palazzo, G. (2016). Managing institutional complexity: A longitudinal study of legitimacy strategies at a sportswear brand company. *Journal of Business Ethics*, *137*(1), 31–51. doi:10.100710551-014-2532-x

Bear, S., Rahman, N., & Post, C. (2010). The Impact of Board Diversity and Gender Composition on Corporate Social Responsibility and Firm Reputation. *Journal of Business Ethics*, *97*(2), 207–221. doi:10.100710551-010-0505-2

Becker, G. S. (1985). Human capital, effort, and the sexual division of labor. *Journal of Labor Economics*, *3*(1, Part 2), S33–S58. doi:10.1086/298075

Belle, F. (1993). *Executivas: Quais as Diferenças na Diferença?* Editora Atlas.

Bénavidès, J., Guilloux, F., Allam, D. E., Uzan, A., Mizoule, J., Renault, C., Dubroeucq, M. C., Guérémy, C., & Le Fur, G. (1984). Opposite effects of an agonist, R05-4864, and an antagonist, PK 11195, of the peripheral type benzodiazepine binding sites on audiogenic seizures in DBA/2J mice. *Life Sciences*, *34*(26), 2613–2620. doi:10.1016/0024-3205(84)90048-1 PMID:6330481

Beniflah, J., & Veloz, J. (2021). Building a multicultural organisation: A conceptual model for organisational change in the 21st century. *Journal of Cultural Marketing Strategy*, *5*(2), 153–168.

Berger, A. N., Kick, T., & Schaeck, K. (2014). Executive board composition and bank risk taking. *Journal of Corporate Finance*, *28*, 48–65. doi:10.1016/j.jcorpfin.2013.11.006

Bernile, G., Bhagwat, V., & Yonker, S. (2018). Board diversity, firm risk, and corporate policies. *Journal of Financial Economics*, *127*(3), 588–612. doi:10.1016/j.jfineco.2017.12.009

Bertrand, M., Goldin, C., & Katz, L. F. (2010). Dynamics of the gender gap for young professionals in the financial and corporate sectors. *American Economic Journal. Applied Economics*, *2*(3), 228–255. doi:10.1257/app.2.3.228

Bethue-Cookman College. (2021). https://www.cookman.edu/history/our-founder.html

Bhadra, C., & Shah, M. T. (2007). Nepal: Country gender profile. *Report prepared for JICA*.

Bhandari, U., Yadav, S., Devkota, N., Paudel, U. R., Rajbhandari, S., & Karki, D. (2021). Private and public bank consumers' preference in Kathmandu Valley: Evidence from customers' satisfaction index. *International Research Journal of Science, Technology. Education and Management*, *1*(1), 67–78.

Bibi, N. (2016). Role of gender diversity in organizational effectiveness and its implications. *International Review of Management and Marketing*, *6*(4), 80–85.

Bilan, Y., Mishchuk, H., Samoliuk, N., & Mishchuk, V. (2020). Gender discrimination and its links with compensations and benefits practices in enterprises. *Entrepreneurial Business and Economics Review*, *8*(3), 189–203. doi:10.15678/EBER.2020.080311

Biography.com Editors. (2018, February 28). *Madam C.J. Walker*. Retrieved from https://www.biography.com/inventor/madam-cj-walker

Birindelli, G., Dell'Atti, S., Iannuzzi, A. P., & Savioli, M. (2018). Composition and activity of the board of directors: Impact on ESG performance in the banking system. *Sustainability*, *10*(12), 4699. doi:10.3390u10124699

Blau, D. (1998). The Well-Being of American Women: 1970-1995. *Journal of Economic Literature*, *36*(1), 112–165.

Blau, F. D., & Kahn, L. M. (2017). The gender wage gap: Extent, trends, and explanations. *Journal of Economic Literature*, *55*(3), 789–865. doi:10.1257/jel.20160995

Blau, F. D., & Winkler, A. E. (2018). *The Economics of Women, Men, and Work* (8th ed.). Oxford University Press.

Blinder, A. S. (1973). Wage discrimination: Reduced form and structural estimates. *The Journal of Human Resources*, *8*(4), 436–455. doi:10.2307/144855

Blue, L. (2015). *Fruitful Inspirations*. Trafford Publishing.

Bodie, Z., Kane, A., & Miller, A. J. (2014). *Investment* (10th ed.). McGraw-Hill Education.

Bøllingtoft, A. (2007). A critical realist approach to quality in observation studies. In H. Neergaard & J. Ulhøi (Eds.), *Handbook of Qualitative Research Methods in Entrepreneurship* (pp. 406–433). Edward Elgar. doi:10.4337/9781847204387.00027

Boniatti, A. O., Souza Velho, A., Pereira, A., Pereira, B. B., & Oliveira, S. M. (2014). A Evolução da Mulher no Mercado Contábil. *Revista Gestão e Desenvolvimento em Contexto*, *2*(1), 19–27.

Bonilla-Priego, M. J., Font, X., & Pacheco-Olivares, M. R. (2014). Corporate sustainability reporting index and baseline data for the cruise industry. *Tourism Management*, *44*, 149–160. doi:10.1016/j.tourman.2014.03.004

Bono, R., Arnau, J., & Vallejo, G. (2008). Analysis techniques applied to longitudinal data in psychology and health sciences in the period 1985-2005. *Papeles del Psicólogo*, *29*, 136–146.

Boraas, S., & Rodgers, W. M. III. (2003). How does gender play a role in the earnings gap-an update. *Monthly Labor Review*, *126*, 9.

Botelho, L. L. R., Schons, C. C. J., Vieira, B., & Cunha, C. J. C. A. (2008). *Desafios gerenciais das mulheres empreendedoras: como exercer a liderança em espaços de identidade masculina? O caso da alpha tecnologia.* Disponível em: https://www.researchgate.net/profile/Cristiano-Cunha/publication/38320124_Desafios_gerenciais_das_mulheres_empreendedoras_como_exercer_a_lideranca_em_espacos_de_identidade_masculina_O_caso_da_Alpha_Tecnologia/links/0c96051abdbc542fb4000000/Desafios-gerenciais-das-mulheres-empreendedoras-como-exercer-a-lideranca-em-espacos-de-identidade-masculina-O-caso-da-Alpha-Tecnologia.pdf

Boubakri, N., Cosset, J. C., & Saffar, W. (2013). The role of state and foreign owners in corporate risk-taking: Evidence from privatization. *Journal of Financial Economics*, *108*(3), 641–658. doi:10.1016/j.jfineco.2012.12.007

Boudreaux, K. J. (1973). 'Managerialism and Risk-Return Performance. *Southern Economic Journal*, *39*(3), 366–372. doi:10.2307/1056402

Bradbury, M. D., & Kellough, J. E. (2008). Representative bureaucracy: Exploring the potential for active representation in local government. *Journal of Public Administration: Research and Theory*, *18*(4), 697–714. doi:10.1093/jopart/mum033

Braga, M. B., & Paulani, L. M. (2020). *A nova contabilidade social: uma introdução à macro economia*. Saraiva.

Brasil, Ministério do Planejamento. (2022). *Painel Estatístico de Pessoal, distribuição por Gênero, Setembro de 2022*. http://painel.pep.planejamento.gov.br/QvAJAXZfc/opendoc.htm?document=painelpep.qvw&lang=en-US&host=Local&anonymous=true

Brasil. Constituição da República Federativa do Brasil. (1998/2020). Planalto, Brasília.

Braun, P. (2010). Going green: Women entrepreneurs and the environment. *International Journal of Gender and Entrepreneurship*, *2*(3), 245–259. doi:10.1108/17566261011079233

Briozzo, A., Cardone-Riportella, C., & García-Olalla, M. (2019). Corporate governance attributes and listed SMEs' debt maturity. *The International Journal of Business in Society*, *19*(4), 735–750. doi:10.1108/CG-11-2017-0272

Brown, L. R. (1981). Building a sustainable society. WW Norton & Company.

Bruna, M. G., Dang, R., Scotto, M. J., & Ammari, A. (2019). Does board gender diversity affect firm risk-taking? Evidence from the French stock market. *The Journal of Management and Governance*, *23*(4), 915–938. doi:10.100710997-019-09473-1

Bruschini, C., & Lombardi, M. R. (2002). Instruídas e trabalhadeiras: Trabalho feminino no final do século XX. *Cadernos Pagu*, *17*(18), 157–196. doi:10.1590/S0104-83332002000100007

Bujor, A., & Avasilcai, S. (2014). Creative Entrepreneurship in Europe: A Framework of Analysis. *Annals of the Oradea University, 1*(1), 151–156. doi:10.15660/AUOFMTE.2014-1.2960

Burke, R. J. (1997). Women on corporate boards of directors: A needed resource. *Journal of Business Ethics, 16*(9), 909–915. doi:10.1023/A:1017987220508

Burnes, B., & Jackson, P. (2011). Success and failure in organizational change: An exploration of the role of values. *Journal of Change Management, 11*(2), 133–162. doi:10.1080/14697017.2010.524655

Buttner, E. H., & Moore, D. P. (1997). Women's organizational exodus to entrepreneurship: Self-reported motivations and correlates with success. *Journal of Small Business Management, 35*, 34–46.

By, R. T. (2005). Organisational change management: A critical review. *Journal of Change Management, 5*(4), 369–380. doi:10.1080/14697010500359250

Byron, K., & Post, C. (2016). Women on Boards of Directors and Corporate Social Performance: A Meta-Analysis. *Corporate Governance, 24*(4), 428–442. doi:10.1111/corg.12165

Cabeza-García, L., Fernández-Gago, R., & Nieto, M. (2018). Do Board Gender Diversity and Director Typology Impact CSR Reporting? *European Management Review, 15*(4), 559–575. doi:10.1111/emre.12143

Campbell, K., & Mínguez-Vera, A. (2008). Gender diversity in the boardroom and firm financial performance. *Journal of Business Ethics, 83*(3), 435–451. doi:10.100710551-007-9630-y

Campos, C. J. G. (2004). Método de Análise de Conteúdo: Ferramentas para a Análise de Dados Qualitativos no Campo da Saúde. *Revista Brasileira de Enfermagem, 57*(5), 611–614. doi:10.1590/S0034-71672004000500019 PMID:15997809

Cardoso, A. R., & Winter-Ebmer, R. (2010). Female-led firms and gender wage policies. *Industrial & Labor Relations Review, 64*(1), 143–163. doi:10.1177/001979391006400107

Carmo, C., Alves, S., & Quaresma, B. (2022). Women on boards in Portuguese listed companies: Does gender diversity influence financial performance? *Sustainability, 14*(10), 6186. doi:10.3390u14106186

Carmona, P., De Fuentes, C., & Ruiz, C. (2016). Risk disclosure analysis in the corporate governance annual report using fuzzy-set qualitative comparative analysis. *RAE Revista de Administracao de Empresas, 56*(3), 342–352. doi:10.1590/S0034-759020160307

Carneiro, L. B., Gomes, D. G., Cruz, A. P. C., & Frare, A. B. (2022). Glass ceiling: A study on the factors of this phenomenon in Brazil from the perception of women managers. *SINERGIA-Revista do Instituto de Ciências Econômicas. Administrativas e Contábeis, 26*(1), 173–185.

Carter, D. A., Simkins, B. J., & Simpson, W. G. (2003). Corporate governance, board diversity and firm value. *Financial Review, 38*(1), 33–53. doi:10.1111/1540-6288.00034

Carter, D., D'Souza, F., Simkins, B., & Simpson, W. (2010). The gender and ethnic diversity of US boards and board committees and firm financial performance. *Corporate Governance*, *18*(5), 396–414. doi:10.1111/j.1467-8683.2010.00809.x

Carter, N. M., Williams, M., & Reynolds, P. D. (1997). Discontinuance among new firms in retail: The influence of initial resources, strategy, and gender. *Journal of Business Venturing*, *12*(2), 125–145. doi:10.1016/S0883-9026(96)00033-X

Casaca, S. F. (2022a). *Os benefícios sociais e económicos da igualdade remuneratória entre mulheres e homens: Economic Case*. https://genderpaygap-elimination.pt/wp-content/uploads/2022/03/Economic-Case_new.pdf

Casaca, S. F. (2022b). *Os benefícios sociais e económicos da igualdade remuneratória entre mulheres e homens: Policy Brief.* https://genderpaygapelimination.pt/wp-content/uploads/2022/03/Policy-Brief_act.pdf

CBS. (2009). Report on the Nepal labour force survey 2008. *Statistical report*. 244.

Chang, R. D., Zuo, J., Zhao, Z. Y., Zillante, G., Gan, X. L., & Soebarto, V. (2017). Evolving theories of sustainability and firms: History, future directions, and implications for renewable energy research. *Renewable & Sustainable Energy Reviews*, *72*, 48–56. doi:10.1016/j.rser.2017.01.029

Chantreuil, F., & Lebon, I. (2015). Gender contribution to income inequality. *Economics Letters*, *133*, 27–30. doi:10.1016/j.econlet.2015.05.009

Chebbia, K., Aliedanb, M. M., & Mohammed, A. (2020). Women on the Board and Environmental Sustainability Reporting: Evidence from France. *International Journal of Innovation. Creativity and Change*, *14*(11), 231–258.

Cheng, S. (2008). Board size and the variability of corporate performance. *Journal of Financial Economics*, *87*(1), 157–176. doi:10.1016/j.jfineco.2006.10.006

Chen, L. H., Gramlich, J., & Houser, K. A. (2019). The effects of board gender diversity on a firm's risk strategies. *Accounting and Finance*, *59*(2), 991–1031. doi:10.1111/acfi.12283

Chen, S., Ni, X., & Tong, J. Y. (2016). Gender diversity in the boardroom and risk management: A case of R&D investment. *Journal of Business Ethics*, *136*(3), 599–621. doi:10.100710551-014-2528-6

Cheruiyot, K. J. (2017). Determinants of technical efficiency in Kenyan manufacturing sector. *African Development Review*, *29*(1), 44–55. doi:10.1111/1467-8268.12237

Chisholm, S. (2010). *Unbought and Unbossed: Expanded 40th Anniversary Edition*. Take Root Media.

Cimini, R. (2022). The effect of female presence on corporate boards of directors on the value relevance of accounting amounts: Empirical evidence from the European Union. *Journal of International Financial Management & Accounting*, *33*(1), 134–153. doi:10.1111/jifm.12138

Cimirotić, R., Duller, V., Feldbauer-Durstmüller, B., Gärtner, B., & Hiebl, M. R. W. (2017). Enabling factors that contribute to women reaching leadership positions in business organizations: The case of management accountants. *Management Research Review*, *40*(2), 165–194. doi:10.1108/MRR-10-2014-0233

Clark, C. E., Arora, P., & Gabaldon, P. (2021). Female Representation on Corporate Boards in Europe: The Interplay of Organizational Social Consciousness and Institutions. *Journal of Business Ethics*. doi:10.100710551-021-04898-x

CNMV. (2006). *Unified Good Governance Code of Listed Companies*. CNMV. https://www.cnmv.es/Portal/~/verDoc.axd?t=18470855-a84c-4b12-b67a-3c77ccef9ea3

CNMV. (2015). *Good governance code of listed companies*. CNMV. https://www.cnmv.es/DocPortal/Publicaciones/CodigoGov/Good_Governanceen.pdf

CNMV. (2020). *Good governance code of listed companies*. CNMV. https://www.cnmv.es/DocPortal/Publicaciones/CodigoGov/CBG_2020.pdf

Coe, I. R., Wiley, R., & Bekker, L. G. (2019). Organisational best practices towards gender equality in science and medicine. *Lancet*, *393*(10171), 587–593. doi:10.1016/S0140-6736(18)33188-X PMID:30739694

Cohen, J. R., Dalton, D. W., Holder-Webb, L. L., & McMillan, J. J. (2020). An analysis of glass ceiling perceptions in the accounting profession. *Journal of Business Ethics*, *164*(1), 17–38. doi:10.100710551-018-4054-4

Cole, J. B. (2011). *Conversations: Straight Talk with America's Sister President. Anchor: Penguin Random*. House.

Coleman, M. G. (2003). Job skill and black male wage discrimination. *Social Science Quarterly*, *84*(4), 892–906. doi:10.1046/j.0038-4941.2003.08404007.x

Comi, S., Grasseni, M., Origo, F., & Pagani, L. (2020). Where Women Make a Difference: Gender Quotas and Firms' Performance in Three European Countries. *ILR Review, 73*(3), 768–793. doi:10.1177/0019793919846450

Cooke, F. L., Cooper, B., Bartram, T., Wang, J., & Mei, H. (2019). Mapping the relationships between high-performance work systems, employee resilience and engagement: A study of the banking industry in China. *International Journal of Human Resource Management*, *30*(8), 1239–1260. doi:10.1080/09585192.2015.1137618

Cooper, K. (2010). Accounting by women: Fear, favour and the path to professional recognition for Australian women accountants. *Accounting History*, *15*(3), 309–336. doi:10.1177/1032373210368422

Corbin, J., & Strauss, A. (1990). Grounded theory research: Procedures, canons and evaluative criteria. *Qualitative Sociology*, *13*(1), 3–21. doi:10.1007/BF00988593

Cornwell, C., Rivera, J., & Schmutte, I. M. (2017). Wage discrimination when identity is subjective evidence from changes in employer-reported race. *The Journal of Human Resources*, *52*(3), 719–755. doi:10.3368/jhr.52.3.0815-7340R1

Cortellese, F. (2022). Does the gender composition of the board of directors have any effect on tax aggressiveness in western countries? &. *Sociology*, *15*(1), 2022. doi:10.14254/2071

Cox, L. A. Jr. (2008). Why risk is not variance: An expository note. *Risk Analysis: An International Journal*, *28*(4), 925–928. doi:10.1111/j.1539-6924.2008.01062.x PMID:18554271

Croson, R., & Gneezy, U. (2009). Gender differences in preferences. *Journal of Economic Literature*, *47*(2), 448–474. doi:10.1257/jel.47.2.448

Cruz, M. H. S. (2012). *Mapeando diferenças de gênero no ensino superior da Universidade Federal de Sergipe*. São Cristóvão: Editora UFS.

Cucari, N., Esposito De Falco, S., & Orlando, B. (2018). Diversity of Board of Directors and Environmental Social Governance: Evidence from Italian Listed Companies. *Corporate Social Responsibility and Environmental Management*, *25*(3), 250–266. doi:10.1002/csr.1452

Cunningham, L. A. (2020). Board gender diversity: debate and practice. *Legal Studies Research Paper Series.* George Washington University Law School.

Daily, C. M., & Dalton, D. R. (2003). Women in the boardroom: A business imperative. *The Journal of Business Strategy*, *24*(5), 8–10. doi:10.1108/jbs.2003.28824eaf.002

Damanpour, F. (2010). An integration of research findings of effects of firm size and market competition on product and process innovations. *British Journal of Management*, *21*(4), 996–1010. doi:10.1111/j.1467-8551.2009.00628.x

Danaj, E. (2016). Gender Wage Gap. Encyclopedia of Family Studies, 1–3.

Đặng, R., Houanti, L. H., Reddy, K., & Simioni, M. (2020). Does board gender diversity influence firm profitability? A control function approach. *Economic Modelling*, *90*, 168–181. doi:10.1016/j.econmod.2020.05.009

Datta, S., Doan, T., & Toscano, F. (2021). Top executive gender, board gender diversity, and financing decisions: Evidence from debt structure choice. *Journal of Banking & Finance*, *125*, 106070. doi:10.1016/j.jbankfin.2021.106070

David, T., & Ely, R. (2005). Making Differences Matter: A new paradigm for managing diversity. *Harvard Business Review on Women in Business, 74*(5), 125–157. https://pdfs.semanticscholar.org/9112/a3e0ebfb74d1418d078093bd4429ffb6bd90.pdf

De Bakker, F. G., Groenewegen, P., & Den Hond, F. (2005). A bibliometric analysis of 30 years of research and theory on corporate social responsibility and corporate social performance. *Business & Society*, *44*(3), 283–317. doi:10.1177/0007650305278086

De Cabo, R. M., Gimeno, R., & Nieto, M. J. (2012). Gender diversity on European bank's board of directors. *Journal of Business Ethics*, *109*(2), 145–162. doi:10.100710551-011-1112-6

De Celis, I. L.-R., Velasco-Balmaseda, E., De Bobadilla, F. S., Alonso-Almeida, M. D., & Intxaurburu-Clemente, G. (2015). Does having women managers lead to increased gender equality practices in corporate social responsibility? *Business Ethics (Oxford, England)*, *24*(1), 91–110. doi:10.1111/beer.12081

de Estatística, N. (INE). (2020). Empresas em Portugal 2018. Lisboa: Instituto Nacional de Estatística

De Masi, S., Słomka-Gołębiowska, A., & Paci, A. (2020). Women on boards and monitoring tasks: An empirical application of Kanter's theory. *Management Decision*, *59*(13), 56–72. doi:10.1108/MD-10-2019-1450

de Sousa, J. F. (1998). O Estado Novo e a Contabilidade: contributo para o estudo do Ensino Técnico e da profissão de Contabilista na década de 30. *Estudos do ISCA, 3/4*, 112–170.

Del Baldo, M., Tiron-Tudor, A., & Faragalla, W. (2018). Women's role in the accounting profession: A comparative study between Italy and Romania. *Administrative Sciences*, *9*(1), 1–23. doi:10.3390/admsci9010002

Del Río, C., Gradín, C., & Cantó, O. (2011). The measurement of gender wage discrimination: The distributional approach revisited. *The Journal of Economic Inequality*, *9*(1), 57–86. doi:10.100710888-010-9130-7

Delgado-Piña. M. I., Rodríguez-Ruiz. Ó., Rodríguez-Duarte. A., & Sastre-Castillo. M. Á. (2020). Gender Diversity in Spanish Banks: Trickle-Down and Productivity Effects. *Sustainability. 12*(5). 2113.

Demetriades, J. (2007). Gender Indicators: What. Why and How? OECD. https://www.oecd.org/dac/gender-development/43041409.pdf

Denis, L., & Julián, M. P. (2022). *Gender pay gaps in the European Union—A statistical analysis*. Publications Office of the European Union.

Detthamrong, U., Chancharat, N., & Vithessonthi, C. (2017). Corporate Governance, Capital Structure and Firm Performance Evidence from Thailand. *Research in International Business and Finance*, *42*, 689–709. doi:10.1016/j.ribaf.2017.07.011

Devkota, N., Paudel, U. R., & Khanal, G. (2021). Is Current Understanding Adequate for Green Banking Practices in Nepal: A Lesson Learned. In Handbook of Research on Climate Change and the Sustainable Financial Sector (pp. 84-98). IGI Global. doi:10.4018/978-1-7998-7967-1.ch006

Devkota, N., Rai, R., Khanal, G., Padda, I. U. H., Paudel, U. R., Parajuli, S., & Bhandari, U. (2022b). Customer Perception and Awareness of Green Banking Practices: An Alternative Strategy of Environmental Sustainability. In Disruptive Technologies and Eco-Innovation for Sustainable Development (pp. 20-41). IGI Global.

Devkota, N., Adhikari, S., Parajuli, S., Bhandari, U., & Poudel, U. R. (2022a). Employees Perception on Gender diversity on banking performance in Kathmandu valley: Status, Challenges and Way-forward. *Qubahan Academic Journal*, *2*(1), 1–7. doi:10.48161/qaj.v2n1a87

Dezsö, C. L., & Ross, D. G. (2012). Does female representation in top management improve firm performance? A panel data investigation. *Strategic Management Journal*, *33*(9), 1072–1089. doi:10.1002mj.1955

Diaz-Iglesias. S.. Blanco-Gonzalez. A.. & Orden-Cruz. C. (2019). Science mapping analysis of change management. *Revista ESPACIOS*. *40*(32).

Dictionary, C. (2021). *Maverick*. https://www.collinsdictionary.com/us/dictionary/english/maverick#:~:text=Word%20forms%3A%20mavericks&text=If%20you%20describe%20someone%20as,individualist%20More%20Synonyms%20of%20maverick

Dictionary, O. (2021). *Resilience*. https://www.oxfordlearnersdictionaries.com/us/definition/english/resilience#:~:text=%E2%80%8Bthe%20ability%20of%20people,position%20to%20win%20the%20game.

Dieese - Departamento Intersindical de Estatística e Estudos Socioeconômicos. (2021). *Especial Mulheres - A inserção das mulheres no mercado de trabalho (Brasil e Regiões)*. Disponível em: https://www.dieese.org.br/outraspublicacoes/2021/graficosMulheresBrasilRegioes2021.html

Dijkstra, A. G., & Hanmer, L. C. (2000). Measuring socio-economic gender inequality: Toward an alternative to the UNDP gender-related development index. *Feminist Economics*, *6*(2), 41–75. doi:10.1080/13545700050076106

Dornelas, J. (2012). Empreendedorismo: transformando ideias em negócios (6th ed.). São Paulo: Editora Atlas.

dos Técnicos Oficiais de Contas, O. (2013). *Relatório e contas 2013*. https://pt.calameo.com/read/000324981fbf34e2f6fe4

dos Técnicos Oficiais de Contas, O. (2014). *Relatório e contas 2014*. https://pt.calameo.com/read/000324981a5991de0c4c9

Duppati, G. R., Scrimgeour, F., & Sune, A. (2019). Relevance of corporate boards in driving performance in the period that covers financial crisis. *Corporate Governance (Bingley)*, *19*(2), 321–338. doi:10.1108/CG-11-2016-0204

Duppati, G., Sune, A., & Samanta, N. (2017). Corporate governance, research and development volatility and firm performance - Evidence from Spain and Ireland. *Cogent Economics and Finance*, *5*(1), 1317117. doi:10.1080/23322039.2017.1317117

Durbin, D. A. (2021, January 27). Black woman CEO: Walgreens taps Starbucks exec, Roz Brewer, for role. *Usa Today*. www.usatoday.com. https://www.usatoday.com/story/money/business/2021/01/27/black-woman-ceo-walgreens-taps-starbucks-exec-roz-brewer-role/4278423001/

Dwyer, S., Richard, O. C., & Chadwick, K. (2003). Gender diversity in management and firm performance: The influence of growth orientation and organizational culture. *Journal of Business Research*, *56*(12), 1009–1019. doi:10.1016/S0148-2963(01)00329-0

Dyllick, T., & Hockerts, K. (2002). Beyond the business case for corporate sustainability. *Business Strategy and the Environment*, *11*(2), 130–141. doi:10.1002/bse.323

Eagly, A. H., Karau, S. J., & Makhijani, M. G. (1995). Gender and the effectiveness of leaders: A meta-analysis. *Psychological Bulletin*, *117*(1), 125–145. doi:10.1037/0033-2909.117.1.125 PMID:7870858

Eagly, A. H., Nater, C., Miller, D. I., Kaufmann, M., & Sczesny, S. (2020). Gender stereotypes have changed: A cross-temporal meta-analysis of US public opinion polls from 1946 to 2018. *The American Psychologist*, *75*(3), 301–315. doi:10.1037/amp0000494 PMID:31318237

Eckel, C. C., & Grossman, P. J. (2008). Differences in the economic decisions of men and women: Experimental evidence. Handbook of experimental economics results, 1, 509-519.

Egbuwe, T. I., & Nwinee, B. F. (2019). Gender Impact on Execution of Business Strategy for Effective Economic Performance in Nigeria. *International Journal of Science and Business*, *3*(3), 141–150.

Eisenhardt, K. M. (1989). Building theories from case study research. *Academy of Management Review*, *14*(4), 532–550. doi:10.2307/258557

Elsevier. (2021). *Scopus: Who uses Scopus*. Elsevier. https://www.elsevier.com/solutions/scopus/who-uses

England, P. (2010). The gender revolution: Uneven and stalled. *Gender & Society*, *24*(2), 149–166. doi:10.1177/0891243210361475

Essence. (2021, June 7). *Two black women CEOs make history on Fortune 500 list*. https://www.essence.com/news/money-career/two-black-women-ceos-make-history-on-fortune-500-list/

Estatuto da Ordem dos Contabilistas Certificados, no. Lei n.º 139/2015, de 7 de setembro, Ordem dos Contabilistas Certificados (2015). https://www.occ.pt/fotos/editor2/dr7setembroocc.pdf

Estatuto dos Técnicos Oficiais de Contas, no. Decreto-Lei 265/95, de 17 de Outubro, Ministério das Finanças, Diário da República n.º 240/1995, Série I-A de 1995-10-17 (1995).

Estes, R., & Hosseini, J. (1988). The gender gap on wall street: An empirical analysis of confidence in investment decision making. *The Journal of Psychology*, *122*(6), 577–590. doi:10.1080/00223980.1988.9915532

European Commission. (2018). *2018 Report on equality between women and men in the EU*. EC. doi:10.2838/21655

European Commission. (2020). *A Union of Equality: Gender Equality Strategy 2020-2025*. Brussels, COM(2020) 152 final.

European Commission. (2020). *Equal Pay? Time to close the gap!* EC. https://ec.europa.eu/info/sites/default/files/aid_development_cooperation_fundamental_rights/2020_factsheet_on_the_gender_pay_gap.pdf

European Commission. (2022). *2022 Report on gender equality on the EU*. Publications Office of the European Union.

EUROSTAT. (2022). *Gender pay gap in the EU down to 13.0%*. https://ec.europa.eu/eurostat/en/web/products-eurostat-news/-/edn-20220307-2

Faccio, M., Marchica, M.-T., & Mura, R. (2016). CEO gender, corporate risk-taking, and the efficiency of capital allocation. *Journal of Corporate Finance*, *39*(August), 193–209. doi:10.1016/j.jcorpfin.2016.02.008

Fama, E. (1980). Agency problems and the theory of the firm. *Journal of Political Economy*, *88*(2), 288–307. doi:10.1086/260866

Fannie Lou Hamer. (n.d.). National Women's History Museum. https://www.womenshistory.org/education-resources/biographies/fannie-lou-hamer

Farag, H., & Mallin, C. (2017). Board diversity and financial fragility: Evidence from European banks. *International Review of Financial Analysis*, *49*, 98–112. doi:10.1016/j.irfa.2016.12.002

Feitosa, Y. S., & Albuquerque, J. S. (2019). Evolução da Mulher no Mercado de Trabalho. *Business Journal*, *1*(1), 1–17. doi:10.6008/CBPC2674-6433.2019.001.0005

Fenoy-Castaño, C., Martínez-Romero, M. J., & Martínez-Alonso, R. (2021). Does the female presence in corporate governance influence the level of indebtedness in agri-food family firms? [Switzerland]. *Agriculture*, *11*(11), 1135. doi:10.3390/agriculture11111135

Fernandez-Feijoo, B., Romero, S., & Ruiz-Blanco, S. (2014). Women on boards: Do they affect sustainability reporting? *Corporate Social Responsibility and Environmental Management*, *21*(6), 351–364. doi:10.1002/csr.1329

Fernández-Gago, R., Cabeza-García, L., & Nieto, M. (2016). Corporate social responsibility, board of directors, and firm performance: An analysis of their relationships. *Review of Managerial Science*, *10*(1), 85–104. doi:10.100711846-014-0141-9

Fernandez-Mateo, I., & Kaplan, S. (2018). Gender and organization science: Introduction to a virtual special issue. *Organization Science*, *29*(6), 1229–1236. doi:10.1287/orsc.2018.1249

Fernández-Temprano, M. A., & Tejerina-Gaite, F. (2020). Types of director, board diversity and firm performance. *Corporate Governance (Bingley)*, *20*(2), 324–342. doi:10.1108/CG-03-2019-0096

Ferrant, G., Pesando, L. M., & Nowacka, K. (2014). *Unpaid Care Work: The missing link in the analysis of gender gaps in labour outcomes. In Boulogne Billancourt*. OECD Development Center.

Ferreira, A. B. D. H. (1986). *Novo dicionário da língua portuguesa*. Editora Nova Fronteira.

Ferreira, D. (2010). Board diversity. Corporate governance: A synthesis of theory, research, and practice, *USA: John Wiley & Sons. Inc*, *225*, 241.

Ferreira, D. (2015). Board diversity: Should we trust research to inform policy? *Corporate Governance*, *23*(2), 108–111. doi:10.1111/corg.12092

Ferreira, G. T. C., Kaetsu, P. T., & Cunha, C. L. (2020). Empreendedorismo na Amazônia brasileira: Uma revisão sistemática da literatura. *Humanidades & Inovação*, *7*(16), 443–455.

Ferreira, M. D. M. (2002). História, Tempo Presente e História Oral. *Topoi (Rio de Janeiro)*, *3*(5), 314–332. doi:10.1590/2237-101X003006013

Figueiredo, M. da C., & Botelho, M. (2013). Decomposition of the gender wage gap in Portugal, 1998–2007: The evidence of gender discrimination. *Portuguese Journal of Social Science*, *12*(3), 287–315. doi:10.1386/pjss.12.3.287_1

Figueroa-Domecq, C., Palomo, J., Flecha-Barrio, M. D., & Segovia-Pérez, M. (2020). Technology double gender gap in tourism business leadership. *Information Technology & Tourism*, *22*(1), 1–32. doi:10.100740558-020-00168-0

Filion, L. J. (1999). Empreendedorismo: Empreendedores e proprietários-gerentes de pequenos negócios. *Revista ADM*, *34*(2), 5–28.

Filipe, G. (2020). *Determinantes da Estrutura de Capital: Efeito de Variáveis Micro e Macroeconómicas no Setor Hoteleiro em Portugal - Uma Análise de Dados em Painel,* [Master's thesis, University of Algarve].

Firmansyah, A., Utami, W., Umar, H., & Mulyani, S. D. (2020). Do Derivative Instruments Increase Firm Risk for Indonesia Non-Financial Companies*? International Journal of Business. Economics and Management*, *7*(2), 81–95.

Firmino, C. R., & Silva, F. H. E. (2015). *Desigualdades de Gênero no Serviço Público do Poder Executivo Federal. Escola Nacional de Administração Pública*. ENAP.

Fischer, E. M., Reuber, A. R., & Dyke, L. S. (1993). A theoretical overview and extension of research on sex, gender, and entrepreneurship. *Journal of Business Venturing*, *8*(2), 151–168. doi:10.1016/0883-9026(93)90017-Y

Fleischer, D. (2022). Does gender diversity in supervisory boards affect gender diversity in management boards in Germany? An empirical analysis. *German Journal of Human Resource Management*, *36*(1), 53–76. doi:10.1177/2397002221997148

Floris, M., Dettori, A., & Dessi, C. (2020). Innovation within tradition: Interesting insights from two small family bakeries. *Piccola Impresa/Small Business, 1*, 70–92.

Flynn, A., Earlie, E. K., & Cross, C. (2015). Gender equality in the accounting profession: One size fits all. *Gender in Management, 30*(6), 479–499. doi:10.1108/GM-06-2015-0048

Fondas, N., & Sassalos, S. (2000). A different voice in the boardroom: How the presence of women directors affects board influence over management. *Global Focus, 12*, 13–22.

Formigoni, H., Segura, L., & Gallego-Álvarez, I. (2021). Board of directors characteristics and disclosure practices of corporate social responsibility: A comparative study between Brazilian and Spanish companies. *Social Responsibility Journal, 17*(2), 282–298. doi:10.1108/SRJ-01-2019-0043

Fornell, C., & Yi, Y. (1992). Assumptions of the two-step approach to latent variable modeling. *Sociological Methods & Research, 20*(3), 291–320. doi:10.1177/0049124192020003001

Freund, A. (2013). História Oral como Processo Gerador de Dados. *Revista Tempos Históricos, 17*(1), 28–62.

Friede, G., Busch, T., & Bassen, A. (2015). ESG and financial performance: Aggregated evidence from more than 2000 empirical studies. *Journal of Sustainable Finance & Investment, 5*(4), 210–233. doi:10.1080/20430795.2015.1118917

Friese, S. (2011). Using ATLAS. ti for analyzing the financial crisis data. *In Forum Qualitative Sozialforschung/Forum: Qualitative. Social Research, 12*(1), 1–24.

Fuente, J. A., García-Sánchez, I. M., & Lozano, M. B. (2017). The role of the board of directors in the adoption of GRI guidelines for the disclosure of CSR information. *Journal of Cleaner Production, 141*, 737–750. doi:10.1016/j.jclepro.2016.09.155

Furlotti, K., Mazza, T., Tibiletti, V., & Triani, S. (2019). Women in top positions on boards of directors: Gender policies disclosed in Italian sustainability reporting. *Corporate Social Responsibility and Environmental Management, 26*(1), 57–70. doi:10.1002/csr.1657

Galbreath, J. (2018). Is Board Gender Diversity Linked to Financial Performance? *The Mediating Mechanism of CSR Business and Society, 57*(5), 863–889.

Galbreath, J. (2018). Is Board Gender Diversity Linked to Financial Performance? The Mediating Mechanism of CSR. *Business & Society, 57*(5), 863–889. doi:10.1177/0007650316647967

Galego, A., & Pereira, J. (2010). Evidence On Gender Wage Discrimination In Portugal: Parametric And Semi-Parametric Approaches. *Review of Income and Wealth, 56*(4), 651–666. doi:10.1111/j.1475-4991.2010.00413.x

Gallego-Álvarez, I., García-Sánchez, I. M., & Rodríguez-Dominguez, L. (2010). The influence of gender diversity on corporate performance. *Revista de Contabilidad-Spanish Accounting Review, 13*(1), 53–88. doi:10.1016/S1138-4891(10)70012-1

Gallego-Álvarez, I., & Pucheta-Martínez, M. C. (2020). Environmental strategy in the global banking industry within the varieties of capitalism approach: The moderating role of gender diversity and board members with specific skills. *Business Strategy and the Environment*, *29*(2), 347–360. doi:10.1002/bse.2368

Gallhofer, S., & Haslam, J. (2002). Accounting and emancipation: some critical interventions. Routledge.

Gallhofer, S., & Haslam, J. (2004). Reply to critique of "accounting and emancipation: some critical interventions.. Emerald Group Publishing Limited.

Gallhofer, S., & Haslam, J. (2017). Critical theory. Routledge.

Gallhofer, S., & Haslam, J. (1996). Accounting/art and the emancipatory project: Some reflections. *Accounting, Auditing & Accountability Journal*, *9*(5), 23–44. doi:10.1108/09513579610151944

Gallhofer, S., & Haslam, J. (1997). Beyond accounting: The possibilities of accounting and "critical" accounting research. *Critical Perspectives on Accounting*, *8*(1-2), 71–95. doi:10.1006/cpac.1996.0087

Gallhofer, S., & Haslam, J. (2009). *Emancipation*. Routledge.

Gallhofer, S., & Haslam, J. (2019). Some reflections on the construct of emancipatory accounting: Shifting meaning and the possibilities of a new pragmatism. *Critical Perspectives on Accounting*, *63*, 1–19. doi:10.1016/j.cpa.2017.01.004

Gallhofer, S., Haslam, J., & Yonekura, A. (2015). Accounting as differentiated universal for emancipatory praxis: Accounting delineation and mobilisation for emancipation(s) recognising democracy and difference. *Accounting, Auditing & Accountability Journal*, *28*(5), 846–874. doi:10.1108/AAAJ-08-2013-1451

Gallup Poll. (2021, March 5). *Lloyd, Camille. Black Women in the Workplace*. Gallup.com

García, C. J., & Herrero, B. (2021). Female directors, capital structure, and financial distress. *Journal of Business Research*, *136*, 592–601. doi:10.1016/j.jbusres.2021.07.061

García-Meca, E., López-Iturriaga, F. J., & Santana-Martín, D. J. (2022). Board gender diversity and dividend payout: The critical mass and the family ties effect. *International Review of Financial Analysis*, *79*, 101973. Advance online publication. doi:10.1016/j.irfa.2021.101973

García-Meca, E., Ramón-Llorens, M. C., & Martínez-Ferrero, J. (2021). Are narcissistic CEOs more tax aggressive? The moderating role of internal audit committees. *Journal of Business Research*, *129*, 223–235. doi:10.1016/j.jbusres.2021.02.043

Garcia-Torea, N., Fernandez-Feijoo, B., & de la Cuesta-González, M. (2017). La influencia de la estructura de propiedad en la transparencia de la información de RSC: Evidencia del caso Español. *Revista Española de Financiación y Contabilidad*, *46*(3), 249–271. doi:10.1080/02102412.2016.1267451

Gartzia, L. (2021). Gender Equality in Business Action: A Multi-Agent Change Management Approach. *Sustainability, 13*(11), 6209. doi:10.3390u13116209

Gem - Global Entrepreneurship Monitor Empreendedorismo no Brasil: 2019. (2020). *Coordenação de Simara Maria de Souza Silveira Greco; diversos autores*. Curitiba: IBQP.

Giannarakis, G. (2014). Corporate governance and financial characteristic effects on the extent of corporate social responsibility disclosure. *Social Responsibility Journal, 10*(4), 569–590. doi:10.1108/SRJ-02-2013-0008

Giannarakis, G., Konteos, G., & Sariannidis, N. (2014). Financial, governance and environmental determinants of corporate social responsible disclosure. *Management Decision, 52*(10), 1928–1951. doi:10.1108/MD-05-2014-0296

Gill, R. (2011, September). Managing People in Organizations: Integrating the Study of HRM and Leadership. *Harvard Business Review, 28*(3), 1–40.

Gomes, A. F., Santana, W. G. P., & Araújo, U. P. (2009). Empreendedorismo feminino: o estado-da-arte. In XXXIII Encontro da Anpad (pp. 1–16). São Paulo.

Gomes, A. S. (2021). A história da contabilidade e a evolução da mulher: Empoderamento e crescimento profissional feminino. *Revista de Estudos Interdisciplinares do Vale do Araguaia, 4*(2), 1–16.

Gomez, L., & Bernet, P. (2019). Diversity improves performance and outcomes. *Journal of the National Medical Association, 111*(4), 383–392. doi:10.1016/j.jnma.2019.01.006 PMID:30765101

Gonçalves, R. C.; Lima, T. K. (2007). Sobre o Método da História Oral em sua Modalidade Trajetórias de Vida. *Revista Katálysis, 10*, 83-92.

Gonçalves, C., Gonçalves, G., & Sequeira, L. (2014). *A Profissão de Técnico Oficial de Contas—Enquadramento normativo*. VidaEconómica.

González, P., Santos, L. D., & Santos, M. C. (2009). Education and gender wage differentials in Portugal: What can we learn from an age cohort analysis? *Education Economics, 17*(2), 263–278. doi:10.1080/09645290802628437

Gram, L., Granados, R., Krockow, E. M., Daruwalla, N., & Osrin, D. (2021). Modelling collective action to change social norms around domestic violence: Social dilemmas and the role of altruism. *Humanities and social sciences communications, 8*(1), 1-15.

Gray, R., Dillard, J., & Spence, C. (2013). Pesquisa em contabilidade social como se o mundo importasse um ensaio sobre postalgia e um novo absurdismo. *Revista de Contabilidade e Organizações, 7*(17), 119–133. doi:10.11606/rco.v7i17.59345

Green, S. (2021, October 31). *Emotional Intelligence: Why It's Important. Life and Health Network*. Lifeandhealth.org

Greenhaus, J. H., & Beutell, N. J. (1985). Sources of conflict between work and family roles. *Academy of Management Review*, *10*(1), 76–88. doi:10.2307/258214

GRI. (2023). *Home*. Global Reporting Initiative. https://www.globalreporting.org/information/sustainability-reporting/Pages/default.aspx

Grosser, K., & Moon, J. (2008). Developments in company reporting on workplace gender equality?: A corporate social responsibility perspective. *Accounting Forum*, *32*(3), 179–198. doi:10.1016/j.accfor.2008.01.004

Guebara, R. K. M. & Ravache, R. L. (2021). Desigualdade de género os desafios encontrados pelas mulheres na sociedade. *Connection line-revista eletrónica do Univag, 24*, 154-159. doi:10.18312/connectionline.v0i24.1642

Guilding, C. (2003). Hotel owner/operator structures: Implications for capital budgeting process. *Management Accounting Research*, *14*(3), 179–199. doi:10.1016/S1044-5005(03)00049-0

Guimaraes, T., & Armstrong, C. (1998). Empirically testing the impact of change management effectiveness on company performance. *European Journal of Innovation Management*, *1*(2), 74–84. doi:10.1108/14601069810217257

Gupta, A. K., & Chen, T. (2001). Goodness-of-fit tests for the skew-normal distribution. *Communications in Statistics. Simulation and Computation*, *30*(4), 907–930. doi:10.1081/SAC-100107788

Gurven, M., & Hill, K. (2009). Why do men hunt? A reevaluation of "man the hunter" and the sexual division of labor. *Current Anthropology*, *50*(1), 51–74. doi:10.1086/595620 PMID:19579355

Guynn, J. (2019). *Amazon names black Starbucks exec Rosalind Brewer to all-white board in 'barrier-breaking; appointment*. https://www.usatoday.com/story/news/2019/02/04/amazon-names-starbucks-exec-rosalind-brewer-first-black-board-member/2769779002/

Haider, J., & Fang, H. X. (2016). Board size, ownership concentration and future firm risk. *Chinese Management Studies*, *10*(4), 692–709. doi:10.1108/CMS-05-2016-0094

Halliday, C. S., Paustian-Underdahl, S. C., & Fainshmidt, S. (2021). Women on Boards of Directors: A Meta-Analytic Examination of the Roles of Organizational Leadership and National Context for Gender Equality. *Journal of Business and Psychology*, *36*(2), 173–191. doi:10.100710869-019-09679-y

Halstead, F. (2018). Leadership skills that inspire incredible results. Career Press, an imprint of Red Wheel Weiser, LLC.

Hambrick, D. C., & Mason, P. A. (1984). Upper echelons: The organization as a reflection of its top managers. *Academy of Management Review*, *9*(2), 193–206. doi:10.2307/258434

Hardies, K., Lennox, C., & Li, B. (2021). Gender discrimination? Evidence from the Belgian public accounting profession. *Contemporary Accounting Research, 38*(3), 1509–1541. doi:10.1111/1911-3846.12667

Harjoto, M. A., Laksmana, I., & Yang, Y. W. (2018). Board diversity and corporate risk taking.

Haslam, J. (2016). Informings for control and emancipatory interests in accounting: new reflections on the intellectual emancipation of accounting and the possibilities of emancipatory accountings. In J. Haslam & P. Sikka (Eds.), *Pioneers of Critical Accounting: A Celebration of the Life of Tony Lowe* (pp. 143–161). Palgrave Macmillan. doi:10.1057/978-1-137-54212-0_8

Hassan, Z. (2018). IMpact of gender diversity on indian firm's financial performance. *International Journal of Management, Accounting and Economics, 5*(5).

Hawi, R., Alkhodary, D., & Hashem, T. (2015). Managerial competencies and organizations performance. *International Journal of Management Sciences, 5*(11), 723–735.

Haynes, K. (2008). Power and politics in gender research: A research note from the discipline of accounting. *Gender in Management, 23*(7), 528–532. doi:10.1108/17542410810908875

Haynes, K. (2017). Accounting as gendering and gendered: A review of 25 years of critical accounting research on gender. *Critical Perspectives on Accounting, 43*, 110–124. doi:10.1016/j.cpa.2016.06.004

Heflin, F., Kolev, K. S., & Whipple, B. C. (2022). The risk-relevance of non-GAAP earnings. *Baruch College Zicklin School of Business Research Paper*, 01.

Hernández-Lara, A. B., & Gonzales-Bustos, J. P. (2019). The impact of interlocking directorates on innovation: The effects of business and social ties. *Management Decision, 57*(10), 2799–2815. doi:10.1108/MD-11-2017-1186

Hernández-Nicolás, C., Martín-Ugedo, J., & Minguez-Vera, A. (2015). The influence of gender on financial decisions: evidence from small start-up firms in Spain. *E & M Economie and Management, 18*(4), 93-107.

Hilderman, J. (n.d.). *Clone yourself: Build a team that understands your vision, shares your passion, and runs your business for you.* Gauvin, Jacques, OverDrive, Inc.

Hillman, A. J. (2015). Board diversity: Beginning to unpeel the onion. *Corporate Governance, 23*(2), 104–107. doi:10.1111/corg.12090

Hillman, A. J., & Dalziel, T. (2003). Boards of directors and firm performance: Integrating agency and resource dependence perspectives. *Academy of Management Review, 28*(3), 383–396. doi:10.2307/30040728

Hillman, A. J., Shropshire, C., & Cannella, A. A. Jr. (2007). Organizational predictors of women on corporate boards. *Academy of Management Journal, 50*(4), 941–952. doi:10.5465/amj.2007.26279222

Hillman, W., & Radel, K. (2021). The social, cultural, economic and political strategies extending women's territory by encroaching on patriarchal embeddedness in tourism in Nepal. *Journal of Sustainable Tourism*, 1–22.

Hinz, R. P., McCarthy, D. D., & Turner, J. A. (1996). *Are Women Conservative Investors? Gender Differences in Participant Directed Pension Investments*. Wharton School Pension Research Council, University of Pennsylvania.

Hoang, T. T., Nguyen, C. V., & Van Tran, H. T. (2019). Are female CEOs more risk averse than male counterparts? Evidence from Vietnam. *Economic Analysis and Policy*, *63*, 57–74. doi:10.1016/j.eap.2019.05.001

Hocking, D. (1979). Be a leader people follow. GL Regal, A Division of G/L Publications.

Hofland-Mol, M., & Poortvliet, M. (2019). Crafts in the Netherlands: From an Economic to a Value-Based Perspective. In A. Mignosa & P. Kotipalli (Eds.), *A Cultural Economic Analysis of Craft* (pp. 129–142). Springer International Publishing. doi:10.1007/978-3-030-02164-1_11

Ho, S., Li, A., Tam, K., & Zhang, F. (2015). CEO gender, ethical leadership, and accounting conservatism. *Journal of Business Ethics*, *127*(2), 351–370. doi:10.100710551-013-2044-0

Huang, J., & Kisgen, D. J. (2013). Gender and corporate finance: Are male executives overconfident relative to female executives? *Journal of Financial Economics*, *108*(3), 822–839. doi:10.1016/j.jfineco.2012.12.005

HubbardE. (2021). https://quoteinvestigator.com/2015/01/09/say-nothing/

Huse, M., & Solberg, A. (2006). How Scandinavian women make and can make contributions on corporate boards. *Women in Management Review*, *21*(2), 113–130. doi:10.1108/09649420610650693

Hussain, N., Rigoni, U., & Orij, R. P. (2018). Corporate governance and sustainability performance: Analysis of triple bottom line performance. *Journal of Business Ethics*, *149*(2), 411–432. doi:10.100710551-016-3099-5

Hutchinson, M., Mack, J., & Plastow, K. (2015). Who selects the 'right' directors? An examination of the association between board selection, gender diversity and outcomes. *Accounting and Finance*, *55*(4), 1071–1103. doi:10.1111/acfi.12082

Ibrahim, M. E., & Al Marri, A. (2015). Role of gender and organizational support in work-family conflict for accountants in UAE. *International Journal of Commerce and Management*, *25*(2), 157–172. doi:10.1108/IJCoMA-03-2013-0026

Ibrahim, N., Angelidis, J., & Tomic, I. M. (2009). Managers' attitudes toward codes of ethics: Are there gender differences? *Journal of Business Ethics*, *90*(3), 343–353. doi:10.100710551-010-0428-y

Ignatius, A. (2021, July – August). I'm here because I'm as good as you. *Harvard Business Review*. https://hbr.org/2021/07/im-here-because-im-as-good-as-you

Ilinitch, A. Y., Soderstrom, N. S., & Thomas, T. E. (1998). Measuring corporate environmental performance. *Journal of Accounting and Public Policy, 17*(4–5), 383–408. doi:10.1016/S0278-4254(98)10012-1

ILO. (2005). *Youth: Pathways to decent work.* ILO. http://www.ilo.org/youthmakingithappen/Resources/01.html%5Cn papers2://publication/uuid/CC56FB32-F1EE-47AF-BF14-72722C4E6 008

Informa D&B. (2022). Diversidade de género nas empresas em Portugal. Informa D&B. https://biblioteca.informadb.pt/read/document.aspx?id=2639# Instituto

Initiative One. (2021). https://www.initiativeone.com/insights/blog/leadership-challenges/

International Finance Corporation. (2016). *Working with Smallholders: A Handbook for Firms Building Sustainable Supply Chains*. World Bank.

Inuwa, M. (2016). Job satisfaction and employee performance: An empirical approach. *The Millennium University Journal, 1*(1), 90–103. doi:10.58908/tmuj.v1i1.10

IPGC. (2018). *Código de Governo das Sociedades*. IPGC. https://cgov.pt/images/ficheiros/2018/codigo_de_governo_das_sociedades_ipcg_vf.pdf

IPGC. (2020). *Código de Governo das Sociedades*. IPGC. https://cam.cgov.pt/images/ficheiros/2020/revisao_codigo_pt_2018_ebook-05.11.2020.pdf

Irfan, M., Bhatti, O. K., & Malik, R. K. (2021). Impact of Compensation on Inclusive Organizations. *Compensation and Benefits Review, 53*(3), 103–129. doi:10.1177/0886368720971922

IRME - Instituto Rede Mulher Empreendedora. (2019). *Pesquisa "Empreendedorismo no Brasil: um recorte de gênero nos negócios"*. Disponível em: https://materiais.rme.net.br/empreendedorismo-no-brasil-um-recorte-de-genero

Iudícibus, S. (2021). *Teoria da Contabilidade*. Atlas.

Iversen, T., & Rosenbluth, F. M. (2011). *Explaining Occupational Gender Inequality: Hours Regulation and Statistical Discrimination.* APSA 2011 Annual Meeting Paper.

Jablonski, B. (1996). Papéis conjugais: conflito e transição. *Relação amorosa, casamento, separação e terapia de casal, 1*(1), 113-123.

Jailaxmi & Gautam, A. (2017). Work life balance of bank employees as related to age, gender and marital status. *International journal of management, and business studies, 7*(1), 44-46.

Jakob, D. (2013). Crafting your way out of the recession? New craft entrepreneurs and the global economic downturn. *Cambridge Journal of Regions, Economy and Society*, *6*(1), 127–140. doi:10.1093/cjres/rss022

Jeff. (2021). *How great leaders communicate*. https://globalleadership.org/articles/leading-others/how-great-leaders-communicate-to-create-movement/?gclid=CjwKCAiAqIKNBhAIEiwAu_ZLDgCtHaSEIFotkIzzIZhT_borcHR8-mgjXzTf1Q_UjveAIrfeFIQYmBoCNc0QAvD_BwE

Jensen, M. C. (1986). Agency Costs of Free Cash Flow, Corporate Finance, and Takeovers. *The American Economic Review*, *76*(2), 323–329.

Jensen, M. C., & Meckling, W. H. (1976). Theory of the firm: Managerial behavior, agency costs and ownership structure. *Journal of Financial Economics*, *3*(4), 305–360. doi:10.1016/0304-405X(76)90026-X

Jeong, S. H., & Harrison, D. A. (2017). Glass breaking, strategy making, and value creating: Meta-analytic outcomes of women as CEOs and TMT members. *Academy of Management Journal*, *60*(4), 1219–1252. doi:10.5465/amj.2014.0716

Jha, P., Kumar, A., & Yamini Mishra, Y. (2020). Labouring Women: Issues and Challenges in Contemporary India. Orient Blackswan.

Jizi, M. I., & Nehme, R. (2017). Board gender diversity and firms' equity risk. *Equality, Diversity and Inclusion*, *36*(7), 590–606. doi:10.1108/EDI-02-2017-0044

Johnson, V. (2019). Black women are natural born leaders quotes from the great Harriet Tubman journal. @Coachvalj journals.

Johnson, J. E., & Powell, P. L. (1994). Decision making, risk and gender: Are managers different? *British Journal of Management*, *5*(2), 123–138. doi:10.1111/j.1467-8551.1994.tb00073.x

Jonathan, E. G. (2005). Mulheres empreendedoras: Medos, conquistas e qualidade de vida. *Psicologia em Estudo*, *10*(3), 373–382. doi:10.1590/S1413-73722005000300005

Joshi, R. (2017). Does Gender Diversity Improve Firm Performance? Evidence from India. *Undp*.

Julien, P. A., Marchesnay, M., & Machado, H. V. (2012). Interdisciplinaridade da pesquisa em empreendedorismo e em PME: Por uma teoria empreendedora que contemple diferenças culturais. *Gestão & Planejamento*, *11*(2), 355–368.

Jung, J. H., & Choi, K.-S. (2017). Gender Discrimination and Worker Selectivity: A Comparison of the Self-employed and Wage Earners. *Global Economic Review*, *46*(3), 251–270. doi:10.1080/1226508X.2017.1305284

Jung, S., Repetti, T., Chatfield, H. K. G., Dalbor, M., & Chatfield, R. (2019). Internationalization and accounting-based risk in the restaurant industry. *Journal of Hospitality and Tourism Management*, *41*, 148–155. doi:10.1016/j.jhtm.2019.11.001

Júnior, L. C. L., da Silveira, N. S. P., & Santini, R. B. (2015). A feminização da área contábil: Um estudo qualitativo básico. *Revista de Educação e Pesquisa Em Contabilidade (REPeC), 9*(1).

Kabeer, N. (1994). *Reversed realities: Gender Hierarchies in Development Thought*. Verso.

Kabeer, N. (1999). Resources, agency, achievements: Reflections on the measurement of women's empowerment. *Development and Change, 30*(3), 435–464. doi:10.1111/1467-7660.00125

Karmakar, A. K., & Bagchi, P. (2022). Gender Inequality, Women Empowerment and Public Action in India. In S. Maiti, T. Gupta, & D. Sharma (Eds.), *Economic Growth, Development and Social Challenges in the New Normal* (pp. 85–99). Kunal Books.

Kassinis, G., Panayiotou, A., Dimou, A., & Katsifaraki, G. (2016). Gender and Environmental Sustainability: A Longitudinal Analysis. *Corporate Social Responsibility and Environmental Management, 23*(6), 399–412. doi:10.1002/csr.1386

Katre, A. (2020). Self-Directed Learning on the Runway to Crafts Entrepreneurship. *Artivate: A Journal of Entrepreneurship in the Arts, 9*(2). doi:10.34053/artivate.9.2.119

Khalifa, R., & Kirkham, L. (2009). Gender. In The Routledge Companion to Accounting History. Routledge.

Khan, H.-U.-Z. (2010). The effect of corporate governance elements on corporate social responsibility (CSR); reporting: Empirical evidence from private commercial banks of Bangladesh. *International Journal of Law and Management, 52*(2), 82–109. doi:10.1108/17542431011029406

Khan, W. A., & Vieito, J. P. (2013). CEO gender and firm performance. *Journal of Economics and Business, 67*, 55–66. doi:10.1016/j.jeconbus.2013.01.003

Khaoula, F., & Moez, D. (2019). The moderating effect of the board of directors on firm value and tax planning: Evidence from European listed firms. *Borsa Istanbul Review, 19*(4), 331–343. doi:10.1016/j.bir.2019.07.005

Khatib, S. F., & Nour, A. N. I. (2021). The impact of corporate governance on firm performance during the COVID-19 pandemic: Evidence from Malaysia. *Journal of Asian Finance, Economics and Business, 8*(2), 0943-0952.

Khidmat, W. B., Habib, M. D., Awan, S., & Raza, K. (2022). Female directors on corporate boards and their impact on corporate social responsibility (CSR): Evidence from China. *Management Research Review, 45*(4), 563–595. doi:10.1108/MRR-09-2020-0560

Khlif, H., & Achek, I. (2017). Gender in accounting research: A review. *Managerial Auditing Journal, 32*(6), 627–655. doi:10.1108/MAJ-02-2016-1319

Kirsch, A. (2018). The gender composition of corporate boards: A review and research agenda. *The Leadership Quarterly, 29*(2), 346–364. doi:10.1016/j.leaqua.2017.06.001

Kirsch, A. (2022). Revolution From Above? Female Directors' Equality-Related Actions in Organizations. *Business & Society, 61*(3), 572–605. doi:10.1177/00076503211001843

Knyazeva, A., Knyazeva, D., & Naveen, L. (2021). Diversity on Corporate Boards. *Annual Review of Financial Economics*, *13*(1), 301–320. doi:10.1146/annurev-financial-101520-065559

Kobeissi, N. (2010). Gender factors and female entrepreneurship: iInternational evidence and policy implications. *Journal of International Entrepreneurship*, *8*(1), 1–35. doi:10.100710843-010-0045-y

Kochhar, K., & Jain-chandra, S. (2017). *Women, work, and economic growth: Leveling the playing field.* e-Library. https://www.elibrary.imf.org/doc/IMF071/23146-9781513516103/23146-9781513516103/Other_formats/Source_PDF/23146-978147557 9062.pdf?redirect=true

Kokot-Blamey, P. (2021). Mothering in accounting: Feminism, motherhood, and making partnership in accountancy in Germany and the UK. *Accounting, Organizations and Society*, *91*, 1–16. doi:10.1016/j.aos.2021.101255

Kosminsky, E. (1986). Pesquisas qualitativas: A utilização da técnica de histórias de vida e de depoimentos pessoais em sociologia. *Ciencia e Cultura*, *38*(1), 30–36.

Kossek, E. E., Su, R., & Wu, L. (2017). "Opting out" or "pushed out"? Integrating perspectives on women's career equality for gender inclusion and interventions. *Journal of Management*, *43*(1), 228–254. doi:10.1177/0149206316671582

Kouzes, J. M., & Posner, B. Z. (2007). The leadership challenge: The most trusted source on becoming a better leader (4th ed.). The Leadership Challenge: A Wiley Brand.

Kulich, C., & Chipeaux, M. (2019). Gender inequality in economic resources. In *The social psychology of inequality* (pp. 35–51). Springer. doi:10.1007/978-3-030-28856-3_3

Kutu, S., Devkota, N., Upretee, S., Paudel, U. R., & Dhakal, K. (2023). Commercial Bank Readiness for Adoption of Marketing 4.0: Evidence From Nepal. In Marketing and Advertising in the Online-to-Offline (O2O) World (pp. 247-266). IGI Global.

La Rocca, M., Neha, N., & La Rocca, T. (2020). Female management, overconfidence and debt maturity: European evidence. *The Journal of Management and Governance*, *24*(3), 713–747. doi:10.100710997-019-09479-9

Labre, J. F., & Lauzier, M. (2021). Studying the influences of organizational learning on turnover intentions, absenteeism, and organizational performance among employees working in a French-Canadian hospital. *International Journal of Training Research*, *19*(1), 1–20. doi:10.1080/14480220.2020.1864439

Lahiri, M. M., Sarkar, S., & Bhargava, M. (2022). A brief history of 'glass ceiling': The past, present & the future. *Academy of Marketing Studies Journal*, *26*(6), 1–5.

Lee, K. W., & Thong, T. Y. (2022). Board gender diversity, firm performance and corporate financial distress risk: international evidence from tourism industry. *Equality, Diversity and Inclusion: An International Journal*, (ahead-of-print).

Lehman, C. (2012). We've come a long way! Maybe! Re-imagining gender and accounting. *Accounting, Auditing & Accountability Journal, 25*(2), 256–294. doi:10.1108/09513571211198764

Lemos, L. C. Junior, Santini, R. B., & Silveira, N. S. P. (2015). A Feminização da Área Contábil: Um Estudo Qualitativo Básico. *Revista de Educação e Pesquisa em Contabilidade, 1*(1), 64–83.

Lenard, M. J., Yu, B., York, E. A., & Wu, S. (2014). Impact of board gender diversity on firm risk. *Managerial Finance, 40*(8), 787–803. doi:10.1108/MF-06-2013-0164

Leslie, L. M., Manchester, C. F., & Dahm, P. C. (2017). Why and when does the gender gap reverse? Diversity goals and the pay premium for high potential women. *Academy of Management Journal, 60*(2), 402–432. doi:10.5465/amj.2015.0195

Leszczyńska, M. (2018). Mandatory quotas for women on boards of directors in the european union: Harmful to or good for company performance? *European Business Organization Law Review, 19*(1), 35–61. doi:10.100740804-017-0095-x

Lewin, K. (1947). Frontiers in group dynamics: II. Channels of group life; social planning and action research. *Human Relations, 1*(2), 143–153. doi:10.1177/001872674700100201

Lewin, K. (1951). *Field theory in social science: selected theoretical papers* (D. Cartwright, Ed.).

Liao, L., Luo, L., & Tang, Q. (2015). Gender diversity. board independence. environmental committee and greenhouse gas disclosure. *The British Accounting Review, 47*(4), 409–424. doi:10.1016/j.bar.2014.01.002

Linstead, S., Brewis, J., & Linstead, A. (2005). Gender in change: Gendering change. *Journal of Organizational Change Management, 18*(6), 542–560. doi:10.1108/09534810510628495

Lisboa, M., Frias, G., Roque, A., & Cerejo, D. (2006). Participação das mulheres nas elites políticas e económicas no Portugal democrático (25 de abril de 1974 a 2004). *Revista da Faculdade de Ciências Sociais e Humanas, 18*, 163–187.

Li, Y., & Zeng, Y. (2019). The impact of top executive gender on asset prices: Evidence from stock price crash risk. *Journal of Corporate Finance, 58*, 528–550. doi:10.1016/j.jcorpfin.2019.07.005

Li, Y., & Zhang, X. (2019). Impact of board gender composition on corporate debt maturity structures. *European Financial Management, 25*(5), 1–35. doi:10.1111/eufm.12214

Llopis, G. (2014). *Leadership Is About Enabling the Full Potential In Others*. Retrieved July 29, 2014, from https://r.search.yahoo.com/_ylt=AwrC3PFwID9fx1kALAkPxQt.;_ylu=X3oDMTEyNTF2dHE4BGNvbG8DYmYxBHBvcwMyBHZ0aWQDQzAxNjVfMQRzZWMDc3I-/RV=2/RE=1598001393/RO=10/RU=https%3a%2f%2fwww.forbes.com%2fsites

Locker, K. O., & Kaczmarek, K. S. (2001). Business communication: Building critical skills. McGraw-Hill Higher Education: A Division of the McGraw-Hill Companies.

Lone, E. J., Ali, A., & Khan, I. (2016). Corporate governance and corporate social responsibility disclosure: Evidence from Pakistan. *Corporate Governance (Bingley), 16*(5), 785–797. doi:10.1108/CG-05-2016-0100

Lonkani, R. (2019). Gender differences and managerial earnings forecast bias: Are female executives less overconfident than male executives? *Emerging Markets Review, 38*, 18–34. doi:10.1016/j.ememar.2018.11.012

Lopes, I. T., Ferraz, D. P., & Martins, M. M. (2016). *The influence of diversity on boards on profitability: an overview across iberian non-financial listed companies* (Vol. 13). Corporate Ownership & Control.

López-Delgado, P., & Diéguez-Soto, J. (2020). Indebtedness in family-managed firms: The moderating role of female directors on the board. *Review of Managerial Science, 14*(4), 727–762. doi:10.100711846-018-0307-y

López-Gracia, J., & Aybar-Arias, C. (2000). An empirical approach to the financial behaviour of small and medium sized companies. *Small Business Economics, 14*(1), 55–63. doi:10.1023/A:1008139518709

Loukil, N., & Yousfi, O. (2016). Does gender diversity on corporate boards increase risk-taking? *Canadian Journal of Administrative Sciences, 33*(1), 66–81. doi:10.1002/cjas.1326

Løyning, T. (2021). Regulating for gender equality in business: The law on gender quotas and the network of interlocking directorates in Norway, 2008–2016. *Review of Social Economy*, 1–27. doi:10.1080/00346764.2021.1901139

Lozano, R. (2012). Towards better embedding sustainability into companies' systems: An analysis of voluntary corporate initiatives. *Journal of Cleaner Production, 25*, 14–26. doi:10.1016/j.jclepro.2011.11.060

Lozano, R., Nummert, B., & Ceulemans, K. (2016). Elucidating the relationship between sustainability reporting and organisational change management for sustainability. *Journal of Cleaner Production, 125*, 168–188. doi:10.1016/j.jclepro.2016.03.021

Lucas, A., & Dias, D. (2020). Glass Ceiling in accounting profession: Myth or reality? *INTED2020 Proceedings, 1*, 5499–5504. 10.21125/inted.2020.1483

Lucas-Pérez, M. E., Mínguez-Vera, A., Baixauli-Soler, J. S., Martín-Ugedo, J. F., & Sánchez-Marín, G. (2015). Women on the Board and Managers' Pay: Evidence from Spain. *Journal of Business Ethics, 129*(2), 265–280. doi:10.100710551-014-2148-1

Lugarinho, M. C. (2013). Masculinidade e colonialismo: em direção ao "homem novo" (subsídios para os estudos de gênero e para os estudos pós-coloniais no contexto de língua portuguesa). *Revista do Núcleo de Estudos de Literatura Portuguesa e Africana (NEPA) da UFF, 5*(10), 15-38.

Lundin, S. C., Paul, H., & Christensen, J. (2000). Fish! A remarkable way to boost morale and improve results. Hyperon.

Madaleno, M., Vieira, E. S., & Teodosio, J. P. C. (2021). Corporate female leadership effects considering PSI20 and IBEX35 companies' performance. In *Research Anthology on Challenges for Women in Leadership Roles* (pp. 711–731). IGI Global., doi:10.4018/978-1-7998-8592-4.ch039

Madalozzo, R. (2011). CEOs e composição do conselho de administração: A falta de identificação pode ser motivo para existência de teto de vidro para mulheres no Brasil? *Revista de Administração Contemporânea*, *15*(1), 126–137. doi:10.1590/S1415-65552011000100008

Majeed, S., Aziz, T., & Saleem, S. (2015). The effect of corporate governance elements on corporate social responsibility (Csr) disclosure: An empirical evidence from listed companies at kse Pakistan. *International Journal of Financial Studies*, *3*(4), 530–556. doi:10.3390/ijfs3040530

Malik, A., Budhwar, P., Patel, C., & Srikanth, N. R. (2022). May the bots be with you! Delivering HR cost-effectiveness and individualised employee experiences in an MNE. *International Journal of Human Resource Management*, *33*(6), 1148–1178. doi:10.1080/09585192.2020.1859582

Mallin, C. A., & Michelon, G. (2011). Board reputation attributes and corporate social performance: An empirical investigation of the US Best Corporate Citizens. *Accounting and Business Research*, *41*(2), 119–144. doi:10.1080/00014788.2011.550740

Manita, R., Bruna, M. G., Dang, R., & Houanti, L. (2018). Board gender diversity and ESG disclosure: Evidence from the USA. *Journal of Applied Accounting Research*, *19*(2), 206–224. doi:10.1108/JAAR-01-2017-0024

Manuel dos Santos, F. F. (2018). *Igualdade de género ao longo da vida: Portugal no contexto Europeu*. FFMS. https://www.ffms.pt/FileDownload/97de6517-2059-46b4-967a-f3b8a15ef139/igualdade-de-genero-ao-longo-da-vida

Mari, M., Poggesi, S., & De Vita, L. (2016). Family embeddedness and business performance: Evidences from women-owned firms. *Management Decision*, *54*(2), 476–500. doi:10.1108/MD-07-2014-0453

Marinova, J., Plantenga, J., & Remery, C. (2016). Gender diversity and firm performance: Evidence from Dutch and Danish boardrooms. *International Journal of Human Resource Management*, *27*(15), 1777–1790. doi:10.1080/09585192.2015.1079229

Marlowe, J., & Clarke, A. (2022). Carbon accounting: A systematic literature review and directions for future research. *Green Finance*, *4*(1), 71–87. doi:10.3934/GF.2022004

Marques, I. A. (2018). *A mulher nas carreiras de topo* [Dissertação de mestrado, Universidade Autónoma de Lisboa]. http://hdl.handle.net/11144/3868

Marques, T. C. N. (2016). A regulação do trabalho feminino em um sistema político masculino, Brasil: 1932-1943. *Estudos Históricos (Rio de Janeiro)*, *29*(59), 667-686.

Marques, C. S., Santos, G., Ratten, V., & Barros, A. B. (2019). Innovation as a booster of rural artisan entrepreneurship: A case study of black pottery. *International Journal of Entrepreneurial Behaviour & Research*, *25*(4), 753–772. doi:10.1108/IJEBR-02-2018-0104

Marques, T. de M. G., & Ferreira, C. M. (2015). Mulheres na gestão de topo: A problemática do gap de gênero e salarial. *Revista Ibero Americana de Estratégia*, *14*(1), 43–59. doi:10.5585/riae.v14i1.2150

Martínez-García, I., Terjesen, S., & Gómez-Ansón, S. (2022). Board Gender Diversity Codes, Quotas and Threats of Supranational Legislation: Impact on Director Characteristics and Corporate Outcomes. *British Journal of Management*, *33*(2), 753–783. doi:10.1111/1467-8551.12517

Martínez, M. (2019). Gender policies on board of directors and sustainable development. *Corporate Social Responsibility and Environmental Management*, *26*(6), 1539–1553. doi:10.1002/csr.1825

Martins, L. C., & Branco, A. U. (2001). Desenvolvimento moral: Considerações teóricas a partir de uma abordagem sociocultural construtivista. *Psicologia: Teoria e Pesquisa (Brasília)*, *17*(2), 169–176. doi:10.1590/S0102-37722001000200009

Martín-Ugedo, J. F., Mínguez-Vera, A., & Rossi, F. (2019). Female directors and firm performance in Italian and Spanish listed firms: Does masculinity matter? *Academia (Caracas)*, *32*(3), 411–436. doi:10.1108/ARLA-06-2018-0124

Mathew, S., Ibrahim, S., & Archbold, S. (2016). Board attributes that increase firm risk-evidence from the UK. *Corporate Governance: The international journal of business in society, 16* (2), 233-258.

Matos, J. S., & Machado, A. F. (2006). Diferencial de Rendimentos por Cor e Sexo no Brasil (1987-2001). *Revista Economica*, *8*(1), 5–27.

Matos, J. S., & Senna, A. K. (2011). História Oral como Fonte: Problemas e Métodos. *Revista Historiæ*, *2*(1), 95–108.

Maxwell, J. C. (2002). *Leadership 101*. Thomas Nelson Publishing.

Mazzucato, M., & Tancioni, M. (2012). R&D, patents and stock return volatility. *Journal of Evolutionary Economics*, *22*(4), 811–832. doi:10.100700191-012-0289-x

McAra, M., & McHattie, L.-S. (2020). Crafting Futures: Inspiring Interdisciplinary Innovation with Young Craft Artisans in Malaysia. *Pages on Arts and Design*, *18*, 306–328.

McGuire, D. (2012, December 1). *Opinion: It's time to free Rosa Parks from the bus*. CNN. https://www.cnn.com/2012/12/01/us/opinion-its-time-to-free-rosa-parks-from-the-bus/index.html

Mellahi, K., & Johnson, M. (2000). Does it pay to be a first mover in e. commerce? The case of Amazon. com. *Management Decision*, *38*(7), 445–452. doi:10.1108/00251740010373458

Mellemvik, F., Monsen, N., & Olson, O. (1988). Functions of accounting - a discussion. *Scandinavian Journal of Management*, *4*(3-4), 101–119. doi:10.1016/0956-5221(88)90003-6

Melón-Izco, Á., Ruiz-Cabestre, F. J., & Ruiz-Olalla, M. C. (2020). Diversity in the board of directors and good governance practices. *Economics and Business Letters*, *9*(2), 97–105. doi:10.17811/ebl.9.2.2020.97-105

Menezes, M. G. D., & Santiago, M. E. (2014). Contribuição do pensamento de Paulo Freire para o paradigma curricular crítico-emancipatório. *Pro-Posições*, *25*(3), 45–62. doi:10.1590/0103-7307201407503

Menicucci, E., & Paolucci, G. (2020). Does gender diversity matter for risk-taking? Evidence from Italian financial institutions. *African Journal of Business Management*, *14*(10), 324–334. doi:10.5897/AJBM2020.9089

Menicucci, E., Paolucci, G., & Paoloni, N. (2019). Does gender matter for hotel performance? Evidence from the Italian hospitality industry. *International Journal of Tourism Research*, *21*(5), 625–638. doi:10.1002/jtr.2286

Meyerson, D. E., & Fletcher, J. K. (2000). A Modest Manifest for Shattering the Glass Ceiling. *Harvard Business Review*, *78*(1), 127–136.

Micky Olutende, O., Wisiuba Bukhala, P., & Wesonga, B. (2018). Exercise Prescription: Practices of Healthcare Professionals in Hospital Setting, Kenya. *Journal of Physical Activity Research*, *3*(1), 47–54. doi:10.12691/jpar-3-1-8

Miller, K., & Vagins, D. (2019). *The simple truth about the gender pay gap*. American Association of University Women.

Minguez-Vera, A., & Martin, A. (2011). Gender and management on Spanish SMEs: An empirical analysis. *International Journal of Tourism Research*, *22*(14), 2852–2873.

Miotto, G., & Vilajoana-Alejandre, S. (2019). Gender equality: a tool for legitimacy in the fast fashion industry. *Harvard Deusto Business Research*. *8*(2), 134–147.

Miranda, A. R. A., Cappelle, M. C. A., Fonseca, F. P., Mafra, F. L. N., & Moreira, L. B. (2013). O Exercício da Gerência Universitária por Docentes Mulheres. *Revista Pretexto*, *14*(1), 106–123.

Miranda, L. C. (2006). *A Percepção da Mulher no Mercado de Trabalho: Emprego, Carreira ou Vocação*. Faculdade IBMEC.

Mirza, S. S., Majeed, M. A., & Ahsan, T. (2020). Board gender diversity, competitive pressure and investment efficiency in Chinese private firms. *Eurasian Business Review*, *10*(3), 417–440. doi:10.100740821-019-00138-5

Mischau, A. (2001). Women in higher education in Europe - A Statistical overview. *The International Journal of Sociology and Social Policy*, *21*(1/2), 20–31. doi:10.1108/01443330110789529

Modigliani, F., & Miller, M. H. (1958). The cost of capital, corporation finance and the theory of investment. *The American Economic Review*, *48*(3), 261–297.

Molina, J., M., C., & Torrado, M., N. (2011). *The efficiency of the financial sector in Spain: a gender focus.* Adm. Bogotá (Colombia).

Monteiro, A. P., Pereira, C., & Barbosa, F. M. (2021). *Environmental disclosure on mandatory and voluntary reporting of Portuguese listed firms: the role of environmental certification, lucratively and corporate governance.* Meditari Accountancy Research. doi:10.1108/MEDAR-09-2020-1001

Monteiro, C. F. D. S., & Souza, I. E. D. O. (2007). Vivência da violência conjugal: Fatos do cotidiano. *Texto & Contexto Enfermagem, 16*(1), 26–31. doi:10.1590/S0104-07072007000100003

Moraes, R. (1999). Análise de conteúdo. *Review of Education, 22*(37), 7–32.

Morais, J. G., Oliveira, C. G., Campos, K. R. S., Viana, G. M., & Fernandes, M. L. R. (2006). Gênero, Raça e Competências de Direção no Serviço Público Federal. *Cadernos Enap, 36*(1), 1–69.

Moreno, Á., Khalil, N., & Tench, R. (2021). Enemy at the (house) gates: Permanence of gender discrimination in public relations career promotion in Latin America. *Communicatio Socialis, 34*(3), 169–183.

Morley, L., & Crossouard, B. (2016). Women's Leadership in the Asian Century: Does Expansion Mean Inclusion? *Studies in Higher Education, 41*(5), 801–814. doi:10.1080/03075079.2016.1147749

Moser, C. (1993). *Gender Planning and Development: Theory, Practice and Training.* Routledge.

Mugaddam, A. (2021). Language shift and gender in Dilling, Sudan: Who leads the process?. *Journal of Arts and Humanities, 10*(03), 01-13.

Mussak, E. (2004). O entusiasmo do empreendedor. *Vencer, 56*(1), 98.

Myers, S. C. (1977). Determinants of corporate borrowing. *Journal of Financial Economics, 5*(2), 147–175. doi:10.1016/0304-405X(77)90015-0

Myers, S. C. (1984). The Capital Structure Puzzle. *The Journal of Finance, 39*(3), 575–592. doi:10.2307/2327916

Nadeem, M., Suleman, T., & Ahmed, A. (2019). Women on boards, firm risk and the profitability nexus: Does gender diversity moderate the risk and return relationship? *International Review of Economics & Finance, 64*, 427–442. doi:10.1016/j.iref.2019.08.007

Nadeem, M., Zaman, R., & Saleem, I. (2017). Boardroom gender diversity and corporate sustainability practices: Evidence from Australian Securities Exchange listed firms. *Journal of Cleaner Production, 149*, 874–885. doi:10.1016/j.jclepro.2017.02.141

Naidu, S., Chand, A., & Southgate, P. (2014). Determinants of innovation in the handicraft industry of Fiji and Tonga: An empirical analysis from a tourism perspective. *Journal of Enterprising Communities: People and Places in the Global Economy, 8*(4), 318–330. doi:10.1108/JEC-11-2013-0033

Nakagawa, Y. (2015). The gender diversity firm performance relationship by industry type, working hours, and inclusiveness: An empirical study of Japanese firms. [JDM]. *Journal of Diversity Management*, *10*(1), 61–78.

Nakano, M., & Nguyen, P. (2012). Board size and corporate risk taking: Further evidence from Japan. *Corporate Governance*, *20*(4), 369–387. doi:10.1111/j.1467-8683.2012.00924.x

Nanzushi, C. (2015). *The effect of workplace environment on employee performance in the mobile telecommunication firms in Nairobi city county* [Doctoral dissertation, University of Nairobi].

Nasir, M. A., & Morgan, J. (2018). The unit root problem: Affinities between ergodicity and stationarity, its practical contradictions for central bank policy, and some consideration of alternatives. *Journal of Post Keynesian Economics*, *41*(3), 339–363. doi:10.1080/01603477.2017.1387060

Nathaniel, F., Ernawati, E., & Mahadwartha, P. A. (2019). The effect of board gender diversity on firm risk. *In 16th International Symposium on Management (INSYMA 2019)* (Vol. 308, pp. 44-47). Atlantis Press. 10.2991/insyma-19.2019.12

Navarro-García, J. C., Ramón-Llorens, M. C., & García-Meca, E. (2020). *Female directors and corporate reputation*. BRQ Business Research Quarterly. doi:10.1177/2340944420972717

Navumau, V., & Matveieva, O. (2021). The gender dimension of the 2020 Belarusian protest: Does female engagement contribute to the establishment of gender equality? *New perspectives*, *29*(3), 230-248.

Nawaz, K., Saeed, H. A., & Sajeel, T. A. (2020). Covid-19 and the state of research from the perspective of psychology. *International Journal of Business and Psychology*, *2*(1), 35–44.

Ndinda, C., & Ndhlovu, T. P. (2018). Gender, poverty and inequality: Exploration from a transformative perspective. *Journal of International Women's Studies*, *19*(5), 1–12.

Nepal, J., & Lertjanyakit, H. (2019). Impact of Gender Based Discrimination on Employee Performance in Case of Nepalese Commercial Banks. *Nepalese Journal of Management Science and Research*, *2*(1), 21–30.

Neuman, S., & Oaxaca, R. L. (2004). Wage decompositions with selectivity-corrected wage equations: A methodological note. *The Journal of Economic Inequality*, *2*(1), 3–10. doi:10.1023/B:JOEI.0000028395.38694.4b

Nicolò, G., Zampone, G., Sannino, G., & De Iorio, S. (2022). Sustainable corporate governance and non-financial disclosure in Europe: Does the gender diversity matter? *Journal of Applied Accounting Research*, *23*(1), 227–249. doi:10.1108/JAAR-04-2021-0100

Nielsen, S., & Huse, M. (2010). The contribution of women on boards of directors: Going beyond the surface. *Corporate Governance*, *18*(2), 136–148. doi:10.1111/j.1467-8683.2010.00784.x

Nisiyama, E. K., & Nakamura, W. T. (2018). Diversidade do Conselho de Administração e a Estrutura de Capital. *Revista de Administração de Empresas*, *58*(6), 551–563. doi:10.15900034-759020180604

Nogueira, M., Alvarez, C., & Urbano, D. (2013). Socio-cultural factors and female entrepreneurship. *The International Entrepreneurship and Management Journal*, *9*(2), 183–197. doi:10.100711365-013-0251-x

Noland, M., Moran, T., & Kotschwar, B. R. (2016). Is gender diversity profitable? Evidence from a Global Survey. SSRN *Electronic Journal*, (March 2019). doi:10.2139/ssrn.2729348

Ntim, C. G., & Soobaroyen, T. (2013). Corporate governance and performance in socially responsible corporations: New empirical insights from a Neo - Institutional framework. *Corporate Governance*, *21*(5), 468–494. doi:10.1111/corg.12026

Nunes, M. T. A. (2007). *Género e cidadania nas imagens de História: estudos de manuais escolares e software educativo*. Comissão para a Cidadania e Igualdade se Género.

Nwokolo, O. O., Coombs, A. A., Eltzschig, H. K., & Butterworth, J. F. IV. (2022). Diversity and inclusion in anesthesiology. *Anesthesia and Analgesia*, *134*(6), 1166–117. doi:10.1213/ANE.0000000000005941 PMID:35130194

Nyström, M., Höög, E., Garvare, R., Weinehall, L., & Ivarsson, A. (2013). Change and learning strategies in large scale change programs: Describing the variation of strategies used in a health promotion program. *Journal of Organizational Change Management*, *26*(6), 1020–1044. doi:10.1108/JOCM-08-2012-0132

Oaxaca, R. (1973). Male-female wage differentials in urban labor markets. *International Economic Review*, *14*(3), 693–709. doi:10.2307/2525981

Oaxaca, R. L., & Ransom, M. R. (1994). On discrimination and the decomposition of wage differentials. *Journal of Econometrics*, *61*(1), 5–21. doi:10.1016/0304-4076(94)90074-4

Oelz, M., Olney, S., & Tomei, M. (2013). *Equal pay: An introductory guide*. Academic Press.

Öge, S., Karasoy, A., & Kara, Ö. (2014). A research on glass ceiling syndrome career barriers of women academics. *International Journal of Economics and Management Engineering*, *8*(9), 3019–3028.

Olabuénaga. J. I. R. (2012). Metodología de la investigación cualitativa. *Universidad de Deusto. 15*.

Oliveira, M. (2011). *Metodologia Científica: um manual para a realização de pesquisas em administração*. UFG. Disponível em: https://d1wqtxts1xzle7.cloudfront.net/52313331/Manual_de_metodologia_cientifica_-_Prof_Maxwell-with-cover-page-v2.pdf?Expires=1656869648&Signature=OZO0RgCClmLiwx2hw0P-mtg52SY4CD5UC2FJk7NYhyfw5-UVPYVIKATThkEO0Mv5OVaZ5hW0SVKyzwfnh~I-GXiOuRYqXsID77voMBUSZkIjfxFD-gpgqu1NqQnnqC-fl7JUPqIt-zpD6nn-KkT-tfixIK9vXeRAZMbwR74nityPiN752L9cGXMGskqkKIP7YPuSlHFfONINXnOCX1~rg~sHi~W0SGU-lXuPaoESCYWPE9BsDwUTqlenTpXtlfsAH1HZWwDUkEDMe5U~0zIUBGFax7dHZXH-qdzSn35pASuCHazSHHqPeNgc8KCHb9n2gBaXbaRoZhnVywcJqP0muQ__&Key-Pair-Id=APKAJLOHF5GGSLRBV4ZA

Oliveira, B. B., & Woida, L. M. (2018). O Fenômeno *Glass Ceiling* e o Acesso à Informação: Estudo sobre Barreiras Invisíveis Impostas às Mulheres no Trabalho. *Revista de Filosofia Temática*, *3*(1), 61–75.

Omri, A., & Boukattaya, S. (2018). Gender diversity and firm performance: Evidence from French boardrooms. *EuroMed J. of Management*, *2*(4), 356. doi:10.1504/EMJM.2018.096456

Ongena, S. (2003). Working Paper Series. *RE:view*, *85*(6). doi:10.20955/r.85.67

Ordem dos Contabilistas, C. (2015). *Relatório e contas 2015*. https://www.occ.pt/fotos/editor2/rc2015d.pdf

Ordem dos Contabilistas, C. (2016). *Relatório e contas 2016*. https://www.occ.pt/fotos/editor2/rc2016_b.pdf

Ordem dos Contabilistas, C. (2017). *Relatório e contas 2017*. https://pt.calameo.com/read/00032498147b319bfa1f4

Ordem dos Contabilistas, C. (2018). *Relatório e contas 2018*. https://pt.calameo.com/read/00032498177cb91926b08

Ordem dos Contabilistas, C. (2019). *Relatório e contas 2019*. https://www.occ.pt/news/DIversos/RC2019.pdf

Ordem dos Contabilistas, C. (2020). *Relatório e contas 2020*. https://pt.calameo.com/read/000324981c94bf0cad338

Ordem dos Contabilistas, C. (2020). *Relatório e Contas 2020*. OCC. https://www.occ.pt/pt/a-ordem/relatorio-e-contas-plano-de-atividades-e-orcamento/

Ordem dos Contabilistas, C. (2021). *Relatório e contas 2021*. https://www.occ.pt/news/Documentos/RC2021.pdf

Ordem dos Contabilistas, C. (2021). *Relatório e Contas 2021*. OCC. https://www.occ.pt/news/Documentos/RC2021.pdf

Organização Internacional do Trabalho. (2021). *Estudo sobre a diferença salarial entre homens e mulheres em Portugal.* https://www.ilo.org/lisbon/publica%C3%A7%C3%B5es/WCMS_836143/lang--pt/index.htm

Othmani, H. (2021). Does board gender diversity matter in the banking sector? Evidence from Tunisia. *African Development Review, 33*(1), 14–24. doi:10.1111/1467-8268.12487

Palacín-Sánchez, M., Ramírez-Herrera, L., & Pietro, F. (2013). Capital structure of SMEs in Spanish Regions. *Small Business Economics, 41*(2), 503–519. doi:10.100711187-012-9439-7

Palotti, P., & Freire, A. (2015). *Perfil, Composição e Remuneração dos Servidores Públicos Federais: Trajetória Recente e Tendências Observadas. Cadernos ENAP, 42.*

Pant, B. (2016). *Financial Inclusion in Nepal: Policy Review and Prescriptions.* 1–18. NRB. https://nrb.org.np/ecorev/articles/2.pdf

Panter-Brick, C. (2002). Sexual division of labor: Energetic and evolutionary scenarios. *American Journal of Human Biology, 14*(5), 627–640. doi:10.1002/ajhb.10074 PMID:12203817

Panwar, R., Paul, K., Nybakk, E., Hansen, E., & Thompson, D. (2014). The Legitimacy of CSR Actions of Publicly Traded Companies Versus Family-Owned Companies. *Journal of Business Ethics, 125*(3), 481–496. doi:10.100710551-013-1933-6

Parajuli, S., Paudel, U. R., & Devkota, N. (2020). Banking communications: A perceptual study of customer relations. *South Asian Journal of Social Studies and Economics, 8*(3), 23–34. doi:10.9734ajsse/2020/v8i330212

Paudel, U. R., & Devkota, N. (2022). Assimilation of Communication Deviance in Customer and Banker Appraisals of Commercial Banks in Kathmandu, Nepal. In Innovative Economic, Social, and Environmental Practices for Progressing Future Sustainability (pp. 1-17). IGI Global.

Paudel, U. R., Parajuli, S., Devkota, N., & Mahapatra, S. K. (2020). What determines customers' perception of banking communication? An empirical evidence from commercial banks of Nepal. *Global Economy Journal, 20*(04), 1–21. doi:10.1142/S2194565920500190

Paudel, U. R., Tamrakar, L., Devkota, N., Maga, S. R., & Parajuli, S. (2021). Promoting Effective Managerial Communication on Banking Sector in Kathmandu Valley: Cross Sectional Analysis. *International Research Journal of Management Science, 6*(1), 110–127. doi:10.3126/irjms.v6i1.42352

Pawer, A. S. (2020). *Agony of the Indian Women.* Dattsons.

Perazzo, P. F. (2015). Narrativas Orais de Histórias de Vida. *Revista Comunicação & Inovação, 16*(30), 121–131.

Perez-Arce, F., & Prados, M. J. (2021). The decline in the US labor force participation rate: A literature review. *Journal of Economic Surveys, 35*(2), 615–652. doi:10.1111/joes.12402

Perryman, A. A., Fernando, G. D., & Tripathy, A. (2016). Do gender differences persist? An examination of gender diversity on firm performance, risk, and executive compensation. *Journal of Business Research*, *69*(2), 579–586. doi:10.1016/j.jbusres.2015.05.013

Pestana, M. H., & Gageiro, J. N. (2014). *Análise de Dados para Ciências Sociais, A complementaridade do SPSS*. Edições Sílabo.

Pfeffer, J., & Salancik, G. R. (2003). *The external control of organizations: A resource dependence perspective*. Stanford University Press.

Pham, T., & Thesis, D. (2017). Gender Diversity Management Polici*es*.

Phillipov, M. (2016). Using media to promote artisan food and beverages: Insights from the television industry. *British Food Journal*, *118*(3), 588–602. doi:10.1108/BFJ-06-2015-0219

Pignatti, N. (2020). Encouraging women's labor force participation in transition countries. *IZA World of Labor: Evidence-Based Policy Making*. Advance online publication. doi:10.15185/izawol.264.v2

Pinto, A. M. (2019). *As Diferenças de Género na Percepção do Conflito Trabalho-Família* [Dissertação de mestrado, Instituto Politécnico de Castelo Branco]. http://hdl.handle.net/10400.11/1226

Post, C., & Byron, K. (2015). Women on boards and firm financial performance: A meta-analysis. *Academy of Management Journal*, *58*(5), 1546–1571. doi:10.5465/amj.2013.0319

Post, C., Rahman, N., & McQuillen, C. (2015). From Board Composition to Corporate Environmental Performance Through Sustainability-Themed Alliances. *Journal of Business Ethics*, *130*(2), 423–435. doi:10.100710551-014-2231-7

Powell, G. N., & Butterfield, A. (1994). Investigating the "Glass Ceiling" Phenomenon: An Empirical Study of Actual Promotions to Top Management. *Academy of Management Journal*, *37*(1), 68–86. doi:10.2307/256770

Prates, S. (2021, 29 de junho). O papel das mulheres na resiliência das empresas. *Lider Magazine*. https://lidermagazine.sapo.pt/o-papel-das-mulheres-na-resiliencia-das-empresas/

Pucheta-Martínez, M. C., Bel-Oms, I., & Olcina-Sempere, G.Pucheta-Martínez. (2016). Corporate governance, female directors and quality of financial information. *Business Ethics (Oxford, England)*, *25*(4), 363–385. doi:10.1111/beer.12123

Pucheta-Martínez, M. C., & Bel-Oms, I.Pucheta-Martínez. (2016). The board of directors and dividend policy: The effect of gender diversity. *Industrial and Corporate Change*, *25*(3), 523–547. doi:10.1093/icc/dtv040

Pucheta-Martínez, M. C., & Bel-Oms, I.Pucheta-Martínez. (2019). What have we learnt about board gender diversity as a business strategy? The appointment of board subcommittees. *Business Strategy and the Environment*, *28*(2), 301–315. doi:10.1002/bse.2226

Pugalia, S., & Cetindamar, D. (2022). Insights on the glass ceiling for immigrant women entrepreneurs in the technology sector. *International Journal of Gender and Entrepreneurship, 14*(1), 44–68. doi:10.1108/IJGE-10-2020-0169

Putnam, L. L. (1979). Women in Management: Leadership Theories, Research Results, and Future Directions. *Annual Meeting of the Central States Speech Association.*

Queiroz, J. L. A. P. (2013). *Trajetória de vida e trabalho das mulheres empreendedoras de Boa Vista, Roraima: avanços e vitórias. Dissertação de Mestrado.* Universidade Federal do Amazonas.

Queiroz, M. I. P. (1991). *Variações sobre a técnica de gravador no registro da informação viva.* T.A. Queiroz.

Queisser, M. (2016). Gender equality and the Sustainable Development Goals. In Love. P. (Ed.). *Debate the Issues: New Approaches to Economic Challenges.* OECD Publishing. Paris.

Quental, C., & Wetzel, U. (2002). Equilíbrio trabalho-vida e empreendedorismo: a experiência das mulheres brasileiras. Encontro Nacional da Associação Nacional de Pós-Graduação e Pesquisa em Administração (EnANPAD), 26.

Rafferty, A. E., Jimmieson, N. L., & Armenakis, A. A. (2013). Change readiness: A multilevel review. *Journal of Management, 39*(1), 110–135. doi:10.1177/0149206312457417

Raigada, J. L. P. (2002). Epistemología. metodología y técnicas del análisis de contenido. *Sociolinguistic Studies, 3*(1), 1–42. doi:10.1558ols.v3i1.1

Rai, R., Kharel, S., Devkota, N., & Paudel, U. R. (2019). Customers perception on green banking practices: A desk. *The Journal of Economic Concerns, 10*(1), 82–95.

Ransom, M., & Oaxaca, R. L. (2005). Intrafirm mobility and sex differences in pay. *Industrial & Labor Relations Review, 58*(2), 219–237. doi:10.1177/001979390505800203

Rao, K., & Tilt, C. (2016). Board composition and corporate social responsibility: The role of diversity, gender, strategy and decision making. *Journal of Business Ethics, 138*(2), 327–347. doi:10.100710551-015-2613-5

Ratten, V. (2022a). Artisan entrepreneurship in Indonesia. In V. Ratten (Ed.), *Entrepreneurship in Indonesia* (pp. 14–31). Routledge.

Ratten, V. (2022b). Food artisan entrepreneurship in Indonesia. In *Entrepreneurship in Indonesia* (pp. 32–44). Routledge.

Rebelo, D. (2011). *As conquistas democráticas da mulher portuguesa.* http://www.25abril.org/a25abril/get_document.php?id=240

Redman, A. (2018). Harnessing the Sustainable Development Goals for businesses: A progressive framework for action. *Business Strategy & Development, 1*(4), 230–243.

Reguera-Alvarado, N., & Bravo-Urquiza, F. (2022). The influence of board social capital on corporate social responsibility reporting. *Journal of Intellectual Capital, 23*(4), 913–935. doi:10.1108/JIC-11-2020-0359

Reguera-Alvarado, N., de Fuentes, P., & Laffarga, J. (2017). Does board gender diversity influence financial performance? Evidence from Spain. *Journal of Business Ethics, 141*(2), 337–350. doi:10.100710551-015-2735-9

Reimann, M., Peters, E., & Diewald, M. (2022). COVID-19 and Work–Family Conflicts in Germany: Risks and Chances Across Gender and Parenthood. *Front. Sociol., 6*, 780740. doi:10.3389/fsoc.2021.780740 PMID:35071402

Ribeiro, M. C., & Machado, A. L. (2014). O Uso do Método História Oral nas Pesquisas Qualitativas: Contribuições para a Temática do Cuidado em Saúde Mental. *Estudos e Pesquisas em Psicologia, 14*(2), 578–591. doi:10.12957/epp.2014.12562

Richard, O. C., Kirby, S. L., & Chadwick, K. (2013). The impact of racial and gender diversity in management on financial performance: How participative strategy making features can unleash a diversity advantage. *International Journal of Human Resource Management, 24*(13), 2571–2582. doi:10.1080/09585192.2012.744335

Ried, G. E., Acken, B. T., & Jancura, E. G. (1987). An historical perspective on women in accounting. *Journal of Accountancy, 163*(5), 338–355.

Robb, A. M., & Watson, J. (2012). Gender differences in firm performance: Evidence from new ventures in the United States. *Journal of Business Venturing, 27*(5), 544–558. doi:10.1016/j.jbusvent.2011.10.002

Robinson, E. (2011). Disintegration: The splintering of Black America. Anchor Books: A Division of Random House, Inc.

Rodrigues, H. E. (2020). *Empreendedorismo feminino no meio rural paraense: estudo com agricultoras familiares em municípios do Baixo Tocantins. Dissertação de Mestrado.* Universidade Federal Rural da Amazônia.

Rodrigues, S. (2016). *Salários e desigualdade de género em Portugal* [Dissertação de mestrado, Universidade dos Açores]. http://hdl.handle.net/10400.3/4093

Rodrigues, L. L., Tejedo-Romero, F., & Craig, R. (2017). Corporate governance and intellectual capital reporting in a period of financial crisis: Evidence from Portugal. *International Journal of Disclosure and Governance, 14*(1), 1–29. doi:10.1057/jdg.2015.20

Rodrigues, S. C., & Silva, G. R. (2015). A Liderança Feminina no Mercado de Trabalho. *Revista Digital de Administração, 1*(4), 1–12.

Rosener, J. B. (1990). Way females lead. *Harvard Business Review, 68*, 119–125. PMID:10107957

Rosener, J. B. (1997). *America's competitive secret: Women managers.* Oxford University Press on Demand.

Rossi, F., & Cebula, R. J. (2015). Does the board of directors affect the extent of corporate R&D? Evidence from Italian listed companies. *Economic Bulletin, 35*(4), 2567–2580.

Rowlands, J. (1997). *Questioning Empowerment: Working with Women in Honduras*. Oxam Publications. doi:10.3362/9780855988364

Sabir, F. S., Maqsood, Z., Tariq, W., & Devkota, N. (2019). Does happiness at work lead to organisation citizenship behaviour with mediating role of organisation learning capacity? A gender perspective study of educational institutes in Sialkot, Pakistan. *International Journal of Work Organisation and Emotion, 10*(4), 281–296. doi:10.1504/IJWOE.2019.106891

Saeed, A., Belghitar, Y., & Yousaf, A. (2016). Firm-level determinants of gender diversity in the boardrooms: Evidence from some emerging markets. *International Business Review, 25*(5), 1076–1088. doi:10.1016/j.ibusrev.2016.01.002

Saeed, A., Riaz, H., Liedong, T. A., & Rajwani, T. (2022). The impact of TMT gender diversity on corporate environmental strategy in emerging economies. *Journal of Business Research, 141*, 536–551. doi:10.1016/j.jbusres.2021.11.057

Sampaio, E. S., Gomes, D. R. R., & Porte, M. S. (2017). História da contabilidade e o gênero feminino: O caso Anna Jansen, a rainha do maranhão (Sec. XIX). *Revista Española de Historia de la Contabilidad, 14*(26), 59–89. doi:10.26784/issn.1886-1881.v14i26.306

Sánchez, P. C., Sánchez-Ballesta, J. P., & García-Meca, E. (2012). Explanatory factors of good governance in Spanish listed firms. *Revista de Contabilidad-Spanish Accounting Review, 15*(2), 237–255. doi:10.1016/S1138-4891(12)70044-4

Santos, C. (2017, Maio). A mulher profissional. *Revista Contabilista - Ordem Dos Contabilistas Certificados, 206*, Article 206.

Santos, C. M. M., Tanure, B., & Carvalho Neto, A. M. (2014). Mulheres executivas brasileiras: oO teto de vidro em questão. *Revista Administração em Diálogo, 16*(3), 56–75.

Santos, M. A., Melo, M. C. D. O. L., & Batinga, G. L. (2021). Representatividade da Mulher Contadora em Escritórios de Contabilidade e a Desigualdade de Gênero na Prática Contábil: Uma Questão ainda em Debate? *Sociedade. Contabilidade e Gestão, 16*(1), 148–163. doi:10.21446cg_ufrj.v0i0.30679

Saona, P., Muro, L., & Alvarado, M. (2020). How do the ownership structure and board of directors' features impact earnings management? The Spanish case. *Journal of International Financial Management & Accounting, 31*(1), 98–133. doi:10.1111/jifm.12114

Sarkar, S. (2010). *Empreendedorismo e inovação*. Forte da Casa: Escolar Editora.

Schlickmann, E., & Pizarro, D. (2013). A Evolução da Mulher no Trabalho: Uma Abordagem sob a Ótica da Liderança. *Revista Borges, 3*(1), 70–89.

Schweitzer, S. (2008). As mulheres e o acesso às profissões superiores: uma comparação européia, séculos XIX e XX. In Mercado de trabalho e gênero: comparações internacionais. Rio de Janeiro: Editora FGV.

Sear, R. (2021). The male breadwinner nuclear family is not the 'traditional' human family, and promotion of this myth may have adverse health consequences. *Philosophical Transactions of the Royal Society B, 376*(1827).

Sebrae - Serviço Brasileiro de Apoio às Micro e Pequenas Empresas. (2018). *Os desafios da mulher empreendedora.* Disponível em: https://www.sebrae.com.br/sites/PortalSebrae/artigos/os-desafios-da-mulher-empreendedora,e74ab85844cb5510VgnVCM1000004c0 0210aRCRD

Sebrae - Serviço Brasileiro de Apoio às Micro e Pequenas Empresas. (2020). *Brasil deve atingir marca histórica de empreendedorismo em 2020.* Disponível em: https://www.agenciasebrae.com.br/sites/asn/uf/NA/brasil-deve-atingir-marca-historica-de-empreendedorismo-em-2020,d9c76d1 0f3e92710VgnVCM1000004c00210aRCRD

Seebeck, A., & Vetter, J. (2021). Not Just a Gender Numbers Game: How Board Gender Diversity Affects Corporate Risk Disclosure. *Journal of Business Ethics, 177*(2), 395–420. doi:10.100710551-020-04690-3

Segalo, P., & Fine, M. (2020). Underlying conditions of gender-based violence—Decolonial feminism meets epistemic ignorance: Critical transnational conversations. *Social and Personality Psychology Compass, 14*(10), 1–10. doi:10.1111pc3.12568

Segovia-Pérez, M., Figueroa-Domecq, C., Fuentes-Moraleda, L., & Muñoz-Mazón, A. (2019). Incorporating a gender approach in the hospitality industry: Female executives' perceptions. *International Journal of Hospitality Management, 76*(Part A), 184–193.

Sen, G., & Crown, C (1987). *Development, Crises and Alternative Visions: Third World Women's Perspectives.* Monthly Review Press.

Sengupta, M., & Harris, L. M. (2022). Interrogating differences: Intersectionality and participatory livelihood development in the upland forest of Tripura (Northeast India). *Geoforum, 130*, 59–68. doi:10.1016/j.geoforum.2022.02.002

Sennett, R. (2008). *The Craftsman.* Yale University Process.

Serra, S., Lemos, K. M., & Matins, M. S. (2022). The Influence of the Board of Directors and the Auditor in the Disclosure of Derivative Financial Instruments: Evidence on Portuguese Capital Market. *International Journal of Professional Business Review, 7*(1), e0240. doi:10.26668/businessreview/2022.v7i1.240

Serrasqueiro, Z., & Caetano, A. (2015). Trade-off theory *versus* pecking order theory: Capital structure decisions in a Peripheral Region of Portugal. *Journal of Business Economics and Management, 16*(2), 445–466. doi:10.3846/16111699.2012.744344

Setó-Pamies, D. (2015). The Relationship between Women Directors and Corporate Social Responsibility. *Corporate Social Responsibility and Environmental Management*, *22*(6), 334–345. doi:10.1002/csr.1349

Sharma, S., & Taneja, M. (2018). The effect of training on employee performance. *International Journal of Recent Technology and Engineering*, *7*(4), 6–13.

Shehata, N., Salhin, A., & El-Helaly, M. (2017). Board diversity and firm performance: Evidence from the UK SMEs. *Applied Economics*, *49*(48), 4817–4832. doi:10.1080/00036846.2017.1293796

Shelton, L. M. (2006). Female entrepreneurs, work–family conflict, and venture performance: nNew insights into the work–family interface. *Journal of Small Business Management*, *44*(2), 285–297. doi:10.1111/j.1540-627X.2006.00168.x

Shoham, A., & Lee, S. M. (2018). The causal impact of grammatical gender marking on gender wage inequality and country income inequality. *Business & Society*, *57*(6), 1216–1251. doi:10.1177/0007650317696231

Shrestha, E., Devkota, N., Paudel, U. R., & Parajuli, S. (2021). Post-merger Employee Satisfaction in Commercial Banks of Nepal: Findings from Employee Satisfaction Index. *Journal of Business and Social Sciences Research*, *6*(1), 45–62. doi:10.3126/jbssr.v6i1.38128

Shrestha, S., Devkota, N., Paudel, U., Bhandari, U., & Parajuli, S. (2020). Bankers' Communication Know-how: An Analysis from Commercial Banks of Kathmandu valley. *Quest Journal of Management and Social Sciences*, *2*(1), 80–99. doi:10.3126/qjmss.v2i1.29023

Shropshire, C., Peterson, S., Bartels, A. L., Amanatullah, E. T., & Lee, P. M. (2021). Are Female CEOs Really More Risk Averse? Examining Economic Downturn and Other-Orientation. *Journal of Leadership & Organizational Studies*, *28*(2), 185–206. doi:10.1177/1548051821997404

Siboni, B., Sangiorgi, D., Farneti, F., & De Villiers, C. (2016). Gender (in) accounting: Insights, gaps and an agenda for future research. *Meditari Accountancy Research*, *24*(2), 158–168. doi:10.1108/MEDAR-04-2016-0054

Sidhu, J. S., Feng, Y., Volberda, H. W., & Van Den Bosch, F. A. J. (2021). In the Shadow of Social Stereotypes: Gender diversity on corporate boards, board chair's gender and strategic change. *Organization Studies*, *42*(11), 1677–1698. doi:10.1177/0170840620944560

Sila, V., Gonzalez, A., & Hagendorff, J. (2016). Women on board: Does boardroom gender diversity affect firm risk? *Journal of Corporate Finance*, *36*, 26–53. doi:10.1016/j.jcorpfin.2015.10.003

Silva, S. M. C. (2016). *Tetos de Vitrais: Gênero e Raça na Contabilidade no Brasil.* Tese de Doutorado, Faculdade de Economia, Administração e Contabilidade, Universidade de São Paulo.

Silva, S. M. C. D. (2016). *Tetos de vitrais: gênero e raça na contabilidade no Brasil. Tese de Doutorado*. Universidade de São Paulo.

Singh, A. K., Kota, H. B., Sardana, V., & Singhania, S. (2021). Does Gender Diversity on Board Promote Corporate Social Responsibility? An Empirical Analysis of Sustainable Development Goals, *Australasian Accounting. Business and Finance Journal, 15*(5), 22–40.

Singh, V., & Point, S. (2006). (Re)presentations of gender and ethnicity in diversity statements on European company Websites. *Journal of Business Ethics, 68*(4), 363–379. doi:10.100710551-006-9028-2

Skała, D., & Weill, L. (2018). Does CEO gender matter for bank risk? *Economic Systems, 42*(1), 64–74. doi:10.1016/j.ecosys.2017.08.005

Smagina, A., & Ludviga, I. (2021). *What is Crafts Entrepreneurship? The Development of its Definition Through Entrepreneurs`and Consumers`Perceptions.* doi:10.22616/REEP.2021.14.045

Smith, M. (2012). Social regulation of the gender pay gap in the EU. *European Journal of Industrial Relations, 18*(4), 365–380. doi:10.1177/0959680112465931

Smithson, J., Lewis, S., Cooper, C., & Dyer, J. (2004). Flexible working and the gender pay gap in the accountancy profession. *Work, Employment and Society, 18*(1), 115–135. doi:10.1177/0950017004040765

Soare, T., Detilleux, C., & Deschacht, N. (2022). The impact of the gender composition of company boards on firm performance. *International Journal of Productivity and Performance Management, 71*(5), 1611–162. doi:10.1108/IJPPM-02-2020-0073

Sobczack, A. (2018). The Queen Bee Syndrome. The paradox of women discrimination on the labour market. *Journal of Gender and Power, 9*(1), 51–61. doi:10.14746/jgp.2018.9.005

Sogorb-Mira, F. (2005). How SME uniqueness affects capital structure: Evidence from a 1994–1998 Spanish data panel. *Small Business Economics, 25*(5), 447–457. doi:10.100711187-004-6486-8

Souza, M. B., Trindade, F. M., Freire, R., & Lyra, F. R. L. R. (2016). Potencial empreendedor de empresárias do setor turístico de Florianópolis (SC). *Revista Alcance, 23*(4), 455–474.

Srinidhi, B., Gul, F. A., & Tsui, J. (2011). Female directors and earnings quality. *Contemporary Accounting Research, 28*(5), 1610–1644. doi:10.1111/j.1911-3846.2011.01071.x

Srivastava, R. V., & Tang, T. (2022). The Matthew effect in talent management strategy: Reducing exhaustion, increasing satisfaction, and inspiring commission among boundary spanning employees. *Journal of Business and Industrial Marketing, 37*(3), 477–496. doi:10.1108/JBIM-06-2020-0296

Stanley, T. D., & Jarrell, S. B. (1998). Gender wage discrimination bias? A meta-regression analysis. *The Journal of Human Resources, 33*(4), 947–973. doi:10.2307/146404

Steil, A. V. (1997). Organizações, Gênero e Posição Hierárquica - Compreendendo o Fenômeno do Teto de Vidro. *Revista ADM, 32*(3), 62–69.

Stojanovic, A., Milosevic, I., Arsic, S., Urosevic, S., & Mihajlovic, I. (2020). Corporate social responsibility as a determinant of employee loyalty and business performance. *Journal of Competitiveness*, *12*(2), 149–166. doi:10.7441/joc.2020.02.09

Strobino, M. R. D. C., & Teixeira, R. M. (2014). Empreendedorismo feminino e o conflito trabalho-família: Estudo de multicasos no setor de comércio de material de construção da cidade de Curitiba. *Revista ADM*, *49*(1), 59–76.

Strøm, R. (2015). Gender discrimination before mandated quotas? Evidence from Norway: 1989–2002. *Scandinavian Journal of Management*, *31*(3), 303–315. doi:10.1016/j.scaman.2015.02.006

Sule, D. F. (2019). Work-family balance and stress management among accountants in Obafemi Awolowo University Ile-Ife, Nigeria. *Gender Actualization of the SDGD: The African experience*, 60.

Sundarasen, S. D., Je-Yen, T., & Rajangam, N. (2016). Board composition and corporate social responsibility in an emerging market. *Corporate Governance (Bingley)*, *16*(1), 35–53. doi:10.1108/CG-05-2015-0059

Tajfel, H. E. (1978). Differentiation between social groups: Studies in the social psychology of intergroup relations. *Academic Press*, *1*(1), 1-10.

Tajfel, H. (1974). Social identity and intergroup behaviour. *Social Sciences Information. Information Sur les Sciences Sociales*, *13*(2), 65–93. doi:10.1177/053901847401300204

Talavera, O., Yin, S., & Zhang, M. (2018). Age diversity, directors' personal values, and bank performance. *International Review of Financial Analysis*, *55*, 60–79. doi:10.1016/j.irfa.2017.10.007

Tamura, R., Kobayashi, K., Takano, Y., Miyashiro, R., Nakata, K., & Matsui, T. (2019). Mixed integer quadratic optimization formulations for eliminating multicollinearity based on variance inflation factor. *Journal of Global Optimization*, *73*(2), 431–446. doi:10.100710898-018-0713-3

Tandukar, H., Devkota, N., Khanal, G., Padda, I. U. H., Paudel, U. R., Bhandari, U., Adhikari, K., & Parajuli, S. (2020). An empirical study in Nepalese commercial bank's performances on green banking: An analysis from the perspective of bankers. *Quest Journal of Management and Social Sciences*, *3*(1), 49–62. doi:10.3126/qjmss.v3i1.37591

Tang, C. H., & Jang, S. (2007). Revisit to the determinants of capital structure: A comparison between lodging firms and software firms. *International Journal of Hospitality Management*, *26*(1), 175–187. doi:10.1016/j.ijhm.2005.08.002

Tapver, T., Laidroo, L., & Gurvitš-Suits, N. A. (2021). Banks' CSR reporting – Do women have a say? *Corporate Governance*, *20*(4), 639–651. doi:10.1108/CG-11-2019-0338

Tejedo-Romero, F., & Araujo, J. F. F. E. (2018). Transparency, Social Responsibility and Corporate Governance: Human capital of companies. *Cuadernos de Gestión*, *18*(2), 133–162. doi:10.5295/cdg.160693ft

Tejedo-Romero, F., Rodrigues, L. L., & Craig, R. (2017). Women directors and disclosure of intellectual capital information. *European Research on Management and Business Economics, 23*(3), 123–131. doi:10.1016/j.iedeen.2017.06.003

Teruel, M., & Agustí, S.-B. (2017). The link between gender diversity and innovation: What is the role of firm size? *International Review of Entrepreneurship, 15*(3), 319–340.

The Newsroom. (2013). *Video: Xerox Chairman and CEO Ursula Burns discusses leadership and pushing past the status quo.* https://business.wfu.edu/newsroom/video-xerox-chairman-and-ceo-ursula-burns-discusses-leadership-and-pushing-past-the-status-quo/

Thomas, L. T., & Ganster, D. C. (1995). Impact of Family-supportive work variables on work-family conflict and strain: A Control perspective. *The Journal of Applied Psychology, 80*(1), 6–15. doi:10.1037/0021-9010.80.1.6

Thompson, C. G., Kim, R. S., Aloe, A. M., & Becker, B. J. (2017). Extracting the variance inflation factor and other multicollinearity diagnostics from typical regression results. *Basic and Applied Social Psychology, 39*(2), 81–90. doi:10.1080/01973533.2016.1277529

Thurnell-Read, T. (2021). Kindred spirits: Doing family through craft entrepreneurship. *The Sociological Review, 69*(1), 37–52. doi:10.1177/0038026120916131

TIAA. (2021). *Announcing our third annual HBCU early career insights program.* TIAA.

Ting, I. W. K., Wang, W., Lu, W., & Chen, Y. (2021). Do female directors will have impact on corporate performance? *Review of Managerial Science, 15*(3), 611–631. doi:10.100711846-019-00351-6

Tiron-Tudor, A., & Faragalla, W. (2018). Women career paths in accounting organizations: Big4 scenario. *Administrative Sciences, 8*(4), 62. doi:10.3390/admsci8040062

To, A. T., Suzuki, Y., Vuong, B. N., Tran, Q. T., & Do, K. (2019). Foreign Ownership and Stock Return Volatility in Vietnam: The Destabilizing Role of Firm Size. *Organizations and Markets in Emerging Economies, 10*(2), 356–377. doi:10.15388/omee.2019.10.18

Todnem, By. R. (2008). Organisational change management: A critical review. *Journal of Change Management, 5*(4), 369–380.

Toker, B., & Erkut, B. (2022). Old Roots into New Trees: Artisan Entrepreneurship in Cyprus. In R. Boateng, S. L. Boateng, & T. Anning-Dorson (Eds.), *Delivering Distinctive Value in Emerging Economies: Efficient and Sustainably Responsible Perspectives from Management Researchers and Practitioners*. Routledge. doi:10.4324/9781003152217-7

Tonin, M., & Vlassopoulos, M. (2015). Corporate philanthropy and productivity: Evidence from an online real effort experiment. *Management Science, 61*(8), 1795–1811. doi:10.1287/mnsc.2014.1985

Tonoyan, V., Strohmeyer, R., & Jennings, J. E. (2020). Gender gaps in perceived start-up ease: Implications of sex-based labor market segregation for entrepreneurship across 22 European countries. *Administrative Science Quarterly*, *65*(1), 181–225. doi:10.1177/0001839219835867

Torres. M. J. M. Izquierdo. M. Á. F. & Olmedo. E. E. (2013). Responsabilidad social corporativa e internacionalización bancaria: el caso de la banca española en Argentina. Brasil y Chile. *Harvard Deusto Business Research, II*(2), 143–164.

Triana, M. D. C., Gu, P., Chapa, O., Richard, O., & Colella, A. (2021). Sixty years of discrimination and diversity research in human resource management: A review with suggestions for future research directions. *Human Resource Management*, *60*(1), 145–204. doi:10.1002/hrm.22052

Truyens, J., De Bosscher, V., & Sotiriadou, P. (2016). An analysis of countries' organizational resources, capacities, and resource configurations in athletics. *Journal of Sport Management*, *30*(5), 566–585. doi:10.1123/jsm.2015-0368

Tsalis, T. A., Malamateniou, K. E., Koulouriotis, D., & Nikolaou, I. E. (2020). New challenges for corporate sustainability reporting: United Nations' 2030 Agenda for sustainable development and the sustainable development goals. *Corporate Social Responsibility and Environmental Management*, *27*(4), 1617–1629. doi:10.1002/csr.1910

Tulaadhar, J. K. (2018). *Status of female employees in banking sector of Nepal: a case study of Kailali district* [Doctoral dissertation].

Tyler, M. (2005). Women in change management: Simone De Beauvoir and the co-optation of women's Otherness. *Journal of Organizational Change Management*, *18*(6), 561–577. doi:10.1108/09534810510628503

U.S. Bureau of Labor Statistics. (2021, March 31). *27-1012 Craft Artists*. Occupational Employment and Wage Statistics.

Ugarte, S. M., & Rubery, J. (2021). Gender pay equity: Exploring the impact of formal, consistent and transparent human resource management practices and information. *Human Resource Management Journal*, *31*(1), 242–258. doi:10.1111/1748-8583.12296

UNESCO (2022a). *Global education monitoring report 2022: gender report, deepening the debate on those still left behind.* Global Education Monitoring Report Team.

UNESCO. (2020). *Gender evolution in education.* UNESCO. https://tellmaps.com/uis/gender/#!/tellmap/79054752

UNESCO. (2022b). *UNESCO in action for gender equality, 2020-2021.* UNESCO.

United Nations Global Compact. (2022). *UN Sustainable Development Goals.* UN. https://www.unglobalcompact.org/sdgs/17-global-goals

United Nations. (2015). *World Summit on Sustainable Development "Transforming our World: The 2030 Agenda for Sustainable Development."* UN. https://www.un.org/sustainabledevelopment/summit/

United Nations. (2019a). *Report of the Secretary-General on SDG Progress*. UN. https://sustainabledevelopment.un.org/content/documents/24978Report_of_the_SG_on_SDG_Progress_2019.pdf

United Nations. (2019b). *Sustainable Development Goal 5: Achieve gender equality and empower all women and girls*. UN. https://sustainabledevelopment.un.org/sdg5

UNRIC. (2021a). *A (des)igualdade de género e o (des)equilíbrio de poder*. UNESCO. https://unric.org/pt/a-desigualdade-de-genero-e-o-desequilibrio-de-poder/

UNRIC. (2021b). *Igualdade de género*. UNRIC. https://unric.org/pt/mensagem-do-secretario-geral-da-onua-conferencia-internacional-contra-o-terrorismoriade-5-8-de-fevereiro-de-2005proferida-pelo-sr-javier-ruperez-director-executivodireccao-do-comite-cont-3

UNRIC. (2021c). *Objetivo 5: Igualdade de género*. UNRIC. https://unric.org/pt/objetivo-5-igualdade-de-genero-2/

Unt, M., Rokicka, M., Täht, K., & Roosalu, T. (2021). "Glass Ceiling" and "Sticky Floor" in Estonian Public and Private Sectors. In *Gendering Post-Soviet Space* (pp. 195–209). Springer. doi:10.1007/978-981-15-9358-1_9

US Department of Commerce. (2000). Best practices in achieving workforce diversity. USDC.

Valles. M. S. (2002). Ventajas y desafíos del uso de programas informáticos (eg ATLAS. Ti y MAXqda) en el análisis cuantitativo: una reflexión metodológica desde la grounded theory y el contexto de la investigación social española. *Fundación Centro de Estudios Andaluces*. 1–26.

Van den Brink, M., & Benschop, Y. (2018). Gender interventions in the Dutch police force: Resistance as a tool for change? *Journal of Change Management*, *18*(3), 181–197. doi:10.1080/14697017.2017.1378695

Van der Voet, J., Kuipers, B., & Groeneveld, S. (2015). Held back and pushed forward: Leading change in a complex public sector environment. *Journal of Organizational Change Management*, *28*(2), 290–300. doi:10.1108/JOCM-09-2013-0182

Van der Walt, N., & Ingley, C. (2003). Board dynamics and the influence of professional background. gender and ethnic diversity of directors. *Corporate Governance*, *11*(3), 218–234. doi:10.1111/1467-8683.00320

Van Knippenberg, D., & Sitkin, S. B. (2013). A critical assessment of charismatic—transformational leadership research: Back to the drawing board? *The Academy of Management Annals*, *7*(1), 1–60. doi:10.5465/19416520.2013.759433

Van Nes, F., Abma, T., Jonsson, H., & Deeg, D. (2010). Language differences in qualitative research: Is meaning lost in translation? *European Journal of Ageing*, *7*(4), 313–316. doi:10.100710433-010-0168-y PMID:21212820

Vaz, D. V. (2013). O Teto de Vidro nas Organizações Públicas: Evidências para o Brasil. *Economia e Sociedade*, *49*(3), 765–790. doi:10.1590/S0104-06182013000300007

Vaz, D. V., & Hoffmann, R. (2011). Segregação Ocupacional por Sexo no Setor Público Brasileiro no Período 1995 e 2008. *Revista da ABET*, *10*(1), 120–141.

Velte, P. (2016). Women on management board and ESG performance. *Journal of Global Responsibility*, *7*(1), 98–109. doi:10.1108/JGR-01-2016-0001

Vicente, A. (2000). *Direitos das mulheres/direitos humanos*. Cadernos Condição Feminina, 59. Comissão para a Igualdade e para os Direitos das Mulheres.

Vidwans, M., & Cohen, D. A. (2019). Women in accounting: Revolution, where art thou? *Accounting History*, *1963*. doi:10.1177/1032373219873686

Vieira, E. S. (2018). Board of directors characteristics and performance in family firms and under the crisis. *Corporate Governance (Bingley)*, *18*(1), 119–142. doi:10.1108/CG-01-2017-0010

Vilela, C. V. (2015). *O acesso das mulheres ao estudo da Contabilidade: comparação entre o caso britânico e o caso português* [Dissertação de mestrado, Instituto Superior de Contabilidade e Administração do Porto]. http://hdl.handle.net/10400.22/7871

Volery, T., Mueller, S., & von Siemens, B. (2015). Entrepreneur ambidexterity: A study of entrepreneur behaviours and competencies in growth-oriented small and medium-sized enterprises. *International Small Business Journal: Researching Entrepreneurship*, *33*(2), 109–129. doi:10.1177/0266242613484777

Walker, S. P. (2008). Accounting histories of women: Beyond recovery? *Accounting, Auditing & Accountability Journal*, *21*(4), 580–610. doi:10.1108/09513570810872932

Wang, C. J. (2012). Board size and firm risk-taking. *Review of Quantitative Finance and Accounting*, *38*(4), 519–542. doi:10.100711156-011-0241-4

Wang, Y., Wilson, C., & Li, Y. (2021). Gender attitudes and the effect of board gender diversity on corporate environmental responsibility. *Emerging Markets Review*, *47*, 100744. doi:10.1016/j.ememar.2020.100744

Watson, J., & Robinson, S. (2003). Adjusting for risk in comparing the performances of male- and female-controlled SMEs. *Journal of Business Venturing*, *18*(6), 773–788. doi:10.1016/S0883-9026(02)00128-3

WEF. (2022). *Global Gender Gap Report 2022—Insight Report*. https://www3.weforum.org/docs/WEF_GGGR_2022.pdf

Weichselbaumer, D., & Winter-Ebmer, R. (2006). Rhetoric in economic research: The case of gender wage differentials. *Industrial Relations*, *45*(3), 416–436. doi:10.1111/j.1468-232X.2006.00431.x

Westcott, M. (2021). Women specialist managers in Australia–Where are we now? Where to next? *The Journal of Industrial Relations*, *63*(4), 501–521. doi:10.1177/00221856211001913

Whelan-Berry, K. S., & Somerville, K. A. (2010). Linking change drivers and the organizational change process: A review and synthesis. *Journal of Change Management, 10*(2), 175–193. doi:10.1080/14697011003795651

White, E. (2004). *Alice Walker: A Life*. W. W. Norton & Company.

Whiting, R. H. (2008). New Zealand chartered accountants' work/family strategies and consequences for career success. *Pacific Accounting Review, 20*(2), 111–137. doi:10.1108/01140580810892472

Wijekoon, A., Salunke, S., & Athaide, G. A. (2021). Customer heterogeneity and innovation-based competitive strategy: A review, synthesis, and research agenda. *Journal of Product Innovation Management, 38*(3), 315–333. doi:10.1111/jpim.12576

Williams, P. (2019). *Tell them who you are*. https://medium.com/@preslaysa/tell-them-who-you-are-c4ab1a4c0f12

Wilson, B. (2021). *Sabotage: Leadership That Overcomes Betrayal, Theft and Deceit*. Propellor Company.

Women Business Collaborative. (2021). *Women CEOs in America*. https://www.wbcollaborative.org/women_leaders_ceo/thasunda-brown-duckett/

Won, D., Hwang, B. G., & Chng, S. J. (2021). Assessing the effects of workforce diversity on project productivity performance for sustainable workplace in the construction industry. *Sustainable Development, 29*(2), 398–418. doi:10.1002d.2155

Wood, G. J., & Lindorff, M. (2001). Sex differences in explanations for career progress. *Women in Management Review, 16*(4), 152–162. doi:10.1108/09649420110392136

Wood, R. C. (2015). *Hospitality management: A brief introduction*. SAGE Publications. doi:10.4135/9781473920521

Wootton, C. W., & Kemmerer, B. E. (2000). The changing genderization of the accounting workforce in the US, 1930–90. *Accounting Business & Financial History, 10*(2), 169–190. doi:10.1080/095852000411023

World Economic Forum. (2017). *The Global Gender Gap Report*. WEF.

World Economic Forum. (2020). *Insight Report: The Global Gender Gap Report 2020*. World Economic Forum: Cologny/Geneva. Switzerland. https://www.weforum.org/reports/gender-gap-2020-report-100-years-pay-equality

Wu, J., Richard, O. C., Triana, M. D. C., & Zhang, X. (2022). The performance impact of gender diversity in the top management team and board of directors: A multiteam systems approach. *Human Resource Management, 61*(2), 157–180. doi:10.1002/hrm.22086

Xia, H., Tan, Q., & Bai, J. (2018). Corruption and technological innovation in private small-medium scale companies: Does female top management play a role? *Sustainability, 10*(7), 2252. doi:10.3390u10072252

Yang, P., Riepe, J., Moser, K., Pull, K., & Terjesen, S. (2019). Women directors, firm performance, and firm risk: A causal perspective. *The Leadership Quarterly, 30*(5), 101297. doi:10.1016/j.leaqua.2019.05.004

Yang, X., Xu, H., & Ni, S. (2021). The creative renewal of a craft cluster: The role of materiality and mobility in cluster evolution. *Regional Studies, 55*(3), 546–555. doi:10.1080/00343404.2020.1802417

Yarram, S. R., & Adapa, S. (2021). Board gender diversity and corporate social responsibility: Is there a case for critical mass?. *Journal of cleaner production*, 278, 123z319.

Ye, D., Deng, J., Liu, Y., Szewczyk, S. H., & Chen, X. (2019). Does board gender diversity increase dividend payouts? Analysis of global evidence. *Journal of Corporate Finance, 58*, 1–26. doi:10.1016/j.jcorpfin.2019.04.002

Yu, B., Lenard, M. J., York, E. A., & Wu, S. (2017). Female leadership in banking and bank risk. *Academy of Accounting and Financial Studies Journal, 21*(3), 1–19.

Yu, J. J., & Madison, G. (2021). Gender quotas and company financial performance: A systematic review. *Economic Affairs, 41*(3), 377–390. doi:10.1111/ecaf.12487

Zerfass, A., Verhoeven, P., Moreno, Á., Tench, R., & Verčič, D. (2020). *European Communication Monitor 2020: Ethical Challenges, Gender Issues, Cyber Security, and Competence Gaps in Strategic Communication: Results of a Survey in 44 Countries*. EUPRERA-European Public Relations Education and Research Association.

Zhang, J. Q., Zhu, H., & Ding, H.-B. (2013). Board Composition and Corporate Social Responsibility: An Empirical Investigation in the Post Sarbanes-Oxley Era. *Journal of Business Ethics, 114*(3), 381–392. doi:10.100710551-012-1352-0

Zhou, G. (2019). Financial distress prevention in China: Does gender of board of directors matter? *Journal of Applied Finance and Banking, 9*(6), 127–153.

Zurdo, R. J. P., Centeno, M. C. G., Fernández, M. G., & Barberis, G. M. F. (2013). Responsabilidad social corporativa y género en los consejos de administración de las cooperativas de crédito españolas. *Prisma Social: Revista de Investigación Social, 10*, 332–360.

About the Contributors

Elisabete S. Vieira is Coordinator Professor, ISCA-UA, University of Aveiro. She is researcher at the Research Unit on Governance, Competitiveness and Public Policies (GOVCOPP), being Vice Coordinator of the Competitiveness, Innovation and Sustainability (CIS) Research Group. She has a Ph.D. in Finance from the ISCTE, Lisbon. Her research topics include corporate finance, corporate behavior finance, and corporate governance.

Mara Madaleno is Assistant Professor of Finance and Economics at the Department of Economics, Management, Industrial Engineering and Tourist at the University of Aveiro. Finished her Ph.D. in 2011 at the University of Aveiro in Economics. Director of the Master in Economics – Branches: Finance + Business Economics. Full researcher at the GOVCOPP – Research Unit on Governance, Competitiveness and Public Policies, and Vice-Coordinator of the research line SAD – Systems for Decision Support at GOVCOPP. She is also Vice-Director of the Master in Data Science for Social Sciences and Vice-Coordinator of Continua-UA. Her research interests include financial markets, financial economics, financial energy markets, environmental economics, energy and environment, sustainability. Participates in several research projects.

João Teodósio is Assistant Professor at the School of Management and Technology from the Polytechnic Institute of Santarém, Portugal. He belongs to the GOVCOPP Research Unit from the University of Aveiro, Portugal. His research interests are related to finance, corporate governance and international business issues.

* * *

Zyed Achour has a PhD in Management Science and is an Assistant Professor at the National Institute of Labor and Social Studies, University of Carthage, Tunisia. He is member in the "Gouvernance d'Entreprise Finance Appliquée et Audit" (GEF2A) Laboratory. Among his Reserach interest are social dimensions of Strategic

Management, Firm Performance, Labor Studies, Gender Diversity, Sustainability and Corporate Social Responsibility.

Georgette Andraz is a senior lecturer of strategic management and entrepreneurship at the School of Management, Hospitality and Tourism of the University of the Algarve. She holds a Master in Economic and Business Administration Sciences from the Faculty of Economics, University of the Algarve and a PhD in Management Sciences from the University of Évora. Her main research interest include Strategy, competitiveness and Performance and Entrepreneurship. She is a member of CEFAGE - Research Center of the University of Évora, has authored, and coauthored various national and international scientific publications. Orcid 0000-0001-5553-7620.

Celísia Baptista is a PhD in Management – Sénior lecturer of Finance and Accounting, Master in Economic and Business Sciences, Assistant Professor at ESGHT/UAlg. Author of several studies in the area of Finance. ORCID id- 0000-0002-6495-9398.

Devid Basyal holds PhD from Department of Public Policy and Administration, Incheon National University, South Korea. He has gained MPhil/MA in Economics from TU, Nepal, and MBA from University of Gloucestershire, UK. Dr. Basyal has has more than 12 years of teaching experience at Graduate and Undergraduate level. He has published some peer-reviewed journal articles about Public Policy, Business management, E-government. His area of research interest is Economics, E-government, Public Policy, Business Management.

Alicia Blanco-González is a Full Professor of Marketing on Rey Juan Carlos University. She is Vice-president of European Academy of Management and Business Economics, Director of Organizational Legitimacy Observatory (Ramón Llull University) and Director of MBEresearch Group (Rey Juan Carlos University). Her research lines are legitimacy, institutional theory, social responsibility, sustainability.

Carla Carvalho holds a PhD in Accounting from the University of Aveiro. She is currently Adjunct Professor at University of Aveiro (ISCA-UA), where she teaches several curricular units in the area of Financial Accounting, Auditing, Corporate Governance, Research Methodologies and Business Simulation, in Accounting and Finance Degrees, and in Accounting Masters. She teaches Accounting and Financial Reporting in the Doctoral Program in Accounting at the University of Aveiro (DEGEIT). Research interest areas: Financial and non-financial reporting; Quality of financial information; International accounting standards; Profession and Teaching in Accounting; Corporate Governance; Intangible assets and goodwill.

Jessika Carvalho is a Master in Applied Economics from UFPA (2021) in the Public Finance research line. Degree in Law from Universidade da Amazônia (2016). Member of the UFPA Ethics Committee (2017-2019). Member of the Social Equity Laboratory Research Group. Mediator in Training at the 7th Judicial Center for Conflict Resolution and Citizenship. Researcher in Law and Economics, especially in matters involving Public Finance, Financial and Tax Law.

Carla Gomes da Costa has a Ph.D. in Management and Human Resources Development (ISCTE-IUL- 2016), a Master's Degree in Social and Organizational Psychology (ISCTE-IUL), a Bachelor's Degree in Sociology, and a Bachelor's Degree in Psychology. She is an Assistant Professor at Universidade Europeia since September 2021, where she is also the Vertical Coordinator for the Management Area and Coordinator of the Master's Degree in HRM and Coordinator of the Bachelor's Degree in HRM. Being a university teacher for 25 years, she has taught in several higher education institutions in Portugal. She has held academic management positions at the undergraduate and master's levels. She also has 25 years of experience as a consultant and trainer in public and private entities in the areas of Organizational Behavior, HRM and Health Promotion.

Niranjan Devkota is an economist with the special focus on cross border activities and climate change related issues focusing adaptation. He has over 10 years of experience in the field of economics related research with varietal dynamics. His recent research focuses ranges from development economics especially in cross-border activities and agriculture. He received his PhD degree from Tribhuvan University Nepal. He has experience in impact analysis and model building. He has worked in terms to prepare strategic and implementation plans of several economic issues as a research associates. He has received high level training and capacity building workshop on international co-operation, natural resource management and trade related activities from several international agencies like SANDEE (ICIMOD), NDRC (China), Hi-Aware (ICIMOD), SANEM (Bangladesh) and from esteemed organizations and universities (online mode). He has command over STATA and basic knowledge of R.

Ivo Dias is an Assistant Professor at Universidade Europeia. He received his Ph.D. degree in Organizational and Economics Sociology from ISEG – Lisbon University and his research are in the fields of Economics, Human Resources Management, and Social Entrepreneurship. He has published several research papers and has extensive practical experience in public and private academies and organizations. He also participates in research projects at the European University, namely the project PASC (Associations Platform of Civil Society), and e-Work, and is a collaborator of the ISCSP – Lisbon University in the development of the Strategic Plan for the Municipality of Santa Cruz (Madeira).

Lidiane Dias holds a PhD in Accounting from the University of Brasília (UnB) and is a researcher and Professor at the Federal University of Pará (UFPA), Brazil, where she coordinates the Laboratory for Innovation and Oversight in the Public Sector (LAIC-UFPA). She is Joint Editor of area Public Accounting of journals 'Evidenciação Contábil & Finanças', of Federal University of Paraíba (UFPB) and 'Sociedade, Contabilidade e Gestão", of Federal University of Rio de Janeiro (UFRJ). In partnership with the University of Essex (UEssex) and University of São Paulo (USP), Lidiane represents the UFPA in the coordination of the project 'Tackling Covid19 Through Co-production: engaging Brazilian vulnerable communities facing the consequences of pandemics', funded by the British agency UK Research Innovation (UKRI) and Newton Fund. Her research focuses on public governance and government openness.

Susana Díaz-Iglesias is a Lecturer in the Business Economics Department at Universidad Rey Juan Carlos (Spain). Ph.D. in Social and Legal Sciences, specializing in Business Economics from the URJC. Research interested lines are change management, sustainability, organizational legitimacy, and education. She has more than 17 years of professional experience in Human Resources Management in national and multinational companies in sectors such as engineering, banking and consulting. Member of Management & Business Economics Research Group and The European Academy of Management and Business Economics.

Burak Erkut is an Associate Professor at the Department of Business, Faculty of Business and Economics, Eastern Mediterranean University.

Asim K. Karmakar (b. 03.01.1955) is currently an Assistant Professor in Economics, School of Professional Studies, Netaji Subhash Open University, Kalyani, West Bengal (Formerly Assistant Professor Department of Economics, Jadavpur University, Kolkata), He obtained his Ph.D. degree in Economics from Jadavpur University, Kolkata. He is presently the Executive Member of the IEA) and formerly the EC member of TIES; formerly the Managing Editor (2011-2014) of Artha Beekshan. Of late, he is the managing editor of Artha Beekshan (2020-23) He has completed four minor research projects sponsored by the CAS, Jadavpur University and the UGC. He has written several co-edited and edited books published by

Springer as well as research articles published by Springer, IGI Global, Emerald and Palgrave Macmillan, ROGE Oxford. U.K. He delivered lectures at home and abroad including in Bejing, Mexico, Oxford University and UNO. He has contributed more than 120 research papers (out of which 40 papers are Scopus Indexing) in reputed journals at home and abroad, and written books on different fields of economics. Titles include Balance of Payments Theory and Policy: The Indian Experience, Capital Account Convertibility in India (Co-edited), Analytical Issues in Trade, Development and Finance (Co-edited), Rural Livelihoods in India (Co-edited) et al. Dr. Karmakar has co- authored 10 text books including B.Com. (Hons.), BA Hons. (Macro-economics under New UGC Syllabus). Over and above he has received two national and four international academic awards for his outstanding contribution to the field of Economics.

Hüseyin Karşılı is an Assistant Professor at the Department of Business, Faculty of Economics, Administrative and Social Sciences, Bahçeşehir Cyprus University.

Ana Lucas is an assistant professor at the European University, in the financial area. She is also a guest adjunct professor at ISCAL. She holds a PhD in Management, a Masters in Accounting and Taxation and a Degree in Business Organization and Management. She attends a second Ph.D., in Accounting. She develops her research activity primarily in the area of the accounting profession and management accounting, being the author of the book Contabilidade de Gestão nas Administrações Públicas (Rei dos Livros) and Ser Contabilista Certificado (Cordeld'Prata). She is also co-author of the book Contabilidade Financeira na Hotelaria e na Restauração (Lídel) and Contabilidade de Gestão Aplicada ao Turismo (Almedina). She is author and co-author of several scientific and technical publications, and reviewer of scientific articles in journals and conferences. She is an integrated researcher at CiTUR – Center for Research, Development, and Innovation in Tourism and a member and ambassador of the GRUDIS-Portuguese Network for Research in Accounting. She has been a Certified Accountant since 1997. Her ORCID ID is 0000-0002-9177-7215

Fernanda Matias is Vice-Rector of the University of the Algarve (2006-2013). PhD in Financial, ISCTE- University Institute of Lisbon, Portugal, 2001 (Special Award), Teacher of Corporate Finance and Financial Math at the University of Algarve. Coordinator of the Master in Corporate Finance. Participation as a teacher of several Master. Co-author of two books on Corporate Finance and Financial Mathematics. Author of articles published in international scientific journals on financial management and business, etc. such as Journal of Family Business Management, Research in International Business and Finance, among others. The current line of investigation is on the financial decisions of companies, family business and capital structure. She is a member of CEFAGE ORCID 0000-0002-5128-7801.

Elisabete Neves is Associate Professor and Coordinator of the Master Degree in Financial Analysis at Coimbra Business School|ISCAC. She is a researcher at the Centre for Transdisciplinary Development Studies (UTAD) and at Polytechnic of Coimbra, Coimbra Business School Research Centre| ISCAC. She received her Ph.D. in Finance from the University of Salamanca (Spain). Her research topics include stock evaluation and performance of investment funds, corporate governance and behavioral characteristics, bank efficiency and performance, green funds, CSR, Corporate Performance. She has several articles published in indexed journals, such as the Journal of Management and Governance; International Journal of Managerial Finance; International Journal of Productivity and Performance Management; International Journal of Accounting and Information Management; Operational Research; Journal Operational Research Society, Social Responsibility Journal, China Finance Review International, Annals of Operations Research, etc.

Carmen Orden-Cruz is Associate Professor in the Business Economics Department at Universidad Rey Juan Carlos (Spain). Master's in Financial Management and Ph.D. in Business Economics, both from Complutense University of Madrid (Spain). Research interests include Behavioural Finance, financial markets, financial system, Islamic Finance, and Education. Previous professional experience includes twenty years as a Fund Manager at Gesmadrid and Economist at the Economics Research Department, both at Caja Madrid Savings Bank Group (currently Caixabank). Member of Management & Business Economics Research Group and The European Academy of Management and Business Economics.

Juliene Pereira is an Accounting Science Student at the Federal University of Pará.

Subrata Ray is a principal of Prabhu jagatbandhu college. He has also served Sabang Sajanikanta Mahavidyalaya as associate professor in Economics. He has published many books (both as editor and writer). He is the member of different institutions Indian Statistical Institute, Indian Economic Association, etc. Presently he is the secretary of Bengal Economic Association. He has also published about 80 articles in books and journals.

Sutapa Ray is Associate Professor and Head of the Department of Philosophy of Prabhu Jagatbandhu College, Andul, Howrah. She is also the Coordinator of IGNOU Study Centre of the college and Course Director and Mentor of National Health Care Academy, Singapore. She is actively involved in research work and has undertaken three Research projects funded by the most prestigious research organisation of the country, University Grants Commission. She has authored a book entitled "A Relatively Real World: Putnam versus Rorty " which addresses epistemological and metaphysical issues. She has also co-authored a book entitled "Yoga: The Art of Living" which shows how practice of yoga and meditation can cure lifestyle diseases like diebetes. She has also edited a book entitled " Combating Covid: Philosophical Reflections". She has co-edited various books like "Paralytic Pandemic: An Emergence of a Human Crisis ", "Marxian Theory: Assessment and Relevance in the Post Reform Era ", "Contemporary Issues and Challenges to the Society " and "The Pursuit of Thoughts ". Further, she has innumerable publications on various topics of Philosophy, Economics, Sociology, Religion, etc.

Sandra Rebelo holds a PhD in Economic and Business Sciences (2017) and a Master's in Business Finance (2003) from the University of Algarve. She has been a professor in the area of financial management at the ESGHT of the University of Algarve since 1997. She is the author of articles published in national and international journals on financial management and a researcher at CITUR-Algarve. ORCID id- 0000-0002-5358-5204.

Rui Robalo holds a PhD in Business Sciences by Faculty of Economics, University of Porto (Portugal). He is Associate Professor of the School of Management and Technology of the Polytechnic Institute of Santarém (Portugal). His teaching covers various accounting topics, in different cycles of studies. He has published research in relevant accounting journals and books.

Aleff Santana is a Full Professor at the Institute of Applied Social Sciences of the Federal University of Pará (ICSA-UFPA). Coordinator of the Laboratory of Critical and Interpretive Studies in Accounting (LECIC) at the Federal University of Pará (UFPA). Researcher and Responsible for the Research Line "Human Rights, Diversity and Inclusion" at the Social Equity Laboratory (LABEQ) of the Federal University of Pará (UFPA). PhD student in Controllership and Accounting at the University of São Paulo (PPGCC-USP). Master in Applied Economics from the Federal University of Pará (PPGEA-UFPA). Specialist in IFRS and Brazilian Accounting Standards from the Legale Faculty of the State of São Paulo (FALEG-SP). Specialist in Public Law from the Legale Faculty of the State of São Paulo (FALEG-SP). Bachelor of Science in Accounting from the Federal University of Pará (ICSA-UFPA). Bachelor of Laws from the University of the Amazon (ICJ-UNAMA).

Adriana Silva is an Adjunct Professor in Management Accounting at the Polytechnic Institute of Santarém. Integrated member researcher of the CICF, School of

Management, IPCA, Barcelos, Portugal. Member researcher of the Laboratory of Critical and Interpretive Studies in Accounting (LECIC) at the Federal University of Pará (UFPA). Associated Editor of journal "Revista Contemporânea de Economia e Gestão". PhD in Accounting from the University of Minho. Research interest focuses on critical and interpretative accounting and accounting history, specifically on themes that give prominence to subordinated voices.

Adelaine Soares is a Master in Applied Economics from the Federal University of Pará (UFPA). Specialist in Financial Management, Auditing and Controlling at Faculdade Estratego. Bachelor in Statistics from the Federal University of Pará (UFPA).

Sahadeb Upretee earned a PhD in Mathematics (Specializations: Actuarial Science; Statistics) from the University of Wisconsin Milwaukee, USA. Dr. Upretee is an assistant professor at the Department of Mathematics, Central Washington University, Ellensburg, WA. He teaches undergraduate courses in Mathematics, Statistics, and Actuarial Science. His research interest includes Data Science, Applied Statistics, Actuarial Science, Loss Data Analytics, Financial Economics, Structural Equations Modeling, Business Analytics, Model Uncertainty, Risk Measures, and Math Education. He collaborates with faculty members and researchers across different countries for scholarly activities.

Index

G

H

I

L

M

N

O

P

R

S

T

W

X

www.ingramcontent.com/pod-product-compliance
Lightning Source LLC
LaVergne TN
LVHW080607300926
849162LV00005B/1068